South-East Asian Social Science Monographs

Balanced Development

Balanced Development
East Java in the New Order

Edited by
Howard Dick, James J. Fox,
and Jamie Mackie

SINGAPORE
OXFORD UNIVERSITY PRESS
OXFORD NEW YORK
1993

Oxford University Press, Walton Street, Oxford OX2 6DP
Oxford New York Toronto
Delhi Bombay Calcutta Madras Karachi
Kuala Lumpur Singapore Hong Kong Tokyo
Nairobi Dar es Salaam Cape Town
Melbourne Auckland Madrid
and associated companies in
Berlin Ibadan

Oxford is a trade mark of Oxford University Press

Published in the United States
by Oxford University Press, New York

British Library Cataloguing in Publication Data
Data available

Library of Congress Cataloging-in-Publication Data
Balanced development: East Java in the new order/edited by Howard Dick, James J. Fox, and Jamie Mackie.
p. cm.—(South-East Asian social science monographs)
Includes bibliographical references and index.
ISBN 0-19-588597-X
1. Jawa Timur (Indonesia)—Economic conditions. 2. Jawa Timur (Indonesia)—Social conditions. I. Dick, H. W. (Howard W.) II. Fox, James J., 1940. III. Mackie, J. A. C. IV. Series.
HC448.J44B34 1993
330.9598'2—dc20
92–1597
CIP

Typeset by Indah Photosetting Centre Sdn. Bhd., Malaysia
Printed in Singapore by Kyodo Printing Co. (S) Pte. Ltd.
Published by Oxford University Press Pte. Ltd.,
Unit 221, Ubi Avenue 4, Singapore 1440

Preface

THIS book examines the economic and social development of East Java during the first twenty-five years of the New Order. During this period, East Java's development has been characterized by an impressive combination of dynamism, discipline, and diversity. This combination of features has contributed to sustained economic growth within a context of 'balanced development'. The focus of this book is on the breadth and variety of this development.

In East Java, there is no one sector of the economy nor one aspect of social or political life that is so prominent as to overshadow all other aspects of provincial life. One can point to remarkable achievements in a wide range of areas. East Java's success in carrying out its family planning programme is a good example, but no less remarkable is East Java's record in increasing rice production and in developing its agricultural base. Surabaya's industrial development has not been as spectacular as that of Jakarta but, perhaps for this very reason, Surabaya does not dominate the rest of the province in the way that Jakarta dominates West Java. Surabaya's situation would thus support a view of balanced development.

The fifteen chapters that comprise this book deal with specific aspects of East Java's development. They examine East Java's overall economy and demography, its 'revolution' in family planning and in education and employment, recent patterns of migration, the variety of the province's agriculture, increasing electrification, and the development of the province's manufacturing industries. These general accounts are flavoured with specific studies—on the workings of the co-operatives in the rice programme in Malang, on the establishment of the industrial complex of Pandaan located on the main road linking Surabaya and Malang, and on the rise of Gudang Garam as a cigarette production centre in Kediri. Finally, special attention is given to regional finance and to the role of Surabaya within the province.

It is important to emphasize that although this book covers a wide range of topics, it does not claim to be comprehensive. No one book can possibly consider all of the important aspects of East Java's development in recent decades. East Java's school system from the primary level to its universities, including its extensive network of Islamic schools, has contributed enormously to the balanced development highlighted in the book. The development of rural credit, particularly in the 1980s, is another subject worthy of special attention, as is the development of East Java's livestock industry. A careful assessment of income distribution as a result of development, an examination of forestry policy in the province with the largest forested area in Java, or an overall analysis of village development, and many more such studies still need to be undertaken. Therefore, in view of the many issues that remain to be considered, we can only offer this volume as an initial contribution to the continuing study of the province as a whole. Since no comparable study of so many aspects of development and change in a single province has yet been attempted, we would hope as well that this initial effort might encourage others to carry out similar studies.

Any discussion that concentrates so specifically on contemporary developments, however, needs to be prefaced with some reminder of the historical context within which these developments have occurred. Although the last few decades have seen enormous change, it is important to recall that East Java is the heartland of a complex culture and society whose historic traditions have deep roots in the past. East Java may well be a new emerging economic region but it is also an area with a great historical heritage.

The international 'Festival of Indonesia', which began in the United States in 1990 with several notable exhibitions, has given prominence to one spectacular icon of East Java's illustrious past. That object is the thirteenth-century sculpture of the goddess of transcendent wisdom taken from Candi Singasari in East Java. This exquisite statue, chosen as the frontispiece for the catalogue volume, *The Sculpture of Indonesia*, is presented as Indonesian sculpture 'at its all-time apogee' (Fontein, 1990). It is a sumptuous, perfectly preserved portrait-statue of the goddess, Prajñapārmitā, in meditation, seated on a lotus cushion. The catalogue records the long-standing popular tradition, already noted at the beginning of the nineteenth century, that claims that this statue is a representation of Ken Dedes, the first queen of Singasari, the maternal ancestor of all the rulers of the great kingdoms of East Java, Singasari, and Majapahit—and of those who claim royal descent from Majapahit.

Although this particular statue embodies, in an extraordinary way, the traditions of East Java's early kingdoms, it represents only a portion of East Java's complex historical traditions. In addition to the Hindu–Buddhist traditions of kingdoms dating from the tenth to the fifteenth centuries, the foundations of Javanese Islam are also to be found in East Java. Thus the tombs of the early Muslim Saints—Sunan Ngampel in Surabaya, Sunan Giri in Gresik, and Sunan Bonang in Tuban, along with the grave of Malik Ibrahim in Gresik—are popular sites for contemporary pilgrims. The extraordinary wood carving that adorns the mausoleums of Giri is an example of continuity with the past, consisting, as it does, of distinctive Islamic ornamentation based on older Javanese decorative traditions. The location of the mausoleums also provides a striking contrast between ancient and modern East Java. The tombs are the object of pious pilgrimage, yet they are set on a hilltop overlooking the modern cement factory at Gresik which is gradually mining the limestone hill of Giri from below.

More important, perhaps, than specific monuments or mausoleums are the common traditions and practices of East Java that maintain a tacit continuity with past endeavours. Thus, for example, East Java's achievement in increasing rice production has been built upon a historic infrastructure. Crucial to the success of the 'Green Revolution' has been the government's extension and improvement of an elaborate irrigation network technically developed by the Dutch. Yet this network is itself a development of a far earlier irrigation system. The Kali Konto, a tributary of the Brantas, forms a part of East Java's network. Directing a flow of water into the Kali Konto is the modern engineering edifice of the Srinjing conduit, whose strategic location is historically confirmed by a succession of inscriptions. The first of these inscriptions, known as the Hariñjing A Charter, records, in Old Javanese, the building of the initial dam and conduit in AD 804. A second inscription from AD 921 reconfirms the rights of the original builders of the dam and conduit, while a third inscription from AD 1350 records the restoration of this dam so that 'it might last forever for all the people of the valley east of Daha [Kediri]' (van Setten van der Meer, 1979: 20). The farmers of this area in their everyday cultivation of irrigated rice are in effect the inheritors of a line of predecessors that can be traced back for over a thousand years.

Given the complexities of the past, it is essential to clarify the reference made to the East Javanese population in this book. This reference is to the entire population of the province, which includes significantly both Javanese and Madurese as well as Chinese. One of the continuing features of East Java is the historical relationship between Madurese- and Javanese-speaking populations and their present prominence in the province. According to the 1980 Census information on daily language usage at home, just under 75 per cent of East Java's population relies principally on Javanese, 23 per cent on Madurese, and only 2 per cent on Indonesian (Fox and Gardiner, 1983). These figures may be compared to those for Central Java and Yogyakarta where 97 per cent or more of the population speaks Javanese. The Chinese of East Java are an economically influential minority who are concentrated in urban areas. Chinese historical evidence (Groeneveldt, 1880) indicates the presence of Chinese in the port towns of Java in the fifteenth century, so the Chinese, too, have contributed crucially to the complex history of East Java. Recent studies of specific Chinese communities such as those in Malang (Rafferty, 1982) and in Pasuruan (Oetomo, 1987) have focused on language usage to illuminate a variety of internal social identities among Chinese of diverse origins. The focus of this book, however, has precluded specific consideration of the various communities of East Java including the distinct Javanese-speaking minority populations of Tengger (Hefner, 1985) or the so-called 'Osek' of Banyuwangi. It is essential, however, to acknowledge this complexity as a crucial feature of social life in East Java.

This book itself has had an unusual history. The main theme which is stressed in it, that of 'balanced development', emerged only in the final stages of its compilation, when the various contributors had completed their research and had begun discussing the overall significance of the broader patterns they discerned. A further problem arose at this stage since the particular developments described by each of the contributors formed part of a continuous and ongoing process. At a certain point, therefore, it became necessary to impose a somewhat arbitrary close to the investigations in order to produce the volume. At each stage of editing, the temptation arose to try to add further information to update the discussion. In most cases, this temptation had to be resisted. The contributors to this book all maintain continuing interests in East Java and are aware of the changes that have been occurring within the province since the writing of their particular chapters.

Essentially this book describes a period of rapid change in East Java's history. This process continues. East Java is still in the midst of changes perhaps just as far-reaching as those described in this book. To some, East Java appears to be on the verge of a new phase in its development: the effects of deregulation since 1988 may well stimulate an even more rapid process of growth and industrialization in the 1990s than that of the 1970–90 period. For this reason, it is all the more important to have examined East Java's recent past developments as the critical foundation for the present.

Canberra
November 1991

JAMES J. FOX

Acknowledgements

RESEARCH for this book was partially funded by a grant provided by the Research School of Pacific Studies under its project for the Study of Industrialisation in Asia. In the early stages of compiling the various typescripts and imposing some degree of coherence upon them, Loene Doube provided tireless editorial assistance and advice for which all contributors to this volume are particularly grateful. Norma Chin with assistance from Ria van de Zandt gave invaluable help in the final stages of editing and finally brought the volume to its completed form. Again all contributors express their thanks for their efforts. We are also indebted to the services of Keith Mitchell of the Cartographic Unit of the Research School of Pacific Studies for the maps, figures, and charts.

Acknowledgement is also due to Oxford University Press for permission to use a rewritten version of a paper by Mackie and Djumilah Zain that appeared as Chapter 2 in *Unity and Diversity: Regional Economic Development in Indonesia since 1970* edited by Hal Hill; to the Biro Pusat Statistik, Jakarta, for permission to use unpublished statistical data in Chapters 3, 4, 5, 10, and 12; and to officials of the Kantor Statistik Jawa Timur for assistance in providing advice and information for this volume.

Canberra
November 1991

HOWARD DICK
JAMES J. FOX
JAMIE MACKIE

Contents

Tables

Figures

Abbreviations and Glossary

ani-ani	a traditional cutting implement used to harvest rice, stalk by stalk
ANIEM	(Algemeene Nederlandsch-Indische Electriciteit Maatschappij) General Netherlands Indies Electricity Company
arek Suraboyo	native-born Surabayans
ASEAN	Association of South-East Asian Nations
Bankop	(Bantuan Koperasi) Co-operative Aid; a credit programme for obtaining cattle provided by the dairy co-operative
Banpres	(Bantuan Presiden) Presidential Aid; a credit programme for obtaining dairy cattle made available by presidential decree
Bantuan Pembangunan Desa	Village Development Grant Scheme
Bappeda	(Badan Perencanaan Pembangunan Daerah) Regional Development Planning Board
Bappenas	(Badan Perencanaan Pembangunan Nasional) National Planning Development Board
bawon	a system of harvesting rice in which the owner of the crop allows his or her neighbours (usually women) to participate in the harvest, and then pays them a set fraction (for example, one-twelfth or one-fifteenth) of the rice that each harvests as their wages
becak	trishaw; a three-wheeled pedicab
beras	milled rice or rice
bergculturen	upland crops; that is, coffee and tea initially, rubber and cocoa later
Bimas	(Bimbingan Massal) Mass Guidance; official agricultural extension programme for rice and later other food crops; the Bimas programme provided both credit and physical inputs for farmers
bimbingan	'guidance'; strongly paternalistic connotations in Indonesian, meaning literally 'to lead [a child] by the hand'

Binnenlands Bestuur	(former) Colonial Civil Service
BKKBN	(Badan Koordinasi Keluarga Berencana Nasional) National Family Planning Co-ordinating Board
BKO	(*badan kontak organisasi*) a body set up at *kabupaten* level to assist development of the KUD
BKPM	(Badan Koordinasi Penanaman Modal) Capital Investment Co-ordinating Board
bladtabak	high-quality leaf tobacco
blok	communal land that could not be committed in small segments but had to be leased in large irrigated blocks
BPP	(Balai Penyuluhan Pertanian) Agricultural Extension Centre; a regional centre at which extension activities of various agricultural agencies are co-ordinated
BPS	(Biro Pusat Statistik) Central Bureau of Statistics
BRI	(Bank Rakyat Indonesia) Indonesian People's Bank; the State-owned bank principally responsible for distributing agricultural credit in rural areas
Bulog	(Badan Urusan Logistik) State Logistics Board, responsible for procuring and distributing basic commodities, the most important of which is rice
bupati	district head (formerly regent); the chief civil official of a *kabupaten*
BUUD	(*badan usaha unit desa*) a government-supported village organization established to assist in distributing farm inputs and purchasing rice and other crops; a preliminary form of the KUD
cabang	districts subdivided into sections or 'branches'
camat	subdistrict officer; the chief civil official of a *kecamatan*
CBR	crude birth rate
CDR	crude death rate
chlamydia	an asymptomatic vaginal infection associated with infertility
CKS	(Centraal Kantoor voor de Statistiek) Central Statistical Office, colonial period
Cultuurstelsel	Cultivation System
desa	village or rural community; often used interchangeably with *kelurahan*
Diperta	(Dinas Pertanian) Department of Agriculture at provincial and district level

Disbun	(Dinas Perkebunan) Service for Estate Crops; a regional agricultural service dealing with industrial crops
DIY	(Daerah Istimewa Yogyakarta) Special Region of Yogyakarta
DKI	(Daerah Khusus Ibukota) Special Capital Region (of Jakarta, which has the administrative status of a province)
dukuh	hamlet; one village usually comprises several *dukuh*
erfpacht	long-lease
FDT	the census category of Food, Drink, and Tobacco
FISIP	Faculty of Social Sciences at Airlangga University, Surabaya
gabah	unmilled rice
gabah kering giling	dry-rice paddy ready for milling
gabah kering lumbung	dry-rice paddy still being dried
gabah kering panen	wet-rice paddy
GDP	gross domestic product
gogol	share of or shareholder in the communal land tenure system
gogolan system	a communal land tenure system
Golkar	(Golongan Karya) a political party whose members were largely government officials
gotong royong	mutual self-help
GRP	gross regional product
gugur gunung	special drives to recruit family planning acceptors
gula merah	'brown', unrefined sugar
HYV	high-yielding variety (of rice)
IAIN	(Institut Agama Islam Negeri) State Islamic Institutes
ICPS	Indonesian Contraceptive Prevalence Survey held in 1987
Inmas	(Intensifikasi Massal) Mass Intensification; an agricultural extension programme for rice and other food crops. The Inmas programme, in contrast to the Bimas programme, supplies participants with subsidized inputs but does not include credit
Inpres	(Instruksi Presiden) Presidential Instruction; development grants from the central government to provincial, *kabupaten*, and village governments, usually for infrastructural works with a substantial job-creation element

Inpres Sekolah Dasar — Inpres programme for the construction of village primary schools

Insus — (Intensifikasi Khusus) Special Intensification (of rice)

Ipeda — (Iuran Pembangunan Daerah) Regional Development Levy; a land tax, replaced by the PBB since 1985

IRRI — International Rice Research Institute

ISIC — International Standard Industry Classification; a census code used to categorize industries; a five-digit code represents the highest and a two-digit code the lowest level of disaggregation

IUD — intra-uterine (contraceptive) device

Jabotabek — the Greater Jakarta area (Jakarta, Bogor, Tangerang, and Bekasi)

jeruk — citrus

kabupaten — regency; district; an administrative area below the level of province

kampung — (urban) village

kanwil — (*kantor wilayah*) regional office of a central government department

kantor statistik — statistics office

kawedanan — district; an administrative unit within a *kabupaten*, comprising several *onderdistrict*/*kecamatan*

kebun — dry-cultivated garden with predominantly perennial crops

kecamatan — subdistrict; an administrative area below the level of *kabupaten*

kejuron — management units that link to local village organizations

kelurahan — villages; often used interchangeably in rural areas with *desa*

KIK — (Kredit Investasi Kecil) Credit for Small Investments; a credit programme providing fixed capital for small and medium-scale enterprises

KNPI — (Komite Nasional Pemuda Indonesia) National Committee of Indonesian Youth; a Golkar-backed youth organization

kontak tani — contact farmer; chairperson of a farmers' group

KOPSAE — (Koperasi Sinau Andandani Ekonomi) Co-operative Learning to Care for the Economy; the dairy co-operative in Pujon, Malang

Koramil — Military Area Command

kotamadya — municipality; it has the same administrative status as a *kabupaten*

kretek	clove cigarette
krosok	'filler' tobacco; low-quality leaf
KRP	Konto River Project; a development co-operation project set up in the Konto River upper watershed area to develop a model for watershed management
kuasa	control
KUD	(*koperasi unit desa*) village unit co-operative; a government-supported rural village co-operative
kV	kilovolt
kW	kilowatt
kWh	kilowatt-hour
L and M sector	Large and Medium-scale sector of manufacturing; factories having 20 or more workers
LFPRs	labour force participation rates
LNG	liquefied natural gas
LIPI	(Lembaga Ilmu Pengetahuan Indonesia) Indonesian Institute of Sciences
MARIF	Malang Agriculture Research Institute for Food Crops
MW	megawatt
MWh	megawatt-hour
Na-oogst	post-harvest tobacco; that is, tobacco grown after the rice harvest, in the dry season
ngenger	to live with a family to look after the cattle and perform other household chores
NIC	newly industrialized country
NIWEM	(Nederlandsch-Indische Waterkracht en Electriciteit Maatschappij) Netherlands Indies Hydropower and Electricity Company
non-teknis	non-technical
NUDS	National Urban Development Strategy of Indonesia
onderdistrict	subdistrict in colonial administration, equivalent to later *kecamatan*
Oosthoek	Eastern Corner; the part of Java east of an imaginary line between Pasuruan and Malang
PAL	the former naval dockyard
palawija	annual food crop other than rice or temperate-climate vegetables; chiefly maize, cassava, sweet potatoes, soya beans, and nuts
Panca Usaha Tani	Five Principles of Good Farming
PBB	(Pajak Bumi dan Bangunan) Land and Building Tax, previously Ipeda
PDI	(Partai Demokrasi Indonesia) Indonesian Democratic Party; a fusion of the Nationalist

	Party with Catholic and other Christian parties
pekarangan	house lot; home garden
pendapatan asli daerah	revenues raised within the region
Pepabri	(Persatuan Purnawirawan Angkatan Bersenjata Republik Indonesia) Association of Retired Army Members, closely linked with Golkar
Perum Perhutani	(Perusahaan Umum Kehutanan) Public Forest Corporation; a public enterprise that manages forest plantations and watershed protection forests in most of Java
pikul	a load, usually weighing about 60 kilograms, attached to both ends of a pole which is carried over the shoulders
PLTD	(*pembangkit listrik tenaga diesel*) a diesel-generating plant
PLKB	(*petugas lapangan keluarga berencana*) family planning fieldworkers
PLN	(Perusahaan Listrik Negara) State Electricity Corporation
PMDN	(*penanaman modal dalam negeri*) domestic investment
pokok murni	net assessment (for tax purposes)
Polsek	(Polis Sektor) Sector Police
PPL	(Penyuluh Pertanian Lapangan) Agricultural Extension Service, including extension officers who work for PPL
PPP	(Partai Persatuan Pembangunan) Development Unity Party; a political party formed by the union of various Islamic groups
PSI	(Partai Sosialis Indonesia) Indonesian Socialist Party, banned by Sukarno in the early 1960s
PUSP	(Proyek Pengembangan Usaha Sapi Perah) Dairy Cattle Development Project; a government dairy cattle introduction scheme
ranting	sub-branches
rasa	flavour (as applied to *kretek*)
Repelita	(Rencana Pembangunan Lima Tahun) Five-Year Development Plan
Repelita I	First Five-Year Development Plan, 1969/70–1973/4
Repelita II	Second Five-Year Development Plan, 1974/5–1978/9
Repelita III	Third Five-Year Development Plan, 1979/80–1983/4
Repelita IV	Fourth Five-Year Development Plan, 1984/5–1988/9

RIN	(Rijksinstituut voor Natuurbeheer) Research Institute for Nature Management
saus	clove sauce used to flavour *kretek*
sawah	level and bunded field which is either irrigated or rain-fed and supports at least one crop of wet-cultivated rice in an annual rotation; in highland areas, any irrigated field
sawah tadah hujan	rain-fed *sawah*
sederhana	simple
sekolah dasar	primary school
setengah teknis	semi-technical
SIER	Surabaya Industrial Estate Rungkut
SMA	(*sekolah menengah atas*) senior high school
SMAM	singulate mean age at marriage
SMP	(*sekolah menengah pertama*) junior high school
Sub-Dolog	(Sub-Depot Logistik) Branch Office of Bulog at *kabupaten* level
Supas	(Survei Penduduk Antar Sensus) Intercensal Population Survey
Supra Insus	(Supra Intensifikasi Khusus) Special Intensification; a new government programme which promulgated markedly higher fertilizer recommendations for particular areas of rice intensification
Susenas	(Survei Sosial Ekonomi Nasional) National Socio-economic Survey
Susisik	an industrial area comprising the *kotamadya* of Surabaya and the *kabupaten* of Sidoarjo and Gresik
swadaya masyarakat	voluntary contributions in labour and in kind to the village government
swadaya	least advanced development status category, 'subsistence'
swakarya	more advanced development status category, 'developing'
swakarsa	unassisted (migrants)
swasembada	most advanced development status category, 'developed'
tahu	bean curd, made from soya bean
tanah bengkok	village land assigned to village officials in lieu of salary
TCF	the census category of Textiles, Clothing, and Footwear
tebasan	the selling of a rice crop by its owner before it is harvested to a contractor, who then brings in his or her own labourers to harvest the crop
tebu rakyat	peasant sugar-cane

tegalan	dry-cultivated (non-irrigated) field cropped largely with secondary annual crops
teknis	technical
tembakau rakyat	peasant tobacco
tempe	soya bean cake
TFR	total fertility rates
TRI	(Tebu Rakyat Intensifikasi) Smallholder Sugarcane Intensification Programme
UNDP	United Nations Development Programme
Unibraw	(Universitas Brawijaya) Brawijaya University
USAID	United States Agency for International Development
VD	venereal disease
Voor-oogst	a variety of cigar tobacco
Vorstenlanden	Dutch term for the Javanese Principalities
warung	small food stall
wereng	a small brown planthopper that infests and destroys rice crops
wilayah	a district or region (usually overlapping administrative boundaries)
yasan	portions of village land

Notes on Contributors

ANNE BOOTH is Professor (Economics of Asia), School of Oriental and African Studies, University of London.

HOWARD DICK is Senior Lecturer, Department of Economics, University of Newcastle.

JAMES J. FOX is Professor of Anthropology, Research School of Pacific Studies, Australian National University.

PATRICK GUINNESS is Senior Lecturer, Department of Sociology, La Trobe University.

TERENCE H. HULL is Senior Research Fellow, Department of Political and Social Change, Research School of Pacific Studies, Australian National University.

IMRON HUSIN is Associate Director for Programs, Center for Policy and Implementation Studies, Jakarta.

GAVIN W. JONES is Professor of Demography, Research School of Social Sciences, Australian National University.

JAMIE MACKIE is Professor Emeritus, Australian National University.

PAUL MEYER is Research Fellow in the Graduate Programme in Demography, National Centre for Development Studies, Australian National University.

J. W. NIBBERING, a doctoral graduate of the Department of Human Geography, Research School of Pacific Studies, Australian National University, is now working as a development consultant.

AMIR SANTOSO is Head of the Department of Political Science, University of Indonesia.

RIWANTO TIRTOSUDARMO is Researcher at the Population and Manpower Studies Center, Indonesian Institute of Social Sciences, Jakarta.

KENNETH YOUNG is Senior Lecturer, Department of Anthropology and Sociology, Monash University.

1
East Java in a Regional Perspective

Howard Dick

Introduction

OF all the provinces of Indonesia, East Java seems in recent years most closely to have approximated the ideal of balanced development (Mackie and Djumilah Zain, 1989).[1] Resource-rich provinces in the Outer Islands, especially those producing oil or timber, have achieved higher growth rates of gross regional product (GRP) but these have been accompanied by sharp cleavages between the 'modern' export-oriented sector and the rest of the provincial economy (Hill, 1989). The national capital, Jakarta (which has the legal status of a province), and the surrounding province of West Java have also achieved higher growth rates, but at the cost of glaring distributional and geographic inequalities (Castles, 1989; Hardjono, 1989). East Java has sustained a growth rate above the national average yet has managed to combine this with a fairly even spread of benefits across sectors, classes, and districts (Mackie, Chapter 2). Wide relative income disparities can still be observed but development has translated into a dramatic reduction in numbers in absolute poverty. Although the proportion of the population falling below a conventional poverty line was still just over one-third in 1984, this had fallen from over two-thirds in 1976 (Hill and Williams, 1989).

The now rapid development of East Java was not predictable in the late 1960s. Indeed, at the outset of the New Order conditions were said to be among the worst in the country (Anon., 1971). The striking features of the province were acute poverty, stagnation of the modern sector of the economy, and very little evidence of potential for self-sustaining economic growth. The province suffered like others from the neglect of infrastructure and deterioration of the productive capacity of the modern sector. Symptomatic of this neglect was the condition of roads (Dick and Forbes, 1992). Even main roads had deteriorated so much by the mid-1960s that journeys of some tens of kilometres could take many hours weaving around pot-holes, through mud, and across makeshift bridges. As late as 1971 it was reported that only 400 kilometres of the province's 3 700 kilometres of national and provincial roads were in good repair (Anon., 1971). What made conditions so critical in East Java was its dense population. Low productivity translated into very low income per capita, with extensive districts of acute poverty. In particular, the southern and northern belts of low limestone hills, extending through to Madura Island, were regarded as among the most poverty-stricken areas in the world (Anon., 1971).

East Java was not well-placed to benefit from the inflow of foreign aid and investment after the New Order came to power in 1966. The small Wonokromo oilfield, dating from the 1890s, was among the oldest in the country and not worthy of rehabilitation (Lindblad, 1989). The province had no untapped timber or mineral resources to attract foreign investors (Mackie, Chapter 2). And, despite a good port, it could not compete with Jakarta and West Java as a location for foreign investment in manufacturing. Until the end of the First Five-Year Development Plan (Rencana Pembangunan Lima Tahun or Repelita I) in 1973/4, East Java remained a backwater. This was exemplified by the contrast between Jakarta, already experiencing a construction boom and whose streets were choked with traffic, and Surabaya, whose appearance was almost unchanged.

This lag in East Java's development may nevertheless have been a blessing in disguise. The province escaped the first phase of New Order development that was perceived to be dominated by foreign investment and characterized by marked inequality in the distribution of benefits. In Jakarta popular discontent boiled over in January 1974 with demonstrations (the so-called Malari riots) during the visit of the Japanese Prime Minister. In East Java, by contrast, officials laboured during the course of the First Five-Year Development Plan to establish what used to be identified as the 'preconditions' for economic growth. Repair of roads was given high priority, so that communications could be restored throughout the province. Rehabilitation of irrigation works helped to support the rice intensification programme (Fox, Chapter 6). A family planning programme was launched with the full backing of the provincial government (Hull, Chapter 3). These and other initiatives enabled the province to exploit its own potential much better and, after 1974 as oil revenues became available to fund development, to spread funds across the whole province instead of concentrating them in the vicinity of the main city, as in Jakarta–West Java (Hardjono, 1989).

This chapter begins with a deconstruction of the concept of the 'national economy' and argues the logic of an alternative approach that recognizes subnational economies as substantive economic systems. From this perspective, East Java can be seen as a major economic region in its own right, not just as a province of Indonesia but in the wider context of South-East Asia. Such a perspective also has implications for the interpretation of inward- and outward-looking development strategies. The next two sections examine some key features of East Java's New Order development: first, growth and specialization, and then administration and policy. The final section briefly reviews the subsequent chapters and explains their place within the structure of the book.

National Economy and Substantive Economy

The concept of the national economy now so pervades our thinking that it requires some effort to recognize that it is nothing more than a category and indeed a fairly new one. Like any category, it has been called into being for convenience and perhaps out of necessity. Emergence of the modern nation-state gave rise to the need to define the economic space within which it governed. For quite some time this economic space was delineated by its frontiers. Goods and people were counted—and taxed—as they moved from one jurisdiction to the next. The need to measure the level of economic activity within those frontiers was not perceived until the Great Depression of the 1930s, which was the catalyst both for the formulation and rapid acceptance of interventionist Keynesian macroeconomic policy and the development of the techniques of national income accounting. If only to meet the requirements of the United Nations, the World Bank, and the International Monetary Fund, every nation now boasts a national statistical bureau which assembles data of dubious provenance and reliability to clothe the national economy in the garments of national income and expenditure statistics. With heroic faith in the significance of these figures and drawing upon ramshackle economic theory, national governments then set the economic policies that impinge upon all members of society.

We all live and work in the national—or international—economy in much the same way as we breathe the air. There is no escaping from it. Yet neither is there any way of relating to something so amorphous. As producers and consumers, we observe and are part of the incessant movement of people and goods from place to place. Amidst all the bustle of daily life, we identify with a village, town, or city. Only in the case of city-states such as Hong Kong, Singapore, or Brunei, however, do these social entities correspond with the abstract national economy. Yet we accept without question that it is somehow meaningful to treat the national economies of these city-states as comparable with such huge countries as China, India, or Indonesia.

As the largest national economy in the Association of South-East Asian Nations (ASEAN) bloc, Indonesia is a good illustration of how arbitrary the national income approach is. On the basis of 1988 GRP figures, about half of the entire national gross domestic product (GDP) was concentrated in the small but populous island of Java, while the balance was dispersed across the rest of a vast and still poorly integrated archipelago (Table 1.1).[2] Of the GRP of Java itself, which was larger than the GDP of the national economies of Pakistan, Malaysia, or the Philippines, half was made up in turn by the national capital of Jakarta and the surrounding province of West Java. On its own the Special Region of Jakarta (Daerah Khusus Ibukota, or DKI), though a smaller economic unit than the recognized Greater Jakarta (Jabotabek) area, had a GRP larger than the GDP of some of the smaller countries of Asia such as Sri Lanka and Nepal. Comparing like with like, the GRP of

TABLE 1.1
Gross Domestic Product, 1988 (US$ billion)

Country/Region	*GDP*
Nepal	2.9
Sri Lanka	6.4
Jakarta	9.5
EAST JAVA	13.0
Bangladesh	19.0
Jakarta–West Java	23.0
Singapore	24.5
Pakistan	34.0
Malaysia	35.0
Philippines	39.0
Java	45.0
Thailand	58.0
Indonesia	83.0

Sources: National figures from World Bank (1990); provincial figures (converted at US$1 = Rp 1,691) from BPS (unpublished data).

Jakarta was estimated to be about 40 per cent of the GDP of the prosperous city-state of Singapore, which is widely regarded as a newly industrialized country (NIC).

Actually there is no compelling reason, aside from force of habit and the availability of statistics, why development should almost invariably be studied from a national perspective. The nation-states of today are the often unstable outcomes of historical compromises. At the end of World War II the large majority of contemporary nation-states did not yet exist as sovereign entities. Recent events such as the disintegration of the Soviet Union and Yugoslavia, the reunification of Germany, ongoing turmoil in the Middle East, civil war in Sri Lanka, Burma, and Ethiopia, and the beginnings of dialogue between China and Taiwan confirm that neither the borders of nations nor even their existence can be taken as immutable. Yet such political vicissitudes can have surprisingly little impact upon the patterns and rhythms of economic life, which is remarkable for its continuity. Like the banks of a river, national boundaries constrain the location and flow of economic activity without transforming its elements. In the phrase 'national economy', the 'economy' is abiding, while the 'nation' is sometimes but a fragile container.

Because they abstract from the spatial dimension, national income statistics also convey the misleading impression that production is distributed uniformly within national boundaries. In the case of agricultural value added, this may vaguely approximate reality. Non-agricultural value added, however, tends to cluster. In South-East Asia this is most apparent in the case of Large- and Medium-scale (L and M) manufacturing, coinciding with the modern sector of manufacturing, which is heavily concentrated in and around the metropolitan regions of each country: Greater Jakarta, Greater Bangkok, Greater Manila, the Kuala

Lumpur–Port Klang corridor, and, ignoring national boundaries, the Singapore–Johor–Batam Island complex.

In terms of the substantive economy of production, trade, and consumption, the main building blocks are cities and their dependent hinterlands, which together constitute a region. A static definition would show regions as articulated by networks of transport and communications, of which towns and cities are the main nodes; a dynamic definition would show regions as articulated by flows of goods and services, which is to say trade, and by flows of the mobile factors of production, capital, and labour. In this way, by building upon revealed patterns of economic activity, economic subsystems can be identified and compared like with like in terms of area, population, production, and trade. For some purposes it may be appropriate to compare the city-state of Singapore with Greater Jakarta, Greater Manila, and Greater Bangkok; for other purposes it may be more appropriate to include Singapore within a Greater Indonesian, Greater Malaysian, or entire ASEAN economy.

Yet for all that has been written about the development of national economies in the Third World, remarkably little has been written about their subnational regions, be they states, provinces, or whatever. From this point of view alone, there is reason enough to write a book about the province and region of East Java. Though it is but one of Indonesia's 27 provinces, East Java would, if independent, be a substantial country in its own right. Its most recent population estimate of some 32.5 million in 1990 was about the same as that of Burma, Zaire, or Argentina and nearly twice that of Malaysia or Australia. In 1988 East Java's GRP of approximately US$13 billion was larger than many countries represented in the United Nations and, within Asia, much larger than the GDP of Nepal and Sri Lanka and about two-thirds that of Bangladesh (Table 1.1).

Of course, just as national boundaries are often arbitrary, so too may provincial boundaries be. While the whole island of Java, now integrated by good communications networks, can certainly be regarded as an economic system, it does not necessarily follow that the administrative territory of East Java should also coincide with an economic subsystem. Perhaps fortuitously, in this case it does, and the provincial economy does have as its focus a major economic core. Historically, East Java's importance has flowed from favourable economic geography, namely the intersection of the main river valleys of the Brantas and Bengawan Solo at the natural harbour of Surabaya at the western end of Madura Strait (Figure 1.1).[3] With about 1 million hectares of irrigated fields and rice production in 1986 of 7.5 million tonnes, East Java, together with Central and West Java, ranks alongside the Chao Phraya Delta of Thailand, the Mekong Delta of Vietnam, and the Irrawaddy Delta of Burma as one of the biggest and most fertile agricultural hinterlands of South-East Asia. The role of Surabaya as the major port city and focus of transport and communications networks corresponds with that of Bangkok, Saigon, and Rangoon. That Jakarta (formerly Batavia)

FIGURE 1.1
Map of East Java

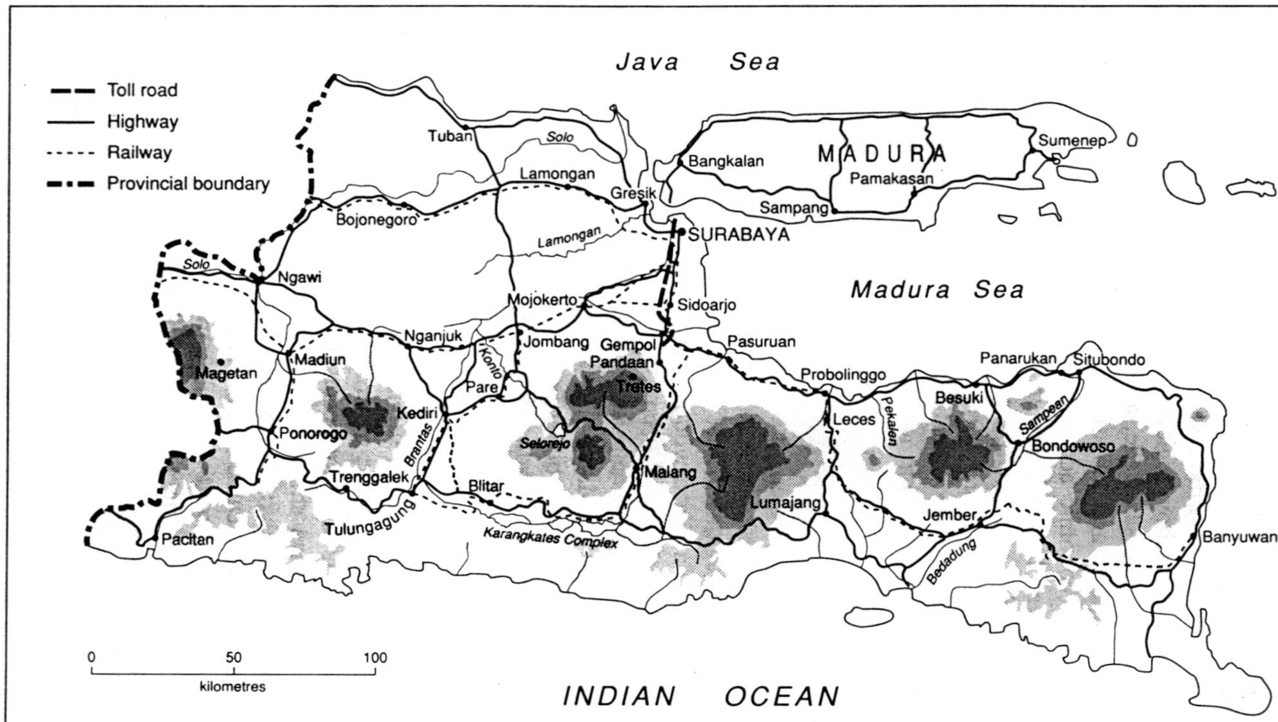

rather than Surabaya became the capital of modern Indonesia owes nothing to economic logic.[4] Nevertheless, the locational advantages of Surabaya have ensured that its political eclipse was not accompanied by economic decline as in the case of other once-prominent port cities such as Malacca, Patani, Cebu, and Zamboanga.

The importance of Surabaya as the core of a major economic region is underlined by population figures (Table 1.2). In 1980 the city's population of about 2 million made it not only the largest non-capital city in South-East Asia but actually much larger than Malaysia's capital city of Kuala Lumpur (including Klang and Petaling Jaya). Among non-metropolitan cities, the only other cities in South-East Asia of a similar order of size are in Indonesia. In the Philippines in 1988 the largest non-metropolitan city of Cebu had a population of only 0.6 million; in Malaysia in 1980 the largest was Ipoh with only 0.3 million; in Thailand in 1980 no non-metropolitan centre reached even 150,000.

East Java's standing as South-East Asia's leading non-metropolitan region has been underpinned since the mid-nineteenth century by the Industrial Revolution. As steam-driven sugar mills, railways, and tramways spread into the hinterland, Surabaya evolved as an industrial centre with a prominent Metals and Machinery sector. In recent decades, industry has spilt over into the adjacent *kabupaten* (districts) of Sidoarjo and Gresik (Figure 1.2) and along the main highways towards the towns of Mojokerto, Pasuruan, and Malang (Dick, Chapter 10). Elsewhere in South-East Asia, the only non-metropolitan concentration

TABLE 1.2
Population of Capital and Main Non-metropolitan Cities in South-East Asia (millions)

City	*Population*	*Notes*
JAKARTA (1980)	6.50	
MANILA (1980)	5.90	Metro-Manila
BANGKOK (1980)	4.70	
SAIGON (1980)	2.70	
SINGAPORE (1988)	2.70	
RANGOON (1980)	2.50	
Surabaya (1980)	2.00	
Bandung (1980)	1.50	
KUALA LUMPUR (1980)	1.30	Includes Klang and Petaling Jaya
Semarang (1980)	1.00	
Cebu (1988)	0.60	
Mandalay (1980)	0.50	
Ipoh (1980)	0.25	
Penang (1980)	0.25	Georgetown only
Songkhla (1980)	0.13	
Chonburi (1980)	0.11	
Chieng Mai (1980)	0.10	

Source: United Nations (1989).

FIGURE 1.2
East Java: *Kabupaten*

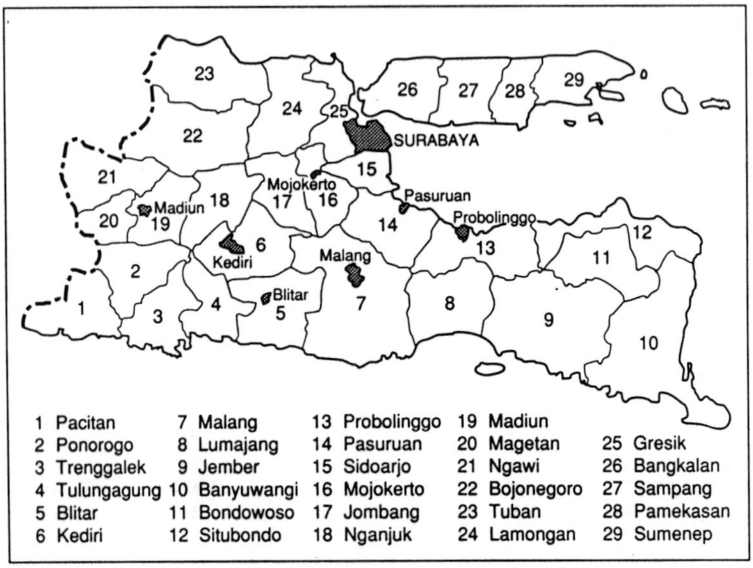

of the same order of magnitude is the Penang Island–Butterworth complex. Although in 1985 employment in L and M manufacturing along the Surabaya–Malang corridor was about 2.5 times as great, these two manufacturing centres were roughly comparable in terms of value added (Table 1.3). The next largest non-metropolitan manufacturing centre of Cebu–Central Visayas had but a small fraction of either employment or value added in the Surabaya–Malang corridor in 1986.

Setting East Java's development in the context of other delta regions of South-East Asia highlights another vital distinction between the perspectives of national economy and substantive economy, namely the specification of comparative advantage. Since cities, almost by definition, are non-agricultural, the Republic of Singapore has followed an orthodox path in specializing in the export of manufactures, to the point where it has gained recognition as an NIC. Were Greater Bangkok, Greater Manila, the Kuala Lumpur–Port Klang corridor, Greater Jakarta, Penang Island–Butterworth, and the Surabaya–Malang corridor also independent republics, it would presumably be orthodox for them to specialize in the export of manufactures as well. Yet because all of these large urban agglomerations are attached to rural hinterlands within much wider national boundaries, their comparative advantage ceases to be clear-cut. In other words, proper specification of comparative advantage requires prior specification of the economic unit, which from a substantive perspective is a major city and its hinterland. Moreover, that hinterland may cut across national boundaries, as in the case of Singapore. Specialization is limited by the size of the total accessible market, regardless of whether it is domestic or international.

In the case of the port city–delta regions such as Bangkok and the

TABLE 1.3
Employment and Value Added in Large and Medium Manufacturing

Country/Region	*Employment*	*Value Added ($ million)*	*Notes*
East Java (1985)			$1 = Rp 1,330
Surabaya–Malang corridor	214,000	670	
Surabaya–Sidoarjo–Gresik (Susisik)	140,000	532	
Malaysia (1984)			$1 = M$2.415
Kuala Lumpur–Selangor	162,000	1,590	
Pulau Pinang	83,000	691	
Johor	68,000	557	
Philippines (1986)[a]			$1= ₱10.5(spot)
Central Visayas	42,000	217	

Sources: Indonesia: BPS (unpublished census tapes).
Malaysia: Jabatan Perangkaan Malaysia, *Industrial Survey, 1984*, Kuala Lumpur.
Philippines: National Statistics Office, *Annual Survey of Establishments, 1986: Manufacturing*, Manila.
Exchange rates from *Far Eastern Economic Review*.
[a]Establishments of more than 10 workers.

Central Plains, Rangoon and the Irrawaddy Delta, Saigon and the Mekong Delta, and Surabaya and the Lower Brantas Valley, the immediate hinterlands are readily identifiable. By the nature of their human and natural resource endowments, these regions are prominent in the production of both agricultural and industrial goods. Their potential for economic growth arises less from specialization according to comparative advantage (as conventionally defined) than from the dynamic interaction between their agricultural and industrial sectors. In other words, it is the *dynamic* potential of these regions that has led to their strategic importance in South-East Asia.

The case of East Java supports the insight that much discussion of (national) comparative advantage and development strategy rests on the shifting sands of misspecification of the substantive economy. Since the mid-1970s East Java has enjoyed rapid economic growth at the rate of about 7 per cent per annum but, at least until recently, this has been achieved with only marginal participation in foreign trade and investment. Although Java used to rank second only to Cuba as the world's leading sugar exporter until the Great Depression of the 1930s and Surabaya was the island's main port of export, post-war sugar exports were at a much reduced level and ceased altogether in 1966. No new export staple emerged to take the place of sugar and East Java's export base has remained weak. In 1983 its commodity exports amounted to only 4 per cent of provincial GRP and 2 per cent of national export earnings (Azis, 1989: 57; Hill, 1989: 38–9). By value the leading export was coffee, followed by prawns, and then a great variety of primary and some secondary exports. Assisted by devaluation, the ratio of commodity exports to GRP had risen to almost 8 per cent by 1987 and manufactured exports were equivalent in value to primary exports (Dick, Chapter 10). In Jakarta–West Java, by contrast, manufactures already constituted four-fifths of non-oil exports by 1986 with Textiles, Clothing, and Footwear alone accounting for about half (Dick, Chapter 10). Only very recently has East Java begun to perform strongly in terms of manufactured exports (Mackie, Chapter 2).

Yet it would be erroneous to portray East Java's economy as inward-looking, thereby ignoring the importance of markets elsewhere in Indonesia. Surabaya has always been the gateway to Eastern Indonesia. Commercial links used to be mainly with South and East Kalimantan, rich in natural resources of oil, coal, and timber, and the much poorer islands of Nusa Tenggara. After Independence, Makassar's decline as an entrepôt allowed the merchants of Surabaya to gain supremacy in Sulawesi and Maluku as well. Surabaya's trade with the Outer Islands used to involve redistribution of imports combined with outward shipments of rice and sugar and return cargoes of copra. With the recent growth of East Java's manufacturing capacity, the Outer Islands have now become a significant increment to the adjacent 'captive' market of East and Central Java. Manufactures are now shipped not only to Eastern Indonesia but also to Sumatra, especially to the rich province of North Sumatra.

A similar analysis needs to be applied to the contribution of external resources to East Java's development. Unlike Jakarta–West Java or North Sumatra, East Java has not enjoyed any large inflow of foreign capital since the 1950s. In fact, over the period 1967 to 1985 it received only 7 per cent of the country's realized foreign investment (Hill, 1988: 41). Although 93 per cent of East Java's foreign investment was concentrated in manufacturing, in 1985 foreign investment accounted for only 10 per cent of value added in L and M manufacturing (Dick, Chapter 10; Hill, 1988: 41). However, the province has received significant but immeasurable inflow of capital, mainly from Jakarta, under the rubric of 'domestic investment'. Also important has been the net inflow of central government revenues, swelled after the mid-1970s by oil tax revenues, though according to the calculations of Booth (Chapter 14), East Java has not been privileged in this respect over other provinces. Together, these various categories of external resources have provided a substantial boost to the provincial economy, but they have not been the main driving force behind development of the province.

East Java's recent development in fact suggests a rather different dynamic from that highlighted by the advocates of outward-looking industrialization. The momentum was provided by the early and rapid introduction of the Green Revolution wet-rice technology. This enabled double and even triple cropping and high yields by comparison with the rest of Indonesia (Fox, Chapter 6). While one dramatic benefit was the increased supply of food, the new technology also raised the real incomes and purchasing power of much of the province's very large population. This increased purchasing power in turn represented a source of demand for goods from the manufacturing sector, which in East Java came to be oriented much more towards the domestic mass market than to the narrow middle-class market so heavily concentrated in Jakarta. The widening of the domestic market was facilitated by the attention of the provincial government to the rehabilitation and improvement of road transport, thereby dramatically reducing the costs of transport for both goods and persons between cities and towns and their rural hinterlands. Improved inter-island shipping facilitated access to markets in the Outer Islands. East Java's size and abundant human resources may thereby have provided a degree of autonomy from the international and even the national economy.

None of this is really surprising. To the economic historian, East Java reveals a familiar pattern of development that is consistent with models of dualistic development used to analyse the interactions between the agricultural and industrial sectors of a closed economy (Fei and Ranis, 1961; Lewis, 1954). More recently, Adelman (1984) has coined the term 'agricultural demand-led industrialization' to distinguish this form of development from the current fashion of export-led industrialization. Booth and Sundrum (1984) have restated the principles of dualistic development and re-emphasized the importance of ensuring balanced development between the agricultural and industrial sectors. In particular, they have emphasized the importance of ensuring that productivity growth and distribution are co-ordinated to achieve consistency between the growth of effective demand and of the demand for labour.

Growth and Specialization

Three features of East Java's development help to explain its relative success in combining fairly rapid growth with the alleviation of mass poverty. First, the province has been able to achieve and maintain high rates of productivity growth in both the agricultural and manufacturing sectors. Secondly, it has been able to achieve a good deal of internal economic specialization, most noticeably between lowland and highland regions. Thirdly, it seems to have benefited from an unusually effective provincial administration. Here the first two features will be considered. While economic historians and development economists have long recognized the importance of supporting the growth of industry by simultaneous growth of agriculture, this favourable conjunction has been difficult to achieve. Agriculture does not always have the potential for large and sustained growth in productivity. New Order Indonesia was very fortunate that the new high-yielding rice varieties became available from the International Rice Research Institute (IRRI) just when a development-oriented government came to power. Moreover, President Suharto, who came from a village background, was personally committed not only to achieving national self-sufficiency in rice but also to raising the welfare of farmers, who soon responded to the new opportunities. Between 1968 and 1983, average rice yields per hectare almost doubled, from 2.72 tonnes to 4.97 tonnes, the highest of any province in Indonesia (Fox, Chapter 6: Table 6.3). Moreover, these productivity gains were widely distributed across the province (Fox, Chapter 6). In the process, lowland agriculture was transformed from a quasi-subsistence to a highly commercialized system of production, with profound consequences for the village economy. These trends established the preconditions for industrial development.

Industrial development is often embraced as an end in itself but its crucial role in development is in providing off-farm employment (Shand, 1986). In 1971 agriculture still occupied two-thirds of East Java's total work-force (Jones, Chapter 4). Since then the labour force has increased at a rate of about 2 per cent per annum but the absorptive capacity of agriculture has been declining. The near doubling of rice output between 1971 and 1983 was counterbalanced by reduction in labour demands per crop, so that between 1971 and 1985 the size of the agricultural work-force remained much the same. Almost the entire burden of labour absorption has therefore fallen on the non-agricultural sectors, although there is no intrinsic reason why off-farm employment should be provided by the secondary (manufacturing) sector rather than by the tertiary (service) sector. Indeed, the service sector tends to be much more labour-intensive than manufacturing, especially large- and medium-scale industry. The potential advantage of manufacturing is that it can lead to large upstream and downstream employment linkages, including linkages with the tertiary sector. The difficulty lies in realizing that potential.

Since the mid-1970s East Java has in fact achieved fairly rapid growth of employment in the L and M sector of manufacturing (establishments of 20 or more employees). Industrial development may have been facilitated by the long-standing existence, mainly around Surabaya, of a small but diverse manufacturing base, though this advantage was not apparent in the early 1970s. Probably much more important was the growth in mass purchasing power flowing from the transformation of agriculture. This was both direct, through higher incomes of farmers, and indirect, through lower real rice prices benefiting virtually all consumers, rural and urban. The evidence of rising consumption per capita, albeit from a very low base, can be found both in national expenditure surveys and in the flood of consumer goods, from plastic buckets to television sets and motor cycles, now pouring into the villages. After the mid-1970s this demand was too great to be met by firms located in and around Jakarta. Competitive pressures led some existing firms and some new market entrants to open plants in East Java (Dick, Chapter 10).

The growth of manufacturing does, however, need to be kept in perspective. First, rapid growth of employment in L and M, as well as Small-scale, industry has not been matched by growth of the Household/Cottage sector, in which employment seems to have remained fairly static. Secondly, the jobs created even in the L and M sector have not necessarily involved high wages. Casual evidence suggests that earnings in large factories, especially for females, are often considerably below those available from self-employed service sector activities. Factory employment nevertheless provides opportunities to marginal groups in the work-force such as young and unmarried women. The highly labour-intensive *kretek* cigarette factories such as that of Gudang Garam in Kediri (Young, Chapter 13), Bentoel in Malang, and Sampurna in Surabaya are spectacular examples of the local impact of manufacturing employment. Guinness and Husin (Chapter 12) suggest that the establishment of new factories along the highway between Surabaya and Malang has also had a marked impact upon villages along that strip.

Overall, however, much more off-farm employment seems to have been provided by the service sector than by manufacturing. Part of the explanation is that manufacturing employment has grown from a very small base. Between 1971 and 1985 the industrial sector (including construction, utilities, and mining) almost doubled its employment share from 6.8 per cent to 13.4 per cent yet created little more than half as many jobs as the service sector (Jones, Chapter 4: Table 4.3). From this point of view, it would be somewhat misleading to speak of the 'industrialization' of East Java as though this were the dominant trend in development. While industrial development was certainly important along the Surabaya–Malang corridor, the general shift across the whole province from agricultural to off-farm employment is better described as a process of economic diversification.

Indeed, the trend towards internal specialization is the key to understanding the dynamism of East Java's development. In the mid-1960s a large proportion of the population had been occupied in subsistence agriculture and had only a very small margin of income left over for the purchase of goods made outside the village. Although East Java had once been a much more prosperous region with a vigorous plantation sector and a good deal of associated manufacturing, the successive blows of the Great Depression of the 1930s, the Japanese Occupation (1941–5) and the Indonesian Revolution (1945–9), followed by the economic chaos of the Sukarno era, had brought about a retrogression to a less sophisticated, subsistence-oriented mode of production (Mackie and Djumilah Zain, 1989: 310–11). The growth in output and incomes generated by the Green Revolution permitted a reintegration of the rural and urban economies. The other necessary precondition was a simultaneous revolution in rural transport that gave all but the most remote villages quick and cheap access to market towns (Dick and Forbes, 1992). By the 1980s villagers in East Java enjoyed an unprecedented degree of mobility.

Yet specialization involved not only the reintegration of countryside and town but also greater diversity in the production of subregions according to their comparative advantage. This latter process was very evident in the highlands, traditionally poor and backward. Nibbering (Chapter 7) shows how improved transport enabled upland villages to move away from subsistence rice production, in which they tended to be less efficient than lowland villages, towards cash crops such as vegetables. In time there emerged further differentiation according to the type of cash crop. Some villages tended to specialize in those vegetables which grew best or could be timed to catch the market, while others switched to the cultivation of coffee or to animal husbandry. The process of specialization was in itself nothing unusual but the speed of adjustment in highland villages was remarkable and helps to explain why real incomes were able to rise quite rapidly even in parts of the province which hitherto had been very poor. It also suggests that the province was able to finance much of the growth in output by ploughing back a proportion of the income gains.

On a provincial scale, the picture is therefore of a massive reallocation of resources to more productive uses, with consequent 'static' and 'dynamic' income gains. The 'static' income gains, which arise from the reallocation of resources to more productive, market-oriented uses, such as the movement of labour from agriculture to manufacturing, are one-off gains. The 'dynamic' gains such as the acquisition of knowledge and skills, widening of the market, and access to economies of scale help to sustain that cumulative process which is identified as economic development. The fact that East Java has been able to generate such specialization internally gives it tremendous strength over other provinces—and indeed over other national economies—which remain heavily dependent upon one or two staple exports. While lacking natural resources such as oil, timber, or minerals, East Java has been able to make the most of geographic diversity, large population, and human resources. Unlike the situation in the enclave economies of the Outer Islands, a substantial part of the growth in income, and hence the multiplier effects upon production and consumption, have been contained within the province rather than leaking away to Jakarta–West Java or overseas.

The trend towards specialization is also reflected in the pattern of labour migration. While towns and villages in both lowland and highland areas have been able to raise productivity and income through specialization, inevitably there are also districts with few natural or man-made advantages and which therefore have difficulty in developing new industries to absorb their growing work-force. In such villages, as in the limestone hills of the south and north-west and of Madura Island, for many years the younger and more adventurous have resorted to migration as the means to employment and higher incomes. Young women migrate to the city as household servants; young men as *becak* (trishaw) drivers, street hawkers, or stevedores. The Madurese especially have long-standing patterns of migration. In the nineteenth century they migrated in large numbers to work on the new tobacco plantations of Besuki and the new coffee plantations of the highlands; the city of Surabaya, just a brief ferry ride from the island, has also been a magnet for Madurese migrants who work as labourers (on the wharves or in construction), as *becak* drivers, and as porters and warehouse guards for Chinese merchants. Under the New Order, improved transport has reduced the cost of migration and made it feasible to return quite frequently to the village (Hugo et al., 1987).

Migration is therefore a dynamic response to the unevenness of economic growth and specialization. In the colonial period, migration was mainly to open up new land for peasant or plantation production, a pattern which in the south-east has persisted until quite recent times (Mackie, Chapter 2). After Independence, the main cities became the poles for migration. Under the New Order, however, the pattern has become more complex than simply rural–urban migration. First, since the mid-1970s there has been a trend among new manufacturing plants to locate along the highways between main cities and towns, such as between Surabaya and Malang (Guinness and Husin, Chapter 12). One of the attractions of such decentralization, apart from cheap land, has been access to village labour but these new industrial corridors have also become magnets for migration from poorer outlying districts (Tirtosudarmo and Meyer, Chapter 5). Secondly, Nibbering (Chapter 7) shows that intra-rural migration is still important, as in the movement of farm labour out of densely settled areas into highland districts. However, regardless of the destinations of migrants, the villages that send out labour enjoy a double benefit—both the reduction in local underemployment (thereby raising the incomes of those who remain) and the receipt of transfer incomes in the form of remittances and goods. Both effects unambiguously alleviate poverty, albeit at the cost of lopsidedness in the village economy.

Administration and Policy

East Java's development from such an unfavourable starting-point seems to owe much to an unusually effective provincial administration. More than other provinces, East Java seems to have maintained the professionalism of the former colonial Civil Service (Binnenlands Bestuur).[5] This was a tradition of achievement, especially in the field of development, combined with a high level of personal integrity and commitment. The survival of such values in East Java may be attributed in part to circumstances in the early years of the New Order. Governor Noer, appointed at the end of 1967, played a crucial role. The only civilian governor at that time, he was a charismatic leader who combined the calm dignity of his noble origins with the highest ideals of the colonial Civil Service. His subordinates, the district heads (*bupati*) and mayors, were in many cases military officers.[6] Those in charge of the remote southern districts acquired the epithet of 'cowboys': not content to sit at their desks issuing orders and receiving homage, they made a point, like Governor Noer himself, of getting to know their districts—going into towns and villages without warning, listening to villagers' concerns, and making sure that some action followed.[7] Their subordinates were in turn expected to perform. The consequence was a remarkable *esprit de corps*, which restored a civil service demoralized by political factionalism and decimated by purges of communists and their alleged sympathizers. Its effectiveness in achieving rehabilitation not only earned grudging popular respect but also helped to reunite a province badly scarred by political violence.

From this time dates another characteristic of the Civil Service of East Java, namely its commitment to independent decision-making. In other provinces, and most notably West Java, officials are appointed primarily for their loyalty to Jakarta and their willingness to implement central government policies. Their success is judged by their ability to placate regional interests rather than in serving them. While officials in East Java can certainly be zealous in implementing national policies, the presumption is none the less that national policies need to be tailored to local needs and conditions and do not preclude simultaneous local initiative (Santoso, Chapter 9). Inappropriate national policies are never resisted outright but fitted into goals and strategies forged at the provincial level. East Java has been far enough away from Jakarta for this to be tolerated by the central government.

Within the provincial government, decision-making has been professionalized. Since the time of Governor Noer, a 'think tank' of specialists has been built up in the governor's office to formulate, co-ordinate, and monitor policy. This role was legitimized by the establishment by the national government in 1974 of Regional Development Planning Boards (Badan Perencanaan Pembangunan Daerah or Bappeda) at the provincial level, followed in 1979 by similar bodies at the district level (Bappeda II) (MacAndrews, Sibero, and Fisher, 1982: 44). The provincial-level Bappeda has become the locus of decision-making but has not relied solely upon its own resources. Academic staff from the two main state universities, Airlangga (Surabaya) and Brawijaya (Malang), are very much involved in policy discussions and seminars. Military officers and members of the provincial parliament are also regularly briefed, once again often involving academic experts. The trend seems to be towards decision-making by consensus, in this case extending well beyond the bureaucracy itself. Another feature is that most decisions are made below the level of governor. While the governor remains a figure of power and authority, the several deputy governors, some of whom have served for long periods, are much more involved in the day-to-day business of government. This is all very different from the accepted view of New Order government as top–down planning.[8]

The effectiveness of East Java's civil government was apparent quite early in the New Order. By 1969, the provincial bureaucracy from the governor's office down to the hamlet level had been mobilized in support of both the Mass Guidance (Bimbingan Massal or Bimas) rice intensification programme, which began in 1967, and the family planning programme, launched in 1968. East Java's early and conspicuous success with these programmes is discussed below by Fox (Chapter 6) and Hull (Chapter 3) respectively. The provincial government also responded with alacrity to the Village Development Grant Scheme (Bantuan Pembangunan Desa or Inpres Desa), introduced in 1969 at the start of the First Five-Year Plan to provide a small grant of

Rp 100,000 to each village. By 1970 grants had been received by all of the more than 8,000 villages in the province, representing some 24,000 projects or more than a quarter of the total for the whole of Indonesia. Moreover, villages in East Java raised from their own resources about 2.5 times the subsidy contributed by the central government, so that total funds available were actually a third of the national total (Anon., 1971: 30). These funds were used mainly for small-scale irrigation projects, the repair of local roads and bridges, and village construction projects (Fox, 1988).

Yet these successes cannot be explained solely in terms of strong administration. They are all cases of opportunity and response. In none of these cases could success have been achieved by general coercion, although coercion certainly was applied by some officials in the early stages of the family planning programme and in rice procurement. The effectiveness of administration lay in making the opportunities widely available and in being able to persuade villagers to lay aside their distrust of both change and of government. That the response to these programmes was more positive in East Java than anywhere else except Bali seems to confirm both the widely observed dynamism of the East Javanese and a perceived legitimacy of provincial administration.

The impact of provincial government policy may have been greatest in the sphere of equity. In view of the great strength of the Indonesian Communist Party in East Java and the fact that the revolt was not defeated until 1968 in the poor southern districts around Blitar, both civil and military leaders were fully aware of the need to ensure that rehabilitation and development were spread across the province rather than confined to the already favoured areas. Geographic equity was therefore a matter of policy from an early stage. Three particular aspects were emphasized. First, Governor Noer realized at the outset the importance of good roads and made their rehabilitation one of his highest priorities. This decision has been thoroughly vindicated by the subsequent revolution in rural–urban transport. Secondly, the provincial government gave full support to national programmes such as the Inpres Desa and Inpres Kabupaten schemes. The former grants were spent mainly on roads while the latter were at first spent mainly on irrigation and communications, but later also on health, welfare, and 'social' facilities (Fox, 1988). Thirdly, the provincial government was careful to avoid undue concentration of public investment in the provincial capital of Surabaya. Indeed, the municipal government of Surabaya has continued to be hard-pressed for funds to overcome its severe infrastructural problems. While the concentration of private investment in the core area of the Lower Brantas, which Mackie (Chapter 2) refers to as the 'Golden Triangle', has certainly involved a bias in development, this may have been offset rather than reinforced by public investment.

The estimates of Ravallion (unpublished) on the distribution of poverty across East Java in 1981 support this view. While pockets of serious poverty remain, and may to some extent be disguised within *kabupaten*, the extent of acute poverty is much less than anyone could have anticipated from the appalling conditions of the mid-1960s. As suggested above, this must be partly an effect of the distribution of public investment and partly the effect of migration away from the districts of acute poverty such as Madura and the southern and northern limestone hills.

Scope of the Book

The primary aim of the book is to outline East Java's rapid development over the 25 years of the New Order and to identify some of the key elements that help to explain it. This chapter has set East Java in its national and international context and indicated some of the issues in development theory or policy upon which its development experience throws some light. The next chapter, a survey by Mackie of 'The East Java Economy', gives a more detailed overview of the province with particular attention to the sectoral dimensions of its development. Later chapters explore these dimensions in more depth under the main headings of Demography, Agriculture, and Manufacturing. A brief summary of these will provide an introductory sketch of the province.

The demographic section focuses upon the crucial dimensions of family planning and fertility, labour force and education, and migration. Introduction of a national family planning programme was an early and at first controversial initiative of the New Order government. Hull ('East Java's Family Planning Revolution, 1961–1987') shows why the programme has been so successful in East Java. Although East Java is still some distance from zero population growth, that target is now foreseeable: Jones ('East Java: Educational Change and Changing Employment Structure') estimates that in the 1990s reduced fertility, together with rising retention rates in secondary and tertiary education, will ensure no growth in the 15–24 age-group of the labour force. Jones also suggests that the achievement of near universal primary education and increasing access to secondary education are accelerating the shift in employment from agriculture to other sectors. Under the New Order, migration has had a big influence on the demography of East Java: net out-migration has dampened the natural rate of growth of population while intraprovincial (including rural–urban) migration has redistributed population within the province. Tirtosudarmo and Meyer ('Migration') summarize the data on East Java's interprovincial migration and use the 1985 intercensal figures to provide the first good overview of intraprovincial migration, confirming the importance of the Surabaya–Malang corridor as the 'growth pole' of the province.

The New Order government never fell into the trap of neglecting the agricultural sector. It responded quickly to the opportunity provided by the new high-yielding rice varieties developed by the IRRI in the mid-1960s. Fox ('The Rice Baskets of East Java: The Ecology and Social Context of *Sawah* Production') traces the course of East Java's Green Revolution in wet rice cultivation in different rice baskets across the province and more briefly reviews the productivity gains achieved in other food crops such as maize and soya bean. Santoso ('The Working of Rural Co-operatives in Malang') shows some of the strengths and weaknesses in the way the rice intensification programme (Bimas) and village co-operatives koperasi *unit desa* or KUD) have been implemented at the village level. Mackie ('Plantations and Cash Crops in East Java: Changing Patterns') reviews the main trends in the production of other cash crops such as sugar, tobacco, and coffee, once dominated by estates but now increasingly the domain of smallholder cultivators. Nibbering ('Agricultural Diversification in the Upper Konto Area') shows that highland regions have also participated in agricultural development through more intensive cultivation of cash crops such as vegetables and coffee and diversification into animal husbandry.

The manufacturing industry has had a long history in East Java and under the New Order has been one of the province's leading sectors. Dick ('Manufacturing') provides an overview of the growth, composition, and spatial distribution of manufacturing, highlighting the importance of the Surabaya–Malang corridor. Husin ('Electricity Supply') shows how the concentration of economic activity in the Lower Brantas region has been reinforced by the historical development of electricity supply, though completion of a Java-wide grid could now facilitate greater decentralization. Guinness and Husin ('Industrial Expansion into a Rural Subdistrict: Pandaan, East Java') give a good example of the kind of ribbon industrial development that has been occurring along the Surabaya–Malang corridor, with rather limited impact upon adjacent rural villages. Young ('Kediri and Gudang Garam: An Industrial Enclave in a Rural Setting') examines the nature and impact of the remarkable industrial complex of the leading clove cigarette (*kretek*) producer, Gudang Garam, in the Lower Brantas town of Kediri. This complex makes a huge contribution to East Java's manufacturing value added and employment yet, in terms of its impact upon Kediri itself, seems to show some of the features of an enclave development.

The final two chapters are concerned with aspects of economic and spatial integration. Booth ('Regional Finance in Indonesia: An East Java Case-study') estimates the size and composition of government spending, highlighting the very weak fiscal effort of the provincial government but suggesting that on balance public spending has facilitated a wider spatial distribution of the benefits of development. Dick ('The Economic Role of Surabaya') looks at the role of the main East Javanese city of Surabaya and suggests that it has promoted rather than retarded the economic development of the rest of the province without giving rise to problems of capital city primacy.

By no means are all the most important dimensions of East Java's development covered by these chapters. For example, more research needs to be done into poverty distribution, social welfare indicators, and environmental problems. The chapters on agriculture and manufacturing would be well complemented by additional studies on the huge and very diverse service sector, especially to identify its contribution to labour absorption of the 'informal sector'. However, this book is intended as an introductory survey of East Java's development and not the final word. If it highlights other issues which demand further research, it will have achieved a useful purpose.

Conclusion

That the basic principles of balanced development have almost had to be rediscovered and restated illustrates just how extreme are the fashions which plague development economics. In the 1950s and 1960s, closed dual sector models were applied in a climate of trade pessimism to justify tariff-induced industrialization. The short-sightedness of extreme autarchic strategies led in the 1970s to a neo-classical reaction that emphasized external markets and 'outward-looking industrialization'. This new fashion, however, is also simplistic, except perhaps for small countries with narrow domestic markets. In their preoccupation with the national economy and trade, the neo-classical development economists have tended to lose sight of the substantive economy. One of the challenges for the 1990s is to set the fundamental logic of dual economy models of development in the context of open economies. This may be done more easily by studying cohesive regional economies rather than amorphous national economies.

Just as equity became a central concern of development economists in the 1970s after a long period of neglect, so one may safely predict that regional development will eventually become a new fashion. However, nothing much can be done on this front until there is at least a minimal literature with enough case-studies to elucidate the differing patterns of regional development, the extent of regional variation, and the scope for policy intervention. Building upon the pioneering work on Indonesia of Hill (1989), this in-depth study of the recent development performance of East Java is intended to contribute to laying foundations of that kind. While in the present state of knowledge almost any regional case-study would be its own justification, as suggested above, the development experience of East Java yields insights of particular value.

Any attempt to *explain* development must inevitably be tentative and somewhat speculative. Being a process of transformation, that is to say, of total change, development cannot easily be disaggregated into discrete sequences of cause and effect. The initial stimulus is often obscure. Many important elements cannot be quantified. Description is therefore much easier than analysis. The problem is compounded when one tries to compare the performance of different economies. For example, there is now a huge literature on the phenomenal growth performance of the 'Four Dragons' of East Asia (see Hughes, 1988) but, despite some splendid insights, we have at best found correlations rather than causes. The elixir of development is still a mystery. At a micro level, as in this case looking at a province instead of a national economy, the task is not much more tractable.

For the time being, we must therefore be content with a few generalizations which appear to be well-founded and may bear closer scrutiny. First, East Java's development over the past 20 or so years has been impressive by any standards, the more so because the initial conditions in the late 1960s were so unfavourable. Secondly, it is a revealing example of development which has not relied on export-led industrialization. While outward-looking industrialization has certainly been very successful in some cases, this is obviously not the only viable approach. Thirdly, and perhaps highlighted by the above, East Java seems to have combined impressive rates of growth with fairly balanced development in terms of sectoral composition, income distribution, and regional equity. Although there is still great inequality in income and expenditure, development seems to have redressed rather than exacerbated the problem. It is intriguing to consider whether these last two generalizations may not in fact be connected. The unbalanced economic structures associated with export-oriented industrialization may well lead, without offsetting policy measures, to unbalanced distribution, whereas more balanced growth less dependent upon the international economy may well be conducive to achievement of greater equity.

Finally, a caveat. This book's fairly positive assessment of East Java's New Order development should not be taken to imply that the province is any paradise. For all the development of the past two decades, millions of East Javanese still live below the poverty line, unable to fulfil their basic needs. Though the benefits of development appear to have been distributed more evenly than in other provinces of Indonesia, that certainly does not mean that there are no extreme inequalities of income and wealth or imbalances between the most advanced and most remote parts of the province (Mackie, Chapter 2). Development could certainly have been pushed much faster had the provincial government put more effort into developing its own sources of revenue instead of relying so heavily on transfers from the central government (Booth, Chapter 14). The environmental problems touched upon by Nibbering (Chapter 7) in respect of upland districts serve as a reminder that in both rural and urban areas, the environmental cost of development has sometimes been alarmingly high.

Nevertheless, development is a 'muddling along' process, like government in general. In terms of public policy, it is important not only to try to understand the process but also to determine how and why some governments do better than others. By comparison with other provinces of Indonesia, East Java's record under the New Order has been an impressive one. It has not been some flash-in-the-pan but the result of getting many things right and not too many wrong. The fact that East Java has now become such a substantial economic region within South-East Asia justifies that achievement being brought to the attention of an audience much wider than Indonesia and Indonesianists.

1. The author is grateful to Heinz Arndt, Jim Fox, Hal Hill, Jamie Mackie, and Thee Kian Wie for comments on earlier drafts.

2. Dick (1990) surveys the slow process of integration of Indonesia's national economy, while Dick (1987) focuses specifically upon the problems of the inter-island shipping industry.

3. During the course of the nineteenth century this pattern was somewhat altered by Dutch engineers: the Bengawan Solo, which used to debouch just north of Gresik, now flows northwards into the Java Sea, while the main flow of the Brantas River has been diverted southwards through Porong.

4. Although Surabaya was arguably the leading centre of the nationalist movement, its bloody seizure by Allied Forces in November 1945 and the subsequent handover to Dutch forces ruled out any possibility that it might become the capital of the new Republic in place of Jakarta, which had been the colonial centre of government since 1619.

5. On the Binnenlands Bestuur, see Sutherland (1979).

6. On the militarization of the provincial Civil Service, see Ward (1974: Chapter 3).

7. The author is grateful to the late Dr Adi Sukadana for drawing his attention to their role.

8. This paragraph has also benefited from the advice of Dr Sukadana.

2
The East Java Economy: From Dualism to Balanced Development

Jamie Mackie

Introduction

AN economic survey of East Java written in 1971 began with the observation that the province combined 'some of the richest potential and some of the direst poverty in Indonesia' (Anon., 1971: 19). Parts of the region were described as 'among the most poverty-stricken in the world ... famine is almost endemic, communication difficult, the road and railway network sparse and in dilapidated condition'. High population densities, among the highest in Java in some regions (averaging nearly 800 persons per square kilometre in most of the Brantas Delta area, and much higher in several parts) then seemed a formidable obstacle to self-generated agricultural development. But that account was written after 40 years of economic stagnation and disinvestment, conditions which have been dramatically reversed since 1970 by the nationwide increases in production brought about under the New Order, particularly by the Green Revolution and in rising oil revenues from the mid-1970s onwards.[1]

By 1990 it was the rapid growth and dynamism of the provincial economy as a whole that stood out, and the relative prosperity of the richer areas, especially in the Brantas Delta itself, far more than poverty elsewhere in the province. Food production had increased substantially, famine had been virtually eliminated, East Java's road and railway networks were among the best in Indonesia, while exports of manufactured goods, the litmus test of successful industrialization, were increasing by more than 15 per cent per annum in the late 1980s. Business firms throughout the province, particularly the local Sino-Indonesian ones, both large and small, were surging ahead vigorously with enterprise and self-confidence.[2]

Some areas still suffered from what seemed like almost endemic poverty, it is true, mainly the drought-prone island of Madura and the dry limestone hill areas along the south-west and north-west coasts of the province; but significant improvements had occurred even in those parts since the 1970s. They have been brought about by higher agricultural productivity, local government development projects, and central government expenditure on infrastructure, as well as by the general recovery of the Indonesian economy under the New Order, which created new possibilities of finding jobs elsewhere through transmigration or intraprovincial migration (see Chapter 5). In those respects, however, East Java has not been notably different from other provinces of Indonesia, for most of them face similar problems and several have been quite successful in tackling them (for example, West Sumatra and Central Java). Where East Java's economy is distinctive is in the character of the development process it has experienced under the New Order. This has been marked by balanced growth, substantially more local investment than foreign, and a high level of diversification of economic activities, ranging from large-scale plantations and manufacturing industries to small-scale commercial farming and flourishing informal-sector activities in the urban areas.

The province has had rates of economic growth averaging 8.1 per cent per annum between 1975 and 1983, fluctuating around 6 per cent during the more troubled years of the mid-1980s, then rising again to about 8 per cent in 1988/9. These growth rates were slightly above the national average, although below those of several other parts of the country (Hill, 1989: 10, 12; Vatikiotis, 1989: 57). But of the various provinces in or near what Hill calls the 'high-growth, high-income group' (Figure 2.1), East Java is the only one that has achieved impressive growth rates and relatively high per capita incomes without the advantages of substantial mineral resources (oil or liquefied natural gas [LNG]) or timber, or special stimuli like tourist dollars or massive external capital investment, such as Jakarta, West Java, and Bali have experienced.[3] East Java achieved its high rate of growth on the basis of internally generated increases in food crops (rice and maize mainly), a variety of plantation and smallholder cash crops, as well as in the manufacturing industry, construction, and the services sector generally, all of them contributing to a degree of diversity that no other province can match (Hill, 1989: 52–3, 316).

This achievement can fairly be described as 'balanced growth' in its true sense, where increases in production and incomes in one sphere have generated new demand and higher production in others, an outcome which has been much harder to achieve in resource-rich provinces with sharply 'dualistic' economic structures that are heavily dependent on one or two crops or commodities (Hill, 1989: Chapters 4, 5, 6, 10, 17, 19). Rates of growth higher than East Java's were also recorded in various low-income provinces during Indonesia's boom years, but mostly from very low base levels (Hill, 1989: 6–10). East Java's singular achievement has been to maintain a steady rate of growth in many fields of agricultural and manufacturing production, and to have done so without relying heavily on external capital.[4] Dependency theories of underdevelopment, which overstress the part played by foreign capital or

FIGURE 2.1
Provincial Economic Performance, 1975–1983

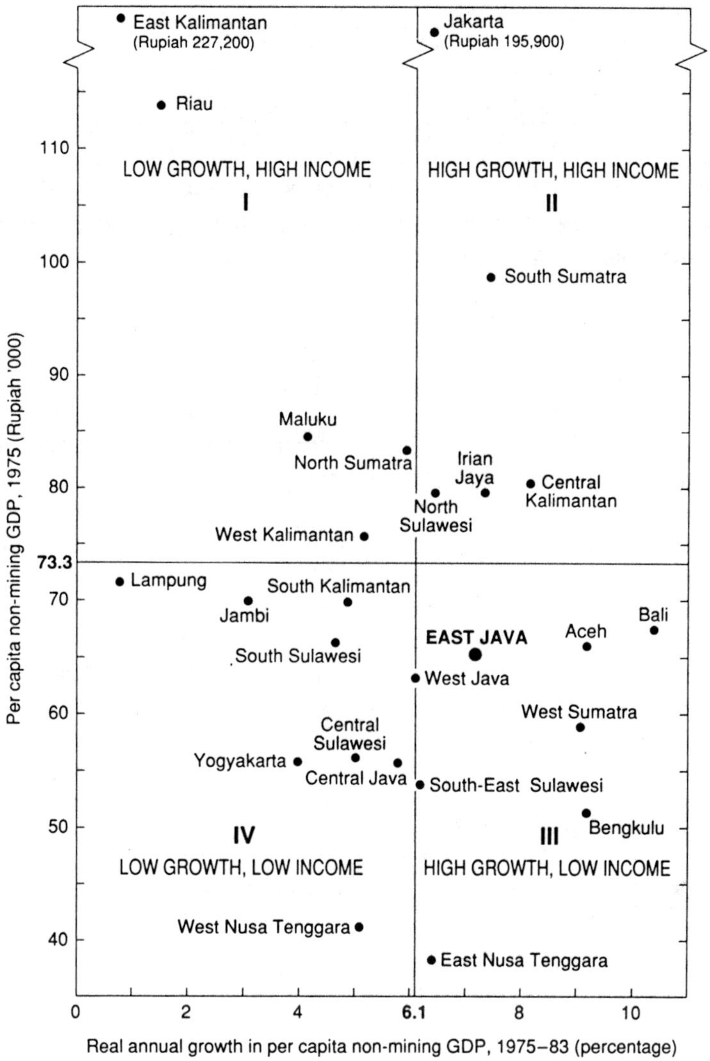

external factors (for example, the oil revenues accruing to the government), simply do not provide adequate explanations here. Although the provincial growth rate dropped slightly in the difficult years when the whole of Indonesia suffered from the collapse of oil prices in 1986/7, the decline was a minor one and by the end of the 1980s the province was again booming in the aftermath of deregulation, despite the much lower oil revenues and tight government budgets.

How and why has East Java, unlike other provinces, been able to achieve this kind of diversified and balanced development? The answer can be given partly in historical terms, and partly by reference to its geography and resources, not forgetting its human resources, for no explanation can leave out of account the distinctive personality traits of the dynamic and forthright *arek Suraboyo* (native-born Surabayans).[5] Much of the resource basis and infrastructure in East Java had been established in colonial times, so it was not a matter of having to create entirely new industries when more ample funds became available during the oil boom of 1974–83, but rather of rehabilitating and expanding existing facilities. Some of the impetus for the development generated in East Java derived from exogenous (that is, external) stimuli, but most of it seems to have come from the endogenous generation of higher incomes within the province, hence increasing local demand for goods and services.

Among the exogenous factors could be listed the big increases in government spending in the 1970s, capital inflows in the form of Jakarta-based and foreign investment, and the expansion of bank credits, new imported technologies (of which the new Green Revolution high-yielding varieties [HYVs] of rice had the most dramatic impact) and the general increase in purchasing power and commercial demand throughout the whole of Indonesia during the oil boom years. But most parts of Indonesia benefited from these same stimuli—and in the case of resource-rich areas from far more—so they alone cannot be regarded as the explanation of why East Java responded so successfully to these changes.

The clue to the puzzle seems to lie in the way various developments in the province have reinforced each other since 1970: economic, administrative, and political changes, different sectors of the economy, and exogenous and endogenous factors. The boost to purchasing power among farmers generated by productivity increases and higher agricultural production has contributed to rising demand for goods and services from the urban manufacturing and services sectors, thereby pushing up the levels of supply and effective demand in all these sectors. Growth has been an interactive and cumulative process in East Java, not just the outcome of increased government spending or inflows of capital from outside.

One of the factors contributing to this outcome has been the shift from a 'dualistic', plantation-based and export-oriented, economic structure in colonial times towards one which is now far more diversified, hence capable of adaptation to the new productive opportunities emerging (see Chapter 8). This important change has occurred mainly in the New Order period. Until about 1970, East Java was still suffering from the adverse consequences of the drying up of Dutch investment and the collapse of the plantation economy in the Great Depression, since no alternative source of dynamism and growth had yet emerged. The provincial economy had simply stagnated for 40 years. Since the late 1960s, however, not only has the Green Revolution transformed the rice economy, but urbanization and industrialization have accelerated, while the plantation sector has also regained strength, at the same time experiencing significant internal changes which have made the entire economic structure of the province less sharply dualistic. East Java has been lucky in that respect, for it has not suffered the lopsided pattern of development that North Sumatra, the other great plantation region, has experienced (Barlow and Thee, 1989). Yet it has been able to rebuild upon the basis of the productive assets and infrastructures, in particular, the unrivalled irrigation works, a sound electricity grid system, and the road-rail network, established by the Dutch in the early twentieth century (Mackie and Djumilah Zain, 1989).

Several geographical factors relevant to East Java's pattern of development must be mentioned. They can be summarized with reference to five main features. First, the central core region of the province, bounded by Surabaya, Malang, Kediri and Pasuruan–Probolinggo (see Figure 1.1), has long been a major plantation area as well as an extremely fertile rice-growing region, especially in the Lower Brantas Valley. In recent years this has been the main centre of manufacturing industry in the province, the so-called 'Golden Triangle'.[6] The diversity of employment opportunities has attracted labour into this region from the poorer outlying areas (Figure 2.2); and both capital investment levels and aggregate earnings are patently much higher there than elsewhere, although precise statistical data to confirm this are not available.

Secondly, the transport network of roads and railways extends from the harbour-city of Surabaya through the central core region to the more distant parts of the province, as does the electricity grid (see Chapter 11), creating a better integrated economic unit than exists in the other provinces of Java or in Sumatra. These facilities help to create relatively cheap, efficient means of moving agricultural commodities from rural areas to the main urban centres where demand is strongest and also of supplying goods from the ports and towns to the villages.

Thirdly, there are several other highly productive regions beyond the core area. The Jember–Lumajang–Banyuwangi plantation belt and 'rice basket' is by far the most prosperous, while some parts of the Bojonegoro tobacco-growing region and of the Nganjuk–Madiun–Magetan–Ngawi rice-growing river valleys are also very productive (see Chapter 6).

Fourthly, East Java is a highly urbanized province, with 8 towns of more than 120,000 people by 1990 and another 40 or so with populations of over 20,000 persons. Such towns are important instruments of economic integration and commercial growth, as well as of state control over economic and political life, diffusion of education and health services and of the various other blessings (or curses) of 'modernization'.

Fifthly, the poorest parts of the province are found on the island of Madura, in the four south-western *kabupaten* (districts) in the remote and relatively isolated limestone hills (Pacitan, Ponorogo, Trenggalek, and Tulungagung), and in the north-western *kabupaten* of Bojonegoro and Tuban, which also have extensive limestone hills, but *sawah* (irrigated or rain-fed field) areas as well, along the Solo River valley. There is limited

FIGURE 2.2
Intercensal Population Growth Rates by *Kabupaten*, 1890–1980

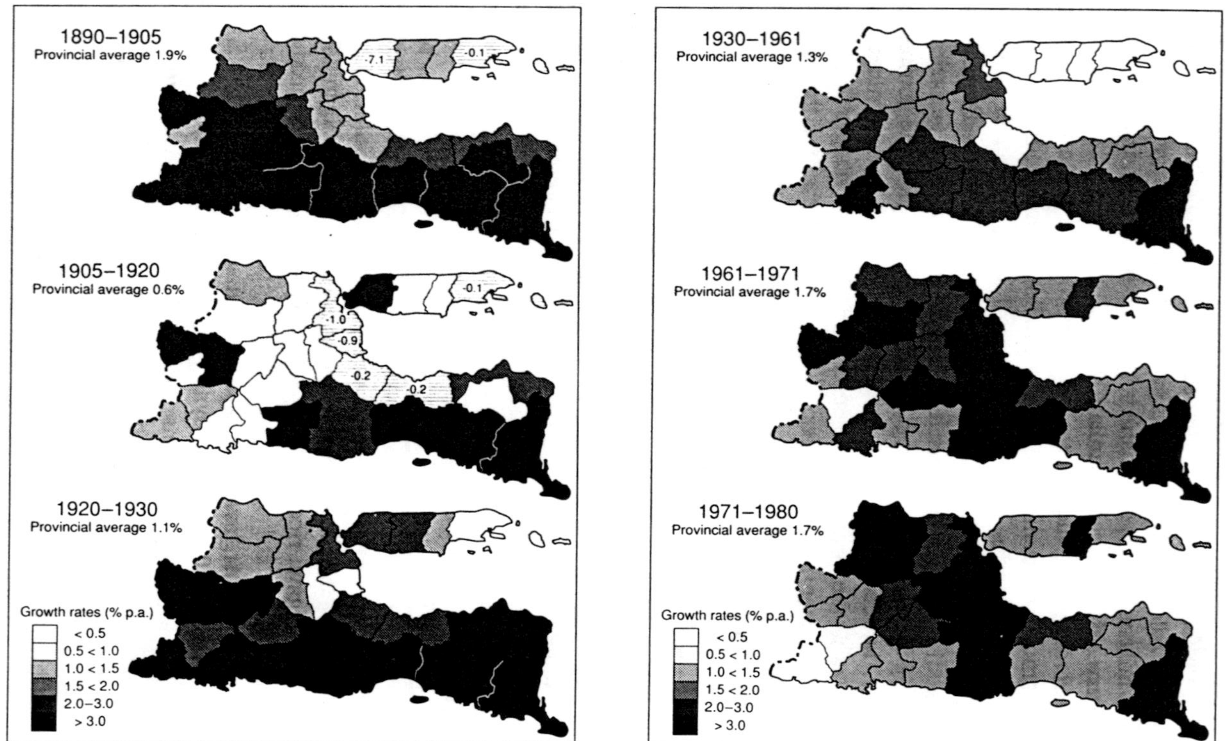

scope for agricultural improvement in these areas because of water shortages (or periodic flooding), and little hope of building up manufacturing industries on any significant scale because of locational disadvantages. People have been moving out of these areas in search of employment throughout this century, especially from Madura, and in several of them little population increase has occurred since 1970. That trend seems likely to continue, since the fast-growth *kabupaten* have been drawing people away from the poorer ones for several decades, especially young people (see Figure 2.2). On the other hand, various provincial government development programmes have benefited the poorer regions economically in some degree. Moreover, the increases in per capita rice production in the poorer *kabupaten* have in some cases been substantial (see Table 2.6). The regional income statistics by *kabupaten*, if they are reliable, indicate that several may even have experienced above-average rates of growth of gross regional product (GRP) between 1983 and 1986.[7] These issues of welfare levels and income distribution will be discussed more fully below.

Structural Changes in the Regional Economy

The most striking changes in the distribution of East Java's GRP among the agricultural (A), manufacturing (M), and services (S) sectors between 1971 and 1988 were the sharp decline in the share contributed by agriculture, from almost 50 per cent in 1971 to less than 30 per cent in 1987, and the equally sharp increase in the M sector (mining and quarrying, manufacturing, utilities, and construction) from 14.6 to nearly 24 per cent over the same period, most of it occurring after 1983 (Table 2.1). There was also a less dramatic increase in the S sector,

TABLE 2.1
Sectoral Distribution of Gross Regional Product and Sectoral Growth Rates, 1971–1987

	Sectoral Distribution (%)				*Growth Rate (%)*			
	A	*M*	*S*		*A*	*M*	*S*	*Total*
1971	49.6	14.6	35.9					
				1971–6	6.5	7.6	2.9	5.2
1976	41.2	13.5	45.3					
				1976–83	4.0	12.8	9.9	8.1
1983	33.7	17.0	49.3					
				1983–7	3.5	7.2	6.4	5.9
1987	30.0	23.7	46.3					

Sources: Hill (1989: 8–10); KSJT, *Jawa Timur dalam Angka, 1988*: 278, 280, 282.
A = Agriculture.
M = Mining and quarrying, manufacturing, utilities, and construction.
S = Services.

mainly in the trade and transport–communications subsectors, from 36 to 46.5 per cent.

Moderate but sustained rates of growth were achieved in all three major sectors during those years, without the erratic spurts recorded by other provinces in various sectors (Hill, 1989: 10), apart from East Java's quite rapid rate of increase in manufacturing between 1976 and 1982. The overall growth rate was relatively low in the early 1970s, with agriculture then growing almost as rapidly as manufacturing. It then grew much faster between 1976 and 1983, especially in the M and S sectors, but declined during the difficult years of low oil prices in the mid-1980s, although there has since been a recovery to around 8 per cent per annum since 1988.[8] The rate of growth in the A sector has declined from the high rates achieved in the early 1970s, although it is still a creditable rate by international standards.

While the share of GRP produced by the S sector as a whole has increased considerably since 1971, the proportion contributed by 'trade, hotels and restaurants' has increased relatively little and appears to have actually declined since 1982 (Table 2.2). Transport and communication has not increased its share much since 1971, according to the GRP

TABLE 2.2
Sectoral Distribution of Gross Regional Product, 1975–1988

	Percentage of Total			
Sector	*1975*	*1980*	*1985*	*1988*
Agriculture	43.0	38.3	30.7	29.8
Food crops	35.0	31.7	22.7	21.0
Smallholders	2.3	2.8	3.0	3.6
Estates	1.8	0.7	0.7	0.8
Livestock	2.7	2.2	3.1	3.1
Forestry	0.4	0.2	0.2	0.3
Fisheries	0.8	0.7	1.0	1.1
Mining	0.2	0.2	0.4	0.4
Manufacturing	11.7	13.8	17.3	18.6
Utilities	0.4	0.6	0.9	0.9
Construction	0.7	1.0	5.0	4.5
Trade, hotels, and restaurants	20.7	23.2	20.2	21.6
Transport and communications	6.3	5.9	6.8	6.7
Banking and finance	1.2	2.1	2.7	1.3
Dwellings	2.3	2.3	2.0	1.9
Government	11.1	11.4	9.3	8.8
Other services	2.3	2.1	5.8	5.5
Total	100.0	100.0	100.0	100.0

Sources: Hill (1989: 317); KSJT, *Jawa Timur dalam Angka, 1988*: 280.

figures, although this seems surprising when one considers the extent of 'the Colt revolution' in rural transportation since the late 1970s. The finance and banking subsector grew slowly until 1982, but its share of the total has more than doubled since then. The share contributed by government services and house rents has declined, although 'other services' may have increased in the 1980s.[9]

All these figures need to be interpreted with caution, since the compilation of regional accounts data at the provincial and lower levels is still a new and far from perfect statistical operation. But the patterns of structural change they reveal accord with the general impression one gets from other sources of information about the way the provincial economy has been developing under the New Order.

Population Growth

With just over 32.5 million people in 1990, East Java has a larger population than Central Java and Yogyakarta combined, but has fallen far behind the Jakarta–West Java complex (BPS, *Statistik Indonesia, 1990*). Its 1.2 per cent per annum rate of population increase in the 1980s (down from 1.5 in the 1970s) was the lowest among Indonesia's provinces, matched only by Central Java (Hugo et al., 1987: 42–3). The rate of increase has been declining steadily since 1961 (see Chapter 3). The family planning programme, which led to a sharp fall in birth rates, has been a major factor in that since about 1975, along with rising age at marriage for women, but out-migration was also a significant factor reducing the rate of population increase in the 1980s. This was due to both the official transmigration scheme and a substantial stream of unassisted (*swakarsa*) migrants leaving the province. Intraprovincial population movements have also been substantial, resulting in a steady flow of rural–urban migration (see Chapter 5) and very low rates of population growth in some rural areas (see Figure 2.2).

East Java's birth rates have been declining steadily since the early 1970s and are well below the national average. Fertility rates declined by 31 per cent between 1967–70 and 1980 (Hugo et al., 1987: 153) and have apparently fallen even further throughout the 1980s. Crude birth rates in rural areas were only marginally higher than in urban areas in the early 1980s (Wilson et al., 1985: 34–5), which indicates that family planning had spread throughout most of the province. Death rates vary a good deal, however, ranging from 5.9 per thousand in urban areas in 1981/2 to 9.1 in rural areas, while infant mortality rates varied even more at that time, from 29 to 73 per thousand in urban and rural areas respectively; they were also much lower for males in urban areas than for females in rural areas (Wilson et al., 1985). This means there is considerable scope for further decline in the mortality rate as health conditions improve, so upward pressure on the rate of population increase can be expected to continue, although it is gradually being offset by the more rapid decline in birth rates.

It is encouraging to note that a comparison of the 0–5 age cohorts revealed by the 1971 and 1980 population censuses (Figure 2.3) indicates that the population pyramid is at last narrowing at its base. But the still very youthful age structure of the population, illustrated graphically by the broadly based population pyramid, which results from the large cohorts born between 1955 and 1975, has been a major factor keeping the crude birth rate higher than it would otherwise be. And the total number of women of childbearing age will be even larger over the next 20 years than it has been hitherto, although it will decline slowly soon after that.

Transmigration to the Outer Islands under government-sponsored schemes was not a significant factor contributing to lower population growth rates until the late 1970s. The total numbers involved were almost negligible between 1930 and 1970 and amounted to only 193,000 between 1969 and 1979, although spontaneous migration to other provinces was probably much higher. But the numbers of registered transmigrants jumped sharply under the Third Five-Year Plan Repelita III, 1979/80–1983/4 to a figure of around 150,000 per annum (including unassisted migrants). An even higher target was set for Repelita IV (190,000 households, or roughly 1 million over five years), although it had to be scaled down due to budgetary constraints soon after 1984.[10] Between 1981 and 1988, a total of approximately 235,000 households (slightly over 1 million people) left East Java as transmigrants, both official and unassisted (BPS, 1988a: 95). It should be noted that if those transmigrants had not left the province, its annual rate of

FIGURE 2.3
East Java: Population Pyramids, 1971, 1980, and 1990

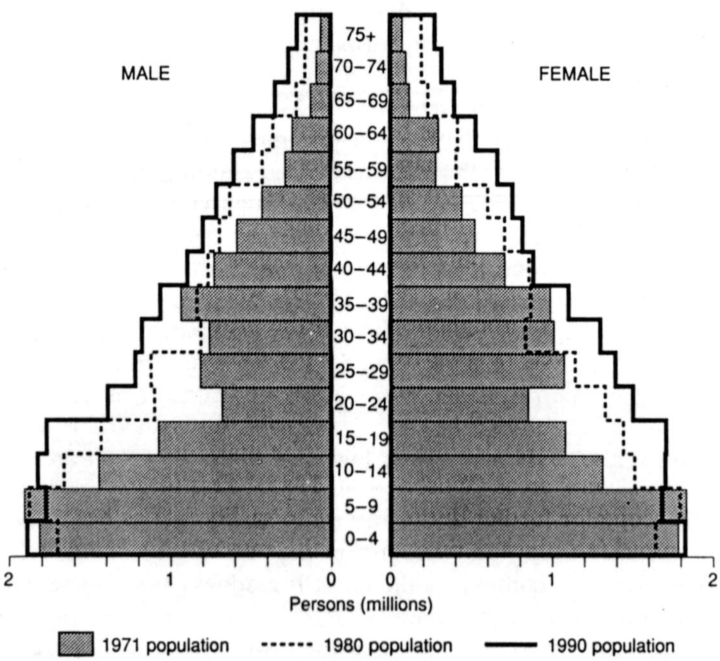

population increase would have been about 0.5 per cent higher, or closer to 1.75 per cent than the 1.24 per cent shown by the official statistics at that time. Such a rate of increase would have been perceptibly higher than the 1961–71 rate (1.5 per cent) and very much higher than the abnormally low 1930–61 figure, despite the impact of the family planning programme from the late 1970s onwards. Although transmigration has not had as great an impact on the population growth rate as the family planning programme (the latter having resulted in a fall in fertility rates of about 2 per cent, judging by figures of a decline in the crude birth rate from 47 to 26 per thousand), it has certainly been an important consideration. Moreover, since the transmigrants are predominantly young families, they represent an even more important reduction in the province's childbearing age cohorts. So transmigration has contributed significantly in the 1980s to the relief of population pressure in the province as a whole, particularly in the main out-migration areas.

Urbanization

With a total urban population of 5.7 million in 1980, about 20 per cent of the total, East Java was a more highly urbanized province than Central Java and Yogyakarta combined, although well behind the Jakarta–West Java complex (NUDS, 1985: Table 4.7). Surabaya, which had been the largest city in the former Dutch colony until 1900 but was surpassed by Jakarta soon after, had a population of just over 2 million in 1980 (including the 'rural' areas within its boundaries) and just over 2.4 million in 1990 (see Chapter 15).[11] Surabaya's population had been growing at more than 4 per cent per annum between 1920 and 1971, then at 3.2 per cent during the 1970s, when Jakarta was growing at 4.5 per cent and some smaller towns even faster (NUDS, 1985: Table 4.6; Hugo et al., 1987: 101–3); in the 1980s its rate of increase rose slightly to 3.6 per cent.

East Java also has three other large towns ranging in size from about 200,000 to 700,000 inhabitants in 1990—that is, Malang, Kediri, and Jember, as well as four between approximately 120,000 and 170,000—that is, Madiun, Pasuruan, Probolinggo, and Blitar. All of these were major centres of plantation enterprise in Dutch times, but have subsequently diversified or languished in varying degrees. Another 40 or so towns ranged from 20,000 to 100,000 in population.

The rate of population increase in all urban centres between 1971 and 1980 was 2.9 per cent, according to the NUDS categorization, which was the lowest rate of all provinces in Indonesia (Table 2.3). Comparable figures for the 1980s are not yet available. That low rate of increase must have been due in part to the fact that East Java was already more highly urbanized than the other provinces before 1971. The rate of increase of the smaller towns was about 0.5 per cent lower than that of the eight major towns, a lesser difference than was recorded before 1971, when the larger towns, Surabaya and Malang in particular, were growing much faster than all but a handful of the smaller ones.

TABLE 2.3
East Java: Population and Population Growth Rates of Eight Main Towns and Other Urban Centres, 1971, 1980, and 1990

	Population ('000)			*Rate of Increase (% p.a.)*	
	1971	*1980*	*1990*	*1971–80*	*1980–90*
Surabaya	1,308.6	1,737.0	2,410	3.2	3.3
Malang	365.3	491.5	650	3.4	2.8
Jember[a]	147.4	171.3	n.a.	1.7	n.a.
Kediri	130.5	176.3	235	3.4	2.9
Madiun	135.7	169.9	166	2.5	–0.2
Probolinggo	76.0	98.1	131	2.8	2.9
Pasuruan	87.0	119.1	134	3.6	1.2
Blitar	71.8	97.9	113	3.4	1.4
Subtotal	2,322	3,061	4,039	3.1	2.8
Other urban centres	2,120	2,659	n.a.	2.6	n.a.
Total urban population	4,442	5,720	n.a.	2.9	n.a.

Sources: 1971 and 1980: NUDS (1985: Tables 4.6, 4.7, App. E1).
1990: BPS, *Statistik Indonesia, 1990*: 35.

[a]1990 data for Jember (a *kota administratif*, not a *kotamadya*) are not yet available; a population of approximately 200,000 is assumed for purposes of the subtotal.

Jember grew very rapidly between 1930 (when it was a relatively minor plantation town of about 21,000 people) and 1970, apparently because of a boom in the local tobacco industry after the nationalization of Dutch enterprises. Kediri's growth has been stimulated since the mid-1970s by the rapid expansion of the giant Gudang Garam factory, Indonesia's largest *kretek* (clove cigarettes) enterprise (see Chapter 13). Previously its rate of increase since 1930 had lagged far behind those of Malang and Jember, due to the collapse of the Dutch plantation economy in that region which had sustained it. Likewise, Madiun, a major railway workshop centre in colonial times, has grown relatively little since then, having not had much new industrial investment to stimulate it.

The Labour Force

East Java's aggregate labour force was 13.6 million in 1985 (see Chapter 4), an increase of nearly 37 per cent over the 1971 figure (9.8 million). The increase in the agricultural labour force in the 1970s was very low, only 771,000, or less than 12 per cent (Table 2.4) and in the 1980s it has had almost no increase at all (see Chapter 4). By then nearly all the growth in the labour force was being taken up by trading activities, 'services' of all kinds, and industry (although the recorded increase in the latter between 1971 and 1980 was surprisingly small). The recorded increase in the construction and transport sector also seems relatively low, casting some doubt on the reliability of the statistics.

In the case of the industrial labour force, it should be noted that sugar milling and the *kretek* industries account for the bulk of the employment. There has not been much increase in the former, but the latter has grown considerably. The number of females engaged in various types of manufacturing activities doubled in both rural and urban areas between 1971 and 1980, which implies a fairly broad geographical spread of female employment; it was not confined to just one or two places (Surabaya–Malang) or particular industries (*kretek* manufacturing or tobacco processing, for example). The number of females engaged in trading activities increased by about 50 per cent in urban areas but by nearly 100 per cent in rural areas (which suggests a process of 'commercial involution' in low-productivity trading activities); but in the services category the opposite was the case—a doubling in rural areas but nearly a fivefold increase in the urban sector. The rates of labour force participation by females appear to have declined since 1930, rather puzzlingly, although less dramatically than in the case of Central Java, where the 1930 figure was presumably inflated by the large numbers of batik workers, of whom there are far fewer in East Java.

Will non-agricultural employment continue to increase as rapidly in the 1990s as it did in the boom conditions of the 1970s? There are various indications that the number of formal-sector jobs outside agriculture did not increase much in the 1980s (at least until the jump in export manufacturing occurred at the end of the decade), hence most of the increase must have been in informal-sector activities at very low income levels. Relatively little is known about the size or character of the informal sector in East Java, but it appears to be of considerable importance in providing various forms of livelihood to millions of people in and around Surabaya and Malang, where the vigorous construction activity of the last 20 years, coupled with a significant but relatively modest growth in large-scale manufacturing industry, has had a multiplier effect in generating all sorts of petty trading and other low-level service activities in the *kampung* (village) that have sprung up around the more established housing estates.

Meanwhile, members of the 1970–4 birth cohort, the biggest ever in East Java (numbering approximately 3.8 million as of 1980) would have been pouring into the labour force in the 1980s, creating an unprecedented pressure for jobs and incomes. The two previous cohorts, born in 1965–9 and 1960–4 or earlier, had been much smaller (see Figure 2.3), so the new entrants into the labour force in the boom years of the 1970s would have found jobs more easily. The demographic effects of the age-distribution pattern upon employment would have been most difficult in the late 1980s; but some relief may be expected during the 1990s, as the smaller 1975–9 birth cohort starts to look for jobs.

TABLE 2.4

East Java: Sectoral Distribution of the Labour Force, 1971, 1980, and 1985

	Total									
	1971		*1980*		*1985*		*Increase, 1971–80*		*Increase, 1980–5*	
Sector	*'000*	*%*	*'000*	*%*	*'000*	*%*	*'000*	*%*	*'000*	*%*
Agriculture	6,503	66.3	7,274	63.2	7,314	54.8	771	11.8	40	0.6
Trade	1,089	11.0	1,957	17.0	2,137	16.0	868	79.7	180	9.2
Industry	541	5.5	702	6.1	1,397	10.5	161	29.7	695	99.0
Services	935	9.6	1,172	10.2	1,699	12.7	237	25.3	527	45.0
Transport	188	1.9	223	1.9	385	2.9	35	18.6	162	72.7
Construction	114	1.2	150	1.3	389	2.9	36	31.6	239	159.3
Other	384	3.9	42	0.3	31	0.2	–	–	–11	–26.2
Total	9,754	100.0	11,520	100.0	13,352	100.0	1,766	18.0	1,832	15.9

	Female									
	1971		1980		1985		Increase, 1971–80		Increase, 1980–5	
Sector	'000	Percentage of Total Labour Force	'000	Percentage of Total Labour Force	'000	Percentage of Total Labour Force	'000	%	'000	%
Agriculture	1,972	30.3	1,936	26.6	2,505	13.6	−36	−1.8	569	29.4
Trade	515	47.3	937	47.9	1,293	7.0	422	81.9	356	38.0
Industry	242	44.7	481	68.5	642	3.5	239	98.8	161	33.5
Services	305	32.6	536	45.7	632	3.5	231	75.7	96	17.9
Transport	3	1.6	4	1.8	4	n.a.	1	33.3	0	0.0
Construction	5	4.4	5	3.3	8	n.a.	0	0	3	60.0
Other	6	44.7	21	49.3	16	0.1	15	250.0	−5	−23.8
Total	3,048	33.8	3,920	34.3	5,098	27.6	872	28.6	1,180	32.16

Sources: 1971: BPS (1974).
1980: BPS (1983a).
1985: BPS (1987a).

Agriculture

Nearly 4 million households were engaged in agricultural activities in East Java in the early 1980s (BPS, 1986b) and the 1980 Population Census recorded slightly more than 7.27 million persons in that category, 63 per cent of the total work-force. But the increase in the agricultural work-force was relatively small in the 1970s, below 12 per cent, and even smaller since then. Since production of the major crops has increased far more rapidly than the agricultural work-force, productivity per farm worker must have risen significantly; so also has productivity per hectare for most crops. The per capita availability of rice and other foods has improved greatly for the province as a whole as well as for nearly all *kabupaten*, including the poorest (Tables 2.5 and 2.6; see Figure 1.2). So even when allowance is made for the substantial quantities of rice, maize, cassava, soya bean, and sugar that are shipped to other provinces or other *kabupaten*, the food supply available for consumption must have increased well above subsistence levels in nearly all parts of the province.

Big increases in agricultural production have been achieved not only in the main food crops but also in most plantation crops in East Java since 1970 (see Chapter 8). Rice production more than doubled between 1968 and 1982 to over 7 million tonnes, after a long period of stagnation throughout the 1950s–60s at an average level of less than 3.4 million tonnes. In 1988, it slightly exceeded 8 million tonnes. East Java has had both the highest rice yields, on average, of all provinces, and the highest rate of increase in yields between 1971 and 1983 (Hill, 1988: 17–18), although West Java exceeded it slightly in total production and area planted.

Maize production has also doubled since the introduction of high-yielding varieties in the late 1970s, with the province now producing more than half the total output of Java (Hill, 1988: 19–20; Timmer,

TABLE 2.5
East Java: Average Annual Production of Main Food Crops, 1952–1988
('000 tonnes)

Crop	*1952–62*	*1970–9*	*1984–8*
Rice (*gabah*)	3 502	4 155	8 150
Maize	1 086	1 293	3 033
Cassava	3 188	3 628	4 109
Sweet potatoes	511	355	266
Peanuts	87	104	128
Soya beans	260	281	448

Sources: 1952–62: Anon. (1971: Table 2).
1970–9: BPS, *Produksi Tanaman Bahan Makanan*.
1984–8: KSJT, *Jawa Timur dalam Angka, 1988*: 9, 92–9.

TABLE 2.6
East Java: Rice Production by *Kabupaten*, 1968, 1981, and 1988

	Rice (kg per capita)		
Kabupaten	*1968*	*1981*	*1988*
Pacitan	49	109	160
Ponorogo	39	149	237
Trenggalek	49	89	96
Tulungagung	50	106	145
Blitar	82	113	182
Kediri	94	117	182
Malang	63	80	76
Lumajang	98	163	248
Jember	117	194	233
Banyuwangi	183	253	307
Bondowoso	113	224	256
Situbondo	125	171	221
Probolinggo	129	140	194
Pasuruan	119	145	198
Sidoarjo	125	131	135
Mojokerto	125	158	180
Jombang	106	178	194
Nganjuk	118	174	245
Madiun	71	178	299
Magetan	82	168	232
Ngawi	153	274	435
Bojonegoro	78	192	336
Tuban	61	132	194
Lamongan	61	247	347
Gresik/Surabaya	31	49	56
Bangkalan	63	76	124
Sampang	39	82	148
Pamekasan	19	55	64
Sumenep	20	48	67
Total	85	140	180

Sources: 1968: Diperta, *Laporan Tahunan, 1968*.
1981: KSJT, *Jawa Timur dalam Angka, 1981*; BPS (1983c).
1988: KSJT, *Jawa Timur dalam Angka, 1988*: 23, 92.

1987). Both maize and rice are now produced as much for the commercial market as for domestic consumption. The same could be said of cassava, which used to be a staple food in the poorer parts of Java, but is increasingly being produced for cash sales (much of it for export as cattle feed, or as tapioca). The total area planted with cassava is now steadily declining, however, for it is no longer as essential to sheer survival among the poor as it was in the 1950s–60s (Falcon et al., 1984). Production of soya bean, a profitable but risky crop, of which nearly half the total output of Java comes from East Java, has also been rising steadily, although with marked fluctuations and in lesser quantities than total demand would warrant. Altogether, the rapid increase in commercial production of these crops has been one of the most striking changes in the rural economy of East Java since Independence.

The regional income statistics show agricultural production in the province as having increased at an average rate of 6.5 per cent per annum between 1971 and 1975, the early years of the Green Revolution, then at a slower rate, around 4 per cent, up to 1982 (a period of severe attacks by *wereng*, the brown planthopper, in the mid-1970s, followed by bumper rice harvests in 1979–81, after those attacks had been overcome), then at nearly 6 per cent between 1982 and 1986. Several other provinces have had higher rates of increase (Hill, 1989: 10), but these are very creditable rates for such a large area. Few countries in the developing world have managed to maintain annual growth rates as high as 4 per cent in agriculture over sustained periods. So East Java's record in this is indeed impressive. Although the share of agriculture in East Java's GRP fell quite sharply between 1971 and 1986, from 59 to 31 per cent, that was due mainly to the more rapid growth of other, predominantly urban, sectors of the economy, a phenomenon that is common in most developing countries.

The increase in rice production is dealt with more fully in Chapter 6 and needs only to be summarized here. It was due largely to dramatic increases in yields per hectare, the earliest and most successful in Indonesia, from a provincial average of 3 tonnes per hectare in 1970/1 to 5.4 by 1988. Higher yields accounted for about 60 per cent of the overall increase in rice production between 1970 and 1982 and higher cropping intensities (more double cropping, and in some areas triple cropping, each year) for about 22 per cent. This is a puzzlingly low figure, considering that the shorter growing season of HYVs is considered one of their main advantages.[12] Some slight increase in *sawah* area has also occurred, about 4 per cent of the total, due largely to the rehabilitation of irrigation facilities. The major rice-producing areas in the province have been Jember, Banyuwangi, Lamongan, and Ngawi, with the highest yields, at or near 6 tonnes per hectare in 1988, being recorded in Jombang, Magetan, Ngawi, Kediri and Malang (KSJT, *Jawa Timur dalam Angka, 1988*: 93). But yield differentials were by that time not very wide, for nearly all regions had gradually experienced big increases in productivity with HYVs and were approaching the limits attainable under current technology. The reasons why East Java has had such success in rice cultivation are complex (see Chapter 6), but the improvements in irrigation facilities and transport services in the first decade of the New Order, as well as the new rice varieties, certainly made an important contribution.

Although plantation crops no longer dominate the agricultural economy of East Java in the way they did in the late colonial era, the province still retains its historic position as a major producer of them. About two-thirds of Indonesia's sugar is grown there and nearly all the

TABLE 2.7
East Java: Major Agricultural Exports, 1970–1988 (US$ million)

		Average	
	1970	*1980–1*	*1987–8*
Coffee	n.a.	51.8	115.3
Rubber	6.2	22.6	34.0
Tobacco and *kretek*	n.a.	35.5	30.0
Cassava chips (*gaplek*)	n.a.	12.9	35.5
Copra cake	2.2	16.0	24.3
Cocoa	n.a.	n.a.	17.0

Sources: 1970: Anon. (1971: 31).
1980–1: KSJT, *Jawa Timur dalam Angka, 1981*: 378.
1987–8: KSJT, *Jawa Timur dalam Angka, 1988*: 168–74.

estate coffee. Yet East Java's export earnings from sugar and tobacco are no longer comparable with those of the late colonial period, for its sugar now goes entirely to domestic consumption, as does most of its tobacco, apart from a small quantity of high-quality cigar tobacco from Besuki. Agricultural exports (if prawns are excluded) accounted for less than half of the total export earnings of the province in the 1980s, the main commodities exported in 1988 being coffee (US$100 million), rubber (US$38 million), coconut oil and other products (US$40 million), cassava pellets (US$37 million), tobacco and *kretek* (US$28 million), and cocoa beans (US$17 million) (KSJT, *Jawa Timur dalam Angka, 1989*). Prawns, plywood, and rattan furniture earned nearly US$380 million in that year (but the last two are merely manufactured there, not grown) and they have risen quite sharply since then. East Java's share of Indonesia's total exports did not exceed 4 per cent at any time in the 1970s–80s and frequently fell below 2 per cent, a far cry from the situation in the 1920s when it was the main source of the colony's export staple, sugar.

The contribution of plantation agriculture to East Java's GRP had fallen to a very low level by the 1980s, only a little over 4 per cent, most of it from the smallholder sector. In fact, the distinction between 'plantation' and 'smallholder' agriculture has become an increasingly blurred and irrelevant one in respect of sugar and tobacco, for the actual cultivation of those crops is no longer the responsibility of estate managers as in colonial times, although it still is for rubber, tea, cocoa, and much of the coffee (see Chapter 8). But the most striking change in East Java's agricultural economy since 1970 is the fact that 'rice is king' in nearly all parts of the province, whereas 60 years ago 'sugar was king' in the most fertile areas, in terms of both its importance in the lives of the millions of rural households involved in its production and its pivotal role in the colonial economic structure (C. Geertz, 1963; Elson, 1984).

Industry

Until the 1970s, East Java could accurately be described as 'the most industrialized province in Indonesia', with a larger fraction of the country's total manufacturing work-force, output, and value added in 1974 than either Jakarta or West Java (Hill, 1987: 86). It has since fallen far behind both of these, with their fast-growing agglomerations of manufacturing industries. In fact the Jakarta–West Java industrial complex was already beginning to exceed the level of manufacturing output in East Java by 1963, although in terms of manufacturing employment it did not do so until the early 1970s. But East Java still has the second largest industrial complex in Indonesia by any measure, with over 3,000 establishments in the large and medium (L and M) category in 1985, employing 412,500 workers, nearly a quarter of Indonesia's total L and M manufacturing work-force, in addition to major sectors of small and household industry, with 165,883 and 556,862 workers respectively (see Chapter 10: Table 10.2). It is also the oldest of them all, an important factor as far as industrial infrastructure is concerned, its long-established metal and machinery workshops in Surabaya having been set up to service the many sugar mills throughout the province in the late nineteenth century. The ship-repair facilities in the harbour were also established then. Since the 1950s, two large, highly capital-intensive cement and fertilizer–petrochemical plants have been established at Gresik, just to the north of Surabaya, to which have been added since 1970 a variety of smaller factories in the Rungkut industrial estate just south of the city and many others along the Surabaya–Malang corridor (see Chapter 14).

A general picture of the major industries of East Java can be seen in Table 2.8. The dominant position of the *kretek* industry is the most striking feature of the industrial structure of the province, accounting for roughly half of total manufacturing output and half of the workers engaged in the 12 major industries, along with more than 60 per cent of their total manufacturing value added. Next in importance came sugar milling, a declining industry on any long-term assessment, since production of sugar-cane peaked in the mid-1980s and is unlikely to increase further. After these came fertilizer, cement, milk products (in each case a single very large factory), weaving, and coconut oil. The fastest growth rates between 1975 and 1983 were recorded by the relatively small toothpaste, cosmetics, and perfume group of industries (a 32-fold growth in value added), coconut oil (26-fold, Bimoli being the main producer), milk products (26-fold, principally the Nestlé factory), and the *kretek* industry (21-fold). Apart from these, only the relatively small yarn and thread spinning industry experienced a high rate of growth (15-fold). East Java's textile industry is very small, however, compared with that of West Java, or even of Central Java–Yogyakarta with its large batik industry. In East Java batik has declined into insignificance, except in a few traditional centres like Lasem, Trenggalek, and Tulungagung.

The five big factories in the Surabaya–Gresik area that loom largest

TABLE 2.8
East Java: Major Industries, 1974/5 and 1985[a]

Industry	Employment		Value Added[b]	
	1974/5	*1985*	*1974/5*	*1985*
Kretek	43,412	84,742	22.3	523.9
Sugar	40,962	37,000	33.1	148.4
Weaving	14,243	16,420	4.4	38.5
Yarn	5,984	6,485	0.7	12.6
Machinery	3,595	5,911	5.4	46.1
Metal structural products	1,398	2,037	2.2	10.0
Fertilizer	1,383	4,012	6.3	83.3
Cosmetics, perfume, and toothpaste	856	2,111	0.3	16.3
Cement	1,105	1,783	9.7	83.3
Coconut oil	1,900	1,921	0.8	51.7
Milk products	176	818	1.3	13.9
Beer	631	353	2.6	7.9

Sources: Hill (1989: Table 12.5); BPS (unpublished data).
[a]Data refer to L and M industries only.
[b]Rp billion, at factor cost.

on the East Java industrial scene are Gresik Cement, Petrokimia (manufacturing fertilizer), Nestlé (milk products), Bimoli (cooking oil and products), and Bintang (beer). The number of jobs they create in the industrial work-force is quite small, however, only about 7,000 in 1983 out of roughly 160,000 in the twelve largest industries. The biggest industrial enterprise in the province—in fact, in the whole of Indonesia—is the unique *kretek* factory, Gudang Garam, located in Kediri, with over 42,000 workers. It accounted for more than half of the *kretek* industry's 50.4 per cent share of total value added in East Java's manufacturing sector in 1983 (Hill, 1989: Table 1.13). It was then almost double the size of East Java's second largest *kretek* company, Bentoel, located in Malang, although there had been intense rivalry for market share between these two throughout the 1980s. Three of the 'Big Four' *kretek* factories in Indonesia are located in East Java, the smallest of them—Sampurna—being a long-established Surabaya firm.

Among the smaller industrial enterprises that deserve mention are the two state-owned paper mills at Leces, near Probolinggo, and Banyuwangi, the Barata (formerly Braat) machinery plant in Surabaya, as well as various others in the Surabaya–Malang corridor; the Surabaya dockyards complex; the Proctor and Gamble coconut oil products factory; several glassware and bottle factories; various car, motor-cycle, and bicycle assembly plants (one of which is Udatin, formerly a major car assembly firm, which went into decline in the 1980s); and a number of printing enterprises.

In addition to all these, a considerable number of large manufacturing enterprises were established during the late 1980s, many of them export-oriented (prawn processing, timber, and rattan furniture factories being the foremost), which represents a new and potentially significant wave of manufacturing investment in East Java and which should give a major boost to the industrial sector in the province in the course of the 1990s. After falling behind the Jakarta–West Java industrial heartland of Indonesia since the late 1960s, East Java may be on the brink of a new phase of dramatic expansion in manufacturing industries.

In assessing the impact of the manufacturing sector on the overall welfare of the society in East Java since the 1960s, one needs to distinguish between the production-income effects, geared largely to levels of productivity, and the employment-generating effects. By far the greatest share of manufacturing value added came from the L and M group. But the total number of workers engaged in that category of enterprises, which tends to be the high-productivity sector with the best growth prospects, was only 270,000 out of a total of nearly 950,000 workers recorded in the 1980 Population Census as engaged in manufacturing industry, although by 1985 it had risen to 36 per cent of the work-force (see Chapter 10: Table 10.2). This means that nearly 700,000 were engaged in small-scale enterprises and household industries, including much informal-sector activity, much of it in highly precarious, low-productivity and low-wage jobs. Even the employment figures give a misleading notion of the wage incomes generated in the L and M sectors, since well over half the workers in this sector would have been engaged in the *kretek*, sugar-milling, and other agriculture-related manufacturing enterprises, where wages tend to be low. The highly capitalized factories that normally pay above-average wage rates require a relatively small work-force in aggregate.

It is impossible to estimate how much secondary employment the larger manufacturing enterprises have generated through small-scale upstream or downstream industries. But it is surely the case that Surabaya would not have experienced its high level of economic activity in the construction and small-scale services and informal sectors without the boost to growth, incomes, and induced investment in other sectors of the Surabaya–Malang region's economy generated by those larger enterprises since 1970. The main employment-generating effects of the growth of manufacturing have probably occurred much more in the services sector and the vast, sprawling, informal sector than in the L and M industry sector. Any comparison between Surabaya and other non-industrialized cities in Indonesia leads to the conclusion that the L and M industries have constituted the leading edge in the development process there since 1965.

It should be remembered, however, that the employment statistics on manufacturing industry in East Java are distorted to some extent by the fact that the two largest industries in the province, *kretek* cigarette production and sugar milling employ very large numbers of workers, as do other establishments involved in the processing of plantation crops (tobacco sorting and curing sheds, and coffee or cocoa fermentation sheds, where large numbers of women are employed in highly labour-intensive work). Since all these industries are essentially ancillary to agricultural production, their scope for expansion is limited and they are no longer a major source of new industrial investment. Neither Central nor West Java has had such a large set of plantation-based industries; on the other hand, a large part of the total manufacturing work-force in those provinces has been employed in the batik and textile weaving industries, both of them highly labour-intensive, which are small in East Java.

These structural features of the industrial complexes of each province must be kept in mind when we are comparing their respective sizes and growth rates, for they affect the aggregate figures greatly. Dick points out that the relative importance of the plantation-based industries has declined sharply since the early 1970s (see Chapter 10) from 33 to 11 per cent of manufacturing value added and from 36 to 28 per cent of employment between 1974 and 1985. New investment in that sector has not played anything like the same part in generating industrial activity and employment as it did before World War II. The main growth sectors in recent years, in value added terms, have been the *kretek* industry, chemicals, and paper. The longer-established industries, like metals and machinery, increased relatively little between 1974 and 1985, although they still constitute a potentially important sector of industry there (see Chapter 10).

The rate of expansion of the manufacturing industry sector in East Java has fallen behind those of West Java and Jakarta since the 1960s for several reasons. The latter have grown from a much lower base level, East Java being the premier industrial centre at that time. And they have since had a vastly greater inflow of foreign investment (US$300 million and US$228 million respectively between 1967 and 1985, compared with US$74 million in East Java) and about four times the level of domestic investment, judging from the investment approval statistics.[13] The share of manufacturing and utilities in East Java's GRP showed only a modest increase between 1978 and 1986 from 14 to 18 per cent (see Chapter 10), although there has been a considerable boom in manufacturing investment there since then. The rate of increase has certainly lagged well behind that of the Jakarta–West Java complex, however, and Dick's observation that the industrial structure of East Java resembles the 'smaller and more backward one of Central Java rather than the larger and more sophisticated one of Jakarta–West Java' is certainly correct. This would not have been true before the 1960s, however, when East Java was still Indonesia's main industrial province.

Foreign and Domestic Investment Levels

Foreign investment in East Java has been a relatively small factor in the overall growth process since 1967, greatly overshadowed by domestic investment. Far from being a major factor behind rapid growth in this

TABLE 2.9
East Java, Java, and Indonesia: Foreign and Domestic Investment Approvals, 1967–1990

	East Java	*Java*	*Indonesia*	*East Java/ Java (%)*	*East Java/ Indonesia (%)*
Foreign Investment Approvals, 1967–October 1990 (US$ million)					
1967–77	29	307	625	9	5
1978–81	46	249	676	18	7
1982–5	14	183	56[a]	8	25
1986–90	422	4,954	5,568	9	8
Domestic Investment Approvals, 1967–October 1990 (Rp billion)					
1967–77	39	169	247	23	16
1978–81	88	927	1,409	9	6
1982–5[a]	431	2,295	3,841	19	11
1985–90	1,695	18,431	27,984	9	6

Sources: BPS, *Indikator Ekonomi*, monthly issues.

Note: These figures are computations from the *Indikator Ekonomi* cumulative series, which have been adjusted at times. They should be regarded as indicators of orders of magnitude only, with an unknown margin of error.

[a]Indonesia total for 1982–5 includes several years of negative investment outside Java.

province, capital formation—both domestic and foreign—has resulted from the boom conditions of the New Order period. Since the figures for approved investments issued by the Capital Investment Co-ordinating Board (Badan Koordinasi Penanaman Modal or BKPM) refer only to approvals, they are merely a rough guide to actual disbursements (Table 2.9). They differ greatly from the estimates by Bank Indonesia of actual foreign capital invested (Hill, pers. com.), the figures for which were US$74 million of realized investments in East Java between 1967 and 1985, or 6 per cent of the national aggregate, and US$258 million by July 1989, indicating a surge of foreign capital in the late 1980s as the local economy boomed.

A calculation of the levels of foreign investment in the various provinces of Indonesia on a per capita basis showed that the figure for East Java was less than half the national average before 1979, a mere Rp 26,600 per person, compared with over Rp 120,000 for West Java and Jakarta (Rietveld, 1988: 80–1). But there was a much higher level of domestic investment, in so far as this can be measured by BKPM approvals, with the bulk of approved investment in East Java being earmarked for manufacturing industry—over 90 per cent of the total. These figures further highlight the observation that domestic capital has played a much larger part in East Java's industrialization under the New Order than foreign capital.

Social Welfare Indicators

Only impressionistic estimates can be made of the extent to which levels of individual welfare in East Java, in terms of income, diet, health, life expectancy, education, employment opportunities, or housing, have improved under the New Order regime. The aggregated nature of official statistics makes it impossible to generalize in a way that takes account of the wide range of differences between the richer parts of the province and the poorer, or the wealthier classes and the landless, although those differences appear to be very great. There can be no doubt that East Java's pattern of economic growth has brought disproportionately large benefits to the wealthy and only modest gains, at most, to the poor. Data and discussion on various aspects of these issues can be found elsewhere in this book (see Chapters 3, 4, 6, and 11). Several others deserve mention here.

Income disparities between the richest and the poorest groups in East Java, whether measured on the basis of regions, economic sectors, or social classes, are still wide by Indonesian standards (although not especially so by comparison with many Third World countries), and are probably even worse at the higher levels of society than they were in the 1960s when poverty was widespread. The reasons for such disparities are basically structural, but they are not easily remediable by government policy. The plantation sector yields quite high incomes to some of its more senior modern-sector employees, but pays very low wages to its non-permanent workers, well below the income levels of most farmers. Much the same can be said for most modern-sector industry, although wages there are generally higher than elsewhere (Manning, 1987: 310). The incomes from informal-sector commercial and service activities, which make up a substantial part of total employment and incomes in East Java, tend to be low, although they are still generally higher than the incomes derived from agricultural labour. In agriculture, the income levels obtainable from rice and high-value crops such as fruit and vegetables are generally higher (although riskier in some cases) than those from dry-season crops like maize, cassava, root crops, and soya beans, which are most likely to be planted by the poorer peasants who do not own *sawah* (or who can get access to it only as sharecroppers or tenants). Very low levels of per capita expenditure in rural areas of East Java were revealed in the 1980 National Socio-economic Survey (Survei Sosial Ekonomi National or Susenas) figures, only marginally higher than those for Central Java and below those of Yogyakarta, Bali, and Nusa Tenggara, both East and West; in urban areas they were slightly higher, but still among the four lowest provincial average figures in Indonesia. The proportion of families below the poverty line (under Sajogyo's definition) was also extremely high (Hill, 1989: 42).

One explanation of East Java's low rural consumption levels may be the relatively high proportion of the population living in the dry, poorly endowed regions along the north and south coasts. Another could be that a substantial part of the work-force is employed as plantation workers at very low wages. But even so, the income levels of millions of the poorer people living in East Java's rural areas are still very low. A more significant issue, however, is the extent to which incomes have risen in the 'Golden Triangle', particularly at the lower levels of society (there can be little question that they have done so at the higher levels), where more abundant employment opportunities have been opening up since the 1970s. But high rates of in-migration have been intensifying the competition for jobs there, or for income-earning niches in the informal sector. Unfortunately, statistical data on such matters are not adequate to answer such questions.

The 1987 Susenas figures showed a considerable improvement in East Java's position relative to other provinces and in comparison with earlier surveys. In terms of per capita expenditure, the province ranked tenth, while the incidence of rural poverty showed a steep decline, from 50 per cent in 1980 to 17.8 per cent in 1987 (Booth, 1992: Table 10.18). Although the extent of rural poverty in East Java was still above that of the other provinces of Java, it was lower than in twelve provinces outside Java. But the Susenas data also indicated quite high rates of regional disparity in expenditure levels (and, by implication, income levels) within the province, so regional inequalities as well as social inequalities remain a serious problem.

The available information on dietary standards reveals that per capita consumption of carbohydrates rose from around 182 kilograms per annum in 1973/4 to 216 in 1979, 235 in 1982, a drought year, and higher levels since then, far above the subsistence minimum of 165 kilograms calculated by the Indonesian Council of Sciences. Consumption of protein was less satisfactory until the 1980s, however, averaging slightly less than the standard minimum figure of 16 kilograms per capita. The increase in meat, fish, egg, milk, and soya bean production in the 1980s has greatly improved dietary levels overall, although they are consumed mainly by the well-to-do, whereas the poor still have limited access to such foodstuffs because of the great distortions in income distribution patterns.

In the provision of educational opportunities, East Java has made dramatic progress since 1970, particularly at the higher levels.[14] It had previously lagged well behind Central and West Java (and even further behind Jakarta and Yogyakarta) in both the educational facilities available and overall participation rates, but it has caught up and now compares favourably with them at nearly all levels. Islamic schools—nearly all of them at an elementary level—were formerly much more numerous than they were elsewhere, and were more important relative to the government school system in East Java. But that situation has changed radically since the introduction in 1974 of the Inpres Sekolah Dasar programme which has resulted in the erection of government-funded primary schools in virtually every village.[15] The number of primary school pupils almost doubled between 1971 and 1984 and nearly all children in the province in that age-group now obtain at least some

TABLE 2.10
East Java: Educational Progress, 1971–1989

	Schools	*Number of Teachers*	*Pupils ('000)*
Primary School (SD) Level			
1971	9,996	69,019	2,414
1975	11,846	83,137	2,616
1984/5	21,488	141,526	4,382
1988/9	22,234	171,961	3,961
Junior High School (SMP) Level			
1971	845	13,268	192
1975	(898)	15,075	264
1984/5	2,655	54,571	896
1988/9	3,079	65,469	1,023
Senior High School (SMA) Level			
1971	173	3,823	46
1975	174	3,972	49
1984/5	924	24,785	331
1988/9	1,324	36,729	469

Sources: BPS, *Statistik Indonesia*, 1971, 1975, and 1984–9.

schooling. The numbers enrolled at primary level have actually been declining since the mid-1980s as the youngest age cohorts have begun to diminish in size, but at the higher levels the expansion of the educational system has continued quite rapidly in respect of number of schools and teachers, as well as of pupils (Table 2.10). Enrolments at junior high school (*sekolah menengah pertama* or SMP) and senior high school (*sekolah menengah atas* or SMA) levels increased around five and seven times respectively between 1971 and 1984, and in both cases has continued to grow rapidly throughout the 1980s (Table 2.10).

The proportion of the population recorded as having had no schooling at all was nearly 70 per cent in 1963 but had fallen to 32 per cent in 1982 (mostly the elderly, it may be assumed) and further during the 1980s. One of the interesting features of East Java's educational development has been the proliferation of non-government schools above the primary level since the 1970s (including many tertiary-level institutions, although most are not of high calibre). Many of these are religious schools of various sorts, including the State Islamic Institutes (Institut Agama Islam Negeri or IAIN)[16] established and funded by the Ministry of Religion (Table 2.11). The number of non-government schools, universities, and training institutes is a striking feature of East Java's educational development, particularly in Surabaya and Malang, and also in Jember and Kediri to a lesser extent.

TABLE 2.11

East Java and Other Provinces of Java: Percentage of Population Aged 10 and Above by Level of Education, 1961–1988/9

	No Schooling		*SD Only*		*SMP and Above*	
	1961	*1963/4*	*1961*	*1963/4*	*1961*	*1963/4*
East Java	67.0	71	30	27	2.8	2.3
Central Java and Yogyakarta	57.5	67	39	31	3.6	2.6
West Java (and Jakarta)	57.2	64	39	34	3.5	2.4
Total Java	60.0	(64)	36	31	3.9	3.0

	No Schooling		*At SD*		*At SMP*		*At SMA*		*At University or Tertiary Institutions*	
	1982/3	*1988/9*	*1982/3*	*1988/9*	*1982/3*	*1988/9*	*1982/3*	*1988/9*	*1982/3*	*1988/9*
East Java	32	27.4	18.3	15.8	3.4	4.3	1.6	2.2	0.1	0.1
Central Java	26	22.4	21.8	19.1	3.5	4.2	1.7	1.9	0.1	0.1
West Java	21	20.7	23.5	19.7	2.9	3.5	1.2	1.6	0.1	0.1
Total Indonesia	24	21.1	23.7	20.4	4.1	4.9	1.9	2.3	0.2	0.2

Sources: BPS, *Statistik Indonesia*, 1961, 1964, 1983, and 1989.
Note: Figures for the 1960s are aggregates and not directly comparable with those for 1982/3 and 1988/9.

SD = *Sekolah dasar* (primary school).
SMP = *Sekolah menengah pertama* (junior high school)—all types included.
SMA = *Sekolah menengah atas* (senior high school)—all types included.

Conclusion

The depth and breadth of the economic transformation that has occurred in East Java under the New Order is better judged in terms of its impact on the living standards of the people there and in the far-reaching changes in daily life it has brought than just in terms of the structural changes revealed by statistics. Production and per capita incomes have been rising steadily since 1970 at rates well above the population growth rate, with output increasing very rapidly in some sectors, in contrast with the stagnation and declining standards of living that afflicted the region during the previous 40 years, when population increased by nearly 70 per cent but gross regional product by nothing like that figure.

Most—perhaps nearly all—of the people in the province at all levels of society are now much better off than they were in the 1960s. Both fertility and mortality levels have been falling dramatically, the former mainly because of the success of the family planning programme, an achievement of historic significance which has eliminated any danger of an imminent Malthusian disaster through population increase outrunning food supplies. Despite the short-term problems of absorbing its still fast-increasing work-force, East Javanese can now look forward to a gradual easing of its population pressures as birth rates decline further and industrialization gains momentum in the 1990s and beyond.

The two major stimulants to East Java's development since the 1960s have clearly been the Green Revolution in rice production, which has nearly trebled since 1968, and the growth of the manufacturing industry, particularly in the late 1980s. But the expansion of the construction and transport sectors, as well as commercial and financial activities more generally, have been complementary to those achievements and have provided vastly more employment. East Java had a great advantage over other provinces in that its manufacturing base was already well developed before World War II, while its transport and irrigation networks and embryonic electricity supply grid had been built up by the Dutch to serve the strong plantation sector. Colonial rule had brought some benefits to the region in that respect, despite the accompanying distortions, suppression, and repression in the processes of socio-economic and political development. But all that infrastructure was of little benefit in the troubled years between 1945 and 1965, for there was insufficient domestic demand to stimulate the manufacturing industry; that came only with the increases in production of agricultural commodities and of the manufacturing industry after 1970. Not only has rice become a very profitable cash crop in the better irrigated parts of the province since then, but so also have maize and cassava (which used to be the poor man's basic diet), tobacco, cloves, and other fruit and vegetables.

Two other great structural changes have been associated with East Java's economic transformation under the New Order. The first is the shift from a rather rigid plantation-based economic system to a more diversified and adaptable smallholder system of agricultural production.

The second is the steady increase in non-agricultural employment. The latter is both an effect and a cause of change through the diversification in job opportunities it brings, since wages and real incomes tend to be higher in the secondary and tertiary sectors, thus generating new forms of demand in both urban and rural areas. With truck and bus transport reaching across so much of East Java, the rural–urban dichotomy that was so sharp before 1970 has become blurred almost to insignificance in many areas.

Growth has entailed social costs, of course, in terms of environmental pressures of many kinds and widening inequalities at the upper levels of the social stratification system, and between the richer and poorer regions. These may prove very difficult to remedy in the years ahead, in so far as the political economy of the distribution of wealth, power, and privilege is likely to have the effect of entrenching social differences rather than eliminating them, at least in the short term. But growth and diversification should bring countervailing tendencies in the longer term, as the middle class becomes stronger and the economy more pluralistic. There are not many signs that the underclasses in East Java are at present being oppressed or exploited so seriously that any major political backlash against the present development strategy is likely to occur. And it is always easier to deal with the problems of redistributing wealth and income in an expanding economy than in a contracting one, as events in the mid-1960s demonstrated dramatically. The major problems of the province in the 1990s are more likely to arise from the pressures of rapid growth upon limited land, water, and soil resources than from the effects of unequal distribution.

Some of these problems will certainly be very difficult to resolve, urban overcrowding especially, although there are grounds for hope that they will not prove intractable, provided the momentum of growth and real development can be maintained through rising levels of productivity. A dramatic example may well be the bridge currently being planned to cross the straits between Surabaya and Madura. It should result in a major redirection of Surabaya's urban overspill from the densely populated Brantas Delta area towards the relatively infertile, thinly populated western end of Madura, stimulating an entirely new pattern of demand for land and labour services there and ultimately alleviating some of the island's grinding poverty. It will not be a panacea to the many problems of urbanization, but it should make a major contribution to the further transformation of East Java's steadily changing economic structure.

1. This chapter is an amended and updated version of the chapter on East Java by Mackie and Djumilah Zain (1989) in the survey of all Indonesian provincial economies edited by Hal Hill (1989). The contributions of Djumilah Zain to the original research on which it was based are gratefully acknowledged.

2. Optimistic reports on the sharp increase in investment in East Java, particularly in Surabaya, after the 1988 deregulation of the banking system are given in the *Asian Wall Street Journal*, 8 March 1989: 1, and the *Far Eastern Economic Review*, 29 June 1989: 57.

'There's an awful lot of money around this town,' commented one European businessman with reference to the establishment of a private Surabaya stock exchange on the initiative of local companies.

3. East Java has no oil deposits apart from a small off-shore field to the north of Madura. It has a few forests with teak and other types of commercial timber (relics of a more flourishing industry in colonial times), but their production is of minor significance to the regional economy these days.

4. East Java accounted for only 7 per cent of Indonesia's foreign investment approvals between 1967 and 1985 but 11 per cent of domestic approvals (Hill, 1988: 41). Between 1984 and 1989, foreign investment approvals totalled barely a quarter of domestic (Vatikiotis, 1989).

5. 'It was said that "real Surabayans" were strong-willed, liked to feel free of social and other obligations, and tended to react violently when pressured; they were also businesslike and hardworking. Vaguely "middle class" in many of their ideals, the *arek Suraboyo* were often "proletarian" by virtue of the types of labor they performed, their lack of economic power in the colonial world, and the vast distances that separated them from both indigenous elites and the favored nonindigenous groups such as Europeans, Chinese and Arabs.' (Frederick, 1989: 6–7.) This account of the personality traits of the *arek Suraboyo* can also be applied to East Javanese in general, particularly the fiery and stubborn Madurese who differ markedly from the more *halus* (refined) Central Javanese.

6. The term 'Golden Triangle' is said to have been coined by officials in the Ministry of Finance to refer to the area bounded by, roughly, Surabaya, Jombang, Pasuruan, and Malang from which an unusually high share of Indonesia's tax revenue is derived.

7. The GRP statistics at the *kabupaten* level published by the provincial statistical office were an innovation in the 1980s, potentially of great value as a guide to regional income levels within East Java; but they have so far been characterized by too many anomalies to be fully accepted at face value.

8. This figure is not yet verifiable from the regional accounts data for 1988–90, but it was cited to the author unofficially by provincial officials in late 1990.

9. The source of the GRP statistics for 1985 and 1988 are from KSJT, *Jawa Timur dalam Angka, 1988* and are based on compilations by the provincial statistical office, which do not always conform with the figures published in the national series by the BPS. The discrepancy in the size of the 'other services' category must be regarded with some suspicion and may be a statistical aberration.

10. The figures on transmigration flows are based on information supplied by the provincial Bappeda office, 1986.

11. The figure for Surabaya's population in 1980 given by Hugo et al. (1987: 101–3) and cited by Dick (see Chapter 15) is 1,737,000; this is based on the NUDS (1985) estimate of the total residing in 'functional urban areas', which are not identical with the administrative definitions of urban areas.

12. The total area cropped with rice in 1984 was reported to be only 1.5 million hectares, barely 25 per cent higher than in 1970.

13. The foreign investment figures cited here are Bank Indonesia estimates of actual outlays (Hill, pers. com.); the domestic investment approval figures are based on Hill (1989: 28).

14. The one exception to this observation prior to 1970 was Surabaya's renowned medical school, established in the colonial period to train 'native doctors', which became the Medical Faculty of Airlangga University after 1950.

15. The Inpres (Instruksi Presiden: Presidential Instruction) system of special-purpose grants to provincial, *kabupaten*, and village authorities was broadened in 1974 to ensure that a primary school (*sekolah dasar*) was established in all villages.

16. The significance of the IAIN system is that the provision of State funding for Islamic higher education enables the Islamic school system to compete for the first time on a basis of something approaching equality in financial terms with the secular system at the higher levels.

3
East Java's Family Planning Revolution, 1961–1987

Terence H. Hull

Introduction

IN the late 1960s the concern over rapid world population growth, typified by such books as Ehrlich's *Population Bomb* (1968), led to a variety of national and international programmes dedicated to the reduction of fertility rates. Massive development assistance was directed to helping governments raise the levels of contraceptive use among their citizens. Evidence of an active family planning programme became one of the accepted international criteria of government commitment to development. By the 1980s this new commitment had begun to bear fruit. Around the world a growing list of nations and regions achieved substantial fertility declines before attaining substantial economic development, demonstrating that government intervention to provide basic family planning services and motivation was a cost efficient means to achieve fertility reduction.

China, Taiwan, South Korea, Singapore, Sri Lanka, and Thailand were among the prominent Asian nations to achieve recognition of this commitment. In the 1980s women in each of these countries experienced fertility levels consistent with an average family size of fewer than three children, and their fertility has continued to decline. To the surprise of many observers, Indonesia's most populous province, East Java, has also joined the ranks of regions experiencing rapid fertility reduction, with recent average fertility levels of 2.6 children per mother. The story of how the province achieved this demographic transition is an important element in understanding the progress made in East Java under the New Order.

Fertility in East Java before 1970

At the time of Independence the population of East Java was almost 20 million, and growing at an average rate of 1.2 per cent per annum. Although in 1930 the province contained a quarter of the population of the entire Netherlands East Indies, its share of the population was falling even then. There was little recognition that fertility was lower in

East Java than elsewhere in the Archipelago. This fact also went largely unnoticed in the early days of Independence, when the attention of the government and the people was on reconstruction following two decades of economic decline, world war, and civil strife. In common with other Indonesian provinces, East Java experienced a post-revolution 'baby boom', as families in more stable social conditions made up for the fertility decline of the 1940s. In spite of this, both East Java's fertility and growth rates were low by national standards. By 1961 the provincial population had fallen to only 22 per cent of the national total. The crude birth rate (CBR), based on data from the 1961 Population Census, was 43 per 1,000 population, and the crude death rate (CDR) was 21, implying an annual rate of natural increase of 2.2 per cent and a doubling of the population every 32 years (Iskandar, 1970). East Javanese women bore around five children on average, but many of these did not survive infancy. The infant mortality rate of 176 per 1,000 live births meant that over one quarter of children born died before reaching school age. As reliable data on fertility became available in the 1970s, it became clear that fertility in East Java had begun to fall in the late 1950s or early 1960s, well before the establishment of the national family planning programme.

Though unrecognized in the 1960s, it appears that women of East Java had long restrained their fertility. The motivation was not necessarily a desire to limit family size. The following were among the most important conditions and behaviours which served to reduce fertility in East Java.

Infecundity

According to the 1971 Population Census the proportion of women in East Java who were apparently sterile was 15 per cent in rural areas and 18 per cent in urban areas, giving the province one of the highest rates of infecundity in Indonesia. The highest rates of childlessness were found in the Surabaya municipality and surrounds, and the *kabupaten* (districts) of the eastern peninsula and mountainous regions (Hull and Tukiran, 1976). Causes of infecundity include venereal disease (particularly gonorrhoea, chlamydia, and genital herpes), tuberculosis, malaria, and malnutrition (McFalls and McFalls, 1984: 258 ff.). Venereal diseases were reported in East Java as early as AD 860 by emissaries from China,[1] but information on the exact nature and extent of infections is extremely limited. There is no doubt that East Java in general and Surabaya in particular had high rates of venereal disease in the early part of this century. This was one of the factors behind the placement of a national venereal disease research institute in Surabaya in 1951 (VD Research Institute of Indonesia, 1953: 16–17). Studies at the time found infection rates of serious forms of venereal disease as high as 18 per cent for both the city and the province as a whole. Such rates of venereal infection were accompanied by even higher rates of non-venereal infections of the reproductive tract which would also impair fertility.

Delayed Marriage

Before Independence marriage records were poorly kept and did not include information on calendric age. Thus studies of trends of age at marriage have to rely on retrospective reporting. Unfortunately, years after the event, when asked their age at first marriage, many women answered with ages reflecting contemporary norms about appropriate ages for marriage rather than their true experience. None the less, from all available indications the traditional pattern of marriage, particularly in rural areas, was to arrange betrothal around the time a girl reached puberty, and then delay consummation and cohabitation until the couple was deemed physically and economically 'ready' (H. Geertz, 1961: 56; Hull and Hull, 1987). Thus women did not begin child-bearing at the earliest opportunity, even under 'traditional' social and economic conditions.

Early in the twentieth century, when schooling and other modernizing influences were spreading through East Java, the ages of betrothal and marriage began to rise (Iskandar, 1970: 80–1), gaining momentum as social movements, nationalist ideology, and secular influences created new notions of roles for young people in Indonesian society. The social and political rebellions which led to the formation of the Indonesian State also encouraged young people to be more independent in the selection of spouses and the timing of marriage. By the early 1960s women were marrying on average at over 17 years of age, compared to around 14 or 15 in previous generations.

Marital Disruption: Divorce and Widowhood

One of the features of Javanese society which has long fascinated foreigners is the high rate of divorce. This contrasts starkly with the general assumptions that marriage in traditional societies is stable and that modernization and Westernization produce the disruptive social conditions that break up marital unions. H. Geertz's study (1961: 71) of an East Javanese town in the early 1950s states simply, 'It is easy to get a divorce in Java ...' and documents a wide variety of cases of divorce initiated by either spouse. Women of East Java have long had a relatively strong social and economic position and do not carry a major stigma if they divorce, or are divorced by, a number of men. The causes of marriage breakup range from serious issues such as infertility, through the common charges of infidelity or incompatibility, to the apparently simple cases of divorce within weeks of the marriage because the girl did not like the appearance of the boy chosen by her parents. Whatever the causes, the effect of high rates of divorce is to depress fertility rates, as many women spend a portion of their potential reproductive period outside a sexual union.

Widowhood is another factor which can interrupt childbearing. In a society with high rates of mortality, even young women are likely to lose their husbands to illness or accident. The risk of widowhood has declined with mortality and with the narrowing of the age gap between husbands and wives. In East Java by the 1950s and 1960s women could expect to spend an average of between 5 and 7 per cent of their potential childbearing years outside a sexual union because of widowhood, and the same proportion due to divorce.

Traditional Post-partum Abstinence

Among many cultures of the Indonesian Archipelago, traditional proscriptions on intercourse in the post-partum period are based on religious formulae which imply that spouses should sleep separately for 35 or 40 days. At times this is related to a ritual cycle and marked out on a lunar calendar, but often it is a piece of advice given by the traditional midwife who assists at the birth. This brief post-partum abstinence period is seen as a time for the young mother to heal and recover from the birth, and is marked as a sign of the husband's respect for the priority of his wife's needs over his own.

Many East and Central Javanese traditionally followed quite different types of post-partum behaviour, with periods of abstinence lasting many months, and sometimes years. In some cases abstinence was linked to the period of breast feeding (from 18 to 36 months), and might be explained in terms of the idea that semen would pollute the breast milk and affect the baby's health. In other cases the duration of abstinence was linked to a woman's amenorrhoea (which is itself a function of the duration and frequency of breast-feeding), with the resumption of sexual relations being delayed until she had resumed regular menstrual cycles. Javanese couples regarded abstinence as an element in preserving the health of the baby, and thought that sexual relations should not be undertaken at 'inauspicious' times, particularly in the post-partum period. Such forbearance was not universal, but was sufficiently widespread to legitimize the practice of prolonged abstinence and undermine the idea that a husband's sexual needs were 'irresistible'. Abstinence within marriage, and particularly post-partum abstinence, was an important factor restraining the fertility of Javanese women. In recent years the duration of post-partum abstinence has been declining, with an attendant reduction in its importance as a factor restraining fertility.

Taken together, these four traditional restraints explain why the women of East Java were bearing only five children on average rather than the six or seven borne by women of North Sumatra, or the ten or so recorded for the most fertile women on record, the Hutterites of North America.

Although traditional restraints acted to keep down fertility rates, some modern developments tended to increase them. The rising age of marriage from the 1930s helped lead to some fertility decline by the late 1960s, but the factors which encouraged people to marry later also worked to reduce the divorce rate and thus the decline in fertility rates.

Modernization was also bringing new medications and economic security, both of which served to reduce overall mortality (and widowhood) and to eliminate many of the causes of infecundity which had plagued earlier generations. As traditional restraints were gradually loosened in the 1960s and 1970s, bringing the health and marriage situation of East Javanese women closer to that experienced elsewhere in Indonesia, the average of five children could have been expected to rise. In addition, many more children survived, creating an increase in family size in East Java, reflected in the data on children ever born recorded in the 1971 Population Census.

While children were traditionally regarded as a source of wealth, parents in East Java in the 1960s were by no means convinced that rising numbers would bring greater welfare for the family. By 1973 parents wanted four children on average (Table 3.1), and underlying this desire was a rapidly changing idea of what kind of life they would like for those children. Parents wanted their children to go to school but they recognized schooling as a great expense.

In the 1960s then, although East Javanese women were having five children on average and a growing proportion of these were surviving infancy, the desire was for a slightly smaller family and that children would be educated. Given the decline in traditional restraints on fertility, it could be foreseen that fertility might rise unless there was a change in the availability of fertility control.

By the mid-1960s a growing number of national leaders saw high fertility as a threat to planned improvements in education, nutrition, hygiene, and employment. It was no longer seen as sufficient just to try to accelerate economic growth; complementary efforts were needed to reduce the rate of population growth. After the 1965/6 coup the New Order government moved decisively to suppress political divisions and implement economic policies which included a commitment to the reduction of population growth rates.

TABLE 3.1

East Java: Reported Ideal Number of Children, 1973 and 1987 (per cent)

Ideal Number	*1973*	*1987*
1	–	2.5
2	–	42.0
3	–	23.1
4	–	17.3
5+	–	4.2
Non-numeric	–	10.9
Total	–	100.0
Average	4.1	2.5

Sources: 1973: Demographic Institute (1974: 34).
1987: BPS (1988a: 21).

By 1968 the National Family Planning Institute had been founded, and within two years it was upgraded to the status of a board, charged with co-ordinating government efforts to reduce fertility. The head of the National Family Planning Co-ordinating Board (Badan Koordinasi Keluarga Berencana Nasional or BKKBN) was both a doctor and an ex-military officer. Although not a minister, he was charged to report directly to the President, who promised the programme his full support. The national body immediately set up offices at provincial and *kabupaten* levels. East Java was one of the first areas chosen for the intensive promotion and distribution of contraceptive materials. Having received instructions from the national government to promote family planning, the provincial government approached the task with great enthusiasm.

Family Planning Programme Strategies in East Java

By 1977 East Java's family planning programme was already clearly a success. Over one-third of married women aged between 15 and 44 were reported to be using modern contraceptives distributed through the programme. Nearly 3 million women were recruited to the programme between 1970 and 1977, and a high proportion of these had maintained their use of contraceptives. Since then the rate of reported current use has risen to over half of married women of childbearing age (Table 3.6).

To achieve this level of acceptance a strong provincial BKKBN office mobilized bureaucratic resources at all levels, from the Governor's office down to the formal and informal leadership of hamlets. From the early days of the programme, the Governor provided strong support, decreeing that every public servant in East Java should promote family planning, and making clear that the government expected public servants to practise family planning themselves as well as preaching it to others. As a result of this top–down mobilization, family planning soon became widely known.

As a first step in implementing the programme, the provincial BKKBN adopted a mass public health intervention model. In many nations, family planning was confined to passive clinic-based services where the staff worked near the seat of local government and waited for clients to come from the surrounding region for treatment. The East Java BKKBN approach was based on the twin assumptions that the population needing family planning services was mainly rural and that people would not seek services in distant clinics, but would gladly receive them if they were offered close to home. To meet the needs of the rural population, two strategies were developed. First, large numbers of family planning fieldworkers (*petugas lapangan keluarga berencana* or PLKB) were recruited to carry messages and supplies directly into people's homes. The second was a series of concentrated efforts to organize medical and administrative resources and mobilize community participation.

Called *gugur gunung* (special drives), these activities were developed by the head of the BKKBN and modelled directly on a series of yaws campaigns he had organized in the 1950s. They succeeded in informing people of the government's support for family planning, and publicizing the types of contraception available through family planning clinics. While the *gugur gunung* reached large numbers of people, they also attracted criticism, the most prominent of which related to their preoccupation with administrative targets. Coinciding with target dates there were peaks in the numbers of new acceptors, and severe troughs thereafter, rather than a steady growth in the number of acceptors.

The army in East Java took up the challenge to support the family planning programme by conducting drives during the month-long anniversary celebrations of the Brawijaja Army Division. Objections were raised when uniformed men began gathering large groups of women who were not yet acceptors and 'encouraging' them to go to the clinic for services. Too often BKKBN officials found themselves faced with a shortage of supplies and a group of unenthusiastic potential clients. Rather than promoting the programme, such tactics tended to undermine its credibility. Gradually the *gugur gunung* were superseded by other strategies, designed to ensure continuous local availability of contraception. These initiatives included the establishment of community contraceptive distribution centres, the promotion of acceptors' clubs where small credit and training schemes were available, and the mobilization of non-government religious and development groups to support the programme.

The BKKBN in East Java was thus both quick to initiate the programme and quick to adapt to changing needs. This commitment is reflected in the expenditure patterns for the first years of the programme: East Java spent US$0.19 per capita on family planning, compared with US$0.15 in both West and Central Java. The greater enrolment in East Java meant the higher per capita cost was transformed into a much lower cost per *acceptor*: US$7.81 compared with US$13.15 in West Java and US$12.31 in Central Java.[2]

One of the early successes of the provincial BKKBN was an effective system for the collection and analysis of monthly statistics on numbers of acceptors and estimated numbers of continuing users. Reports originating in clinics were forwarded to Jakarta within a few days of the end of the month. A random sample of the reports was immediately entered into a computer and tables were distributed back to the provincial BKKBN offices within one or two weeks. The simple tabulations and graphs provided the provincial authorities with a clear picture of the standing of their efforts in comparison with other provinces. Fuller tabulations of data on a broad range of clinic inputs and outputs were produced to the level of *kabupaten*, *kecamatan* (subdistrict), and even villages and clinics.

The effectiveness of the data system has varied since it was put in place in the early 1970s. On a number of occasions large numbers of errors were made by new staff who had not been properly trained in the system. Training programmes were quickly developed. At other times administrative pressures to meet unrealistic targets led to overstatement of acceptor numbers. These problems are difficult to correct at the provincial level, since they reflect on the wisdom of the national leadership responsible for setting the original targets. None the less it has been obvious to BKKBN officials that gross overstatement of achievement undermines the efficiency of their own organization. It removes their ability to plan the logistic needs of the programme and makes them vulnerable to charges of cheating by the Central Bureau of Statistics (Biro Pusat Statistik or BPS) and academics who carry out independent surveys of contraceptive use and knowledge. Despite serious data errors the family planning statistics of East Java have been more accurate and consistent over the years than many other economic and social statistics generated at the village level. The data warrant serious consideration to gain insight into the rapidly changing reproductive behaviour of the East Javanese.

Characteristics of New Acceptors of Contraceptives

The number of new acceptors has risen steadily and dramatically over time, to the point where by 1990 the majority of East Javanese couples of childbearing age was using contraceptives which, a mere two decades ago, were illegal in Indonesia.

The couples attracted to family planning have been younger, of lower parity and better educated with each passing year. None the less they continue to represent a broad cross-section of the population of East Java—including urban and rural dwellers, rich and poor, and people from all walks of life. They enjoy access to a range of contraceptives, but continue to rely fairly heavily on hormonal preparations, whether taken as pills or injected. The major characteristics of new acceptors are discussed below.

Age of Acceptors

At the formation of the family planning programme there was a large latent demand for fertility control among the women of East Java. As might be expected, the women who most wanted to take advantage of the new contraceptive technology were those who had already borne a number of children and did not want to increase their family size. They tended to be in the middle or at the end of their reproductive life: that is, over 25 (Table 3.2). Successive groups of new clients displayed different needs. They were more likely to be seeking contraception to increase the time between births or to delay the first birth until they felt more secure economically. This group was drawn from the mid-range of the reproductive span, the 20–29 age-group. Programme managers worried about providing pills or intra-uterine devices (IUDs) to young women who had not yet borne any children, lest any later difficulties in conceiving would be blamed on the contraceptives and give the programme a bad name. However, by the early 1980s birth control was so widely used and the programme so well established that even adolescent

TABLE 3.2
East Java: Age Distribution of New Acceptors for Selected Years
(per cent)

Age-group	*1971–2*	*1975–6*	*1979–80*	*1984–5*
10–14	0.0	0.0	0.3	0.0
15–19	4.3	8.7	12.1	10.7
20–24	18.4	31.1	35.7	38.9
25–29	28.5	28.5	27.3	26.8
30–34	28.5	18.2	13.7	15.0
35–39	16.7	10.8	8.7	6.4
40–44	3.1	2.4	2.1	1.8
45–49	0.4	0.2	0.2	0.2

Source: BKKBN, quarterly acceptors' reports.

married women were being encouraged to use contraceptives to delay their first child. By 1984/5 half the new acceptors were under 25 years of age.

Parity

The decline in the average age of acceptors has been accompanied by a decline in the average family size attained prior to the adoption of family planning.

TABLE 3.3
East Java: Educational Distribution of New Acceptors, Third Quarter of Selected Fiscal Years (per cent)

		Reads Latin Script	*Years of Schooling*					
	Illiterate		*6*	*9*	*12*	*Tertiary*	*Unknown*	*Sample Size*
1971/2	47.1	22.9	20.3	6.9	2.4	0.2	0.2	4,288
1972/3	49.6	23.4	20.3	4.9	1.5	0.2	0.0	7,929
1973/4	47.9	25.6	20.4	4.0	1.7	0.3	0.0	11,725
1974/5	42.9	29.9	22.5	3.3	1.3	0.1	0.0	21,683
1975/6	37.8	30.0	26.6	3.8	1.6	0.2	0.0	23,925
1976/7	34.4	31.2	28.6	3.7	1.9	0.2	0.0	15,185
1977/8	30.9	31.9	31.0	3.9	2.1	0.2	0.0	16,836
1978/9	23.9	32.1	36.0	5.1	2.5	0.3	0.1	13,155
1979/80	24.1	30.7	37.9	4.3	2.6	0.2	0.3	13,891
1980/1	19.0	32.0	40.6	5.4	2.7	0.2	0.2	14,409
1981/2	16.6	29.8	44.6	5.0	3.0	0.4	0.6	23,896
1983/4	10.8	24.6	50.9	7.0	6.0	0.8	0.0	22,951
1984/5	11.9	26.3	51.4	6.1	4.0	0.3	0.0	12,429

Source: BKKBN, quarterly acceptors' reports.

Education

In the early years of the programme great pride was taken in the high proportion of illiterates among acceptors, an indication that the services were not going just to middle-class urban women. Over time the level of education of acceptors has risen dramatically (Table 3.3). By the mid-1980s nearly two-thirds of the acceptors had completed elementary school. This does not mean that the programme had ceased to serve the needs of poor rural women but rather that poor rural women seeking birth control services were now comparatively well educated, due to the government's success in providing primary education to the rural areas of East Java in the 1960s and 1970s. Where the programme had formerly relied on face-to-face communication and pictorial presentations, it became possible to give information on birth control through more sophisticated written messages.

Husband's Occupation

Evidence that the programme appeals to the rural masses is shown in Table 3.4, where the occupations of the acceptors' husbands are shown for the period between 1971 and 1985. The distribution has changed little over time: well over three-quarters of the husbands have been farmers or labourers.

Method of Contraception Chosen

In the first years of the BKKBN only three contraceptive methods were widely available: the IUD, the oral contraceptive pill, and the condom. Officials preferred women to use the IUD, which was regarded as cheap, effective, and not subject to client 'forgetfulness'. Clients, on the other hand, tended to prefer the pill, which did not require an uncomfortable or intrusive medical procedure like the IUD insertion. Condoms were not popular among either group (Table 3.5). Over the years the pill has maintained its dominance in East Java, but some new options have proved very popular. The Depoprovera injection has attracted a rapidly growing number of users who like a method which is as effective as the pill but requires quarterly injections rather than daily ingestion of tablets. Women who have completed their childbearing are attracted to the idea of sterilization, which settles their family planning needs permanently. Many more women than men are sterilized, and in part this is due to the hesitance of officials, who assume that men will not accept sterilization. This attitude is probably misguided, since Indonesian men have consistently responded well when sterilization facilities have been made available and after they have been told that vasectomies are easier, safer, and cheaper than tubal ligations. The fact that Islam contains teachings inimical to sterilization adds to the pressures which limit the availability of the operations.

TABLE 3.4

East Java: Occupational Distribution of Husbands of New Acceptors, Third Quarter of Selected Fiscal Years (per cent)

	Government Employee	*Private Employee*	*Armed Forces*	*Pensioner*	*Tradesman*	*Fisherman*	*Farmer*	*Manual Labourer*	*Unemployed*	*Unknown*	*Sample Size*
1971/2	11.4	5.6	4.0	0.4	4.7	1.7	63.0	8.6	0.5	0.0	4,288
1973/4	6.6	3.1	2.5	0.2	2.4	1.2	76.7	7.1	0.2	0.0	11,725
1974/5	4.3	3.4	1.3	0.3	2.7	1.6	78.9	7.4	0.2	0.0	21,683
1975/6	4.4	3.8	1.8	0.2	2.6	1.3	76.9	8.9	0.2	0.0	23,925
1976/7	5.4	3.7	1.9	0.2	2.0	1.3	75.9	9.3	0.2	0.0	15,185
1977/8	4.8	4.3	1.5	0.3	2.7	1.4	74.6	10.1	0.2	0.1	16,836
1978/9	5.3	5.2	1.6	0.2	2.4	2.0	71.1	11.2	0.3	0.7	13,155
1979/80	4.5	5.3	1.4	0.2	2.5	1.7	72.9	10.5	0.3	0.8	13,891
1980/1	5.3	5.7	1.3	0.1	2.4	1.2	71.5	11.4	0.3	0.7	14,409
1981/2	4.5	5.8	1.8	0.1	2.3	1.4	71.7	9.1	0.7	2.6	23,896
1983/4	5.0	6.9	1.4	0.2	2.5	1.3	73.4	9.1	0.2	0.1	22,951
1984/5	5.2	8.6	1.6	0.1	2.6	1.3	70.6	9.7	0.3	0.1	12,429

Source: BKKBN, quarterly acceptors' report.

TABLE 3.5

East Java: Recorded Annual Number of Family Planning Acceptors by Method of Contraception, 1969/70–1983/4

	Reversible Methods					Sterilization		
	IUD	*Pill*	*Condom*	*Depoprovera Injection*	*Vaginal Tablet*	*Vasectomy*	*Tubectomy*	*Total*
1969/70	5,921	4,260	2,558	–	–	–	–	12,739
1970/1	25,578	31,856	7,910	–	–	–	–	65,344
1971/2	87,569	139,548	3,576	–	2,789	–	–	233,482
1972/3	205,736	298,731	15,428	–	4,745	–	–	524,640
1973/4	140,800	427,239	71,810	–	2,456	–	–	642,305
1974/5	70,112	500,628	80,337	500	631	68	1,487	653,763
1975/6	119,041	448,128	76,958	2,059	162	110	2,347	648,805
1976/7	234,380	331,837	44,731	5,430	86	359	4,102	620,925
1977/8	155,373	325,847	21,408	10,404	37	420	6,049	519,538
1978/9	138,878	274,046	16,470	9,883	39	232	8,070	447,618
1979/80	127,020	283,896	15,842	6,516	46	163	9,138	442,630
1980/1	130,823	293,597	21,685	12,718	73	143	11,033	470,072
1981/2	137,686	336,402	20,021	21,375	53	103	13,085	528,672
1982/3	170,832	372,756	21,741	38,502	167	569	18,072	622,639
1983/4	277,298	414,787	33,445	107,253	115	273	24,803	857,974

Source: BKKBN, monthly service statistics.
– = Method not available under the programme.

Patterns of Contraceptive Use and Non-use

A large survey of family planning practice in East Java, the Indonesian Contraceptive Prevalence Survey (ICPS), was conducted in 1987 by the BPS, the Westinghouse Institute for Resource Development, and the BKKBN. It showed that just under half the women of reproductive age in East Java were using methods of birth control, with one-third using either the pill or the IUD (Table 3.6). Injectible forms of contraception were used by over 8 per cent of women, while around 4 per cent had been sterilized. These levels represent a huge increase on the situation recorded in the Fertility–Mortality Survey just a decade and a half earlier in 1973. The service statistics for January 1989 show a similar pattern of contraceptive use to that recorded in 1987 but at a substantially higher level. It is unlikely that contraceptive use really climbed from 50 to nearly 70 per cent in 14 months, but it is likely that levels of use are rising.

The dwindling numbers of women who have never used contraceptives constitute a very mixed group with a variety of attitudes (Table 3.7). A quarter would like to become pregnant, while around 7 per cent are currently pregnant. Around 15 per cent are menopausal or currently breast-feeding and do not feel a need for contraception. Only small numbers of those with no experience of contraceptive use actively oppose contraception or regard childbearing as beyond their control.

TABLE 3.6
East Java: Reported Use of Methods of Birth Control by Women of Reproductive Age, 1973, 1987, and 1989 (per cent)

	Survey Results		*BKKBN Report, January*
Method	*1973*	*1987*	*1989*
Pill	6.9	17.8	33.0
IUD	4.5	15.2	22.0
Injection	–	8.5	6.0
Condom	0.3	1.5	1.0
Tubectomy	–	3.8	–
Vasectomy	–	0.0	–
Norplant implant	–	0.8	1.0
Traditional	–	2.3	–
Other methods	0.9	–	3.0
Total users	12.6	49.8	69.1
No method reported	87.4	50.2	30.9

Sources: 1973: Demographic Institute (1974: 52).
1987: BPS (1989a: 34).
1989: BKKBN, monthly service statistics.

TABLE 3.7
East Java: Reported Reasons for Never Using Contraceptives, 1987

Reason	*Per Cent*[a] (*n = 867*)
Wants pregnancy	26.2
Breast-feeding	6.7
Menopause	8.6
Currently pregnant	7.4
Lacks knowledge	7.8
Sexual relations infrequent	1.4
Health concerns	2.3
Problems of access/availability	0.6
Inconvenient	0.8
Too costly	0.2
Fatalistic	4.9
Religion	0.2
Opposes family planning	1.4
Husband opposes family planning	3.7
Others oppose family planning	1.0
Other	14.9
Don't know	11.5
Total	99.6

Source: BPS (1988a: 13).
[a]Percentage of married women who have never used contraceptives.

More remarkable is the fact that over half the women not currently using contraceptives (a quarter of all women of reproductive age) say that they want no more children, and over a fifth want to delay their next birth (Table 3.8): there remains a substantial potential demand for contraceptives which should carry the service provided by the family planning programme to higher levels in coming years.

TABLE 3.8
East Java: Reported Fertility Desires of Women Not Using Contraceptives, 1987

Response	*Per Cent*
Want no more children	51.8
Want more later[a]	22.6
Want more soon[b]	14.5
Want more, unspecified time	8.1
Don't know	3.0

Source: BPS (1988a: 20).
[a]Later = Over two years.
[b]Soon = Within two years.

Fertility Decline, 1965–1985

There has been a revolution in family formation patterns in East Java which began as early as the colonial period with a rise in the age at marriage and culminated in the 1980s in a major reduction in childbearing brought about by the use of modern contraceptive methods. Women in East Java formerly bore five to six children on average, and while some of these died in infancy, women could still expect to have three or four children when they completed childbearing. Today women bear only two or three children, and the chances of one of them dying in childhood has dropped to less than 10 per cent.

While the broad outlines of the fertility decline are clear, some basic problems of measuring fertility have confused many observers and led some to an unwarranted rejection of the evidence for rapid fertility decline. Before examining the evidence of fertility change in East Java, it is important to understand how fertility estimates are generated and the bases for comparison of different calculations.

Because there is no reliable system of birth registration in Indonesia, fertility data are not available on an annual basis. Analysts must rely on the results of periodic surveys and censuses. These all involve sampling, and demographic estimates will be subject to normal sampling errors. In addition the sample sizes and frames for each enumeration are different, so that the size and the direction of sampling errors will be different for each estimate. More important than sampling errors are errors which arise from differences in question formats, interviewer skill, language of interview, the member of the household chosen to provide the information, procedures for coding and verifying responses, and the style of tabulation of the results. Over the years women in East Java have been asked questions about childbearing in a variety of ways. Apparent changes in fertility would reflect differences in their reactions to the clarity and detail of the questions as well as real changes in their behaviour. As the skill of the surveyors increased in the 1970s and 1980s, births which might have been overlooked in earlier enumerations would have been more likely to be counted.

Aside from various errors and biases arising during data collection, analysts must take care to specify the reference period to which estimates of fertility rates pertain. Surveys ask women about births for a number of years before the survey date, and their answers are analysed using various demographic techniques to generate fertility estimates for those periods. Information on the date of a woman's latest birth can produce an estimate of fertility for the year prior to the survey, while data on all the children ever born to a woman are used to estimate fertility three or more years before the enumeration. Some techniques use data on the ratio of young children (0–4 years old) to adult women to produce estimates of average fertility levels two and a half years before the enumeration. Confusion often arises when different techniques are applied to the same survey, producing a variety of different results. In fact all these apparently contradictory estimates might be correct, but merely refer to different periods in the past, over which fertility has been changing rapidly. It is important to examine the method of estimation and the reference period.

Age-specific and Total Fertility Rates

Table 3.9 presents estimates of age-specific fertility rates for East Java from 1964 to 1987. By and large the fertility rates for each age-group show regular declines, with the exception of the age-group 45–49, where small sample sizes and reporting problems disturb the results. Of particular interest are the rates for the age-groups 15–19 and 30–39, for which there have been substantial declines from the earliest days of the family planning programme. For women aged 20–24 fertility decline started later and accelerated in the 1980s. These patterns accord with the data on characteristics of acceptors, which show that contraceptives were used first by older women, and were only later adopted by younger women, in the middle of their reproductive life.

Overall fertility trends can be seen more clearly in Figure 3.1 which plots the total fertility rates (TFRs) from Table 3.9. In East Java family sizes have been halved over the two decades of the government-sponsored family planning programme. Current trends indicate that East Java will reach replacement levels of fertility (a TFR of about 2.2) well before 1995. If the experience of other societies is any guide, East Java's fertility transition will not stop at replacement levels, but will drift below them. The speed and extent of fertility declines will depend on the continuation of social changes which have become characteristic of the New Order period. In particular, the changes in the schooling system and the composition of the work-force will have a strong influence on the proportion of women marrying and the average age of marriage.

FIGURE 3.1
East Java: Total Fertility Rates, 1965–1985

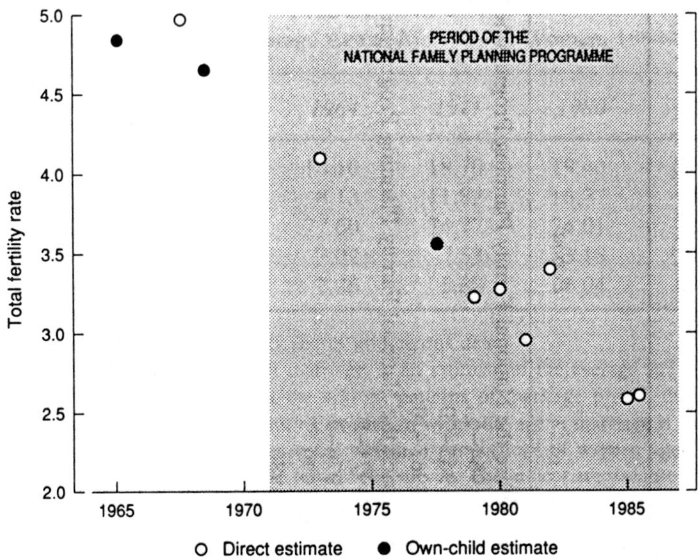

TABLE 3.9

East Java: Age-specific Fertility Rates, 1964–1987 (number of births per 1,000 women in each age-group)

Period	Age							Total Fertility Rate
	15–19	*20–24*	*25–29*	*30–34*	*35–39*	*40–44*	*45–49*	
Before the National Family Planning Programme								
1964–6	177	245	231	170	99	45	–	4.8
1965–70	164	254	219	170	114	63	9	5.0
1967–70	149	246	225	169	96	45	14	4.7
During the National Family Planning Programme								
1971–5	117	221	180	151	81	45	24	4.1
1976–9	114	207	172	115	65	29	9	3.6
1979	81	185	161	118	64	27	8	3.2
1980	91	193	157	111	65	26	8	3.3
1981	86	171	153	100	55	20	9	3.0
1981–3								3.4
1984–7								2.6
1985	52	157	134	90	55	19	6	2.6

Notes: Methods and sources for estimates:

1964–6, 1967–70: Own-child technique (Cho et al., 1976: 1).
1965–70: Pregnancy history (McDonald, Mohammad Yassin, and Jones, 1976: 50).
1971–5: Pregnancy history (BPS, 1978b).
1976–9: Own-child technique (Mamas, 1983: 3–5).
1979, 1980: Last birth method (Unpublished calculations).
1981: Last birth method (Sullivan and Wilson, 1982: 33).
1981–3, 1984–7: Pregnancy history (BPS, 1989a: 52).
1985: Last birth method (Hull and Dasvarma, 1988: 119).

The Rising Age at Marriage

Between 1964 and 1985 the estimated average age at marriage of East Javanese women rose from 18.1 to 20.3 (Table 3.10). It is generally accepted that before 1940 women married much younger than 18, but precise data are not available. An assumed average age of around 14 or 15 would imply a substantial increase in the average age even before 1967, when the government family planning programme was first mooted. Since that time women increasingly have delayed marriage and spent more of their adolescent years in the work-force or in school. This changed behaviour is illustrated by the index I_s in Table 3.10, which shows the weighted proportion of women aged 15–49 who are single. The index rose dramatically from 8 per cent to nearly 20 per cent between 1964 and 1985. Had this been the only change in marriage patterns fertility might have plummeted during the period from the simple effect of fewer women being married at young ages. But as discussed above, marital patterns also depend on the proportion of women who are widowed or divorced. Indices for these two marital statuses (I_w and I_d) have both fallen over the period, indicating that women are less likely to lose potential reproductive time due to the death of a spouse or marital breakdown. Thus the fertility reduction attributable to the rising age at marriage is somewhat offset by the declines in marital disruption.

The changes outlined above have not been uniform throughout the province. Some *kabupaten* still have relatively high fertility, while in others it is declining rapidly to replacement levels. Data on this point are available only from the censuses of 1971 and 1980. Figure 3.2 provides a picture of fertility patterns in 1964–66 and 1976–80, and shows the general decline, as well as the remaining pockets of high fertility in the *kabupaten* of Pamekasan, Jombang, and Sampang. Situbondo had lower fertility in the earlier period (TFR = 3.8), and by 1980 had the lowest

TABLE 3.10
East Java: Trends in the Average Age at Marriage of Women, 1964–1985

Index	*1964*	*1971*	*1980*	*1985*
SMAM[a]	18.10	18.70	19.40	20.30
I_s (single)[b]	8.13	11.82	16.77	19.40
I_m (married)	77.60	74.77	74.01	72.94
I_w (widowed)	7.02	7.53	3.18	2.57
I_d (divorced)	7.26	5.88	6.04	5.09

Source: Calculated from BPS fertility survey and census data.

[a]SMAM, the singulate mean age at marriage, is an estimate of the average age at which women will marry, assuming that the current patterns of marriage prevail throughout their lifetime. It is slightly biased during periods in which the age at marriage is rising.

[b]The indices of marriage patterns are the weighted proportions of women aged 15–49 who are in each marital status at the time of the survey. The indices are weighted according to the distribution of maximum fecundity potential by age and thus reflect the degree to which marriage patterns are likely to restrict natural fertility patterns.

FIGURE 3.2
East Java: Fertility Patterns, 1964–1966 and 1976–1980

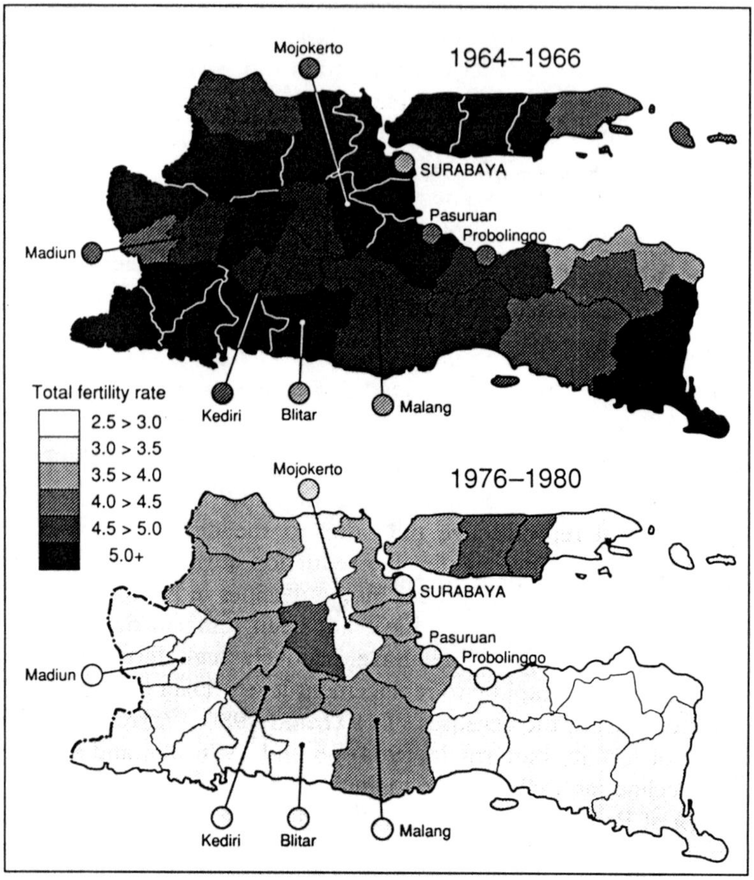

fertility in the province (TFR = 2.75). For most of the province, the 1976–80 figures indicate a fairly uniform achievement of a three-child family. The results of the 1990 Census will determine how the further reduction of total fertility to below 2.5 children on average is reflected in changes in *kabupaten* fertility.

Conclusion

The rate of population growth will decline inevitably as an increasing proportion of women delay marriage, use contraceptives, and limit the size of their completed families. If the current trends persist fertility will continue to fall but the population will still increase and may well exceed 35 million before the year 2000 (Table 3.11). The reduction of growth rates would be intensified if the high rates of out-migration from East Java, assumed in government projections and promoted in policies, are achieved, but it is difficult to be certain of the volume and direction of future migration flows.

TABLE 3.11
East Java: Population Projections (millions)

Year	*Source of Projections*		
	BPS-84[a]	*NUDS-85*[b]	*BPS-88*[c]
1985	31.3	30.2	31.3
1986	–	–	31.8
1987	–	–	32.2
1988	–	–	32.5
1989	–	–	32.9
1990	33.4	31.0	33.2
1991	–	–	33.5
1992	–	–	33.8
1993	–	–	34.1
1994	–	–	34.4
1995	35.4	31.5	34.7
2000	37.1	32.0	–

Sources: BPS-84: BPS (1984a: 39).
NUDS-85: Gardiner (1985: 71).
BPS-88: BPS (1988a: 73).

[a]Based on the 1980 Population Census and assumes a decline of fertility to TFR = 2.9 in 1990–5 and 2.7 in 1995–2000.

[b]Based on the 1980 Population Census and assumes the medium transmigration variant (that is, failure of the Fourth Five-Year Development Plan (Repelita IV) to meet targets) and a smooth decline of fertility to TFR = 2.4 in 1990–5 and 2.3 in 1995–2000.

[c]Based on the 1985 Supas (Intercensal Survey) and assumes TFR = 2.6 in 1990–5.

East Java has achieved a very different population and faces a very different future from those indicated by the prognoses of the late 1950s. These changes represent the culmination of a myriad of political, social, and economic decisions taken both by the people of East Java and by committed government officials in Jakarta. For decades, decision-making over issues of schooling, marriage partners, marriage timing, breast-feeding, sexual behaviour, birth control, divorce, and desired family size has been changing. More recently some critical shifts in government policy have allowed access to modern, efficient forms of birth control.

This vision of demographic change points to an important lesson which, while arising from the experience of East Java, is applicable to the rest of Indonesia. The transition from high to low rates of fertility and mortality can be accelerated through a joint commitment to modernization and development by both the people and the government. Lack of such commitment inhibits the process, as was found in the 1950s and 1960s. It is clear that the success of family planning in East Java in the 1970s lay in the fact that the government was providing services and technologies which responded to the needs of couples who wanted to change the way they formed their families and raised their children.

While the perceptions of the nature of needs were different for government officials and young couples—and at times involved significant moral and social dilemmas—they were sufficiently compatible to reinforce behaviour leading to lower fertility.

1. 'In this country there are poisonous girls; when one has intercourse with them, he gets painful ulcers and dies, but his body does not decay.' (Coedès, 1975: 126.)
2. 1973/4 estimates, using 1973 exchange rates.

4
East Java: Educational Change and Changing Employment Structure

Gavin W. Jones

Introduction

IN the quarter century since the New Order regime took power, the growth and increasing maturity of the Indonesian economy have transformed the structure of employment (Bakir and Manning, 1984; Jones, 1984, 1986; Hugo et al., 1987: Chapter 8). The employment share of primary industries (agriculture, forestry, hunting, and fishing) has declined, the range of occupations has widened, and the education level of the work-force has risen. The declining share of primary industries has been accompanied by a decline in the proportion of the work-force living in rural areas. At the same time the structure of rural employment has become increasingly complex and many workers now move regularly between village-based and urban employment (Hugo, et al., 1987).

As the most populous province in Indonesia, with about one-fifth of the total Indonesian labour force, East Java reflects these national trends. Nevertheless, this large and complex province has special characteristics which have ensured that employment trends have not been a mere carbon copy of those in the nation as a whole. Notable among these characteristics are the size and diversity of the economy, the transmigration of workers to areas outside Java, and cultural traits which affect the work patterns of women. This chapter will explore those trends in employment and education which are specific to East Java and will note some geographic differences within the province.

Growth of the Labour Force and Changing Employment Structure

Recent and Projected Growth of the Labour Force

The growth of the working-age population and of the labour force in East Java between 1971 and 1985 are shown in Table 4.1.[1] The average annual rate of increase of the population aged 10 years and above

TABLE 4.1
East Java: Growth of the Labour Force, 1971–1985

	Male	*Female*	*Both Sexes*
Population aged 10 and above ('000)			
1971	8,547	9,351	17,898
1980	10,516	11,304	21,820
1985	11,573	12,467	24,040
Average annual rate of increase (%)			
1971–80	2.3	2.1	2.2
1980–5	1.9	2.0	1.9
Labour force ('000)			
1971	6,297	3,458	9,755
1980	7,508	4,001	11,509
1985	8,390	5,181	13,571
Average annual increase ('000)			
1971–80	135	60	195
1980–5	177	236	413
Average annual rate of increase (%)			
1971–80	2.0	1.6	1.8
1980–5	2.2	5.4	3.3

Sources: BPS (1974: Table 29; 1983a: Table 28; 1987a: Table 17).

slackened over the period, not so much because of declining fertility (which could hardly yet have affected this measure) but because of accelerated out-migration from the province. Conversion of these population figures into labour force figures reveals some surprising irregularities. Between 1980 and 1985 both the male and the female labour force apparently grew more rapidly than the working-age population, implying a rise in the economically active proportion of this population. The rise was particularly sharp in the case of females. However, as noted by Jones (1987), much of this rise was apparently spurious: it occurred mainly in the category of 'unpaid family workers' and reflected the tendency of the better trained interviewers in the intercensal surveys to identify a higher proportion of the working population than in the censuses.

The labour force remains predominantly rural, but the urban share has been growing: from 13 per cent in 1971 to 17 per cent in 1980 and to almost 20 per cent in 1985. Annual urban growth rates of 5.3 per cent per annum between 1971 and 1980 and 5.5 per cent per annum between 1980 and 1985 were obviously boosted by in-migration to East Java's cities and towns.

In recent years East Java's working-age population has grown more slowly than the Indonesian average, reflecting both the long-standing lower rate of natural increase in East Java (see Chapter 3)[2] and continuing net out-migration. The effect of these two factors is highlighted in Table 4.2, which shows the projected growth (up to the year 2000) of

TABLE 4.2

East Java and the Rest of Indonesia: Projected Growth of Working-age Population by Age-group, 1980–2000

Age-group	*Working-age Population ('000)*			*Percentage Increase*		
	1980	*1990*	*2000*	*1980–90*	*1980–2000*	*1990–2000*
East Java						
15–24	5,768	6,583	6,584	14.1	14.1	0.0
25–44	7,568	9,187	11,170	21.4	47.6	21.6
45–64	4,173	5,241	6,027	25.6	44.4	15.0
65+	1,160	1,477	2,146	27.3	85.0	45.3
15+	18,669	22,488	25,927	20.5	38.9	15.3
Rest of Indonesia						
15–24	29,486	36,356	43,576	25.5	56.0	24.2
25–44	36,160	47,535	62,619	34.1	79.9	34.2
45–64	17,784	24,135	30,747	38.8	81.6	30.8
65+	4,918	6,335	9,573	29.3	97.6	52.9
15+	88,348	114,361	146,515	31.8	73.1	31.3

Source: BPS (1984a).

the working-age population in broad age-groups. The most striking features of these projections are the zero growth projected in the 15–24 age-group for the 1990s (compared with a projected 24 per cent increase for the rest of Indonesia) and the projected growth of the working-age population for the same period at only half the rate of the rest of Indonesia. Given that the entry of young people into the labour force will be delayed by rising levels of schooling, it can be predicted safely that the youthful segment of the East Java labour force will actually decline during the 1990s.[3]

Participation Rates

Male labour force participation rates show little variation between provinces. East Java actually had the highest rate of any province in the 1985 Supas (Survei Penduduk antar Sensus or Intercensal Population Survey) (72.5 per cent among the population aged 10 and above, compared with a national figure of 68.9 per cent), though when standardized for age, it was exceeded by the rate for eight other provinces. For women there is more interprovincial variation. East Java ranks amongst the highest provinces (41.6 per cent of women aged 10 and above were in the labour force in 1985, compared with the national figure of 37.6 per cent), though it cannot match the much higher figures in Yogyakarta and Bali.

Figure 4.1 illustrates the age patterns of the economic activity of women as measured in the 1971, 1980, and 1985 population censuses. They reveal a consistent trend, with participation rates already around 30 per cent in the age-group 15–19, and climbing steadily thereafter to reach a maximum of close to 50 per cent around ages 40–55. The occupational patterns of younger and older working women will be examined later.

Figure 4.2 illustrates female labour force participation rates (LFPRs) in the *kabupaten* (district) and *kotamadya* (municipalities) of Java in 1980. East Java and Central Java show much higher participation rates than West Java. Two exceptions are the low rates in Probolinggo and an area of northern East Java bordering Central Java (Madiun and Bojonegoro). The latter area had constricted since 1971, when it was bounded by Sragen and Kertosono in the south and Blora and Tuban in the north.

There are economic and cultural reasons for differences between *kabupaten* in East Java. For example, the high female LFPR in Kediri is almost certainly due to the incentive provided by employment opportunities in the huge Gudang Garam *kretek* cigarette factory (see Chapter 13). The area of low participation rates in Madiun and Bojonegoro includes Java's main area of teak forests and an extremely poor region in the north, dependent largely on cassava cultivation. In these areas agricultural employment opportunities for women appear to be limited. However, this does not explain why they do not as readily turn their hand to trade or handicrafts as in Central Java–Yogyakarta.

FIGURE 4.1
East Java: Female Labour Force Participation Rates by Place of Residence, 1971, 1980, and 1985

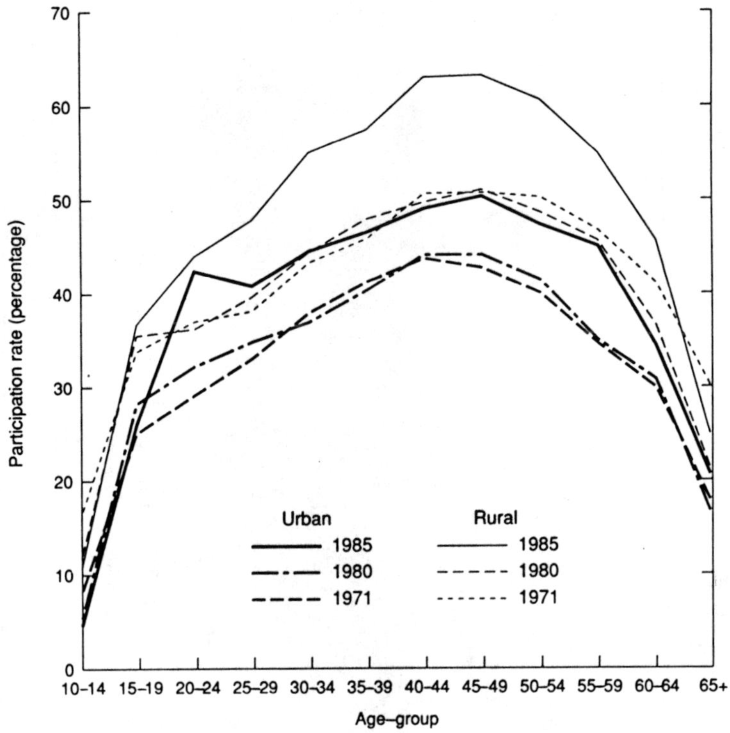

Perhaps the high concentration of devout Muslims in this region helps explain the reluctance of women to engage in the typically Javanese female activity of petty trading. Finally, the low rate in Probolinggo seems hard to explain on economic grounds, while the 'cultural' explanation that it contains a large proportion of Madurese does not suffice, since participation rates in Madura itself are higher.

Changing Employment Structure by Industry

The striking shifts in the distribution of employment across industries between 1971 and 1985 are shown in Table 4.3. The overall growth of employment (column 3) is exaggerated because of the tendency for the 1985 Supas to record higher economic activity rates than the censuses. Bearing this in mind, the total number employed in agriculture increased very little over the period. The share of this sector in total employment suffered a 12 percentage point decline over the period, balanced by a rise in the share of both the industrial and service sectors.

Trends in agricultural employment were not, however, steady over the period. Manning (1988) noted an upsurge in agricultural employment among men in Java in the early 1980s. Although some of this recorded

FIGURE 4.2
Java: Female Labour Force Participation Rates by *Kabupaten* and *Kotamadya*, 1980

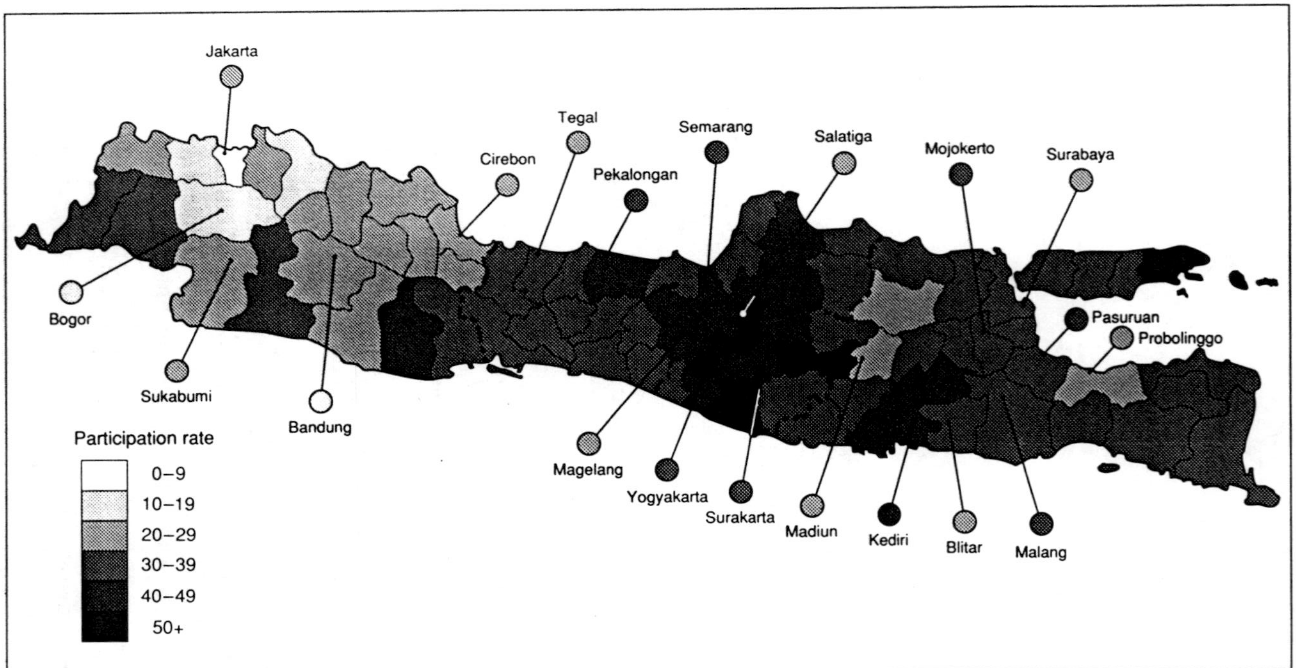

TABLE 4.3
East Java: Trends in the Structure of Employment by Industry, 1971–1985

	Number ('000)		*Percentage Increase*	*Percentage Distribution*	
	1971	*1985*	*1971–85*	*1971*	*1985*
Agriculture	6,503	7,314	12	66.7	54.8
Industrial sector	666	1,785	156	6.8	13.4
Manufacturing	541	1,299	139	5.5	9.8
Construction	114	389	242	1.2	2.9
Utilities/mining	11	97	791	0.1	0.7
Service sector	2,224	4,221	90	22.6	31.6
Transport	188	385	104	1.9	2.9
Trade	1,089	2,137	96	11.2	16.0
Finance	12	56	359	0.1	0.4
Public services	935	1,643	76	9.6	12.3
Unknown	361	29	−91	3.7	0.2
Total	9,754	13,353	37	100.0	100.0

Sources: BPS (1974: Table 39; 1987a: Table 18.9).

growth may be spurious for the reasons noted earlier (see also Nagib and Jones, 1987), there does seem to be some real growth. This may be a response to the difficulty of finding non-farm work in a period of slower economic growth. Yet it also suggests (contrary to the view of Jones (1984: 148), based on trends over the 1960s and 1970s), that the capacity of the agricultural sector to provide more work is not yet exhausted. The trends for East Java support this conclusion even more strongly: recorded male rural employment grew by only 0.3 per cent per annum in the 1970–80 period but by 2.3 per cent per annum in the 1980–5 period. In fact agriculture accounted for 36 per cent of total male employment growth over this period.

In the course of economic development the rising proportion of employment in non-agricultural activities is typically associated with both an increase in urbanization and a shift in the structure of employment within rural areas (United Nations, 1980: 70). In 1985 non-agricultural employment provided 35 per cent of total employment in rural East Java, a large increase over the 23 per cent of 1971. Admittedly, definitions of urban and rural areas changed between those dates and the coverage of family workers also differed. Nevertheless, non-agricultural employment was increasing in importance in rural areas, especially over the 1970s.

Manning (1988: Table 4) has shown that changes in Java's rural employment structure were responsible for more than two-thirds of the growth in non-agricultural employment between 1971 and 1980, and urbanization for only one-third. In East Java over the 1971–85 period, changes in the rural employment structure were responsible for almost three-quarters of the growth in non-agricultural employment for both males and females, and urbanization for between one-quarter and one-third (Table 4.4). When different non-agricultural industries are analysed separately, the contribution of the different factors varies more, but changes in the rural employment structure remain the dominant influence.

Rural areas have long provided much of East Java's non-agricultural employment, in fact a consistently higher proportion than in the remainder of Indonesia. In 1985, 62 per cent of non-agricultural employment in East Java was in rural areas, compared with 55 per cent elsewhere in Indonesia.

The geographic pattern of the changing employment structure between 1971 and 1980 is shown in Figure 4.3. Agricultural employment declined in most *kabupaten* in East Java over the period. The main belts where increases occurred were the *kabupaten* bordering Central Java and those on the north coast of the Oosthoek (Eastern Corner) area (that is, the area east of a line running from Malang to Pasuruan). Within rural areas the lowest percentages of employment in agriculture were found in the Greater Surabaya area, stretching to Mojokerto and Pasuruan. Reasons for the high proportion of non-agricultural employment in this region include (a) urban overspill which fails to be classified as urban areas; (b) the tendency to locate factories on cheaper land outside city boundaries; and (c) commuting to urban jobs from surrounding rural areas.

Between 1971 and 1980 the growth of employment in trade, transportation, finance, and services (the S sector) was widespread throughout East Java. By 1980 only the island of Madura and a few *kabupaten* bordering Central Java had less than 20 per cent of employment in the S sector. In Java as a whole, there was a strong inverse relationship

FIGURE 4.3
East Java: Percentage Increase in Employment in Agriculture in *Kabupaten* and *Kotamadya*, 1971–1980

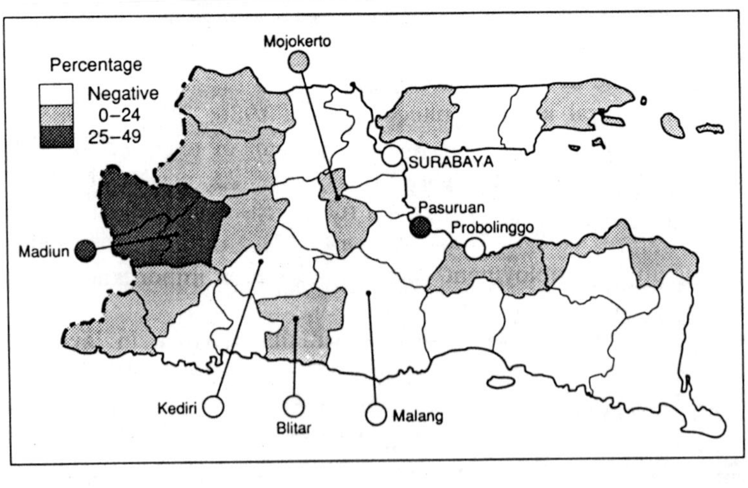

TABLE 4.4

East Java: Distribution of Components of Employment Change in Various Non-agricultural Sectors, 1971–1985 (per cent)

Component	*All Non-agriculture*		*Manufacturing*		*Trade*	
	Male	*Female*	*Male*	*Female*	*Male*	*Female*
Changes in rural employment structure	71	74	60	87	67	77
Urbanization	31	25	20	8	39	20
Changes in urban employment structure[a]	–2	1	20	5	–6	3
Increase in employment in sector as percentage of total employment increase	82	84	18	24	17	40
Number ('000)	1,614	1,372	347	388	332	663

Source: Author's calculations from BPS (1987a).
Note: See United Nations (1980) for methods of calculation.

[a]Some of these changes are due to sampling errors or changes in the definition of rural areas.

between the initial share of the S sector in total employment and its rate of employment growth over the 1971–80 period. The same was true for the growth of employment in mining, manufacturing, construction, and utilities (the M sector). This indicates a levelling in the spread of S- and M-sector employment. The only *kabupaten* of East Java in which absolute growth of finance and service employment exceeded 30,000 and relative growth exceeded 100 per cent were Sidoarjo and Pasuruan, highlighting the expansion of the Greater Surabaya metropolis (Jones, 1984).

Most of the northern areas of East Java (including Madura) recorded high rates of increase in M-sector employment, though this was sometimes from a small base. Figure 4.4 shows the percentage of total manufacturing employment in large and medium (L and M) firms in 1980. Compared with other parts of Java, East Java shows a wider 'spread' of areas where L and M firms provide a substantial share of all employment in manufacturing. Such areas include the Oosthoek area and Ngawi and Bojonegoro (where the absolute numbers employed in manufacturing are rather small). Sawmilling could be a major factor in Ngawi and Bojonegoro, and tobacco processing in the Oosthoek, as well as a large paper factory in Leces.

In 1980, 45 per cent of employment in L and M firms in East Java was in the *kotamadya*, and a further 26 per cent in *kabupaten* surrounding large cities, leaving 29 per cent in all other *kabupaten*. In West Java–Jakarta, such employment was highly concentrated around large cities. By contrast, in Central Java–Yogyakarta, 67 per cent of it was located in 'all other *kabupaten*'. East Java occupied an intermediate position (Jones, 1984).

FIGURE 4.4
East Java: Percentage of Total Manufacturing Employment in Large and Medium Firms, 1980

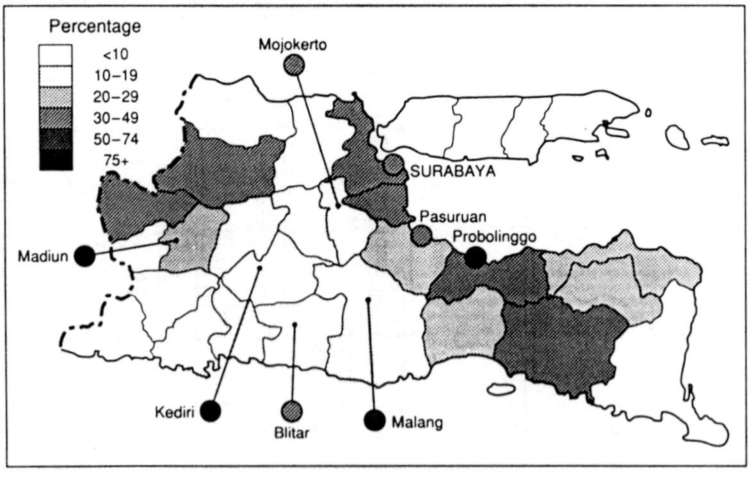

Changing Occupational Structure

The decline since 1971 in the share of the work-force in farming occupations in East Java (most of which occurred before 1980) was largely offset for males by a rise in the share of production process workers, and for females by a rise in the share of both production and sales workers (Table 4.5). The proportion of workers in the professions rose steadily,

TABLE 4.5
East Java: Employed Population by Main Occupation, 1971, 1980, and 1985

	Percentage Distribution			*Change in Percentage Share*	
	1971	*1980*	*1985*	*1971–80*	*1980–5*
Males					
Professional	1.7	2.2	2.7	+0.5	+0.5
Managerial	0.5	0.1	0.1	+0.4	–
Clerical	3.9	3.7	3.7	−0.2	–
Sales	8.1	9.3	10.3	+1.2	+1.0
Services	3.3	2.8	2.2	+0.5	−0.6
Farming	71.2	61.4	59.3	−9.8	−2.1
Production	11.3	20.5	21.7	+9.2	+1.2
Total	100.0	100.0	100.0		
Females					
Professional	1.7	2.6	2.7	+0.9	+0.1
Managerial	0.1	*	*	−0.1	*
Clerical	0.8	1.0	1.2	+0.2	+0.2
Sales	18.9	23.9	25.3	+5.0	+1.4
Services	7.4	8.0	6.8	+0.6	−1.2
Farming	63.5	49.3	49.7	−14.2	+0.4
Production	7.6	15.2	14.3	+7.6	−0.9
Total	100.0	100.0	100.0		
Both sexes					
Professional	1.7	2.4	2.7	+0.7	+0.3
Managerial	0.4	0.1	0.1	−0.3	0
Clerical	2.8	2.8	2.8	0	0
Sales	11.8	14.4	16.1	+2.6	+1.7
Services	4.7	4.6	3.9	−0.1	−0.7
Farming	68.6	57.1	55.6	−11.5	−1.5
Production	10.0	18.8	+8.6	+8.6	+0.2
Total	100.0	100.0	100.0		

Sources: Computed from BPS (1974, 1983a, and 1987a).

Notes: Those with occupations unclassified were excluded for the purposes of these estimates. The numbers (and percentages of total employment) in this category were: 1971: 310,198 (3.8%); 1980: 151,182 (1.4%); 1985: 145,869 (1.1%).

* = Less than 0.05%.

though it was still only 2.7 per cent in 1985. Surprisingly, clerical occupations did not increase their share at all. Later in the chapter, occupational trends will be related to changes in the educational levels of the work-force.

Trends in Unemployment

Unemployment data from censuses and surveys provide disappointingly little information about the actual utilization of labour in Indonesia. Open unemployment is not characteristic either of rural areas or of the urban poor, and in any case is difficult to measure consistently. A more realistic estimate of underemployment levels can be obtained by using information such as the proportion of the employed who work less than 35 hours per week and want more work, and the proportion of males who are categorized as having the economic activity status of 'others' (that is, not working, looking for work, in school, or doing housework). However, time trends cannot be obtained using most of these indicators. The 1971 Population Census did not collect data on hours of work, and the 1980 Population Census did not ask whether those working short hours wanted more work.

Data on regional differences in some measures of labour utilization in 1980 show particularly high unemployment in Madura and in many of the coastal areas facing Madura, and low rates in all the major cities except Pasuruan (Figure 4.5). Figure 4.6, which adds to the unemployed those working less than 35 hours, continues to suggest serious labour underutilization in Madura and to a lesser extent in the entire Oosthoek area, and much lower levels in the cities.

Figures 4.7 and 4.8 show unemployment rates and a more general

FIGURE 4.5
East Java: The Unemployed as a Percentage of the Economically Active Population, 1980

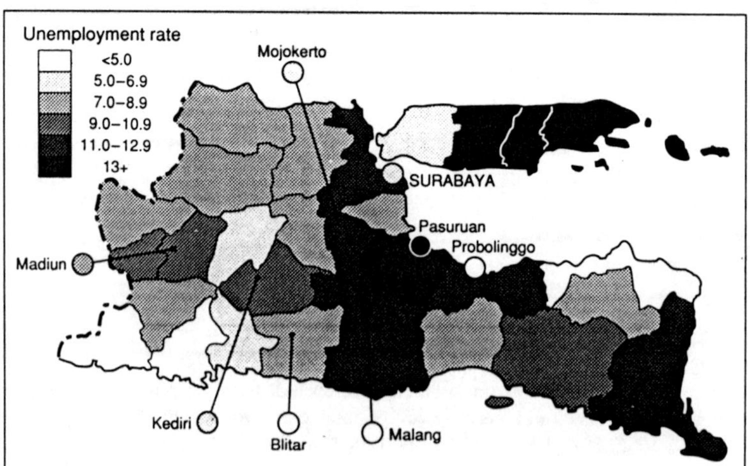

FIGURE 4.6
East Java: Percentage of the Economically Active Population Unemployed or Working Less than 35 Hours in the Reference Week, 1980

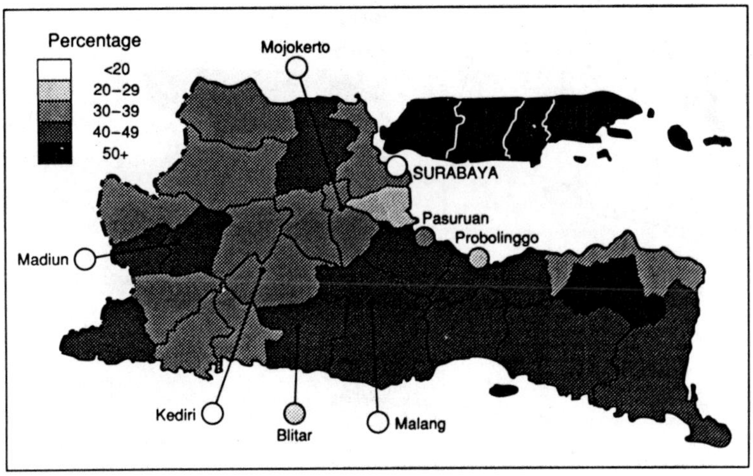

measure of underutilization of potential labour respectively, both for males. The measure of underutilization (comprising the unemployed, those who worked less than 35 hours in the reference week, and 'others') is more relevant as an indicator of underemployment for males than for females, because more females who are categorized as 'others' are likely, for social and cultural reasons, to be unavailable for work.

The patterns of unemployment and of underutilization shown in Figures 4.7 and 4.8 are quite similar.[4] The problematic area is Madura. All the cities and the entire section of East Java west of a line from

FIGURE 4.7
East Java: Unemployment Rates for Males, 1980 (per cent)

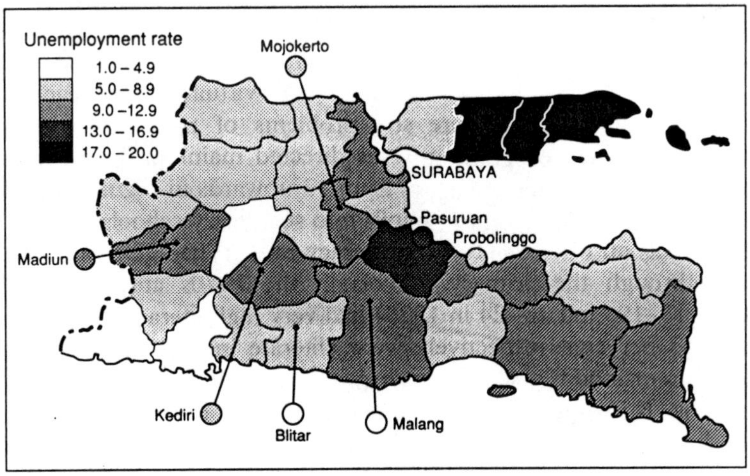

FIGURE 4.8
East Java: Rates of Underutilization of Males in the Labour Force, 1980 (per cent)

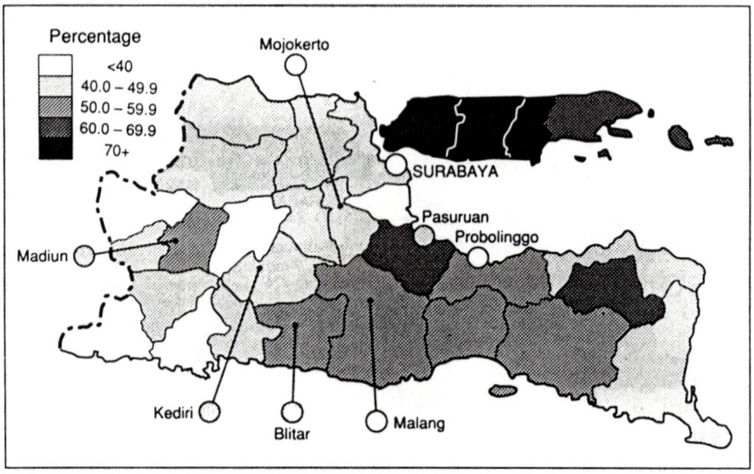

Pasuruan to Blitar have relatively low levels of underutilization of labour. The analysis would be much sharper, however, if one knew the proportion of those working less than 35 hours a week who wanted more work. This will be possible using data tapes from the 1985 Supas.

Educational Trends and Employment

Trends in Education

Over a long period Java lagged behind the rest of Indonesia in the proportion of its children in school and the educational attainment of its population (Jones, 1976). However, during the 1970s and early 1980s the proportion of children attending school in East Java rose dramatically (Figure 4.9). During this period the Inpres Sekolah Dasar programme, funded by revenue from oil, financed the construction of new primary schools throughout rural areas in Indonesia. By the mid-1980s, the goal of universal primary education had virtually been reached in East Java, though there were still problems of premature dropout. Although the Inpres programme was directed mainly towards primary education, the figures for the ages from 13 upwards in Figure 4.9 indicate that there was a flow-on of pupils into secondary schools.

There was an obvious effect on literacy rates. The age-groups which passed through the primary schools in the 1970s and early 1980s (10–14, 15–19, and 20–24 in 1985) had very high literacy rates: only 3, 7, and 13 per cent respectively were illiterate in 1985 (Figure 4.10). Illiteracy remained higher than in Indonesia as a whole but the gap was narrowing. It is surprising that any gap remained at the young ages: by 1980 there was essentially no difference between East Java and the rest of Indonesia in the proportion of children in school (see Figure 4.9).

FIGURE 4.9
Percentage of Children Currently Attending School by Age in East Java, 1971, 1980, and 1985, and in Indonesia, 1980

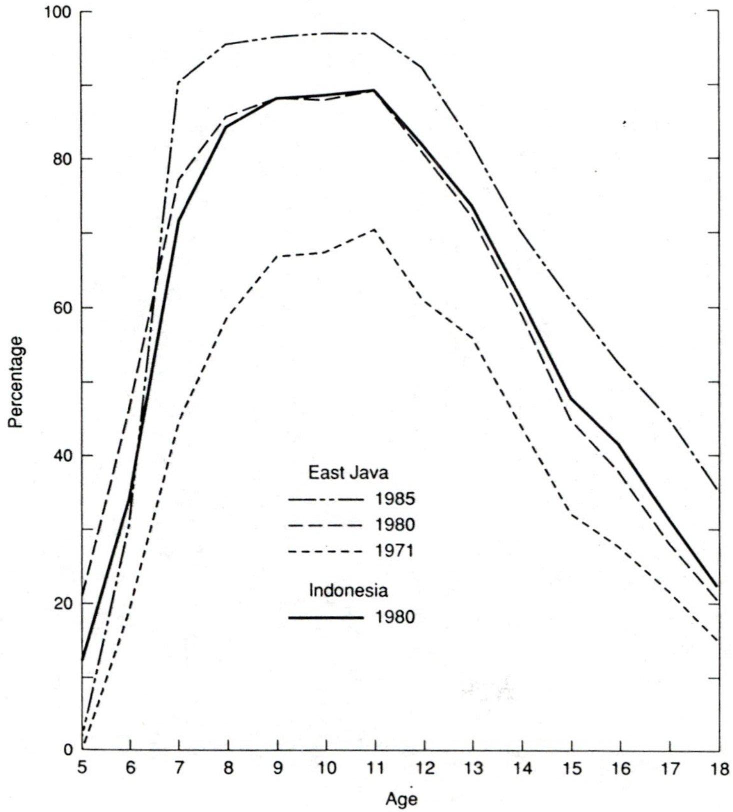

FIGURE 4.10
East Java and All Indonesia: Percentage of the Illiterate Population by Age-group, 1985

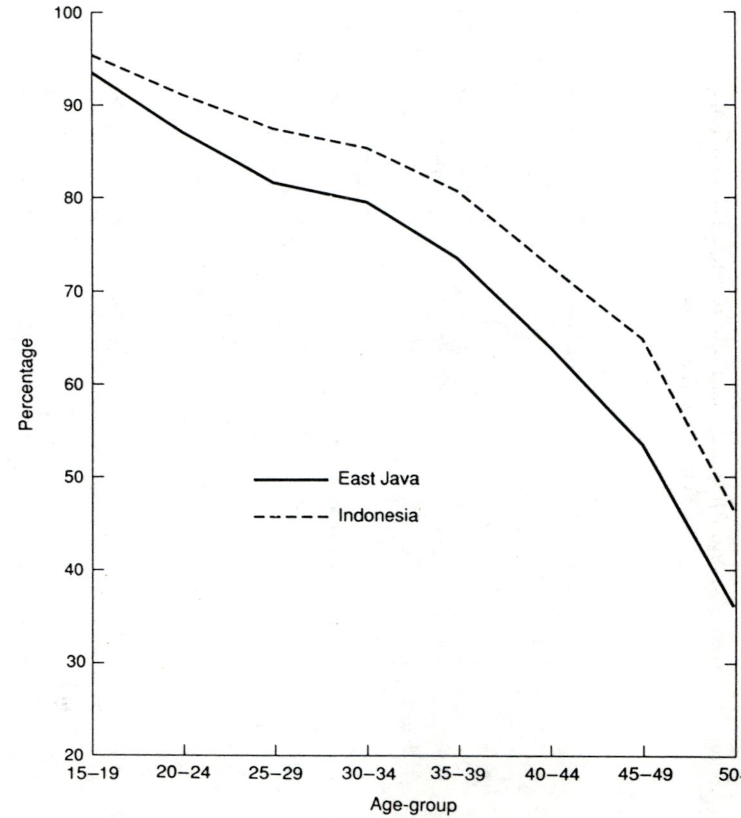

FIGURE 4.11
East Java and All Indonesia: Ratio of Male Literacy Rates to Female by Age-group, 1985

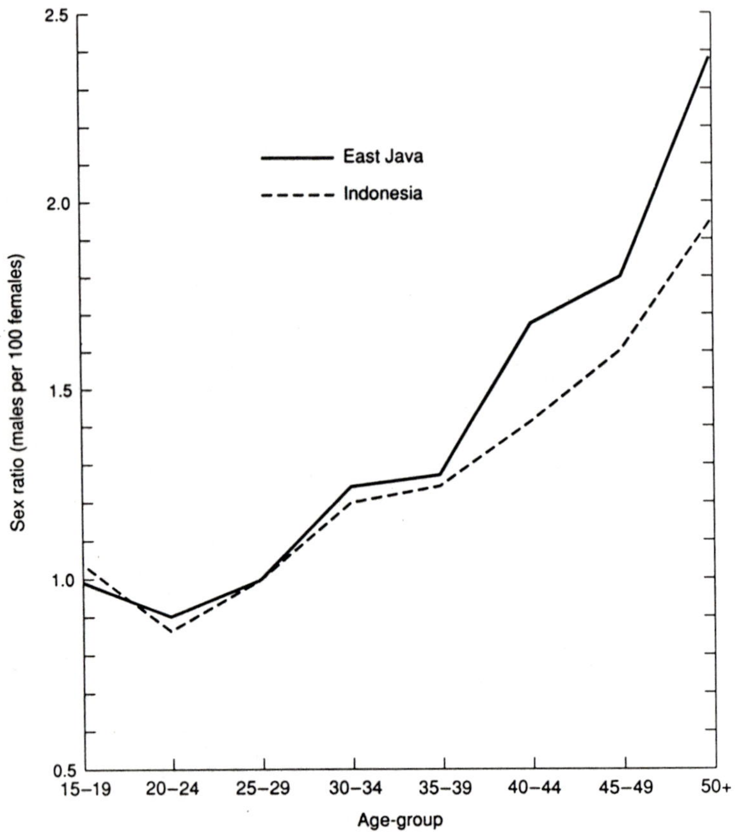

Male literacy rates continue to exceed female but by 1985 the difference was very small at the youngest ages (Figure 4.11). By age 25–29 the gap had widened to more than 10 percentage points, with a male literacy rate of 89 per cent and a female rate of 76 per cent. Beyond this point the gap widened as age increased, with a male rate of 72 per cent and a female rate of 41 per cent at ages above 30.

One measure of the educational attainment of the population—the percentage having completed junior secondary school—is shown by age-groups in Figure 4.12. The difference between older and younger age-groups is striking, more so than the modest but consistent difference between East Java and Indonesia as a whole. Even so, the potential for further improvements in education is evident: the highest percentage having completed junior secondary school is a little over 20 per cent in the 20–24 age-group; even a doubling of this figure would leave it well below that reached in many other countries. Relative access by girls to secondary education still leaves room for improvement, though progress has been striking (Figure 4.13). In this respect East Java differs little from Indonesia as a whole.

FIGURE 4.12

East Java and All Indonesia: Percentage of Population with Completed Junior Secondary School Education by Age-group, 1985

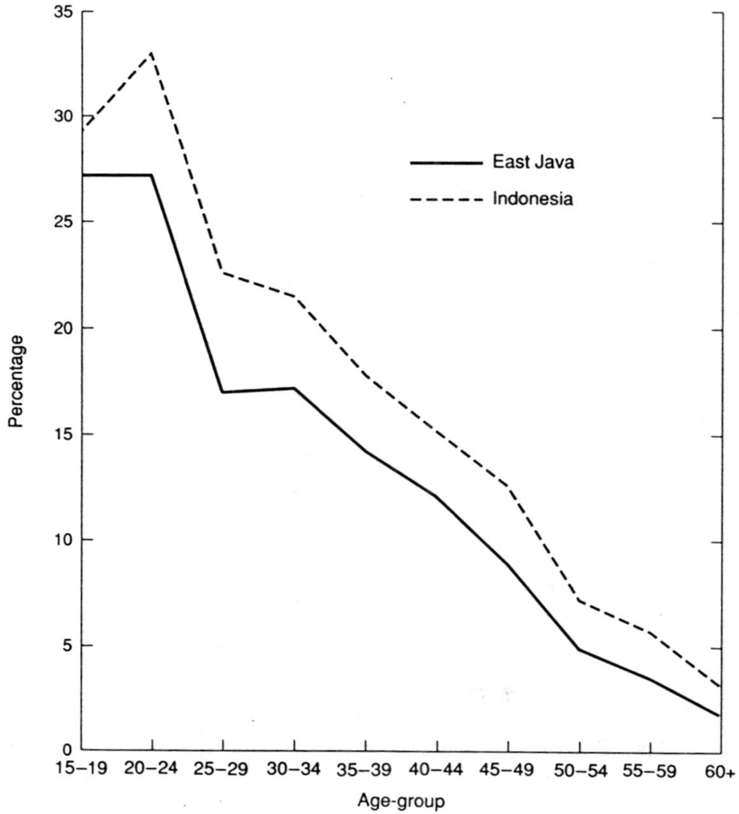

FIGURE 4.13

East Java and All Indonesia: Sex Ratio of Population with Completed Junior Secondary School Education, 1985

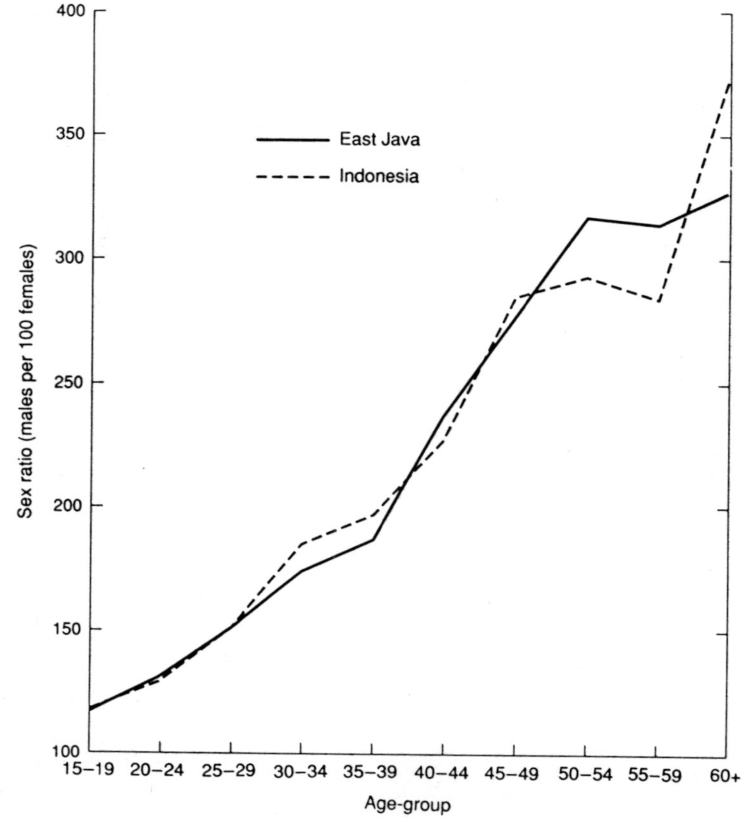

TABLE 4.6
East Java and the Rest of Indonesia: Change in Educational Attainment of Population Aged 10–59, 1971–1985 (per cent)

	East Java			*Rest of Indonesia*		
	1971	*1985*	*Increase*	*1971*	*1985*	*Increase*
Completed primary school at least	23.7	41.3	17.6	28.8	46.9	18.1
Completed junior secondary school at least	5.5	14.2	8.7	7.6	18.3	10.7

Sources: BPS (1974, 1987a, 1987c).

Summary measures of the change in educational attainment of the working-age population over the period are given in Table 4.6. The low educational attainment in the older age-groups weights the figures downwards. Nevertheless, the rise in the proportion of the population which had completed primary school matched that for Indonesia as a whole. By 1985 this proportion was more than 40 per cent. The relative increase in the proportion which had completed junior secondary school was even greater, though this proportion had still reached only 14 per cent in 1985.

The exceptionally rapid fertility decline in East Java (see Chapter 3) which has led to the beginning of a decline in the absolute numbers reaching secondary school age should facilitate efforts to raise participation rates in secondary education. It can therefore be anticipated that the share of the work-force with secondary education will grow even more rapidly than in the recent past.

Work-force Participation by Educational Attainment

Work-force participation differs markedly according to education, particularly for women. Those with the lowest and highest levels of education have much higher participation rates than those in between, the lowest rates being at the completed junior secondary school level (Table 4.7). This pattern holds in each 5-year age-group in the main working ages (20–54), though not in the age-groups 15–19 and above 55 (Table 4.8). The high participation rates among the uneducated and the highly educated have very different explanations (Jones, 1986). Poor and uneducated women probably work because family needs require it. For the better-off, typically the better-educated, attractive work opportunities are likely to be more relevant.[5]

Will these differentials in labour force participation between educational groups persist? The rapid expansion of education is altering the social composition of the different educational groups. The uneducated, who in 1971 comprised 60 per cent of all women, during the 1990s will

TABLE 4.7

East Java: Female Labour Force Participation Rates for Population Aged 10 and Above by Level of Education Completed and Place of Residence, 1971–1985

	Urban		*Rural*		*Total*			*Number ('000)*		
Level of Education	*1971*	*1980*	*1971*	*1980*	*1971*	*1980*	*1985*	*1971*	*1980*	*1985*
No schooling	39.6	39.5	31.7	42.7	31.6	42.3	50.8	5,574	5,050	4,352
Incomplete primary	22.6	27.4	27.2	30.3	26.5	29.8	36.7	2,305	3,793	4,103
Primary	22.8	24.2	30.1	33.2	28.6	30.5	37.2	1,150	1,777	2,770
Junior secondary	20.6	17.9	21.8	23.5	21.1	20.1	22.3	231	411	749
Senior secondary and higher	37.5	44.9	75.8	58.5	46.9	49.4	54.1	91	270	495

Sources: BPS (1974: Tables 16, 37, 37A; 1983a: Table 32; 1987a: Table 19.2).

TABLE 4.8

Urban Areas of East Java: Age-specific Female Labour Force Participation by Level of Education Completed, 1980 (per cent)

Age-group	*No Schooling*	*Incomplete Primary School*	*Primary School*	*Junior High School*	*Senior High School and Higher*
10–14	32.8	4.2	5.1	–	*
15–19	52.9	48.4	25.3	6.5	21.6
20–24	39.1	36.3	28.2	22.4	42.1
25–29	37.8	35.6	27.2	24.2	51.1
30–34	43.7	37.8	28.5	27.8	50.9
35–39	45.9	41.4	33.1	32.9	49.4
40–44	49.3	43.8	31.8	29.8	53.7
45–49	48.8	41.7	31.9	26.8	66.9
50–54	46.0	37.8	25.8	24.6	41.9
55–59	39.2	32.7	20.9	10.8	22.7
60–64	32.6	30.5	16.0	14.0	18.1
65+	17.6	12.2	6.2	11.1	12.2
Number ('000)	627	679	532	250	182

Source: Kristianto (1985: Appendix Table II.3, based on BPS, unpublished tabulation, May 1984).

* = Less than 0.05%.

represent a much smaller and disadvantaged group of older and poor rural women. In 1971 those who had completed primary school and junior secondary school constituted a select and quite privileged group. By 1985 this group had grown to 28 per cent of all women, and will continue to grow rapidly. It cannot be expected that their decision about whether to work will be driven by the same considerations as those which influenced the more select 1971 group. For one thing, possession of these medium levels of education will have lost much of its status, and a wider range of jobs may be thought suitable for women with such levels of education.

Women with medium levels of education represent a much underused resource. As their numbers grow, this underuse will be an increasingly serious loss to the nation unless the participation rates for such women rise. The sharp declines in fertility will mean that the child-rearing contribution of such women will become much less significant, and this should facilitate their increased participation in economic activities.

Four factors are likely to influence future work-force participation of women in East Java: urbanization, education, employment opportunities, and perceptions of appropriate female roles. Because labour force participation rates for urban women and those with lower secondary school education are lower than those for other women, urbanization and educational advance would lower labour force participation, other things being equal. But other things will not be equal, and this brings us to a consideration of the final two factors: changing employment opportunities and changing perceptions of female roles. In particular, how might these affect the work-force participation of the rapidly growing group of young women in East Java with completed primary and junior secondary education?

The middle-class—and increasingly the lower middle-class—women who achieve medium levels of education tend to be drawn from groups which value traditional female roles and for whom it is important to demonstrate the husband's ability to support his family without the need for his wife to work (Raharjo and Hull, 1984). Women with primary school or lower secondary education often cannot find work that is sufficiently remunerative or of high enough status to justify (in their own eyes or in those of their husbands) their entering the work-force. With rising numbers achieving senior secondary school and college education, there will be a 'pushdown' effect (to be described later in the chapter), and the attractiveness of jobs open to primary and lower secondary graduates must decrease unless very high rates of economic growth are achieved. Therefore, unless there is a marked change in attitudes, whereby work of even a fairly mundane kind is seen as suitable for women with these levels of education, a substantial rise in their low participation rates is unlikely. On the other hand, as more women achieve this level of education, it may cease to signify that they are from a 'bourgeois' group concerned to maintain its social status by keeping its women at home.

The Education–Occupation Matrix

The rising education levels of the work-force should facilitate rapid increases in productivity, while the rising proportion of the total population in the work-force should enable such increases to be translated into even more rapid increases in real income per head. Both of these desirable outcomes, however, are contingent on suitable work being available for the rapidly growing work-force.

Whether the educational trends in East Java are consistent with the evolving demand for labour could be assessed by looking at the present jobs of workers with different levels of education and estimating whether the expected increase in these jobs is consistent with the expected growth in the number of workers with different levels of education, thus leaving the education–occupation matrix unchanged. This by no means suggests that prevailing education–occupation matrices are necessarily ideal. If the underlying trends in education and in employment opportunities make it impossible for them to be maintained unchanged, this implies merely that the 'mix' of occupations engaged in by people with given levels of education will have to alter. This is not a problem unless people are inflexible about the kind of work they are willing to do, or unless economic growth is too slow and employment elasticities too small to raise total job opportunities fast enough to absorb all of the growing work-force.

Table 4.9 shows the education–occupation matrix for East Java. Workers with primary school education or less are heavily concentrated in agriculture, production, and sales occupations, whereas those with secondary school education (especially senior and vocational secondary school) tend to be employed in clerical and professional occupations. At the top end of the educational range, among those with academy or university education, well over half are in the professions (according to the 1985 data) and fewer than one-fifth are outside professional, managerial, or clerical occupations.

Farmers remain a very large component of the East Java labour force. Contrary to popular belief, the education of farmers makes an important contribution to their productivity (Colclough, 1982; Oshima, 1983). Given the impressive gains in agricultural productivity over the 1970s and 1980s and the need for continued increases in productivity, it is worth examining the trends in educational attainment of East Java's farmers (Table 4.10). Since 1971, there has been a sharp decline in the proportion of farmers with no schooling (though more than one-third remained unschooled in 1985), matched by a sharp increase in the proportion with some or completed primary school. There was also a sharp rise in the proportion with secondary school education, but from the very low base of 0.7 per cent to 3.3 per cent. The important trend from the point of view of agricultural productivity is undoubtedly the rise from 41 per cent to 64 per cent in the proportion with at least some primary schooling, and the rise in literacy this implies.

East Java: Distribution of Occupations of Employed Population at Each Educational Level, 1980 and 1985 (per cent)

				General High School					
Occupations	*No Schooling*	*Incomplete Primary*	*Primary*	*Junior*	*Senior*	*Vocational High School*	*Academy*	*University*	*All Education Levels*
1980									
Professional	0.3	0.3	1.0	5.9	14.8	36.8	34.0	52.8	2.3
Managerial	0.0	0.0	0.0	0.2	0.7	0.2	1.5	3.4	0.1
Clerical	0.2	1.1	3.5	13.6	31.7	16.1	34.5	26.2	2.7
Sales	15.1	13.4	15.0	18.7	16.8	7.0	5.6	4.7	14.3
Service	4.5	4.3	5.4	6.0	4.4	3.1	2.5	0.7	4.6
Agriculture	67.7	61.1	48.0	18.2	8.4	8.8	4.8	4.3	56.8
Production	12.1	19.7	26.0	30.5	18.5	24.0	9.1	5.7	18.5
Others	0.0	0.1	1.0	7.0	4.6	3.8	8.1	2.2	0.7
Total	100.0	100.0	100.0	100.0	100.0	100.0	100.0	100.0	100.0
Number('000)	4,246	3,915	2,263	332	169	413	30	27	11,397
1985									
Professional	0.1	0.2	0.5	3.1	10.9	32.7	57.5	60.4	2.7
Managerial	0.0	0.0	0.0	0.1	0.7	0.2	3.3	0.8	0.1
Clerical	0.1	0.5	2.2	9.8	28.3	14.7	24.6	27.9	2.7
Sales	16.3	15.7	16.6	23.0	17.6	8.8	3.3	2.3	16.0
Service	4.2	2.9	4.6	6.2	4.7	3.2	2.2	0.8	3.9
Agriculture	68.8	62.4	50.4	23.8	11.1	11.7	0.6	2.4	55.3
Production	10.5	18.2	25.4	30.2	22.8	26.4	5.7	4.6	18.7
Others	0.0	0.0	0.3	3.8	3.9	2.3	2.8	0.8	0.5
Total	100.0	100.0	100.0	100.0	100.0	100.0	100.0	100.0	100.0
Number ('000)	3,864	4,396	3,460	567	291	653	70	50	13,353

Sources: BPS (1984a: Table 37; 1987a: Table 25.3).
Note: A small 'not stated' group was excluded from the denominator in calculating percentages.

TABLE 4.10

East Java: Educational Attainment of Farmers, 1971, 1980, and 1985[a]

	1971	*1980*	*1985*
No school	58.6	44.5	36.0
Incomplete primary	24.8	36.9	37.1
Completed primary	15.9	16.8	23.6
Junior secondary			
General	0.4	0.9	1.8
Vocational	10.1	0.3	0.6
Senior secondary			
General	10.1	0.2	0.4
Vocational	0.1	0.3	0.5
Academy	*	*	*
University	*	*	*
Total	100.0	100.0	100.0
Number ('000)	6,248	6,429	7,342

Sources: BPS (1974: Table 37; 1987a: Table 37; includes 1987c: Table 25.3).

[a]'Farmers' includes agricultural workers.

* = Less than 0.05%.

Issues in the Expansion of Secondary and Higher Education

Over the 1971–85 period professional, managerial, and clerical occupations provided only 7 per cent of the net increase in employment in East Java (compared with 11 per cent in Indonesia as a whole). As already noted, these occupations provide a high proportion of employment for the better-educated, who in turn dominate employment in these occupations. If the share of these occupations in total employment continues to rise only slowly, this will mean too few new jobs in these occupations for all new upper secondary and tertiary graduates, because the supply of secondary and tertiary graduates will be growing much faster than other segments of the work-force. A study of Indonesia, taking into account recent trends and educational targets of the Fifth Plan (Jones, 1992), projected the following rates of increase in the working-age population (20–64) with different levels of education over the 1985–95 period:

None or primary	1.2 per cent
Lower secondary	6.5 per cent
Upper secondary	7.5 per cent
Tertiary	13.6 per cent

If employment in East Java were to grow by 3 per cent a year[6] and if the occupational structure were to remain unchanged, then growth in job opportunities in occupations traditionally employing those with secondary school and university education would clearly lag behind the rapidly growing numbers with these levels of education. Even if, as expected, development of the economy favours occupations requiring further education, and growth of these occupations reaches 4 or 5 per cent per annum, a large gap would remain. Such a situation would result in either rising unemployment and underemployment of the better-educated or increasing absorption of upper secondary and tertiary graduates into occupations which they have hitherto regarded as inferior. The latter outcome would involve a 'pushdown' in the status and earning prospects of occupations available to the better-educated or, viewed differently, a rise in the qualifications needed for a wide variety of jobs. This implies the need for a painful readjustment of expectations and aspirations by those who have viewed education as a passport to high-status, white-collar employment.

The prospective shortfall of professional, managerial, and clerical work for the better-educated does not mean that the expansion of higher education should be delayed, but it does suggest the need for careful evaluation of the purposes of secondary and higher education. Rates-of-return studies in South-East Asia generally support further expansion of secondary and higher education. However, such estimates have little predictive value when structural economic change is occurring and secondary education is changing rapidly from an élite to a mass base (Jones, 1988). Perhaps the more important point to stress is that education plays such diverse roles in a society (Jones, 1988) that its contribution to the welfare of individuals and society should not be judged only on the basis of its contribution to their economic welfare, even if that could be measured accurately.

Conclusion

The employment structure in East Java is still in the early stages of diversification from an agricultural base to a more complex urban–industrial base. Traditional agriculture and illiteracy went hand in hand. Rising levels of education are now leading young people to desert the agricultural sector. Thanks to the earlier decline in birth rates, in the 1990s the youngest age-groups in the work-force (15–24) will not grow at all. The consequent ageing of the work-force will be most pronounced in agriculture.

Nevertheless, educated young people will find it hard to fulfil their job aspirations because of the very rapid growth expected in the number of junior and senior secondary school and college graduates. It is doubtful whether many of them will settle for agricultural work. Longer periods of job search, higher levels of open unemployment, and a rise in mobility as job prospects in other regions are tested are more likely results. For many, the end result will be a lowering of expectations as they settle for the jobs actually available. What these jobs will be will depend on how rapidly the economy grows and on the technological level and labour intensity of the growth areas of the economy.

1. Comparable data for Indonesia as a whole can be found in Jones (1987) and Manning (1988).

2. East Java has long had lower fertility than the Indonesian average. In addition, the recent fertility decline was earlier and more rapid in East Java than elsewhere in Indonesia.

3. It should be noted that the BPS projections on which Table 4.2 is based understate the decline which has occurred—not only in East Java, but also in Indonesia as a whole. This should make little difference to the growth of the labour force up to the year 2000, but to the extent that it does, the impact will be on the youngest labour force age-group. This lends additional conviction to the conclusion that the youthful segment of East Java's labour force will decline in numbers during the 1990s.

4. A regression analysis showed that there was a close association between the rate of open unemployment and the measure of underutilization used in Figure 4.8.

5. Between 1971 and 1980, among women with senior high school education, work-force participation rates rose in urban areas but fell in rural areas, the latter despite a general rise at all other levels of education. Before making too much of this, however, it should be noted that in 1971 there were only 22,000 of these highly educated women in rural areas, representing only a quarter of all women with this level of education in East Java. (By 1980 the number had reached 85,000.)

6. This is about as good as could be expected, given current economic prospects and an incremental employment–output ratio of about 0.5.

5
Migration

Riwanto Tirtosudarmo and Paul Meyer

Introduction

PEOPLE change their place of residence—they 'migrate'—for a variety of reasons: to get a better job, to attend a better school, to establish a new household upon marriage, to live in a more congenial area upon retirement, or to leave a situation of hardship or natural disaster. All of these motivations are (of course) found among the people of East Java, but the focus in this chapter is on the 'economic' incentives for moving. Specifically, it is proposed here that the migration patterns in East Java reflect the underlying patterns of industrialization and that the main migration flows during the New Order period have been towards those areas experiencing industrial growth and away from areas dominated by low-productivity activities such as dry-land agriculture. Equally important, the migration flows also include quantitative shifts of human resources, since the younger and better-educated people tend to be overrepresented in such migration streams.

Until recently it has not been possible to undertake an examination of these propositions on a large scale in Indonesia because of the nature of the questions on migration in the national censuses and surveys. The only people considered to be migrants were those who moved at some stage from one province to another. This resulted in a misleading impression that Indonesians had low levels of mobility. For example, the results of the 1980 Population Census indicated that only 2.4 per cent of the population had 'migrated' during the five-year period preceding the Census. Examinations of migration within provinces were limited to surveys using much smaller samples (such as Hugo, 1978 and Tukiran, 1986) or to studies of migrant communities, mainly in urban areas (such as McCutcheon, 1977 and Steele, 1980).

The 1985 Supas (Survei Penduduk antar Sensus; or Intercensal Population Survey) broadened the definition of migration to include movements between *kabupaten* (districts). Based on preliminary tabulations from the 1985 Supas, the Biro Pusat Statistik (BPS or Central Bureau of Statistics) estimated that nearly 11 per cent of the population had ever moved from one *kabupaten* to another (BPS, 1986a: Table 8). Calculations using figures on numbers of movers between *kabupaten* and their length of stay in *kabupaten* where they were enumerated in 1985 (Mantra, 1986–7: Table 3.8) indicate that nearly 10 per cent of the population aged 10 and above had moved in the previous ten years, and nearly 5 per cent of those aged 5 and above had moved in the previous five years.

To gain a clearer picture of the nature of migration, particularly as it relates to changing economic activities in East Java, the results of a number of small-scale studies of population mobility in East Java are reviewed and then tabulations from the 1980 Population Census of the recent migrants into the province and of those who moved between *kabupaten* from the 1985 Supas are analysed.

Population Mobility in East Java

Most of the studies of population mobility in East Java are concerned with what Zelinsky (1971: 225–6) has defined as conventional migration; that is 'any permanent or semi-permanent change of residence'. Affandy (1987–8) and Slamet (1985) analysed overall trends from various censuses and Supas data sets. Immigrant communities in Surabaya were studied by McCutcheon (1977), Steele (1980), and Wibowo (1983), while Bandiyono (1987) and Tirtosudarmo (1985) used survey data from throughout the province in their examinations of permanent migration. Several other studies (Tukiran, 1986; Wasono and Partosudjono, 1986; Wibowo, 1983) examine non-permanent or circular migration, defined by Zelinsky (1971: 226) as movements which are 'usually short term, repetitive or cyclical in nature, ... [with] the lack of any declared intention of permanent or long-lasting change in residence'.

The findings of these studies can be divided into three main categories. First, population mobility in East Java, permanent or non-permanent, is generally from rural to urban areas, with Surabaya as the main destination. Second, a large number of migrants is involved in informal-sector activities in urban areas; this is particularly true of the non-permanent migrants. Third, the mobility patterns reflect the wider social and economic structural changes which have taken place in East Java during the New Order period.

Migration from Rural to Urban Areas

Two studies of migrants in Surabaya conducted in the mid-1970s found that the majority of them had come from rural areas of the province. McCutcheon (1977: 81), in her 1975 study of adjustment among 600 migrants, found that two-thirds of them had come from rural backgrounds. Steele's (1980) study, carried out in 1974, examined occupational mobility of migrants and found that around 60 per cent of the sample (n = 399) had rural origins. Bandiyono (1987), using a larger survey (n = 2,490) of migrants throughout the province, reports that in Surabaya 40 per cent of the respondents came from rural areas of East Java, and about one-third of the migrants in other urban areas in the survey also reported their places of origin as rural areas of East Java.

Research on migration in most parts of the world has established that people between their late teens and early thirties are more migratory than older people, and this is also true of single people in comparison with those who are married (Todaro, 1976: 27). Young single people are more likely to migrate because they have lower costs (direct, opportunity, and psychic), and they are seen as being more readily disposed to take advantage of new opportunities provided by migration than are older married people. The latter are more likely to be restrained by a host of stronger social and economic ties. The studies in East Java of the characteristics of people who move from rural to urban areas found these propositions to hold there as well: most migrants of both sexes made their first move between ages 15 and 34, and the majority were unmarried when they first moved (Steele, 1980; Tirtosudarmo, 1985: 56–8; Wibowo, 1983). Wasono and Partosudjono (1986), who studied circular migrants located in Surabaya, also found these general characteristics in their sample.

Most of the studies in East Java have also investigated migrants' reasons for moving to urban areas. The reasons given by men were mostly related to work opportunities, while women tended to move for family reasons (McCutcheon, 1977; Tirtosudarmo, 1985: 70; Tukiran, 1986; Wibowo, 1983).

Dominance of Informal-sector Activities

Wibowo's study (1983) of migrants in a squatter settlement in Surabaya found a prevalence of informal-sector activities, as have studies of such communities in other urban centres in Java (see, for example, Hugo, 1978: 225–9). Such migrants often report that jobs were not as readily available in the city as they had been led to believe. They had to use their resourcefulness to create income-generating activities, such as hawking, or to become involved in low-skilled occupations such as manual labour, driving pedicabs, or domestic service. Most of these were 'informal' occupations in the sense that this sector was beyond the regulation, control, and administration of the government.

Two other studies of migrants in Surabaya also found high levels of informal-sector employment. In McCutcheon's sample (1977), over 85 per cent of self-employed people were working in informal-sector jobs (mainly as pedicab drivers or hawkers). Steele (1980: 454) found that a significant proportion of the female migrants in his sample were socially and economically disadvantaged compared with the male migrants. On arrival in Surabaya, many women worked as domestic servants or prostitutes.

Structural Changes and Mobility

Migration flows in East Java, as in many developing areas, can be expected to reflect patterns of economic opportunity, which tend to vary geographically according to resource endowments and population densities. Areas with surplus labour tend to be sources for out-migration, while areas requiring labourers usually attract migrants. The basic structural changes that have occurred during the New Order period in East Java have led to changes in the migration patterns to and within the province. Two main aspects of these structural changes are examined here in the context of their contributions to the migration patterns. These are the changes which have occurred in agricultural areas to produce surplus labour and the development of industries and urban centres to absorb the rural surplus.

In the 1970s scholars began to note changes in the agricultural systems in Java, which could be interpreted as breaking down the static pattern described as 'agricultural involution' by C. Geertz (1963). Most of these later writers emphasized the consequences of the 'Green Revolution' and the application of new agricultural technologies. These changes included an increased level of socio-economic differentiation within rural society (Collier, 1981; Sinaga, 1978; Singarimbun and Penny, 1976; White, 1979), increasing commercialization of farming among those owning larger amounts of land (Edmundson and Edmundson, 1983), and the changing responses of landless farmers in coping with decreased job opportunities (Bryant, 1974; Montgomery, 1975; Soelistyo, 1975; White, 1976).

Early studies on the effects of the introduction of high-yielding varieties of rice in Java indicated that less labour was required for their successful cultivation than was required for traditional varieties (Collier, 1981: 156). In some areas this was due mainly to the concomitant introduction of hand tractors, which was facilitated by the credit policies accompanying the Green Revolution, making them competitive with even the low wages existing in rural areas (Sinaga, 1978: 102–11). Changes in harvesting practices, especially the use of contractors with teams of harvesters (the *tebasan* system) instead of the people (particularly women) of the local village (the *bawon* system), further reduced labour needs, as did the introduction of mechanical rice hullers (Collier, 1981). Agricultural activity, to which the dense populations in rural Java once had relatively easy access, rapidly became more restricted for the large landless portion of the populace. Those with small amounts of land, who had to supplement their incomes with labouring on the land of others, similarly were squeezed out of the agricultural production process. Expanding non-farm activities were able to absorb some of the ensuing surplus rural workers (McDonald and Sontosudarmo, 1976: 84), but others had to look elsewhere for their livelihood.

Some of those forced out of rural parts of Java had some hope of continuing their farming lifestyles by joining the government's transmigration programme, which would resettle them in other parts of Indonesia on lands cleared for agriculture. Although many of these new agricultural settlements were unsuccessful, this programme succeeded in almost countering the migratory flow from the rest of Indonesia to Java (Hugo et al., 1987: 195). Others forced off the land would move to the cities and smaller urban areas in Java.

In East Java the *kotamadya* of Surabaya, Malang, Pasuruan, Kediri, and Probolinggo and the *kabupaten* of Sidoarjo and Gresik have shown high rates of population growth (Tirtosudarmo, 1985: 43). Most (77 per cent; $n = 396$) of the new industrial projects in East Java from 1967 to 1976 were located in the contiguous corridor of administrative districts from Gresik through Surabaya, Sidoarjo, and Pasuruan to Malang (Tirtosudarmo, 1985: 44–6). Kediri, located just to the west of this region, and Probolinggo to the east, had somewhat less industrial development during the same period (6 per cent of new projects), but already had strong industrial bases in the form of large tobacco, sugar, and other refining industries.

In contrast to this growing core region, peripheral parts of the province have had declining rates of population growth. These areas, with a few exceptions, are predominantly rural and have lower levels of industrial activity. They appear to have become more or less permanent sources of migrants, some of whom move to other provinces, but many of whom go to the core region, presumably because the development of industrial projects since the 1960s has provided a strong attraction for job seekers. Other factors encouraging migration from the peripheral areas have been the rising expectations of those who have benefited from the greatly expanded access to education (see Chapter 4) and the ready availability of cheap transport, two other accomplishments of the provincial and national governments during the New Order period.

Little data on migrants throughout the province have been available until the 1985 Supas. The information available from Supas about the characteristics of migrants will be examined in an effort to learn more about the interactions between migration and structural changes, particularly industrialization. But first the data from the 1980 Population Census on the people who moved into East Java during the previous five years will be studied to establish their destinations in East Java and to see whether their particular characteristics indicate that interprovincial migrants at that time were also seeking opportunities in the industrializing areas.

Migrants to East Java, 1975–1980

The data collected in the 1971 and 1980 population censuses indicate that East Java experienced a net population loss through migration throughout the New Order period; that is, there were more out-migrants from the province than in-migrants. Slamet's (1985: 74–8) analysis of the census data on lifetime migrants (people living in a province other than their province of birth) found that the net migration rate (net migrants as a percentage of total population) increased from −1.77 in 1971 to −3.87 in 1980, mainly because of an increase in the out-migration rate (from 2.94 to 5.47), while the in-migration rate increased only slightly (from 1.17 to 1.60). East Java has a relatively high rate of net lifetime migration loss, but its rate is still much lower than West Sumatra, South Sulawesi, and Central Java, the three provinces with the highest rates of negative net migration. East Java and Central

Java are both major sources of candidates for the transmigration programme, and this has been one of the main reasons for the high level of out-migration from both areas.

The net loss in migrants is even more dramatically reflected in the figures for recent migrants (people who moved into or out of East Java in the previous five years). In the 1980 Population Census the number of recent out-migrants (571,000) was nearly three times the number of in-migrants (194,000) (Slamet, 1985: 78). These figures were lower by 1985: 336,000 and 165,000 respectively (Affandy, 1987–8: Tables 3.10 and 3.11).

In 1980 nearly half (45 per cent) of the out-migrants from East Java went to Sumatra, especially to the provinces in the southern half of that island, where most of the transmigration areas are located. Over a quarter (28 per cent) went to other provinces in Java, in particular to Jakarta (13 per cent), which was the second highest destination province after Lampung, an indication that the improved transportation network in Java was also a factor in the dynamics of migration. East Java had a net gain in recent migrants from Central Java and East and West Nusa Tenggara. The migrants from Central Java were probably coming in search of employment, while those from East and West Nusa Tenggara appear to be return migrants (people born in East Java returning home), since the number of recent migrants exceeds that of lifetime migrants from these two provinces (Slamet, 1985: 78–81).

Tabulations from the 1980 Population Census of recent migrants show that over half (53 per cent) of them settled in the core region, where industrialization was increasing rapidly during this period. Over half the migrants to this region (60,000, or 31 per cent of all recent migrants) were found in Surabaya city.

A comparison of the age and gender structure of the recent migrants aged 5 years and above with the total population of East Java in 1980 reveals that the recent migrants were distinctive in several ways (Table 5.1). First, males dominated the migrant group, being 55 per cent of the total, a common characteristic of migrant groups, while the reverse was true of the whole population. Males also outnumbered females in each age-group except those under 14 and over 60. The predominance of males (over 60 per cent) was most pronounced in the age-group 20–24. Over half of all migrants aged 5 years and above were concentrated in the age-groups between 15 and 34 (57 per cent of the male migrants and 51 per cent of the females), compared with less than 40 per cent of the same age and gender groups of the total population. Again, this concentration of migrants in the young working ages is not unexpected and is an indication that the recent migrants to East Java were coming there primarily in search of new opportunities.

Two other comparisons of the recent migrant group with the rest of East Java's population are also in accordance with general theories regarding migration: their education levels are much higher and they are much less likely to be employed in agriculture. The measure of education used here (Table 5.2) is the proportion of males and females who

TABLE 5.1
East Java: Distribution of Recent Migrants and All Residents Aged 5 and Above by Age-group and Sex, 1980 (per cent)

	Migrants		*All East Java*	
Age-group	*Males*	*Females*	*Males*	*Females*
5–9	10.8	12.5	15.7	14.3
10–14	9.3	12.5	13.8	12.1
15–19	15.1	14.8	11.8	11.6
20–24	20.6	16.3	9.2	10.6
25–29	12.1	11.6	9.2	9.1
30–34	8.7	8.0	6.6	6.7
35–39	6.7	5.6	7.0	7.1
40–44	5.0	4.9	6.2	6.7
45–49	2.9	3.0	5.5	5.6
50–54	2.9	3.5	5.0	4.9
55–59	2.2	1.8	3.3	3.1
60–64	1.4	1.9	2.8	3.2
65+	2.3	3.6	3.8	5.1
Total	100.0	100.0	99.9	100.1
Number	106,258	87,497	12,470,765	13,194,589

Sources: Migrants: Analysis of the 1980 Population Census tape.
All East Java: BPS (1981: Table 2).

have completed senior high school in the age-groups from 20 to 49. Male migrants were four to six times more likely than the general population to have achieved this level of schooling and the comparison for females is even more strongly in favour of the migrant group.

The distribution of the labour force (people aged 10 years and above who worked at least one hour in the week before the 1980 Population Census) (Table 5.3) shows that half the female workers and over 60 per

TABLE 5.2
East Java: Distribution of Recent Migrants and All Residents Aged 20–49 with Completed Senior High School Education by Age-group and Sex, 1980 (per cent)

	Migrants		*All East Java*	
Age-group	*Males*	*Females*	*Males*	*Females*
20–29	43	31	11	6
30–39	41	25	9	4
40–49	33	14	5	1

Sources: Migrants: Analysis of the 1980 Population Census tape.
All East Java: BPS (1981: Tables 5.1 and 5.2).

cent of male workers in East Java were in the agricultural sector, compared with less than one-quarter of the migrants of both sexes. The migrants tended to be much more concentrated in the services and public administration sector, and male migrants were also more likely to be employed in trading than were the general population. Migrants were only slightly more likely to be employed in the manufacturing sector than were the total population. One tentative conclusion that can be drawn from these figures is that the new industrial opportunities in East Java were attracting some migrants from outside the province in the late 1970s, but migrants to the province were more likely to be seeking employment in the tertiary sectors than in factory work.

A more detailed examination of the recent migrants in the labour force according to age-groups (Table 5.4) indicates that younger migrants (aged 20–39 for males and 10–29 for females) were a little more likely to be employed in manufacturing than were older migrants, but the differences are not strong enough to indicate that the industries had an exceptionally strong attraction for interprovincial migrants at that time. In fact, at those ages migrants were only marginally more likely to be in the manufacturing sector than in agriculture. In contrast, older migrants were much more concentrated in agriculture. A more striking finding is that male migrants to East Java, especially those aged 20–49, were heavily involved in public administration. This indicates that the employment policies of the government, whereby public servants can be transferred between national and provincial or regional offices, are an important aspect of migration dynamics in Indonesia.

The area of origin of the recent migrants to East Java in 1980 is also useful in understanding the migration process in the province. Over half the working-age migrants came from other parts of the island of Java

TABLE 5.3
East Java: Sectoral Distribution of the Labour Force of Recent Migrants and All Residents by Sex, 1980 (per cent)

	Migrants		*All East Java*	
Industrial Sector	*Males*	*Females*	*Males*	*Females*
Agriculture	25	23	61	49
Manufacturing	17	14	13	13
Trade	17	25	9	24
Transport, services, and public administration	41	38	17	14
Total	100	100	100	100
Number	57,920	21,812	7,420,796	3,920,301

Sources: Migrants: Analysis of the 1980 Population Census tape.
All East Java: BPS (1982: Table 39).

TABLE 5.4

East Java: Sectoral Distribution of Recent Migrants in the Labour Force by Age-group and Sex, 1980 (per cent)

Age-group	*Agriculture*	*Manufacturing*	*Trade*	*Transport and Services*	*Public Administration*	*Total*	*Number*
Males							
10–19	37	16	22	21	4	101	6,759
20–29	18	18	21	27	17	101	22,829
30–39	19	17	16	23	25	100	14,708
40–49	27	16	11	25	22	101	7,460
50+	53	10	12	17	8	100	6,164
All ages	25	17	17	24	17	100	57,920
Females							
10–19	15	18	18	49	0	100	4,970
20–29	16	17	21	38	9	101	7,814
30–39	24	12	31	29	4	100	3,341
40–49	32	10	34	22	2	100	2,653
50+	43	8	31	17	1	100	3,024
All ages	23	14	25	34	4	100	21,812

Source: Analysis of the 1980 Population Census tape.

TABLE 5.5

East Java: Distribution of Recent Migrants Aged 10 and Above by Place of Residence in 1975, Age-group, and Sex, 1980 (per cent)

	Place of Residence in 1975						
Age-group	*Sumatra*	*West Java and Jakarta*	*Central Java and Yogyakarta*	*Bali and Nusa Tenggara*	*Kalimantan, Sulawesi, Maluku, and Irian Jaya*	*Total*	*Number*
Males							
10–19	14	21	34	20	12	101	25,881
20–29	12	21	42	14	11	100	34,772
30–39	12	25	32	15	16	100	16,404
40–49	17	20	24	27	12	100	8,363
50+	10	9	28	43	11	101	9,354
All ages	13	20	35	20	12	100	94,774
Females							
10–19	13	19	34	21	13	100	23,844
20–29	11	21	38	18	13	101	24,408
30–39	8	24	31	22	15	100	11,916
40–49	18	17	22	32	11	100	6,909
50+	6	9	29	49	7	100	9,466
All ages	11	19	33	25	12	100	76,543
Males and females	12	20	34	22	12	100	171,317

Source: Analysis of the 1980 Population Census tape.

(Table 5.5), which have easy road access to East Java. One-fifth came from the less populated provinces to the south-east, Bali, and West and East Nusa Tenggara. The large group of migrants from the central parts of Java were overrepresented in the young working ages (20–29), which again indicates that workers from nearby areas were seeking employment opportunities in East Java. The relatively large group from Bali and Nusa Tenggara is heavily concentrated in the older age-groups, which supports the authors' proposition that these are people originally from East Java who are returning to the province as they approach retirement age.

The education levels of the recent migrants from the south-eastern provinces were lower than those of other recent migrants (Table 5.6), which reflects their older age distribution, older people in Indonesia having had fewer opportunities than younger people to obtain an education. The Sumatran migrants also had lower than average educational achievement, while those from the western parts of Java (Jakarta and West Java) and from the north-eastern islands (Kalimantan, Sulawesi, Maluku, and Irian Jaya) were above average.

These trends are reflected in the sectoral employment of the migrants according to their area of origin (Table 5.7). Migrants from Sumatra and the south-east, who on average were older and had lower educational qualifications, were heavily concentrated in agriculture. (The ones from Sumatra, about 3,200 men and 700 women, could be people originally from rural parts of East Java who went to Sumatra as transmigrants or on their own, became discouraged with farming conditions there, and then decided to return to their home areas.) On the other hand, those from western Java and the north-east, with higher education, were more likely to be employed in tertiary activities (transport, trade, services, and public administration). The large group of male migrants from the nearby central provinces of Java did not differ greatly in their sectoral distribution from the total, but the female migrants from this area were concentrated in the services sector. Many of these may have

TABLE 5.6
East Java: Distribution of Recent Migrants Aged 15–64 with Completed Secondary Education by Place of Residence in 1975 and Sex, 1980 (per cent)

Place of Residence in 1975	*Males*	*Females*
Sumatra	28	20
West Java and Jakarta	37	25
Central Java and Yogyakarta	29	21
Bali and Nusa Tenggara	27	12
Kalimantan, Sulawesi, Maluku, and Irian Jaya	41	23
All migrants	31	20

Source: Analysis of the 1980 Population Census tape.

TABLE 5.7
East Java: Sectoral Distribution of Recent Migrants Aged 15–64 and in the Labour Force by Place of Residence in 1975 and Sex, 1980 (per cent)

Industrial Sector	*Place of Residence in 1975*					
	Sumatra	*West Java and Jakarta*	*Central Java and Yogyakarta*	*Bali and Nusa Tenggara*	*Kalimantan, Sulawesi, Maluku, and Irian Jaya*	*All Places*
Males						
Agriculture	46	8	19	45	15	24
Manufacturing	17	16	18	13	17	17
Trade	10	27	19	12	12	17
Transport and services	17	25	26	21	34	24
Public administration	11	25	18	9	22	18
Total	101	101	100	100	100	100
Number	7,032	11,585	21,230	9,773	6,115	55,735
Females						
Agriculture	28	13	10	47	6	22
Manufacturing	16	13	14	15	14	14
Trade	28	24	26	21	33	25
Services	24	42	45	15	39	34
Public administration	4	7	5	2	8	5
Total	100	99	100	100	100	100
Number	2,419	2,500	8,652	5,149	1,238	19,958

Source: Analysis of the 1980 Population Census tape.

been in domestic service, part of the informal sector discussed above, but those with secondary education may have been employed in other parts of the informal sector, such as financial and social services.

This investigation of characteristics of the migrants who moved to East Java between 1975 and 1980 demonstrates that the group of about 75,000 working migrants (out of a total of 194,000 migrants) is similar in many ways to other migration streams. They tend to be younger and better educated than the population into which they have moved and they are more likely to work in tertiary industries. That part of this stream that came the furthest distance, from the north-eastern islands of Indonesia, had the highest education levels and propensity to be in the service and administration sectors. However, these interprovincial migrants did not appear to have much impact on the manufacturing sector, at least as far as the factory work-force was concerned. The next section will examine the inter-*kabupaten* migrants identified in the 1985 Supas, who were predominantly migrants from areas within East Java, to gauge whether this group has had some role in the recent industrialization processes in East Java.

Migrants in East Java, 1975–1985

The best opportunity to date to obtain a profile of migrants in Indonesia is provided by the 1985 Supas data, from which people in East Java who have migrated from one *kabupaten* to another have been identified, including those who migrated from a different province, within the 10-year period before the survey (a factor which limits this analysis to migrants over 10 years old). The size of the sample was only 3,446, but when sampling weights are applied this produces an estimate of over 1.35 million migrants aged 10 and above, or about 6 per cent of that age-group in the province in 1985. This compares with the figure of around 10 per cent for all of Indonesia given earlier. In part the lower figure for East Java may be due to the very large base population (over 24 million aged 10 and above, and over 31 million in all in 1985) but the size of the difference leads to the conclusion that the level of migration in East Java is lower than in the country as a whole.

For a picture of the geographical pattern of migration in East Java, the province has been divided into five regions: the industrial core described above, the island of Madura, and the areas to the east, south-west, and north-west of the core. The industrial region was clearly the most attractive destination for migrants, with nearly 60 per cent (a total of over 790,000 people) being located there and relatively few in any one of the other regions (Table 5.8). Furthermore, 71 per cent of the migrants in the core region came from outside that region, while in three other regions the figure was 63 to 65 per cent. The remaining region was the south-west, in which only 16 per cent of the migrants came from within the region itself. This may reflect the relatively poor economic conditions throughout that region, so that people there who decided to move generally looked for better opportunities elsewhere.

TABLE 5.8

East Java: Current Region of Residence of Recent Migrants Aged 10 and Above by Place of Previous Residence and Sex, 1985 (per cent)

Previous Location	*Industrial Region*	*Eastern Region*	*Madura Region*	*South-west Region*	*North-west Region*	*All*
Males						
Industrial	29	30	28	24	27	28
Eastern	7	35	10	5	2	9
Madura	9	8	33	1	2	8
South-west	8	9	8	18	6	9
North-west	19	5	2	10	36	19
Other provinces	28	13	20	43	26	27
Total	100	100	101	101	99	100
Number	391,114	81,480	24,501	70,853	112,814	680,762
Row percentage	57	12	4	10	17	100
Females						
Industrial	29	29	31	30	28	29
Eastern	6	37	11	3	1	9
Madura	7	3	36	1	2	6
South-west	13	9	7	14	10	2
North-west	24	7	0	9	38	22
Other provinces	21	16	15	43	20	22
Total	100	101	100	100	99	100
Number	400,613	79,547	21,754	59,613	109,332	670,859
Row percentage	60	12	3	9	16	100
Males and females (%)	59	12	3	10	16	100
Percentage of all residents aged 10+ in 1985	34	19	9	13	26	101

Source: Analysis of the 1985 Supas tape.

The industrial region also tended to attract a greater proportion of the migrants from outside the province than did the other areas, with about 57 per cent of the interprovincial migrants settling there, despite the fact that it does not border on other provinces. Madura, which is in a similar situation, had less than 3 per cent of the interprovincial migrants. The north-west and south-west regions, which border on Central Java (from where East Java gains most migrants, as noted above) each had 16 to 17 per cent of the interprovincial migrants, while the eastern region, which could be expected to gain most of the migrants from Bali and Nusa Tenggara, gained 7 per cent of all interprovincial migrants.

The age and gender composition of the migrants in 1985 and the total population of East Java aged 10 and above are given in Table 5.9. Males did not dominate this group as they did the recent interprovincial migrants in 1980, analysed above. Just over half the migrants were males (compared with 48 per cent of all people in East Java aged 10 and above). Neither did males dominate the migrant group in the industrial region: only 49 per cent of the migrants there were males, compared with 52 per cent in the non-industrial areas. Thus, women may also have been moving to the industrial region for purposes of employment.

TABLE 5.9
East Java: Distribution of Recent Migrants and All Residents Aged 10 and Above by Age-group and Sex, 1985 (per cent)

	Migrants			
Age-group	*Industrial Region*	*Other Regions*	*All Migrants*	*All East Java Residents*
Males				
10–19	18	23	21	29
20–29	43	37	40	22
30–39	24	24	24	18
40–49	9	10	9	14
50 and above	6	6	6	18
Total	100	100	100	101
Number	391,114	289,648	680,762	11,573,255
Females				
10–19	26	25	26	27
20–29	46	46	46	24
30–39	16	16	16	16
40–49	6	8	7	13
50 and above	5	6	5	20
Total	99	101	100	100
Number	400,613	270,246	670,859	12,467,425

Sources: Migrants: Analysis of the 1985 Supas tape.
All East Java: BPS (1987a: Table 3.8).

More significant is the high proportion (43 per cent) of migrants in the age-group 20–29 in 1985, nearly double the figure for the province as a whole (Table 5.9) and higher than the comparable figures for 1980 (see Table 5.1). This concentration of migrants in the early working ages is not unexpected but the magnitude of the figures is surprising, especially for women: nearly three-quarters of the female migrants were under 30 years of age.

As was found with the interprovincial migrants in 1980, these migrants had much higher levels of education than the population as a whole. Among those aged 20 and over, half the males and one-third of the females had completed lower secondary school (junior high school), figures which are three times higher than the comparable ones for the whole province (Table 5.10). Furthermore, higher proportions of the migrants to the industrial region had junior high school attainment than did migrants in the other regions. The figures on attainment of upper secondary (senior high school) level are even more striking: 42 per cent of male migrants and 23 per cent of female migrants in the industrial region had this qualification. A significant proportion of the migrants may have gone to that region in search of higher salaried employment and not just to engage in factory work.

Overall participation in the labour force by migrants, both males and females, was the same as for the whole population aged 10 and above—71 per cent for males and 41 per cent for females (Table 5.11).

TABLE 5.10
East Java: Distribution of Recent Migrants and All Residents Aged 20 and Above by Highest Level of Education Completed and Sex, 1985 (per cent)

	Migrants			
Educational Level	*Industrial Region*	*Other Regions*	*All Migrants*	*All East Java Residents*
Males				
Primary or less	46	57	50	82
Lower secondary	13	15	14	8
Upper secondary	42	28	36	10
Total	101	100	100	100
Number	319,121	222,292	541,413	8,818,879
Females				
Primary or less	64	72	67	90
Lower secondary	13	11	12	4
Upper secondary	23	18	21	5
Total	100	101	100	99
Number	294,686	203,904	498,590	9,163,393

Sources: Migrants: Analysis of the 1985 Supas tape.
All East Java: BPS (1987a: Tables 8.7 and 8.8).

TABLE 5.11

East Java: Sectoral Distribution of Recent Migrants and All Residents in the Labour Force by Sex, 1985 (per cent)

Industrial Sector	*Migrants*			*All East Java Residents*
	Industrial Region	*Other Regions*	*All Migrants*	
Males				
Agriculture	8	33	19	58
Manufacturing	21	6	15	9
Transport and construction	15	12	14	9
Trade	20	17	19	10
Services	36	32	34	13
Total	100	100	101	100
Number	274,094	210,641	484,735	8,254,468
Percentage of population aged 10+	70	73	71	71
Females				
Agriculture	5	25	13	49
Manufacturing	14	6	10	13
Transport and construction	1	0	1	0
Trade	23	29	25	25
Services	58	40	51	13
Total	101	100	100	100
Number	163,069	109,155	272,224	5,098,138
Percentage of population aged 10+	41	40	41	41

Sources: Migrants: Analysis of the 1985 Supas tape.
All East Java: BPS (1987a: Tables 21.1 and 21.2).

Furthermore, participation rates of migrants in the industrial and other regions were similar, although male migrants in the industrial area are slightly less likely to be working. This may be a factor of their higher levels of education, since educated people may be more inclined to be temporarily unemployed while waiting for a suitable position, rather than to work in lower status on informal-sector activities.

Participation in agriculture by migrants was much lower than for the population as a whole, especially in the industrial region (Table 5.11), and also lower than it was among the 1980 group of interprovincial migrants. Participation in the services sector was correspondingly higher compared with both East Java as a whole and the 1980 group of migrants. Male migrants were more likely to be involved in trade than were other males in East Java; female migrants had the same high level of participation in this sector (25 per cent) as did other women in the province. It is likely that much of the service and trading activity involves low levels of skills and status—petty trading and domestic service—but it is not possible to estimate this for the whole population since such a breakdown is not included in the published reports of the 1985 Supas. For the migrants 'personal and domestic services' was by far the largest component of the services sector for women, as was 'retail trade' for the trading sector, both of which imply, in the Indonesian setting, informal-sector activity.

The manufacturing sector in East Java employs over 10 per cent of the total labour force. Among the migrants as a whole, more males, and relatively fewer females, were found in this sector, in comparison to the whole labour force. In the industrial region, male migrants were very likely to be working in industry (21 per cent), and female migrants just as likely as elsewhere in East Java. The comparison between migrants in industrial and non-industrial areas demonstrates clearly that many migrants (especially males) who settled in the industrial region were shifting away from agriculture into industry, but many others were probably being forced to take up jobs in the informal sector.

Conclusion

Migrants in East Java undoubtedly are settling more in the industrializing region than in other parts of the province. This appeared in the data on the interprovincial migrants in 1980 and on all migrants in 1985, with large proportions of both groups being found in that part of East Java with the bulk of the new industrial projects. Both of these groups had some of the characteristics normally associated with migrants—they were generally younger than the population as a whole, were much better educated and tended to avoid employment in agriculture. Some of the migrants were employed in the industrial sector but this was by no means their only source of employment. The tendency for migrants to be employed in industry was little greater than for the population as a whole and significant numbers were also to be found in trade and services, sectors which contain many 'informal' activities.

Thus the migration streams into and within East Java, even to the industrial region, are heterogeneous in nature. Many of the young and relatively well-educated migrants may well be attracted to the industrializing areas to seek work in higher status tertiary jobs that develop within and alongside new industries, rather than in the factories themselves. Other migrants, with lower endowments of human capital, and quite likely those who are being squeezed out of farming activities in their home areas, may be going to the industrial areas in the hope of finding paid employment, but many of them end up as hawkers or domestic servants. On balance, however, migration appears to be a necessary component of the development of the industrial region of East Java and migrants are a positive factor in this development.

6
The Rice Baskets of East Java: The Ecology and Social Context of *Sawah* Production*

James J. Fox

Introduction

EAST JAVA has been at the forefront of the rice intensification programme that has, since 1967, transformed Indonesia's economy. The success of this programme in East Java is widely regarded as one of the most impressive examples of agricultural development during the New Order. In less than 20 years, irrigated wet-rice production in East Java more than doubled. Production grew from just over 3 million tonnes of unhusked rice in 1968 to nearly 7.5 million tonnes by the mid-1980s and then to over 8 million tonnes in 1989.[1]

This spectacular increase was the result of (1) the introduction of new high-yielding, faster maturing varieties of rice; (2) the generous supply of subsidized fertilizer; (3) the rehabilitation and improvement of irrigation networks; and (4) a commitment at all levels of the government bureaucracy to promoting the production of rice through the extension of farmer training, the provision of subsidized credit, the maintenance of support prices and, at times, by heavier-handed interventions in rice farming. The government programme that subsumed and co-ordinated Indonesia's rice intensification was known as Bimas (Bimbingan Massal or Mass Guidance).

The combination of more-productive genetic material, enhanced nutrient supply, and improved water management was applied to a specific, relatively stable cultivated environment—the *sawah*.[2] The response was an increased cropping intensity and a substantial increment in rice yields per hectare. The pattern of East Java's response was

*The author would like to thank the members of the agricultural group at the Center for Policy and Implementation Studies (CPIS) in Jakarta, in particular Suyanto and Hania Rahma, for their support and assistance in compiling some of the data on which sections of this chapter are based. Thanks are also due to Professor Dr Ali Wardhana and Drs Marzuki Usman for their support of this research in CPIS.

no different from that of other provinces of Indonesia with large areas of irrigated *sawah*. However, for East Java the combined response of increased cropping intensity and yield per hectare was, particularly after 1980, greater than in any other province of Indonesia.[3] One result of this production increase is that Indonesia's State Logistics Board (Badan Urusan Logistik or Bulog) has concentrated its procurement efforts in East Java, and so the province has become the major supplier of rice to the rest of the country. Thus in 1989 East Java exported rice to 19 of Indonesia's 27 provinces.

East Java's overall response to rice intensification was immediate, rapid, and sustained. One of the reasons for this response was the existence of an already substantial infrastructure in irrigation and in transport that could be further developed to support an existing and productive *sawah* ecosystem. The existence of this infrastructure was the result of developments in the colonial period. Equally crucial to the transformation in *sawah* production were fundamental changes in agrarian institutions at the village level. Changes in the legal structure of *sawah* ownership led to major changes in patterns of work and relations of production. These changes, which began to take effect just as the Bimas programme was taking shape, put an end to some of the principal village institutions of the colonial period.

Beside rice, East Java's *sawah* also continued to produce sugar-cane as well as high-quality tobacco. Both of these previously important colonial crops, however, had to be accommodated to the principal goal of rice production and, as a result, both declined in relative importance, first in relation to rice and then in relation to other *sawah* crops. From the late 1960s most *sawah* produced increasingly greater amounts of a variety of other secondary crops. Thus, for example, between 1969 and 1985, soya bean production, mainly from *sawah*, increased by over 44 per cent, making East Java by far the largest producer of soya bean in the nation. Although shaped in the colonial period primarily for the production of rice and sugar-cane, the *sawah* systems of East Java became more complex multi-cropping environments.

This chapter focuses on the *sawah* of East Java as production areas. The first section examines East Java's rice production from a national perspective and then goes on to consider the development of those factors that contributed most substantially to East Java's achievements in rice production. This discussion involves an examination of developments in East Java's *sawah* over a period of more than 20 years: the transformation of the physical environment—through irrigation, the use of new seed varieties and enhanced nutrient supply. Special emphasis is given to the mid-1980s (1984–6). This was the period when Indonesia attained technical self-sufficiency in rice production and thus it marks an appropriate point for comparative assessment of rice intensification.

With some perspective on East Java's production as a whole, it is possible to examine the province's internal production in terms of what are defined here as its eight distinct 'rice baskets'. The intention is to present a succinct summary of the basic structure of East Java's *sawah* production systems. Consideration of the specific cropping patterns of the different rice baskets provides further understanding of overall production in the province.

A final section focuses on the social transformation of the lowlands of East Java that has accompanied changes in production systems and agrarian institutions. These changes are harder to specify with the same precision as changes in the planting of rice varieties or in the increased use of fertilizer. Yet an understanding of these changes is vital to comprehending present-day East Java.

Rice Production in National Perspective

As a first step to establish a perspective on East Java's rice production, it is necessary to consider: (1) how Indonesia's rice production has changed over the past 20 years; (2) how Java's rice production has developed as a part of national production; and (3) how East Java's production relates to that of Java as a whole.

Indonesia can be regarded as a single rice-producing system. Within this system the rice production of Indonesia's various islands can be compared to one another. From this perspective, Java's contribution to Indonesia's total rice production has declined only slightly in relation to the Outer Islands even after 20 years of considerable effort to foster rice production throughout the country. Thus Java has consistently produced over 63 per cent of Indonesia's total rice since the beginning of the Bimas programme (Table 6.1).

While Java's share of total national rice production declined slightly, East Java has more or less maintained its percentage share of national production. West Java, with its much larger cropping area, has continued to produce more rice than East Java, but its production relative to

TABLE 6.1
Java and the Outer Islands: Comparative Rice Production and Relative Share of Total National Production, 1968–1986[a]

	1968		*1980*		*1986*	
	Tonnes ('000)	*%*	*Tonnes ('000)*	*%*	*Tonnes ('000)*	*%*
Java	9 801	64.7	18 025	64.4	23 688	63.3
West Java	3 681	24.3	6 412	22.9	8 746	23.4
Central Java/ Yogyakarta	3 120	20.6	5 532	19.8	7 401	19.8
East Java	3 000	19.8	6 020	21.5	7 510	20.1
Outer Islands	5 338	35.3	9 968	35.6	13 748	36.7
Indonesia	15 139	100.0	27 993	100.0	37 437	100.0

Sources: BPS (1968, 1980, 1986b).
[a]Rice form: *Gabah kering giling* (dry-rice paddy).

TABLE 6.2
Java and Bali: Average Rice Yields, 1968–1989 (tonnes per hectare)

	1968	*1971*	*1974*	*1977*	*1980*	*1983*	*1986*	*1989*
West Java	2.53	2.87	2.89	3.09	3.68	4.42	4.53	5.05
Central Java/ Yogyakarta	2.53	3.03	3.04	3.16	3.96	4.77	4.80	5.17
East Java	2.72	3.02	3.27	3.50	4.40	4.97	4.97	5.27
Bali	2.79	3.16	3.68	3.63	4.10	4.47	4.71	5.06

Sources: BPS, *Statistik Indonesia*, various years.

national production diminished between 1968 and 1986.

The key to East Java's success has not been the result of opening new production areas but rather of the more effective utilization of existing areas—increased cropping and increased yields from established *sawah*. Already in 1968 East Java had higher yields per hectare than either West Java or Central Java, but it also improved these yields more rapidly and to a higher level than either of these other two provinces (Table 6.2). By contrast, East Java had lower average yields than Bali in 1968, but within 10 years East Java's average yields had surpassed Bali's and continued to improve thereafter.

Irrigation: The Setting for Sawah Production

East Java has three main rivers: the Bengawan Solo, the Brantas, and the Pekalen–Sampean. Each of these 'rivers' consists, in effect, of a complex river basin dominating a particular area. The Bengawan Solo river basin extends over a considerable portion of the north-west of the province; the Brantas forms an even more extensive basin running roughly through the middle of the province from the south to the north; while the Pekalen–Sampean basin covers a wide area at the eastern end or 'hook' of the province.

The courses of East Java's main rivers and the dense network of tributaries that feed into them are set by a spine of volcanic mountains that transects the province from east to west. The elevation of the peaks of some of these volcanoes exceeds 3 000 metres, but these levels drop rapidly and can flatten out to less than 100 metres in elevation within 10 kilometres. By convention, 'lowlands' are defined as areas at or below 500 metres; 'highlands' as those areas above 500 metres. The lowland regions are the primary areas of intensive *sawah* cultivation, but given the complex topography of the province, some excellent *sawah* are also to be found well up on mountain slopes. Thus, in East Java, productive *sawah* range from steep, terraced plots to flat deltaic stretches of land. Since for six months of the year East Java has a pronounced 'dry' season in which the average monthly rainfall is less than 60 millimetres, 'run-of-river' irrigation is essential to achieve high cropping intensities and high crop yields.

Not all of East Java's *sawah* are irrigated. Approximately 23 per cent are classified as 'rain-fed *sawah*' (*sawah tadah hujan*). Eighty per cent of this rain-fed *sawah*, however, is to be found either on the island of Madura or in a large area on the north coast of the mainland comprising the *kabupaten* of Bojonegoro, Lamongan, Tuban, and Gresik. The particularities of this area are distinguishable from the rest of East Java, where *sawah* are predominantly irrigated.

Since Dutch times East Java has had the most extensive and elaborate irrigation structure on the island. In recent years this irrigation structure has undergone major rehabilitation (Vivekananthan, 1987).[4] At present, the East Java Irrigation Service manages an area of roughly 950 000 hectares divided into 10 districts (*wilayah*) based on East Java's three river basins. The Bengawan Solo basin comprises two districts; the Pekalen–Sampean, three districts; and the Brantas basin, four districts. (The island of Madura has its own separate district, which will not be considered here.) These districts are in turn subdivided into sections or 'branches' (*cabang*), subsections or 'sub-branches' (*ranting*), and finally, *kejuron*, which are the management units that link to local village organizations.

Irrigation systems throughout Indonesia are classified according to their technical quality and management. Thus, in official documents, irrigation networks are designated as 'technical' (*teknis*), 'semi-technical' (*setengah teknis*), and 'simple' (*sederhana*) or 'non-technical' (*non-teknis*). Technical and semi-technical systems differ in the quality of their facilities, but both are managed and controlled by the Irrigation Service down to the tertiary canal heads from which village systems draw their supplies. Simple, non-technical systems refer to village-constructed intake systems which are found mainly on the upper reaches of rivers or streams.

Since the early 1970s significant investment has been made in developing and rehabilitating East Java's irrigation network. It is estimated that East Java has over 1 000 kilometres of primary canals, over 5 000 kilometres of secondary canals, and over 10 000 kilometres of drainage canals. The improvement of the irrigation network has had a progressive character: simple, non-technical irrigation has been developed to a semi-technical state while semi-technical irrigation has been enhanced to a fully technical standard. The result has been an overall increase in what are classified as technical systems. Between 1970 and 1983 East Java's area of technically irrigated *sawah* increased by more than 13 per cent, from 576 000 hectares to over 654 000 hectares.[5] This means that by the mid-1980s almost 69 per cent of East Java's *sawah* were technically irrigated and almost 83 per cent were either technically or semi-technically irrigated.

Table 6.3 sets out the structure of East Java's irrigation systems classified according to their technical capacity. There are considerable differences in the quality of irrigation in the three river basins. More than 80 per cent of the Pekalen–Sampean system is technically irrigated compared with about 69 per cent of the Brantas and 56 per cent of the

TABLE 6.3
East Java: The Irrigation System, 1982/3 (hectares)

River System	*District*	*Technical*	*Semi-technical*	*Non-technical*	*Total*
Bengawan Solo	Madiun	109 525	15 345	32 336	157 206
	Bojonegoro	38 608	7 654	30 359	106 621
Total		148 133	52 999	62 695	263 827
Brantas	Mojokerto	54 217	20 285	4 966	79 468
	Jombang	57 835	–	8 929	66 764
	Kediri	91 998	16 623	31 284	139 905
	Malang	53 281	17 703	17 724	88 708
Total		257 331	54 611	62 903	374 845
Pekalen–Sampean	Lumajang	76 711	14 314	13 239	104 264
	Bondowoso	91 340	5 037	17 783	114 160
	Banyuwangi	62 395	245	5 218	67 858
Total		230 446	19 596	36 240	286 282
Island East Java		635 910	127 206	161 838	924 954
Island Madura		18 319	3 990	2 924	25 233
Total Province		654 229	131 196	164 762	950 187

Source: Vivekananthan (1987: 153, Figure 3).

Bengawan Solo systems. There are also significant differences within these systems. In the Bengawan Solo basin only 36 per cent of the Bojonegoro irrigation district has technical irrigation compared with 70 per cent for Madiun. In the Brantas 86 per cent of Jombang's irrigation is of a technical standard, whereas the much larger district of Kediri has only 66 per cent technical irrigation. In Pekalen–Sampean, Banyuwangi has 92 per cent technical irrigation compared with 74 per cent in Lumajang.

Improved irrigation provides for better management of water supplies to cropping environments: less direct crop dependence on rainfall, better control of flooding in the rainy season, and an enhanced capacity to direct available water in the dry season. The careful management of water is essential to increasing rice yields.

Throughout most of Indonesia the main rice crop has always been the crop that coincides with the west monsoon rainy season. In East Java, with its six months 'dry' season, the rainy-season crop has always been particularly pronounced. Improved irrigation has lessened this dependence and allowed more rice to be grown as a second crop, after the main rainy season. During this second cropping season there are fewer cloudy days and therefore greater sunlight, less flooding, and an overall better supply of water to technically irrigated *sawah*. As a result, yields can often be as high as, if not higher than, those from the same *sawah* in the rainy season.[6] Irrigation improvement in East Java has led not just to an increased cropping intensity—the capacity to grow more crops, on an

FIGURE 6.1
East Java: *Sawah* Harvesting Patterns, 1955 and 1985

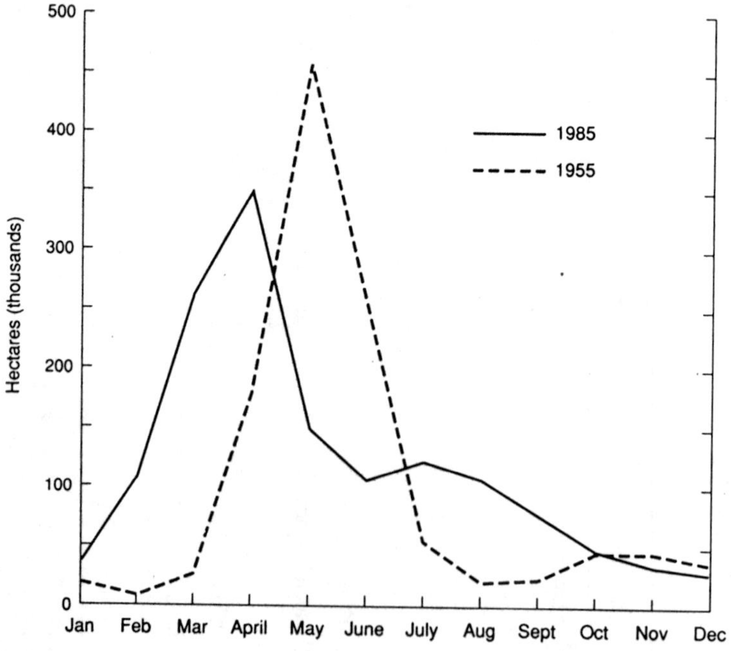

annual basis, on the same land—but also to an improvement in yields from these second crops.

Figure 6.1 illustrates the dramatic change in the pattern of wet-rice harvesting in East Java over the past thirty years. In 1955 the harvest pattern for East Java was dominated by a single sharp peak that began in March, reached its high point in May and then dropped precipitously to a low point between July and August. With the introduction of new, faster maturing varieties of rice, this pattern changed. The harvesting pattern for 1985 shows this change. Harvesting began to rise in January and reached a peak in April—though not as sharp a peak as in 1955. A low point occurred in June, but shortly thereafter the second crop began to be harvested. In general this harvest and that of a subsequent third crop of rice declines to a low point in November and December when rainy-season planting begins again.

New Seed Varieties, 1968–1989

The story of East Java's rice intensification programme can best be traced in terms of the changing varieties of seeds[7] that were adopted in the province to increase production. Significant changes began in the early twentieth century with the introduction of new varieties and the establishment in Bogor in 1905 of a rice-breeding programme to develop new varieties.

Prior to this period, rice in Indonesia was divided into two major types: *javanica* rice, referred to in Indonesia as *bulu* (with a subclass known as *gundil*), and *indica* rice, known as *cereh* (*tjereh*), with *javanica* varieties more likely to be found on volcanic soil and *indica* varieties on other soil formations.

The great achievement of the Dutch–Indonesian breeding programme—indeed one of the most far-reaching events in the history of rice breeding—came about by crossing a Chinese *indica* variety, Cina (which was originally introduced to Java in 1914), with a Bengal variety of rice known as Latisail. The progeny of Cina/Latisail were vigorous, tall, sturdy-stemmed varieties with shorter maturing times than earlier, traditional varieties.

By the early 1940s these varieties, which included named varieties such as Bengawan, Cahaya, Fajar, Intan, Mas, Pelopor, and Peta, were widely diffused and relatively well established in irrigated *sawah*, particularly in Java. Crosses between Bengawan and an Indonesian variety known as Sigadis produced the next generation of rice, including varieties such as Arimbi, Dara, and Syntha (or Shinta). All of these 'improved varieties' were distributed and became established in Indonesia in the 1950s and early 1960s.

Records from the seed stations of East Java in the early 1950s show that Bengawan was overwhelmingly the most important rice variety planted in *sawah* throughout the province from Madiun to Banyuwangi at that time. Cahaya, Mas, and Cina were also widely planted.[8] These varieties had come to be regarded as the 'traditional' rice of the lowland *sawah* of East Java. By the 1960s approximately 10 per cent of rice planted in Indonesia consisted of four varieties: Peta, Bengawan, Intan, and Mas.

Until the 1960s the development of new varieties confronted what could appropriately be described as a 'nitrogen to yield threshold'. Tall-stalked varieties were only responsive to nitrogen fertilizer to a certain threshold level. Beyond this level the application of additional fertilizer resulted in serious lodging. Added nitrogen developed the stalk rather than the panicle of the plant, and the stalk tended to sag sadly. The Dutch–Indonesian breeding programme succeeded in shortening the growing time of Indonesian rice but was unable to overcome the problems of the nitrogen : yield threshold and the problem of lodging.

The breakthrough came in 1962 at the International Rice Research Institute (IRRI) in the Philippines from the eighth of 38 crosses between a semi-dwarf variety of rice, Dee-geo-woo-gen (DGWG), and Peta, one of the tall, vigorous hybrids of the former Dutch–Indonesian breeding programme. The marriage of these two remarkably different rice varieties led to the 'Green Revolution' in South and South-East Asia (Chang, 1979: 188). The resulting short-statured progeny of this contrived marriage, known officially as IR 8-288-3, popularly as IR 8 and in Indonesia as Peta Baru (PB 8), proved to be a remarkable rice variety. In response to applications of nitrogen, IR 8 tillered profusely. Its thick culms and persistent leaf sheaths conferred great straw strength at high nitrogen levels. These qualities allowed IR 8 to produce and support numerous heavy panicles of grain without lodging.

In 1966 IR 8 was released for distribution and was rapidly adopted throughout Asia. A second taller (non-semi-dwarf) variety, IR 5 (or PB 5), was released in 1967, followed by another, C 4 (C4-63), developed separately by University of the Philippines rice breeders, and another two IRRI varieties, IR 20 and IR 22. The introduction of the 'new' high-yielding varieties (HYVs) that began in the late 1960s marked a major change in rice cultivation. Yet the new varieties were part of a continuing breeding genealogy that was already established in East Java.

It was with modern high-yielding varieties—all of them derived, in different ways, from the genetic material of Peta—that Indonesia began its Bimas programme of rice intensification in the late 1960s. Both IR 5 and IR 8 were released in 1967 as essential components of the 'New Bimas' programme (Bimas Baru). In 1971 Indonesia introduced further high-yielding varieties from its own breeding programme. These closely related varieties, Pelita I-1 and Pelita I-2, were selections from crosses between IR 5 and the Indonesian improved variety, Syntha.

The spread of these varieties was rapid. By 1974/5, approximately 53 per cent of Indonesia's irrigated rice consisted of four basic varieties: IR 5, IR 8, C 4, and Pelita (PI-1 and PI-2). Pelita varieties alone accounted for 26 per cent of all irrigated rice. Although the general availability and use of fertilizer were not at a level to achieve the full potential of these seed varieties, yields and production began to increase significantly.

Table 6.4, based on seasonal planting data compiled by the Directorate for Plant Protection, provides a comparison of the percentage of total wet-season rice that was planted to the new high-yielding varieties of rice in West, Central, and East Java and in Bali. These figures show that high-yielding varieties were adopted sooner and more extensively in East Java than in West or Central Java or even in Bali. Despite setbacks from 1976 to 1979, by the rainy season of 1979/80, East Java was overwhelmingly reliant on high-yielding varieties of rice—a fact that is reflected in the markedly higher yield levels that began in 1979 (see Table 6.4) and continued through the 1980s.

The years covered by the data in Table 6.4 represent a critical period in Indonesia's rice intensification programme, marked by a succession of severe brown planthopper outbreaks that required a shift to the use of 'resistant' seed varieties in the attempt to gain protection against planthopper devastation.

The brown planthopper (BPH: *Nilaparvata lugens* Stal.) had its first serious effect on Java's rice crop in the 1974/5 season, destroying both new and 'traditional' rice varieties. Estimates indicate that in the 1974/5 rainy season over 62 000 hectares of rice were damaged by brown planthopper infestations in East Java, with even greater damage in the 1975/6 wet season (Dyck and Thomas, 1979: 7–8). Severe damage continued through 1977/8 not just in East Java but throughout the island, with the greatest losses in Central Java.

In support of Indonesia's floundering rice intensification programme IRRI was able to release new varieties of rice, again involving further breeding via Peta, that were resistant to the brown planthopper. Six of these 'BPH-resistant' varieties—IR 26 and IR 30, released in 1975, and IR 24, IR 28, IR 32, and IR 34, released in 1976—were quickly adopted in Java to replace earlier high-yielding but non-resistant varieties.

With the introduction of 'BPH-resistant' varieties, crop losses to the brown planthopper declined in those areas planted with these varieties,

TABLE 6.4

Java and Bali: Percentage of Rainy Season *Sawah* Planted to High-yielding Varieties, 1975/6–1981/2

	1975/6	*1976/7*	*1977/8*	*1978/9*	*1979/80*	*1980/1*	*1981/2*
West Java	56.4	53.1	47.5	44.7	52.0	51.2	66.7
Central Java	49.9	46.4	55.0	61.6	80.9	74.9	80.0
East Java	66.1	65.3	60.4	56.7	87.8	87.8	87.9
Bali	57.0	64.7	63.0	70.4	81.8	86.3	89.7

Source: Directorate for Plant Protection.

but within one year of their introduction, the resistance of the 'BPH-resistant' varieties began to break down. Rapid changes in the population structure of the brown planthopper produced new 'biotypes' capable of feeding upon the newly introduced 'BPH-resistant' varieties.

In response to early evidence of resistance breakdown, IRRI was again able to release two new varieties in 1977. These varieties were IR 36 and IR 38, both of which possessed genetic resistance to BPH Biotype II. These new high-yielding modern varieties (again involving breeding from Peta) produced the resistance that finally overcame the brown planthopper outbreaks of the 1970s.

Table 6.5 shows the principal modern varieties of rice planted in East Java from the rainy season of 1975/6 to 1988/9. These data cover the difficult years of the late 1970s and the transition to stable and increasing production that began in the early 1980s. In the 1975/6 rainy season East Java was heavily reliant (for 57 per cent of its rice) on Pelita varieties, IR 5 and C 4. By the next rainy season the newly introduced BPH-resistant varieties, IR 26 and IR 30, accounted for almost 36 per cent of rice planting, compared with only 29 per cent for Pelita, IR 5 and C 4 combined.

The following season, 1977/8, was the beginning of a major transition. IR 32 had taken over as the most important new variety, but planting with IR 36 had begun. Together, four new IRRI varieties (IR 32, IR 36, IR 26, and IR 30) accounted for over 53 per cent of the wet rice planted in East Java, with Pelita of only minor importance. From this season onward, planting figures show a steady increase in the reliance on IR 36: from approximately 11 per cent of total rice planted in the 1977/8 rainy season to over 77 per cent in the 1981/2 rainy season. Dry-season planting of IR 36 was substantially higher than wet-season planting for each of these years, surpassing 85 per cent by 1982. Thus, for a critical period IR 36 was overwhelmingly the most important high-yielding, resistant rice variety in East Java.

As critically important as IR 36 proved to be, it was not, and could not be, the ideal rice variety for all of Java's rice-growing environments. IR 36 was far more suitable for drier, less rainy conditions; under wetter conditions, it tended to become vulnerable to several serious diseases. Thus, in general terms, IR 36 was more suitable for East Java than West Java, where the combined planting of IR 36 and IR 38 never exceeded 40 per cent of total rainy-season planting. As a consequence, rice production in West Java took longer to recover from the effects of the brown planthopper than in East or even Central Java.

In 1980/1 Indonesia's own rice breeding programme came to the fore with the release of a series of rice varieties specially suited to Javanese conditions. Many of these varieties bore the names of water sources in West Java: Cisadane, Cimandiri, Cipunegara, Citarum, and Citandui. Others bore the names of other Indonesian localities: Semeru, Sadang, and Krueng Aceh. The two most remarkable of these 'new Indonesian varieties' were Cisadane and Krueng Aceh. In taste characteristics and in yield potential, both of these varieties surpassed IR 36. In a wide

TABLE 6.5
East Java: The Five Most Widely Planted Rice Varieties in the Rainy Season, 1975/6–1988/9

1975/6	%[a]	*1976/7*	%	*1977/8*	%
1. PI-1	28.1	1. IR 26	27.1	1. IR 32	22.4
2. IR 5	16.6	2. PI-1	16.1	2. IR 36	10.8
3. C4-63	9.7	3. IR 30	8.8	3. IR 26	10.1
4. IR 26	8.6	4. C4-63	7.6	4. IR 30	10.1
5. PI-2	3.1	5. IR 5	5.7	5. PI-1	7.0
	66.1		65.3		60.4
1978/9	%	*1979/80*	%	*1980/1*	%
1. IR 36	36.8	1. IR 36	75.1	1. IR 36	75.3
2. IR 32	6.9	2. IR 38	7.4	2. C4-63	5.2
3. IR 38	6.3	3. IR 32	4.4	3. PI-1	2.9
4. PI-1	5.7	4. C4-63	0.6	4. Semeru	2.2
5. IR 28	1.0	5. PI-1	0.3	5. IR 38	2.2
	56.7		87.8		87.8
1981/2	%	*1982/3*	%	*1983/4*	%
1. IR 36	77.4	1. IR 36	65.7	1. IR 36	64.8
2. Cisadane	4.0	2. Cisadane	9.7	2. Cisadane	9.8
3. Semeru	2.5	3. Krueng Aceh	4.9	3. Krueng Aceh	6.3
4. PI-1	2.1	4. IR 50	3.3	4. Semeru	2.9
5. IR 38	1.9	5. Semeru	2.0	5. IR 50	2.2
	87.9		85.6		86.0
1984/5	%	*1985/6*	%	*1986/7*	%
1. IR 36	55.0	1. IR 36	58.5	1. IR 36	51.5
2. Krueng Aceh	20.7	2. Krueng Aceh	14.2	2. Krueng Aceh	12.6
3. Cisadane	7.6	3. Cisadane	10.0	3. Semeru	7.6
4. Semeru	2.3	4. Semeru	4.9	4. Cisadane	7.4
5. Cipunagara	1.3	5. Sadang	1.3	5. Sadang	2.2
	86.9		88.9		81.3
1987/8	%	*1988/9*	%		
1. IR 36	32.7	1. IR 36	29.4		
2. IR 64	15.8	2. IR 64	22.0		
3. Krueng Aceh	9.9	3. Krueng Aceh	14.5		
4. Semeru	7.3	4. Semeru	10.0		
5. Cisadane	7.8	5. Cisadane	7.7		
	73.5		83.6		

Source: Directorate for Plant Protection.

[a]Figures here refer to *sawah* planting. Percentages represent the relative proportion of each variety among all varieties planted during the rainy season. Generally since 1979/80, the 'top five' rice varieties have accounted for over 80% of total planting.

range of growing environments, Cisadane and Krueng Aceh produced yields 10 to 20 per cent higher than IR 36 in the same environment.

The release and effective distribution of these new varieties decreased the heavy reliance on IR 36. Cisadane was particularly well suited to the rainier areas of West Java and the western half of Central Java, and was quickly adopted by farmers in these areas, going from about 30 per cent of rainy-season planting in 1981/2 to well over 80 per cent by 1984/5. In East Java, Cisadane was planted in particular, well-irrigated pockets such as in Sidoarjo and Blitar. Krueng Aceh, on the other hand, responded better to drier conditions and hence was more readily adopted throughout East Java and in parts of the eastern half of Central Java. By the 1984/5 rainy season Krueng Aceh accounted for about 20 per cent of planting in East Java, thus reducing reliance on IR 36. Higher yields from Krueng Aceh and Cisadane, together with IR 36, gave the boost to Indonesia's production that carried the country to rice self-sufficiency in 1985.

After 1986 another excellent IRRI variety, IR 64, was introduced in East Java and gained considerable popularity, further reducing reliance on IR 36. Because of its high yields and desirable taste, IR 64 became the premier rice of the province, quickly increasing in importance to account for over 20 per cent of rainy-season planting by 1988/9. Another IRRI variety, given the name Semeru when it was introduced in the early 1980s, became progressively more important, particularly for East Java's higher altitude *sawah*. However, after 10 years IR 36 still remained the most widely planted rice variety of East Java.

Figure 6.2 is a consolidated pedigree of most of the principal rice varieties planted in East Java since the 1940s. This pedigree traces relations among varieties according to their maternal (cytoplasmic) derivation, which originates from the rice variety known as Cina. Since this pedigree traces a female lineage, certain rice varieties, such as Semeru, which derive genetic material from Cina through the male line, are not included. This pedigree shows graphically both the breeding continuity underlying East Java's rice varieties and the high degree of cytoplasmic uniformity among them.

Fertilizer: Nitrogen, Phosphorus, and Potassium

All the new rice seed varieties were nitrogen responsive and, from the beginning of the Bimas programme, nitrogen (primarily in the form of urea) was intended as the main subsidized fertilizer. By regulating the subsidy on urea in relation to the floor price of unmilled rice (*gabah*), the Indonesian government endeavoured to provide appropriate incentives to the increased production of rice. As the Bimas programme developed, however, other forms of fertilizer were also included within the framework of the subsidy, to allow them to be sold to farmers at the same retail price as urea. Beside urea, the three main fertilizers given subsidies were ammonium sulphate (abbreviated in Indonesia, following a Dutch form, as 'ZA'), triple superphosphate (TSP), and potassium

FIGURE 6.2
East Java: Consolidated Pedigree of Major Rice Varieties with Cina Cytoplasm Planted since the 1940s

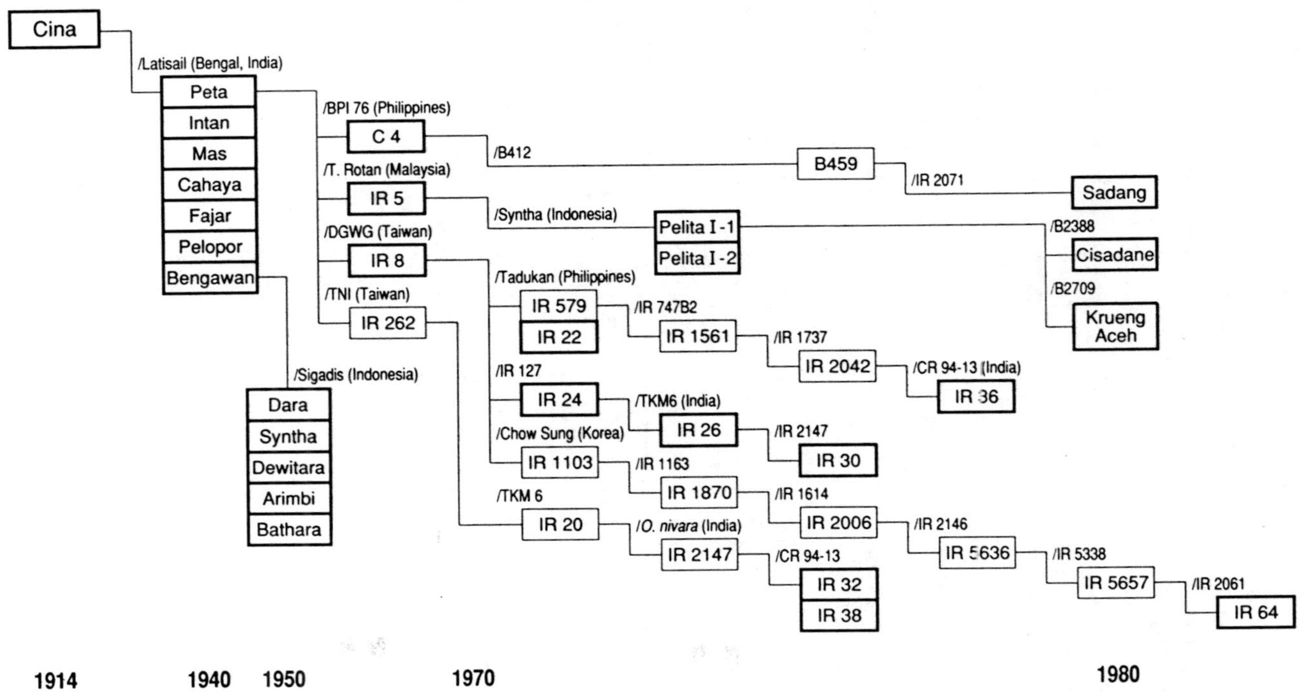

chloride (KCl). By the late 1970s the original nitrogen to *gabah* ratio had become obscured within a general fertilizer subsidy arrangement which promoted the increased use of all fertilizers.

By 1979 Indonesia had the capacity to produce over 2 million tonnes of urea (Table 6.6); by 1986 this capacity had increased to well over 4 million tonnes. In 1979 Indonesia's first TSP plant at Gresik in East Java was opened. By 1983 a second unit began production. Similarly, two new production units for the manufacture of ammonium sulphate were added to the existing facility at Gresik, in 1984 and 1986. Of the main fertilizers, only potassium chloride continued to be imported.

From the early 1970s East Java's farmers were, on average, applying more urea fertilizer than farmers in West or Central Java or in Bali (Table 6.7). This is roughly consistent with yield levels per hectare in the three Javanese provinces, though Bali's yield levels per hectare through the 1970s were higher than East Java's despite the use of less fertilizer. A significant increase in fertilizer use occurred throughout Java in the mid-1970s, again in East Java after 1979 when IR 36 became established, and some years later in Central and West Java when Cisadane was introduced. Comparison between East and West Java is

TABLE 6.6
The Development of Indonesia's Domestic Fertilizer Production Capacity

Production Plant	*Production Capacity (tonnes p.a.)*	*Commencement Date*
Urea fertilizer plants		
Pusri I	100 000	1963
Pusri II	380 000	1974
Pusri III	570 000	1977
Pusri IV	570 000	1978
Kujang	570 000	1978
Kaltim I	570 000	1987
Kaltim II	570 000	1985
Kaltim III	570 000	1988
PIM (Iskandar Muda)	570 000	1985
AAF (ASEAN Aceh)	570 000	1983
Triple superphosphate (TSP)/ ammonium sulphate (ZA) (PT Petrokimia Gresik)		
TSP unit I	500 000	1979
TSP unit II	500 000	1983
ZA unit I	150 000	1972
ZA unit II	250 000	1984
ZA unit III	250 000	1986

Source: Department of Industry.

TABLE 6.7

Java and Bali: Urea Use, 1971–1986 (kilograms per hectare)

	1971		*1974*		*1977*		*1980*		*1983*		*1986*
West Java	109.64		113.36		173.26		180.45		210.18		207.00
Increase (%)		3		53		4		16		–1.5	
Central Java	95.52		114.17		179.83		199.55		250.35		227.37
Increase (%)		20		58		11		25		–9.0	
East Java	114.32		133.48		228.85		267.64		303.47		296.98
Increase (%)		17		71		17		13		–2.0	
Bali	52.50		100.20		151.32		191.98		212.64		207.88
Increase (%)		91		51		27		11		–2.0	

Sources: BPS, *Statistik Indonesia*, 1971, 1974, 1977, 1980, 1983, and 1986.

particularly instructive. In 1971 East Javanese farmers used only slightly more urea per hectare than West Javanese farmers (ratio of urea use, East Java : West Java = 1.04). By 1980 East Javanese farmers were using half as much again (ratio = 1.48), whereas by 1986 they were still using significantly more urea than West Javanese farmers (ratio = 1.43). Fertilizer use began to decline in Java from a peak in 1983/4. This change had much to do with a relative reduction of the subsidy for fertilizer in relation to rice price.

With the initiation in 1985/6 of a new government programme, known as Supra Insus (Supra Intensifikasi Khusus or Special Intensification), which promulgated markedly higher fertilizer recommendations for particular areas of rice intensification, levels of fertilizer use began to rise again. In 1988, in response to increasing—and, in many parts of Java particularly East Java, excessive—use of fertilizer, the government introduced a more nuanced subsidy policy that distinguished between nitrogen and non-nitrogen (mainly phosphate and potassium) fertilizers. For nitrogen fertilizer (urea and ammonium sulphate) the government returned to the original basis of its subsidy programme by carefully calibrating a reduction of its subsidy to an increase in the floor price of unmilled rice. For non-nitrogen fertilizers, which for more than a decade had contributed to a considerable accumulation of soil nutrients, subsidies were reduced more substantially. This policy produced a two-tiered retail price structure for fertilizer that was intended to promote a more efficient use of different sources of nutrient-supply.

Although East Java's rice production increases were the result of (1) better technical irrigation, (2) the rapid adoption of new seed varieties that were generally appropriate to growing conditions, and (3) the use of high quantities of nitrogen and other fertilizer, it is by no means the case that East Java's rice production was uniform throughout the province. There are distinct regional differences in East Java's *sawah* ecosystems. To understand East Java's *sawah* ecology, therefore, it is essential to define the different 'rice baskets' of the province.

Internal Production: The Rice Baskets of East Java

A 'rice basket' defines a contiguous or nearly contiguous growing environment: a *sawah* ecosystem with similar characteristics that can be approximately defined. The concept is used here as an heuristic device for examining East Java's internal *sawah* production. Eight distinct rice baskets have been identified (Figure 6.3) and are used as the framework for differentiating *kabupaten*-level data on seasonal production.[9]

East Java's seasonal rice production is a reflection of its rain patterns. Most rice is grown on irrigated or rain-fed *sawah*. Only about one-quarter of 1 per cent of East Java's rice was grown on dry fields in 1985. Almost half of this dry-field rice was grown either on the island of Madura or in Pacitan, the one *kabupaten* in East Java that has too little irrigated rice to be included in a specific rice basket. Thus East Java's

FIGURE 6.3
East Java: The Rice Baskets

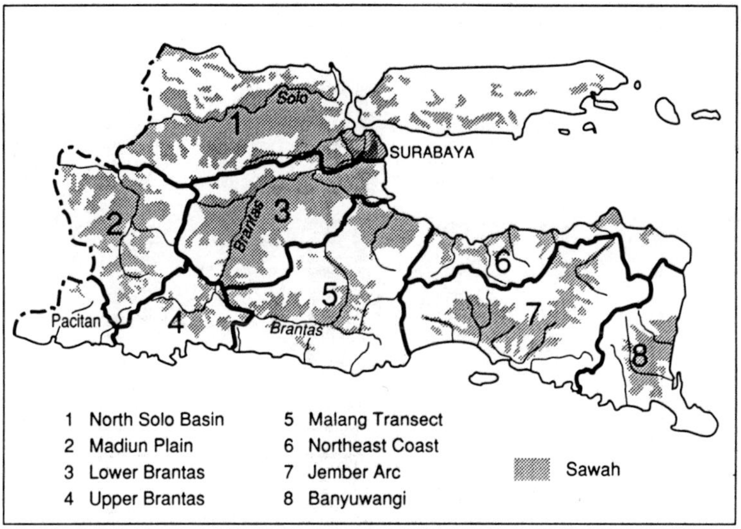

production is overwhelmingly *sawah* rice.

With irrigation, triple cropping is possible and harvesting can occur throughout the year. Double cropping—or in some areas five crops over a two-year period—is the more common pattern. East Java's first harvest peak occurs in April, with a second peak (involving approximately one-third the area of the first harvest) in July. Thereafter harvesting declines (see Figure 6.1). This pattern is slightly staggered for different rice baskets: peak harvests at the western end of the province occur about a month earlier than those at the far eastern end of the island.

Irrigation alone does not provide an adequate criterion for identifying and distinguishing the rice baskets of East Java. Over 3 per cent of irrigated *sawah* occurs in scattered pockets outside the official Department of Public Works' irrigation network. In addition, over 20 per cent of *sawah* in East Java is rain-fed. This rain-fed *sawah* is particularly concentrated in four *kabupaten*—Bojonegoro, Tuban, Lamongan, and Gresik—on the north coast. Statistics from different official sources, however, differ in how much land is classified as non-technically irrigated *sawah* and how much as rain-fed *sawah*.

Table 6.8 identifies the eight rice baskets of East Java, their constituent *kabupaten*, and their respective areas of irrigated and rain-fed *sawah*. The rice baskets are well distributed across the island. The rice baskets that constitute major production areas are, from west to east, the Madiun Plain, the North Solo Basin, the Lower Brantas, the Malang Transect, and the Jember Arc. These rice baskets range in size from 133 000 hectares to over 250 000 hectares of *sawah*. The rice baskets of lesser size and productive importance are the Upper Brantas, the Northeast Coast, and Banyuwangi. These rice baskets range in area from 34 000 hectares to over 68 000 hectares of *sawah*.

TABLE 6.8
East Java: The Rice Baskets, 1988

Rice Basket	*Kabupaten*	*Irrigated Area*		*Rain-fed Area*		*Total Area (ha)*
		Ha	*%*	*Ha*	*%*	
Bengawan Solo Basin						
Madiun Plain		133 577	(88.8)	16 835	(11.2)	150 412
	Madiun	32 024	(92.7)	2 535	(7.3)	34 559
	Magetan	28 172	(94.6)	1 619	(5.4)	29 791
	Ponorogo	32 338	(91.9)	2 867	(8.1)	35 205
	Ngawi	41 043	(80.7)	9 814	(19.3)	50 857
North Solo Basin		97 531	(38.5)	156 019	(61.5)	253 550
	Bojonegoro	26 172	(35.3)	48 001	(64.7)	74 173
	Lamongan	45 554	(55.6)	36 438	(44.4)	81 992
	Tuban	18 669	(33.6)	36 819	(66.4)	55 488
	Gresik	7 136	(17.0)	34 761	(83.0)	41 897
Brantas River Basin						
Lower Brantas		194 105	(92.3)	16 287	(7.7)	210 392
	Kediri	50 262	(97.7)	1 174	(2.3)	51 436
	Jombang	43 889	(90.1)	4 842	(9.9)	48 731
	Mojokerto	31 571	(84.4)	5 835	(15.6)	37 406
	Nganjuk	38 691	(89.8)	4 382	(10.2)	43 073
	Sidoarjo	29 692	(99.8)	54	(0.2)	29 746

Upper Brantas		30 644	(89.6)	3 563	(10.4)	34 207
	Tulungagung	20 720	(92.6)	1 657	(7.4)	22 377
	Trenggalek	9 924	(83.9)	1 906	(16.1)	11 830
Malang Transect		125 909	(95.1)	6 453	(4.8)	132 362
	Pasuruan	41 568	(93.1)	3 080	(6.9)	44 648
	Malang	50 689	(96.2)	2 028	(3.8)	52 717
	Blitar	33 652	(96.2)	1 345	(3.8)	34 997
Pekalen–Sampean Basin						
Jember Arc		149 916	(99.0)	1 492	(1.0)	151 408
	Lumajang	38 179	(100.0)	18	(0.0)	38 197
	Jember	82 960	(99.1)	784	(0.9)	83 744
	Bondowoso	28 777	(97.7)	690	(2.3)	29 467
North-east Coast		65 262	(97.6)	1 600	(2.4)	66 862
	Situbondo	26 853	(97.3)	756	(2.7)	26 609
	Probolinggo	38 409	(97.8)	844	(2.2)	39 253
Banyuwangi						
	Banyuwangi	67 665	(98.9)	755	(1.1)	68 420
East Java	Rice Baskets	864 609	(81.0)	203 004	(19.0)	1 066 613

Source: Diperta Jawa Timur, *Laporan Tahunan, 1988.*

TABLE 6.9

East Java: Rice Production, Area Harvested, and Yields per Hectare in the Rice Baskets, 1985

Rice Basket	*Kabupaten*	*Production ('000 tonnes)*	*Harvested Area (ha)*	*Yield per Hectare (tonnes)*
Bengawan Solo Basin				
Madiun Plain		1 124.9	218 548	5.15
	Madiun	259.1	48 538	5.34
	Magetan	192.8	37 014	5.21
	Ponorogo	253.4	50 977	4.97
	Ngawi	419.6	82 019	5.12
North Solo Basin		1 314.2	276 510	4.75
	Bojonegoro	375.1	74 195	5.06
	Lamongan	501.6	106 373	4.71
	Tuban	238.0	56 790	4.19
	Gresik	199.6	39 152	5.10
Brantas River Basin				
Lower Brantas		1 320.6	256 820	5.14
	Kediri	334.7	62 414	5.36
	Jombang	285.3	54 269	5.26
	Mojokerto	226.8	43 653	5.19
	Nganjuk	272.4	56 152	4.85
	Sidoarjo	201.4	40 332	4.99

Upper Brantas		238.6	47 518	5.02
	Tulungagung	152.6	29 931	5.10
	Trenggalek	86.0	17 587	4.89
Malang Transect		930.5	178 777	5.20
	Pasuruan	341.1	64 557	5.28
	Malang	350.5	66 091	5.30
	Blitar	238.8	48 129	4.96
Pekalen–Sampean Basin				
Jember Arc		1 115.1	240 308	4.64
	Lumajang	265.8	60 481	4.39
	Jember	631.9	133 102	4.75
	Bondowoso	217.4	46 725	4.65
North-east Coast		396.9	84 350	4.70
	Situbondo	156.3	35 009	4.46
	Probolinggo	240.6	49 341	4.88
Banyuwangi				
	Banyuwangi	607.8	119 759	5.07
East Java		7 048.7	1 422 590	4.95

Source: Diperta Jawa Timur, *Laporan Tahunan, 1985*.

Of the major rice baskets, the Madiun Plain and the Lower Brantas are productively similar, with good irrigation and virtually identical yields per hectare (Table 6.9). The North Solo Basin, by contrast, consists predominantly of rain-fed *sawah*. It is the largest rice basket in the province but its annual rice production is less than that of the better irrigated Lower Brantas. The third most important rice basket, the Jember Arc, is highly productive and consists almost entirely of irrigated *sawah*. The Malang Transect, which runs from Blitar to Pasuruan, is somewhat smaller than the Jember Arc, but is similar to Jember in that it consists mainly of irrigated *sawah*. This rice basket has some of the highest annual rice yields per hectare in East Java.

Of the smaller rice baskets, the North-east Coast and Banyuwangi are of approximately the same size and consist mainly of irrigated *sawah*. The Upper Brantas, though small, is predominantly irrigated and has relatively high yields per hectare.

Although the predominant crop in all these rice baskets is indeed rice, it is not the only crop grown in the *sawah* of these areas. Just as they differ in their rice cropping patterns, their irrigation and in average yields, these rice baskets also differ in their cropping patterns of sugar-cane and soya bean, East Java's other two main *sawah* crops.

Sugar-cane and Soya Bean

Since the nineteenth century, East Java has been a major production area for sugar-cane. Sugar-cane has continued to be planted as a major *sawah* crop in the province, although its relative importance in relation to rice and other secondary crops has declined. None the less, in 1984 East Java still produced 63 per cent of Indonesia's total sugar-cane.

The Lower Brantas has always been the leading sugar-cane producing area in the province and this dominance has continued. In 1984 the Lower Brantas produced 32 per cent of East Java's sugar-cane, followed by the Jember Arc with 21 per cent, the Malang Transect with 19 per cent, and the Madiun Plain with 15 per cent of production (Table 6.10). Together, these four rice baskets produced 87 per cent of total provincial production. The North-east Coast produced an additional 8 per cent, while for the rest of East Java's rice baskets sugar-cane was of minor importance.

Sugar-cane is a crop grown over an 18-month period, during which time two harvests are obtained. Depending on when the crop is planted, sugar-cane may replace five or more crops of rice or other secondary crops. Although sugar-cane is not a significant crop in all the rice baskets of East Java, where it is extensively planted it has a considerable effect on the production of other crops. Using available statistics gathered from different sources it is possible to estimate, for some rice baskets, the approximate proportion of land allocated to sugar-cane. Thus for both the Lower Brantas and the Jember Arc, as much as 19 per cent of *sawah* is planted to sugar-cane, while for the Madiun Plain this figure is roughly 15 per cent. On the other hand, for the

North-east Coast, more than 21 per cent of *sawah* is committed to sugar-cane.

Soya bean constitutes a major secondary crop in East Java, making it the largest producer in Indonesia. Soya bean is planted throughout most of the province, but there are areas of special concentration, and cropping patterns vary from rice basket to rice basket. Soya bean is planted in *sawah* either after the first or the second crop of rice. In general a somewhat larger area is harvested as a third seasonal crop from September through November than as a second seasonal crop from April to August. While soya bean can be highly profitable, it is also a high-risk crop, since it is frequently plagued by a variety of viruses and insect pests.

Data for the 1986 soya bean crop reveal the patterns of cultivation in the different rice baskets. Table 6.11 provides data on the harvested areas in each rice basket. The Lower Brantas has the largest area planted to soya bean, with substantial soya bean growing areas in all *kabupaten* except Sidoarjo. In the Lower Brantas, Jombang and Nganjuk account for 66 per cent of the total soya bean area. The soya bean harvest in the Lower Brantas resembles that of the province as a whole, with a larger area harvested in the third season than in the second. The Madiun Plain has the second largest area planted to soya bean, with a heavy concentration in Ponorogo. A high percentage of its crop is harvested in September and October. The Jember Arc ranks third in soya bean cropping area, with 88 per cent of the crop planted in Kabupaten Jember. The Jember Arc has nearly equal soya bean harvests in both the second and third seasons. The North Solo Basin is next in soya bean planting area, but in this rice basket, with its extensive rain-fed *sawah*, soya bean is overwhelmingly a second-season crop, planted after rice. The pattern for this rice basket is set by concentrated planting in Lamongan which is harvested in May and June. Banyuwangi is the next in order of cropping area, with nearly equal second- and third-season harvested areas. In the Malang Transect, Pasuruan accounts for 91 per cent of the soya bean area. Like Jember and Banyuwangi, its harvested area is virtually the same in the second and third seasons.

On the basis of the composite evidence on the three principal crops grown in *sawah* in the different rice baskets of East Java in the mid-1980s, one can venture a few observations about the province's internal production areas. Table 6.12 sets out East Java's rice baskets in rank order based on their area of irrigated *sawah*. This rank order corresponds with irrigated rather than total *sawah*. Among the major rice baskets, the Lower Brantas is clearly the leading production area in rice, sugar-cane, and soya bean. The Jember Arc and the Madiun Plain are similar in total *sawah* area and productive capacity. The Jember Arc, however, has a larger percentage of irrigated land and more land than the Madiun Plain planted to sugar-cane. The Malang Transect is interesting in that one part, Malang, is heavily planted to sugar-cane while another part, Pasuruan, is heavily planted to soya bean. The North Solo

TABLE 6.10
East Java: Sugar-cane Production, Area Harvested, and Yields per Hectare in the Rice Baskets, 1984

Rice Basket	*Kabupaten*	*Production ('000 tonnes)*	*Harvested Area (ha)*	*Yield per Hectare (tonnes)*
Bengawan Solo Basin				
Madiun Plain		134.15	21 877	6.13
	Madiun	35.78	7 313	4.89
	Magetan	38.53	5 571	6.91
	Ponorogo	28.48	4 179	6.81
	Ngawi	31.36	4 814	6.51
North Solo Basin		7.85	1 459	5.38
	Bojonegoro	5.06	902	5.61
	Lamongan	0.04	93	0.48
	Tuban	–	–	–
	Gresik	2.74	464	5.91
Brantas River Basin				
Lower Brantas		278.97	38 093	7.32
	Kediri	84.82	12 264	6.91
	Jombang	69.67	9 457	7.37
	Mojokerto	33.18	5 172	6.41
	Nganjuk	30.02	4 470	6.71
	Sidoarjo	61.28	6 730	9.11

Upper Brantas		20.37	3 045	6.69
	Tulungagung	11.06	1 698	6.51
	Trenggalek	9.31	1 347	6.91
Malang Transect		162.94	31 889	5.11
	Pasuruan	18.95	4 891	3.87
	Malang	100.12	20 563	4.87
	Blitar	43.87	6 435	6.81
Pekalen–Sampean Basin				
Jember Arc		186.86	28 988	6.45
	Lumajang	73.71	11 314	6.51
	Jember	75.79	11 551	6.56
	Bondowoso	37.36	6 123	6.10
North-east Coast		73.45	14 682	5.00
	Situbondo	36.08	5 625	6.41
	Probolinggo	37.36	9 057	4.12
Banyuwangi				
	Banyuwangi	8.01	1 289	6.21
East Java		872.62	141 322	6.17

Source: Diperta Jawa Timur, *Laporan Tahunan, 1984*.

TABLE 6.11
East Java: Areas of Soya Bean Harvested in the Rice Baskets, 1986

Rice Basket	*Kabupaten*	*Harvested Area (ha)*
Bengawan Solo Basin		
Madiun Plain		51 044
	Madiun	14 118
	Magetan	4 986
	Ponorogo	21 839
	Ngawi	10 101
North Solo Basin		46 270
	Bojonegoro	8 887
	Lamongan	21 408
	Tuban	8 068
	Gresik	7 907
Brantas River Basin		
Lower Brantas		56 232
	Kediri	7 390
	Jombang	17 784
	Mojokerto	9 943
	Nganjuk	19 436
	Sidoarjo	1 679
Upper Brantas		8 508
	Tulungagung	5 882
	Trenggalek	2 626
Malang Transect		27 947
	Pasuruan	25 399
	Malang	1 043
	Blitar	1 505
Pekalen–Sampean Basin		
Jember Arc		48 161
	Lumajang	4 990
	Jember	42 150
	Bondowoso	1 021
North-east Coast		5 670
	Situbondo	2 604
	Probolinggo	3 066
Banyuwangi		
	Banyuwangi	36 298
East Java	Rice baskets	280 130
Other		2 334

Source: Diperta Jawa Timur, *Laporan Tahunan, 1986.*

Basin covers the largest total *sawah* area but has significantly less irrigated *sawah* than the Malang Transect. Little sugar-cane is grown in this rice basket, but a large area is allocated to soya bean. Banyuwangi, which is a single-*kabupaten* rice basket, comprises mainly irrigated *sawah* which might be suitable for sugar-cane. Yet Banyuwangi has the

TABLE 6.12

East Java: The Rice Baskets as Production Areas, Mid-1980s (hectares)

Rice Basket	*Irrigated Sawah*	*Total Sawah*	*Harvested Rice Area*	*Rice Crop Ratio*[a]	*Sugar-cane Area*	*Soya Bean Area*
Banyuwangi	67 665	68 420	119 759	1.75	1 289	36 298
Jember Arc	149 916	151 408	240 308	1.59	28 988	48 161
Madiun Plain	133 577	150 412	218 548	1.45	21 877	51 044
Upper Brantas	30 644	34 207	47 518	1.39	3 045	8 508
Malang Transect	125 909	132 362	178 777	1.35	31 889	27 947
North-east Coast	65 262	66 862	84 350	1.26	14 682	5 670
Lower Brantas	194 105	210 393	256 820	1.22	38 093	56 232
North Solo Basin	97 531	253 550	276 510	1.09	1 459	46 270

Source: Derived from Tables 6.8 to 6.11.

[a]Crop Ratio: Annual harvested rice crop area to total *sawah* area.

smallest area of sugar-cane of all the rice baskets in East Java. By contrast, the North-east Coast, while similar to Banyuwangi in irrigated as well as total *sawah*, has proportionally the largest area planted to sugar-cane of any rice basket. The smallest of the rice baskets, the Upper Brantas, is planted to both sugar-cane and soya bean in a relatively high proportion.

Comparing the areas planted to these three crops does not involve equivalent comparison, because sugar-cane takes a minimum of 18 months to produce two crops. In the nearly continual cropping environments of most rice baskets, sugar-cane is roughly equivalent to four or five other crops. The commitment of large areas to sugar-cane, such as in the Lower Brantas, the Jember Arc, the Malang Transect, and the North-east Coast, has a multiplier effect, constraining the possibilities of planting rice and soya bean.

Thus, an interesting difference among the rice baskets is their rice cropping ratio (Table 6.12). This ratio is indicative of how often land is cropped to rice in a year. A ratio of 1.00 would mean that the equivalent of all of the rice basket's land was planted with one crop of rice. All the rice baskets in East Java have a rice cropping ratio greater than one. The most striking difference is between the North Solo Basin, whose rice cropping ratio is close to 1.00, and Banyuwangi, which has the highest rice cropping ratio (1.75) in the province. Interestingly, the Lower Brantas has the second lowest cropping ratio in East Java, because of its heavy commitment to sugar-cane and soya bean, as well as to other secondary crops.

The Social Transformation of *Sawah* Production in East Java

When C. Geertz wrote his important study of the *sawah* economy of Java, *Agricultural Involution* (1963), he was undoubtedly influenced by his fieldwork in Kediri in the Lower Brantas. His descriptions of *sawah* and of the combination of rice and sugar-cane produced from these *sawah* fit precisely the Brantas pattern of production that became well established from the 1870s and was enhanced by substantially improved irrigation beginning in the 1890s. The pattern continued through the period of C. Geertz's field study.

The critical feature of this pattern of production was a particular form of communal land tenure, known in the Brantas as the *gogolan* system. A similar communal land system extended through most of lowland East Java, as far east as Besuki, but with some local variation in usage and terminology. C. Geertz describes the working of the *gogolan* system from the point of view of the European sugar-mill lessor whose arrangements with surrounding villages were based on 21-year contracts (C. Geertz, 1963: 86–9). According to this system one-third of the communally owned *sawah* of each village was leased for planting to sugar-cane. After 18 months, this land was returned to the village, by which time another third of the village's *gogolan* was already allocated to sugar-cane.

From the perspective of the mill, this system followed a simple model of regular, rotational order. Accommodating this system at the village level, however, necessitated complex social arrangements and adjustments to maintain it. Communal land could not be committed in small segments but had to be leased in large irrigated blocks (*blok*). All communal land, which generally included all productive *sawah*, was divided into shares (*gogol*). These shares were further divided into small parcels of land which were generally located in different blocks within the village. Since all village land was officially 'classified' according to its quality, which often varied from one part of the village to another, the system of the 'subdividing of shares' was intended to achieve a rough equality among all shares. Thus one *gogol* would have a certain portion of first-class land combined with third-class; another might consist of several parcels of second-class land, all resulting in an approximate productive similarity. A consequence of the distribution of parcels in different blocks of the village was that farmers were often able to retain a portion of land for subsistence while another portion of their land was given over to sugar-cane.

The number of shares of communal land in a village was, at any one time, fixed and limited. This number could increase—and indeed in some areas did increase—when new land within the village boundaries was brought under irrigation. Access to communal land was limited to a single share per household, and as the population increased and more households were formed, an ever-smaller minority of households was able to hold shares in the village's communal land. Provided that the obligations attached to the holding of communal land were properly fulfilled, village shareholders could—and usually did—reallocate tenancy rights to parts of parcels of their land. The combination of the formal parcelling of shares and the informal allocation of rights to parts of these parcels by pawning, renting, rotational use or share-cropping finally produced, by the 1950s, a system of landholding so fragmented that C. Geertz could aptly describe it as 'lilliputian'.

In 1960 new agrarian laws changed this situation and established a new institutional basis for land tenure. Shareholders who held communal land at the time of the passage of these laws were given individual rights to their holdings and were allowed to sell them after a certain period of time. No longer limited to a single share, individuals were permitted legally to hold up to 5 hectares of *sawah*.

Through the 1950s and most of the 1960s the profitability of growing either rice or sugar-cane was limited, and the constrained production systems that developed during this period were not simply, as C. Geertz has argued, 'self-defeating'. These production systems were also 'self-protecting', since they involved the sharing by cultivators of both the costs and the risks of production, including the risk of being seen by communist sympathizers of the period as landholding reactionaries.

The establishment of the New Order and the implementation of the New Order rice intensification programme, which began to take effect in East Java by 1969, prompted substantial changes in local land tenure. In areas where the planting of sugar-cane was important, there were also profound changes in the relationship between farmers and the local mill. Various schemes were introduced and production targets for sugar-cane were set—and in some instances rigorously implemented—but negotiations had to be worked out between individual cultivators and the mill. Mills were no longer able to lease large blocks of land on long-term contracts. Sugar-cane growing became an arrangement between a mill and individual smallholders, mediated through a particular government programme (see Chapter 8).

The first stages of changes in land tenure occurred at such miniscule and informal levels that official records can provide little evidence. Fragments of land held under the same title that had previously been dispersed along family lines but were too small to be worked profitably, were consolidated. Rights to these fragments of *gogol* holdings had to be consolidated before title could be bought or sold.

In most East Javanese villages, various portions of village land, known in some places as *yasan* land, were individually owned. This non-communal land could be legally bought and sold even during the colonial period. Only after passage of the 1960 Agrarian Law was it possible, however, to sell portions of communal land (*gogol*). Since ownership was no longer limited to a single *gogol*, and individual holdings of up to 5 hectares were legally allowed, there began to occur, in the late 1960s and early 1970s, a further consolidation of landholdings. One of the common local mechanisms for such transactions was the renting of a parcel of land on a long-term contract which eventually led to the outright sale of the land to the person renting it.

Already in the colonial period, households holding full rights to communal *sawah* constituted a minority in lowland villages in areas with high sugar-cane production. Elsewhere, this concentration of landownership was less pronounced but was none the less a feature of social life. In the areas of what the Dutch called the Oosthoek (Eastern Corner), the region from Besuki through to Banyuwangi, the *gogolan* system was never introduced and land tenure developed according to a different pattern from most of the rest of East Java. Everywhere, however, as the population increased, the proportion of village households owning or controlling *sawah* decreased. Detailed village studies indicate that in many areas of East Java this proportion is less than half of the village population. In these areas, the majority of households consist of farm labourers.

There exists no reliable systematic evidence on how far this consolidation of land ownership has gone during the course of the 1980s, nor how widespread it is in different areas of East Java, especially in the vicinity of large urban centres. Most of the available evidence derives from specific village studies. In a few years' time, it may be possible to use new population and farm census data to discern the pattern of changes through the 1980s. For the present, however, data from the Population Census of 1980 and the Agricultural Census of 1983 provide a glimpse of some of the social differences among the rice baskets of East Java at the beginning of the decade.

Social Differences among the Rice Baskets of East Java

Among the different rice baskets of East Java there are marked differences in population densities. These differences provide a primary context in which to evaluate other important social differences. Table 6.13 lists the rice baskets in order of their rural population densities in 1980. Not surprisingly, the population density of the Lower Brantas stands out from the rest. By 1980 the rural population of the Lower Brantas was already approaching an average of a thousand persons per square kilometre. This is the kind of social density that is often considered to epitomize the Javanese landscape. By contrast both Madiun and the Upper Brantas, with only about two-thirds the population density of the Lower Brantas, form a second demographic tier within the province. To the east of the Brantas and in the North Solo Basin population densities are roughly half or less, whereas Banyuwangi has only about one-quarter of the rural density of the Lower Brantas.

In view of these densities, the data published by the Agricultural Census of 1983 are particularly revealing. It is assumed that as the population increases, the pressure on land also increases, and as a result, a smaller proportion of the rural population is able to control productive land. The Agricultural Census wisely adopts the notion of 'control'

TABLE 6.13
East Java: Rural Population Densities in the Rice Baskets, 1980[a]

Rice Basket	*Area (sq. km)*	*Population*	*Density (persons per sq. km)*
Lower Brantas	4 733	4,618,654	977
Madiun Plain	4 263	2,801,788	657
Upper Brantas	2 260	1,397,697	618
Malang Transect	7 762	4,117,584	531
Jember Arc	6 300	3,136,910	498
North-east Coast	2 887	1,391,096	482
North Solo Basin	7 689	3,649,183	475
Banyuwangi	5 783	1,420,532	246

Sources: Area: KSJT, *Jawa Timur dalam Angka, 1981.*
Population: KSJT (1983).

[a]These figures are intended to represent the rural population. They do not include the urban population of the official *kotamadya*. The town of Jember is not yet classified as a *kotamadya*. Hence the sizeable population of this large and rapidly growing town is included in the statistics for the rural population of Kabupaten Jember. To correct for this the population of rural Jember has been decreased by a figure of 230,000 persons, which is the estimated population of the town of Jember (Mackie and Djumilah Zain, 1989: 314). It must be realized that all of these figures are an approximation intended to give a relative representation of the average densities in the different rice baskets.

(*kuasa*) as its criterion for categorizing land. Use of this criterion avoids the problem of landownership where titles to land are difficult to ascertain and are complicated by numerous formal and informal renting, leasing, and sharing arrangements. Control is what is recognized in the villages of East Java, and is acknowledged in terms of who ultimately decides what is planted on a piece of land. Using this notion of control, the Agricultural Census identifies what percentage of the total rural population actually controls land. This controlled land is then distinguished according to farm size.

The rice baskets of East Java are listed in Table 6.14 in order of the percentage of their land-controlling households. Banyuwangi has the lowest percentage of households that actually control land (33 per cent of rural households) whereas the North Solo Basin has the highest (68 per cent). Differences between these two rice baskets are, however, even more pronounced than these figures indicate.

Table 6.14 also shows the percentage of households with farms above or below a half hectare. The figures on farm size for Banyuwangi and the North Solo Basin are nearly identical but if one takes into account quality of the land controlled in these two rice baskets, these similar figures point to further significant differences.

The figures in Table 6.14 represent all forms of landholding, not just *sawah*. Table 6.12, however, provides information on irrigated *sawah* and total *sawah* for each of the rice baskets. While in some rice baskets, such as Banyuwangi, most *sawah* is irrigated *sawah*; in other rice baskets, such as the North Solo Basin, a large percentage of *sawah* is non-irrigated rain-fed *sawah*. Using the data on irrigated *sawah* in Table 6.12 as a reference point, it is possible to assess how much of the land identified in Table 6.14 is in fact prime *sawah* land. This offers a further perspective on landholding patterns in the different rice baskets.

Thus Banyuwangi has the lowest percentage of land-controlling households. This means that this rice basket has the highest percentage of rural households who control no land. Consistent with this pattern, the Agricultural Census (Table 53) reports that 21 per cent of land-controlling households have landholdings of 1 hectare or more. This is the highest percentage in any of the rice baskets. And of the land controlled in this rice basket, 74 per cent is irrigated *sawah*.

By contrast, the North Solo Basin has the highest percentage of land-controlling households but only 24 per cent of the land they control is irrigated *sawah*. Thus, whereas in the North Solo Basin 20 per cent of land-controlling households have more than 1 hectare of land (Agricultural Census: Table 53), this land is clearly of poorer quality than in Banyuwangi since most of it is either non-irrigated *sawah* or is not *sawah* at all.

The other rice baskets of East Java range between these extremes. The contrast between the Lower Brantas and the Madiun Plain is instructive since these two rice baskets have the highest and second highest population densities in East Java. The population density in the Lower Brantas is, however, almost a third higher than that of the Madiun Plain. As one

TABLE 6.14

East Java: Rural Households, Land-controlling Households, and the Pattern of Landholding in the Rice Baskets, 1983

Rice Basket	Rural Households (no.)	Land-controlling Households		Land Controlled (ha)	Percentage of Households Controlling[a]	
		No.	%		<0.5 ha	>0.5 ha
Banyuwangi	344,103	116,020	33	91 556	52	46
Lower Brantas	1,029,941	449,100	44	279 495	61	36
Jember Arc[b]	837,732	383,640	46	222 259	65	33
North-east Coast	373,376	190,233	51	105 864	64	30
Malang Transect	935,114	519,066	56	327 566	60	38
Upper Brantas	310,025	206,522	67	97 635	72	24
Madiun Plain	640,633	431,127	67	232 880	66	32
North Solo Basin	792,640	542,622	68	406 774	51	48

Source: BPS (1986b).

[a]Farm size percentages do not add to 100 because by the definitions used in the Agricultural Survey 'controlled land' had to be operated in the period designated by the Survey. A percentage of land left fallow or otherwise not used was not therefore registered as 'controlled'.

[b]The figures for the Jember Arc have been corrected by the same population factor as in Table 6.13 (230,000 persons = 56,373 households) to take account of the town of Jember.

might expect in any area of such concentrated population, the Lower Brantas shows a considerable concentration of land control. Only 44 per cent of rural households control land, 69 per cent of which is irrigated *sawah.* However, 61 per cent of the land-controlling households have farms of less than 1 hectare. By contrast, in the Madiun Plain, 67 per cent of rural households control land, of which 57 per cent is irrigated *sawah.* A higher percentage of these households (66 per cent) compared to 61 per cent in the Lower Brantas have farms of less than 0.5 hectare.

The range of differences in landholding among the rice baskets of East Java reflect more than differences in ecology. On the basis of these figures, it is possible to venture some observations about Java's social past as well as its future. Those rice baskets—Banyuwangi, Jember, and to some extent, the North-east Coast—that were never historically subjected to a communal land tenure system show relatively high concentrations of land control. In other rice baskets where, during the colonial period, the communal land system acted as a check on land accumulation and consolidation, the relative percentages of land-controlling households are higher. Thus, in the early 1980s, landholding patterns in East Java still clearly reflected a colonial inheritance. The impact of the new Agrarian Law and of the agricultural transformation of the province under the various programmes for intensification had not yet taken full effect. During the 1980s, there were greater changes than in the 1970s but adequate data to evaluate these changes are not yet available. However, one can still perceive certain tendencies. One of these is toward greater concentration of land-control and especially the consolidation of landholdings of less than a quarter hectare. In the Upper Brantas, for example, where 72 per cent of farms were less than half a hectare (and where 45 per cent of all farms were less than one-quarter of a hectare), some process of consolidation has undoubtedly occurred. Other rice baskets, such as the Jember Arc where land-control is already relatively concentrated, still show a high percentage of small farms (with 38 per cent of farms less than one-quarter of a hectare). Here, too, the trend is toward further consolidation. This process, however, depends on the possibility of increasing opportunities for off-farm employment. Hence it is to the rest of the economy of East Java that one must look to appreciate the transformation of the province's rice baskets.

Conclusion

During the New Order, the productive capacity of East Java's *sawah* was enhanced enormously. In a little over two decades, under strong government direction, East Java adopted and then adapted the technology of the 'Green Revolution' to a steadily improving network of irrigated environments. The initial and most evident result was a significant increase in rice production. From its proportional contribution of 20 per cent of national rice production, East Java became Indonesia's major supplier of rice to the rest of the country. At the same time, less spectacularly but no less significantly, the production of other secondary *sawah* crops also increased. Although still important, sugar-cane, whose production in colonial times helped to shape the principal *sawah* environments of East Java, declined relative to rice and other crops such as soya bean or maize. The escape from the previous regimen of regulations designed to promote sugar-cane production contributed to the potential for diversification of various *sawah* environments.

Seen in aggregate, the achievements in East Java's agricultural production tend to obscure the notable diversity of the province's *sawah* environments from which this production derives. All too often the Lower Brantas provides the main image of East Java's *sawah* agriculture. In charting the achievements of East Java agriculture, this chapter has attempted to distinguish its different *sawah* environments and to compare them to one another. These various 'rice baskets' by their diversity are East Java's great strength. Not just as growing environments but as social environments, these rice baskets show different patterns of development. Perhaps therefore the greatest achievement of East Java in the past two decades has been to harness this diversity in a singular development effort.

1. Rice production figures are given by weight. Rice, however, goes through various stages of drying before it is milled. At each stage, the grain loses some of its weight. Hence it is necessary to specify what stage of rice processing is referred to when a set of figures is cited. Conversion ratios are therefore at the heart of all discussion of rice production. An excellent starting-point for an understanding of these factors and their relevance to official Indonesian publications on rice production is Mears (1961, Appendix VI).

The Central Bureau of Statistics (Biro Pusat Statistik or BPS) uses (or has used) the following set of categories:

(a) *gabah kering panen* (wet-rice paddy)
(b) *gagang kering giling* (dry-stalk paddy)
(c) *gabah kering giling* (dry-rice paddy)
(d) *beras* (milled rice or rice).

In official BPS documents to 1973, production figures were generally given in dry-stalk paddy with official conversion ratios as follows:

(a) dry-stalk paddy : dry-rice paddy (100 : 76.5)
(b) dry-stalk paddy : milled rice (100 : 52.0).

After 1973 production figures from BPS were more consistently reported in dry-rice paddy. A three-tiered reference system was created. Wet-rice paddy (*gabah kering panen*) was used to refer to the undried crop; dry-rice paddy (*gabah kering giling*) to the crop dried sufficiently to be ready for milling; whereas rice (*beras*) referred to the milled crop. Conversion ratios were set as follows:

(a) wet-rice paddy : dry-rice paddy (100 : 85)
(b) dry-rice paddy : milled rice (100 : 68).

In 1989, however, BPS changed its conversion ratio for dry-rice paddy (*gabah kering giling*) : milled rice (*beras*) to 0.65. The figures in this chapter still follow the pre-1989 conversion ratio. Discrepancies in production figures may be encountered in official documents because different conversion ratios were used by different government agencies at different times. Because this chapter uses statistics from different sources, some discrepancies are unavoidable.

Javanese villagers distinguish more stages to the drying of rice than do official government sources. For example, a stage between *gabah kering panen* and *gabah kering giling* is recognized, when the crop has been harvested and is still in the process of being dried. This stage is sometimes referred to as *gabah kering lumbung*.

2. *Sawah* are classified in official statistics as either irrigated or rain-fed. With good rain, rain-fed *sawah* can sometimes be almost as productive as irrigated *sawah* but only for the first (rainy season) crop. These *sawah*, if they are used at all in the dry season, are planted to secondary crops. Official figures include production from both rain-fed and irrigated *sawah*. This chapter concentrates on irrigated *sawah* which comprise almost 80 per cent of the *sawah* of East Java.

3. This assertion requires some clarification. East Java increased its rice cropping area by 35 per cent between 1968 and 1986. This was done mainly by increasing cropping intensity rather than by bringing new land under cultivation. By contrast, South Sumatra more than doubled its rice cropping area over the same period, but yields have been at least 1.5 tonnes per hectare less than those of East Java. Although Bali and Yogyakarta, with only one-tenth or less of East Java's cropping area, kept pace in increasing yields through the 1970s, East Java's yields per hectare surged ahead by 1980. Yogyakarta's yields caught up with East Java's in 1983, but its cropping area of rice hardly increased between 1974 and 1989. Bali's yields have been below East Java's since the 1980s; the island has increased its rice cropping area by only about 27 per cent since 1968.

4. This section follows closely the work of M. N. Vivekananthan, an associate of Sir M. MacDonald and Partners, whose knowledge of East Java's irrigation—and willingness to share that knowledge—is truly remarkable. The author has benefited from Vivekananthan's published work and his unpublished reports as well as from discussions with him. Here the author would like to express his gratitude to Vivekananthan for all his assistance.

5. Whether an irrigation system is 'technical' or 'semi-technical' involves certain evaluation criteria. For consistency the author has followed the 1982/3 figures from Vivekananthan (1987) rather than those published in KSJT, *Jawa Timur dalam Angka, 1985*. Rehabilitation continued through the 1980s under the auspices of the East Java Irrigation Project. Figures in *Jawa Timur dalam Angka, 1985* show a 16 per cent increase in technically irrigated *sawah* since 1970, with semi-technical irrigation only slightly diminished and non-technical substantially diminished. The two sets of figures are as follows:

Year	*Technical (ha)*	*Semi-technical (ha)*	*Non-technical (ha)*	*Total (ha)*
Jawa Timur dalam Angka				
1970	576 100	120 729	199 505	896 334
1985	670 039	117 041	143 663	930 743
Vivekananthan				
1982/3	654 229	131 196	164 762	950 187

6. This statement is based on repeated comments from farmers in the Brantas evaluating their own crop yields. Statistics on yields for East Java, published by BPS, do not, however, appear to bear this out. These statistics divide the production year into three four-month periods. Average yields for the first four months (January through April) are higher than those for the next four months (May through August). Average yields for the third four-month period (September through December) are higher than for the second four-month period (May through August) and until 1982 were consistently higher than for the first period.

7. For a longer and more detailed discussion of the development of new seed varieties in Indonesia, see Fox (1991).

8. According to documents from East Java's information service, 48 per cent of the then irrigated *sawah* of East Java was planted with Bengawan (KSJT, *Jawa Timur dalam Angka, 1952*: 274). Besides Bengawan, Cahaya, Mas, and Cina, a number of other varieties also continued to be produced in East Java's rice breeding stations; namely, Andelsiem, Genjah beton, and Gropak gede.

9. The concept of a 'rice basket' is still in an early stage of formulation. If better disaggregated production data were readily available and if such data could, for example, be linked to specific sections and subsections of East Java's irrigation network and to data on soil, rainfall, and so on, it would—and should—be possible to present a more differentiated understanding of a 'rice basket'. Here the author would like to acknowledge discussions with Dr Wolfgang Linser in 1985 and 1986 that led to the initial formulation of this concept in relation to Java as a whole.

7
Agricultural Diversification in the Upper Konto Area*

J. W. Nibbering

Introduction

HIGHLANDS form only 14 per cent of the total area of East Java (Diperta, 1976–86),[1] but they derive their importance from their specific roles in the regional economy and in regulating the hydrological balance. The importance of the highlands in the regional economies of East Java has been growing over the 1970s and 1980s, as the example of the Upper Konto area, discussed in this chapter, demonstrates.

While East Java's lowlands have been undergoing rapid economic and social development, the highlands too have shown considerable change in the 1970s and 1980s. Agricultural development of the Upper Konto area under the New Order has been induced by government policy, world market trends, and spillovers from economic growth in the province as a whole. Agriculture has become increasingly commercialized and more diversified, with impacts on productivity, income, and employment levels. This chapter describes the changes in agriculture in a highland area and indicates parallels and differences with the lowlands. It examines to what extent these developments are sustainable and considers their significance for the wider region.

The Upper Konto area is taken as a case-study which demonstrates specific features and issues relating to highland areas.[2] The area is made up of two altitudinal zones where developments have followed distinct courses. These will be discussed separately and then brought together in a final section.

The Upper Konto Area

The Upper Konto area comprises the Konto River watershed upstream from the Selorejo dam. The area covers approximately 250 square kilometres at an altitude ranging between 620 and 2 868 metres

*The author wishes to extend his gratitude to Jan de Graaff for giving permission to use the results from the agro-economic survey conducted in 1986, as well as for updating some of the official statistical data on crop and livestock production in the two *kecamatan*, and also to Henk Munneke and Eduard Vorsterman van Oyen for providing some of the unpublished data from their socio-economic survey in the hamlet of Cukal, Pujon.

FIGURE 7.1
Highland Areas in East Java and the Upper Konto Area

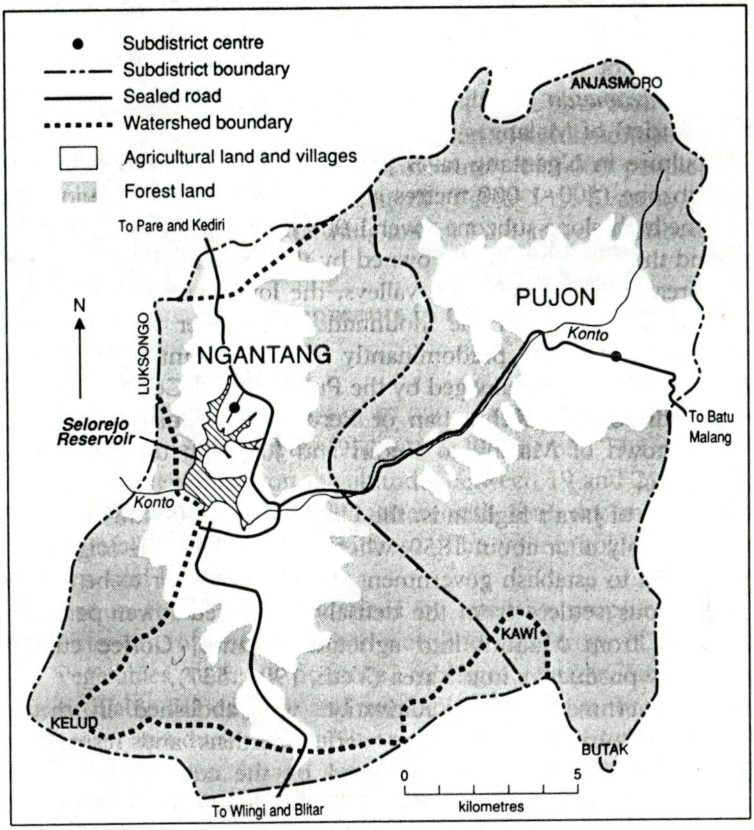

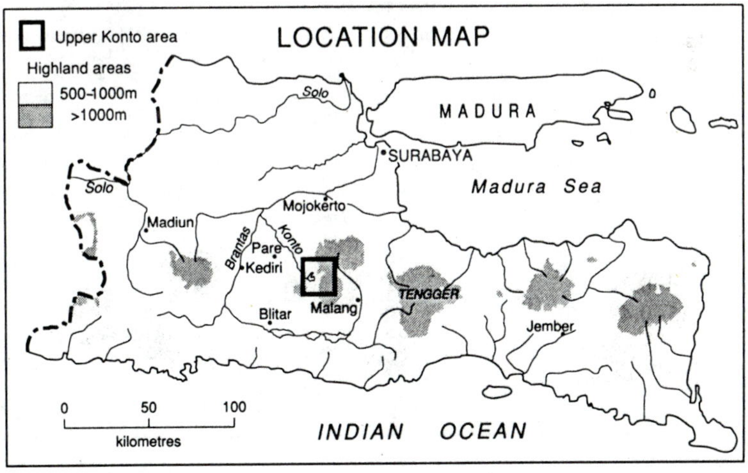

(Figure 7.1). In the past the Konto River regularly caused floods in its lower reaches and those of the Brantas River to which it is the largest tributary. Between 1965 and 1970 the Selorejo dam was constructed across the Konto River in Ngantang, forming a large reservoir in the western part of the area. Administratively, the area coincides roughly with two *kecamatan* (subdistricts), Ngantang and Pujon, in the *kabupaten* (district) of Malang.

Agriculture in Ngantang takes place within the agro-ecological mid-slope subzone (500–1 000 metres above sea level) and in Pujon largely within the high-slope subzone (over 1 000 metres) (Figure 7.1). The villages and the agricultural land owned by the population cover one-third of the area. This occupies the valleys, the lower and middle plateaux, and the lower slopes of the mountains. The other two-thirds of the Upper Konto area are predominantly hilly or mountainous and comprise State forest land managed by the Public Forest Corporation of Java (Perusahaan Umum Kehutanan or Perum Perhutani). A sealed road from the town of Malang to Kediri and Jombang traverses the area (Figure 7.1).

Like most of Java's highlands, the Upper Konto area was settled on a large scale only after about 1850, when large parts of the original forest were cleared to establish government coffee gardens or to be converted by indigenous settlers from the densely populated lower parts of the island and from Madura into agricultural land.[3] Coffee cultivation proved very productive in the area (Veth, 1903: 537).

After government coffee cultivation was abolished in the early twentieth century, the remaining coffee gardens and reserves were added to the forest reserves managed by the colonial forest service (Altona, 1914). On the remaining agricultural land, permanent cultivation systems developed, with maize and cassava on *tegalan* (dry-cultivated

TABLE 7.1
Land Distribution in the Upper Konto Area and the Entire *Kabupaten* of Malang, 1983 (per cent)

Landholding[a] *Size (ha)*	*Ngantang*	*Pujon*	*Kabupaten Malang*[b]
> 1	9	7	11
0.75–0.99	6	4	5
0.50–0.74	11	9	9
0.25–0.49	18	16	15
< 0.25	22	33	18
No land	34	31	43
Total	100	100	101

Source: KSM (1985).
[a]Land owned, rented or share-cropped.
[b]Rural areas only.

fields cropped largely with annuals) and rice on *sawah* (rain-fed or irrigated fields). In the cooler part of the area (Pujon and the adjacent *kecamatan* of Batu), vegetable cropping started at the beginning of the twentieth century to meet the demands of a growing urban population, especially of Europeans (Meijer, 1915).

Between 1920 and 1970 the population of the Upper Konto doubled to 82,000, leading to continued fragmentation of landholdings. The two *kecamatan* are now inhabited by approximately 100,000 people, about one-third of whom control no land at all (Table 7.1). Even so, most of the population is engaged in farming and/or land and cattle labour.

Developments in Pujon

The Setting

The population of Pujon numbered 47,000 in 1985. Its agricultural land is at an altitude ranging between 950 and 1 300 metres. The mean temperature varies, depending on the altitude, between 19 and 21 °C. Average annual rainfall is 2 200 millimetres, with four dry months (with monthly rainfall below 100 millimetres). The young volcanic soils are fertile, deep, and highly permeable.

Land use in Pujon is characterized by intensive cropping systems, with subsistence crops of maize and rice, and cash crops of temperate-climate vegetables such as potatoes, cabbages, carrots, and recently asparagus (Table 7.2). Maize and vegetables are grown throughout the year on *sawah* and during the eight or so wettest months of the year on the *tegalan*. In the wet season some rice is grown on *sawah*. Intricate intercropping and relay cropping are often used in which different crops are grown on the same field simultaneously or with some overlap in time. Many farmers also keep dairy cattle. Perennial gardens, usually

TABLE 7.2
Land Use in Pujon, 1983

Land Use	*Area (ha)*	*Percentage of Agricultural Land*	*Percentage of Total Land*
Irrigated land (*sawah*)	891	26	
Dry-cultivated land			
with annuals (*tegalan*)	1 754	50	
with perennials (*kebun*)	427	12	
House lots (*pekarangan*)	430	12	
Total agricultural land	3 499	100	29
State forest land	8 594	0	71
Total	12 093	100	

Source: KSM, *Kabupaten Malang dalam Angka, 1983.*

planted with coffee, are rare in Pujon. The *pekarangan* (house lots containing home gardens) are small. The limited number of trees on the *pekarangan* and on the *tegalan* is conspicuous.

The surrounding 'forest' land is largely denuded of natural forest and covered with exotic shrubs. Only on the higher slopes and less accessible sites can remnants of the natural forest be found. Some plantation forests, mainly of pines (*Pinus merkusii*) and *Agathis* species have been established on the lower slopes. Many of them show signs of human disturbance.

Changes in Agricultural Production

In Pujon there have been changes in cropping patterns and in livestock numbers and composition. The use of modern farm inputs has increased and a greater proportion of the produce is marketed.

The cultivation of vegetables (all of them cash crops) increased during the late 1960s and early 1970s in response to increasing demand, improved transport, and a more abundant and cheaper supply of fertilizers and pesticides. During the early 1980s, however, production declined (Figure 7.2), due partly to competition from other highland areas which depressed prices.[4] Farmers then turned their attention to dairy cattle.

Maize must have become an increasingly important staple in the area during the first half of the twentieth century. Its cultivation has remained fairly constant. Harvested areas on *tegalan* seem to be little affected by the fluctuations in vegetable cultivation, since maize can often be grown in conjunction with vegetables, using relay cropping. In 1983 about half the farmers in both Ngantang and Pujon used new, improved varieties of maize, the principal constraint being their cost (BPP Ngantang, 1983). Although new varieties give lower yields than in the lowlands, their use has led to an increase in yields from less than 1 tonne to about 1.7 tonnes of dry grain per hectare, which is about the average for Kabupaten Malang (MARIF, 1986: 20). This increased yield has been promoted by increased use of fertilizer, extension, and the Bimas (Bimbingan Massal or Mass Guidance) maize credit programme in which some farmers have participated.

Rice cultivation, on the other hand, has shown a steady decline since the late 1960s. The cooler climate renders the area unsuitable for growing high-yielding varieties (HYVs), which have been introduced successfully at lower altitudes. A longer growing period, higher soil permeability, the smaller and more fluctuating supply of irrigation water during the dry season, and the relatively low market value of rice all tend to discourage rice cultivation in favour of vegetable cultivation. Where still grown, rice is a subsistence crop and only traditional varieties are used.

Small but fairly constant amounts of tuber crops such as cassava, sweet potato, and edible canna are grown as additional food and fodder sources.[5] Growth of these crops for commercial use is very restricted.

FIGURE 7.2
Harvested Areas of Various Crops in Pujon, 1967–1986

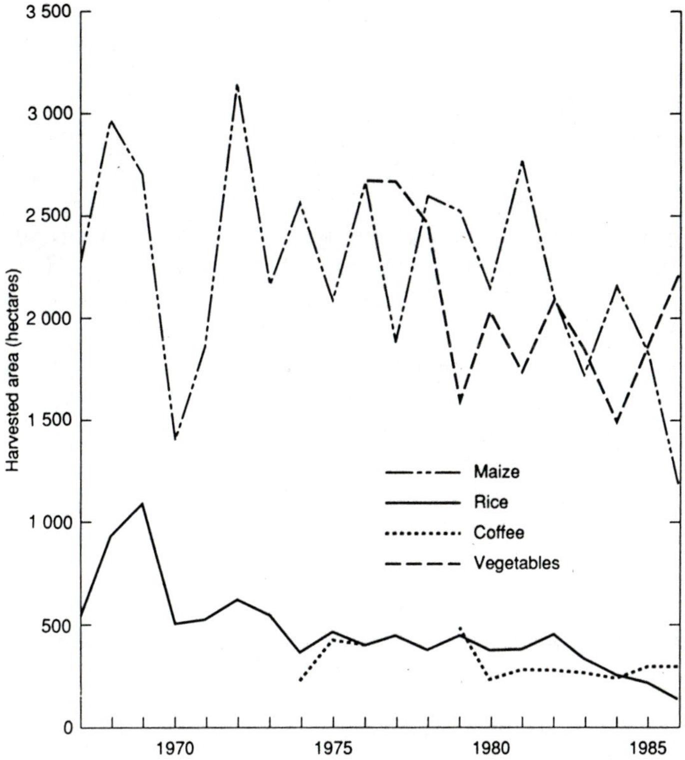

Soya beans and groundnuts, commonly grown in lower regions, are virtually absent. Coffee cultivation has not thrived as much as in Ngantang because varieties well suited to the high altitude were long unavailable and because vegetable and maize cultivation provide higher revenues and greater flexibility.[6] For cloves, coconut, and various fruit trees, the area is too cool.

Before 1978 livestock in Pujon comprised mainly chickens, goats, sheep, and traditional draught cattle, and few farmers engaged in dairy farming. Since then, under the stimulus of the national Dairy Cattle Development Project (Proyek Pengembangan Usaha Sapi Perah or PUSP), the number of dairy cattle has increased rapidly, from 2,646 in 1978 to 12,415 in 1986 (data from village administrations). The aims of the project were to save foreign exchange through self-sufficiency in animal protein foodstuffs, to increase farmers' incomes and create job opportunities. Friesian cattle were imported and allocated to farmers under various credit schemes. By 1982 the total number of dairy cattle in East Java was 58,107, of which 32 per cent were in Kabupaten Malang (KSJT, *Jawa Timur dalam Angka, 1982*), largely concentrated in Pujon and Batu. Competition for feed and labour caused the number of draught cattle in Pujon to decline dramatically from 1,049 in 1978 to 41 in 1986 (data from village administrations).

Vegetable Cultivation and Marketing

Vegetable cultivation puts great demands on farmers' resources and exposes them to considerable risks. The crops require much more labour and capital than do rice and maize. Seed, which has to be imported from abroad, is expensive, and crop management entails intensive fertilizer application and spraying of chemicals for crop protection. Increasing resistance of insects and other pathogens to chemicals is a common problem. Excessive and incorrect use of pesticides, due to lack of information, education, and the practice of manufacturers promoting the use of particular products, threatens the stability of cropping, as insects and pathogens become increasingly resistant.

Farmers have a choice of market channels. They can sell their crops to urban traders, to traders based at the local assembly markets, or to field traders who buy standing crops shortly before harvest time and harvest them themselves (*tebasan*). Farmers often deal with field traders to avoid problems with harvesting, transport, and finding a buyer, and as a safeguard against the risk of a crop perishing.

Although a number of traders of each type operate in the area, they often come together at the assembly market to fix a maximum price

FIGURE 7.3
Price Fluctuations from August 1982 to January 1983 for Several Commodities at the Assembly Market in Pujon

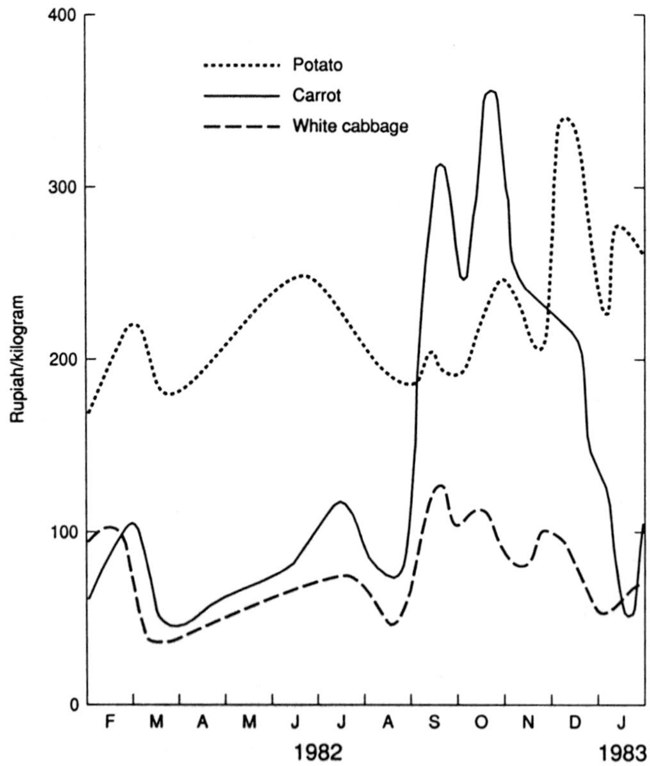

which none of them will exceed. The bargaining power of the farmers depends most of all upon the supply of vegetables at the provincial market in Surabaya. Fluctuations in supply occur largely with season, and local prices vary accordingly (Figure 7.3). Since neither farmers nor traders store any part of the crop, these seasonal fluctuations are not dampened. They are aggravated by a 'hog cycle' effect, whereby farmers tend to shift into whatever commanded high prices in the previous season.

Although the distance between the production area and the major market at Surabaya is only 100 kilometres, the market channel is usually quite long. Often five or six intermediaries are involved before the vegetables reach consumers in Surabaya. Consequently, marketing costs and the risk of damage between farmgate and consumer are high, which may depress farmgate prices (Hamim Washsulfallah et al., 1979: 23).

While there is no processing or canning of vegetable produce in the Upper Konto area, a cannery in Batu handles fruit and asparagus, and some of the latter may come from Pujon.

Dairy Farming

Since 1978, when the government's dairy cattle introduction schemes began, Pujon farmers have responded eagerly to the income-earning opportunity of dairy farming, but production is still constrained largely by the lack of high-quality feed.

Like other ruminants in the area, dairy cattle are stall-fed, using grass and leaves collected from fields, road verges, and the forest, as well as crop residues, primarily fresh maize stalks and leaves, which has given maize cultivation an important additional function. Farmers have also recently started to grow elephant grass (*Pennisetum purpureum*) on the edges of their home yards and *tegalan* and occasionally even in their *sawah* for use as cattle fodder. During the dry season when it is difficult to obtain fodder, imported maize stalks and leaves from the Pare–Kediri lowlands bring some relief.

No local fodder provides the levels of protein required by the dairy cattle (Netherlands Mission, 1982: Chapter 4). Most farmers give expensive supplements, mostly imported rice bran, but not enough to make up for protein deficiencies in the local fodder, and too little to achieve high milk yields. Consequently, lactation periods are short and milk yields are low. Low yields in turn prevent farmers from purchasing more fodder of high quality. Other factors contributing to low milk yields are lack of experience among farmers, inadequate extension and training activities, an infant veterinary service, and the prohibitive price of veterinary supplies.

Little milk is used for home consumption or finds its way to local retailers. Nearly the entire production is collected at the assembly plant of the Pujon dairy co-operative (Koperasi Sinau Andandani Ekonomi or KOPSAE), where it is pasteurized and forwarded to the Nestlé processing plants near Surabaya, and converted into dairy powder. The price paid to the Pujon dairy co-operative is established by the government and was in 1983 considerably higher than the cost price of recombined milk.[7] Farmers benefit from the artificially high prices, but at the cost of a slower growth in national milk consumption (Netherlands Mission, 1982: Chapter 3: 34–42; Remenyi, 1986). Dairy farming in the Upper Konto area therefore owes its profitability so far to the artificially high, regulated farmgate price, the use of family labour, low remuneration of hired labour, and free fodder collection.

Farming Strategies

Monetary returns for vegetable cultivation are considerably higher than those for the cultivation of staple crops (if sold) (Table 7.3). Receipts from cash crops also exceed the cost of purchasing food which the farmer cannot produce if he grows cash crops.

The decline in self-sufficiency resulting from the increase in vegetable cultivation and the decline in rice production have been offset partially by improved maize yields. The stability of maize cultivation suggests that security of food supply may still be a factor in crop choice. Furthermore, prices for vegetables are at times too low to warrant growing vegetables on *tegalan*, especially during the rainy season when the bulk of vegetables is harvested. Many farmers prefer to grow vegetables on their *sawah* during the dry season only. Many do not grow vegetables on their *tegalan* towards the end of the rainy season when rainfall is unreliable, and grow maize instead. Maize is inserted easily

TABLE 7.3
Estimates of Average Costs and Returns of Various Annual Crops in the Upper Konto Area, 1983 (Rp '000 per ha; US$1 = Rp 988)[a]

		Variable Costs			*Farmers' Income*	
	Cropping Days	*Material Inputs*	*Hired Labour*	*Total Revenue*	*Total*	*Per 100 Cropping Days*[b]
Rice	150	29	96	420	295	197
Maize	105	27	24	176	125	119
Cassava	300	18	44	225	163	54
Potatoes	90	362	99	1105	644	788
Cabbages	85	168	68	720	484	569
Carrots	90	47	59	400	294	327
Shallots	90	623	117	1375	635	706
Chillies	100	207	84	650	359	359
Coffee	365	24	87	780	669	183

Source: Adapted from Nibbering (1986).
[a]Averages for irrigated and dry-cultivated fields.
[b]Income is compared on the basis of 100 cropping days to account for different cropping periods.

into crop rotations before, after, or between two vegetable crops by way of intercropping or relay cropping. It is also an important source of fodder. The crop is often planted at high densities, a practice which does not favour optimal grain yields, but enables farmers to collect fodder from a number of thinnings.

Farming households can be differentiated by crop choice. The hamlet of Cukal provides an example of the differences in crop choice in Pujon (Figure 7.4). Farmers with small holdings tend to grow relatively more maize and fewer vegetables than those with larger holdings. Moreover, the vegetables grown by those with small holdings are usually the less risky ones requiring less capital, like carrots and French beans. On smaller holdings root crops tend to make up a larger proportion of total staple food production. Small farmers also tend to grow less rice. In Pujon the time required to grow a rice crop (five months) is long

FIGURE 7.4
Crop Combinations per Landholding Category in Cukal Hamlet, Pujon, 1986

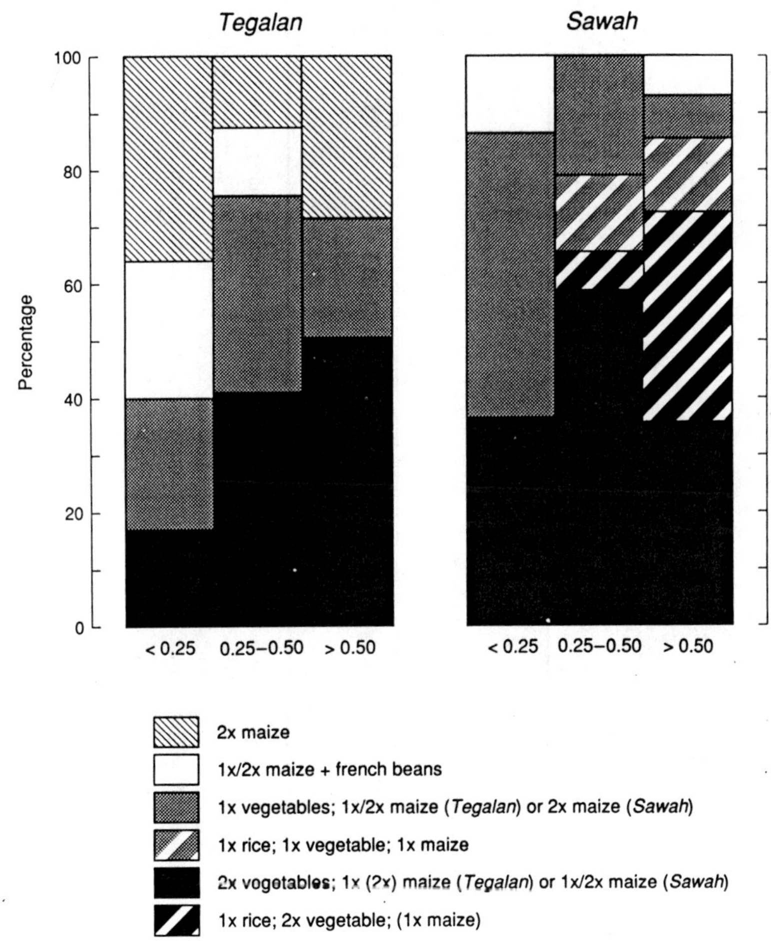

TABLE 7.4
Annual Staple Food Production for Different Landholding Size Categories, Cukal Hamlet, Pujon, 1986–1987

Landholding		*Rice* *(dry grain)*		*Maize* *(dry grain)*		*Casava*[a] *(peeled and dried)*[b]		*Total*	*Need*[c]
Size (ha)	*n*	*Kg*	*%*	*Kg*	*%*	*Kg*	*%*	*(kg)*	*(kg)*
> 0.5	15	410	20	1 513	75	104	5	2 027	901
0.26–0.5	29	90	13	489	71	14	17	693	816
< 0.25	37	–	–	364	81	86	19	450	731

Source: Computed from unpublished survey data collected by Munneke and Vorsterman van Oyen, 1986–7.

[a]Including small quantities of sweet potato and edible canna.

[b]Yields were recorded in fresh tubers. A 40% conversion rate has been applied. One kilogram of peeled and dried cassava has approximately the same calorific value as 1 kilogram of rice or maize.

[c]It has been assumed that one person requires 170 kilograms per annum.

enough to grow maize and a vegetable crop. Growing rice becomes a luxury small farmers can ill afford.

Households with large holdings (more than 0.5 hectares) in Cukal produce enough staple crop to be self-sufficient (Table 7.4). This is not the case with the smallest landholders. While these farmers sacrifice part of their potential food production to meet their need for cash, self-sufficiency in staple food would not be achievable anyway for most of them. Moreover, they often invest their small capital almost entirely in vegetables, neglecting their maize crop. An increase in maize yields would provide a greater food supply, allowing farmers to allocate less land to maize cultivation and more to cash crops.

Dairy farming began as an activity of farmers with large holdings, due to the in-built and operational biases in some cattle credit schemes,[8] and to the inability and unwillingness of small farmers to participate in formal credit schemes. Nevertheless, many small farmers and even some landless households have now obtained animals through purchase and sharing arrangements.

Dairy farming has proved much more profitable than raising traditional cattle. Breeding is even more lucrative. A three-year-old traditional cow in 1985 sold for Rp 300,000 while the market value of a productive dairy cow of the same age was at least Rp 600,000. Furthermore, revenue from milk adds substantially to farmers' incomes (Table 7.5). Even the supply of manure was increased by the shift to dairy cattle. Given the constraints on fodder and family labour, the considerable difference in income has enticed most farmers to replace traditional cattle, which were kept as a means of saving rather than a means of production, with dairy cattle.

The need to use draught cattle for tillage is relatively small, since tillage still requires a great deal of hand spading on the steep terraced

TABLE 7.5
Dairy Production and Income in Pujon: Results of a Survey among 41 Dairy Farmers, 1982 (US$1 = Rp 661)

Number of cattle per household	3.6
Number of adult cows	2.0
Calving interval	13.2 months
Milk yield	9.1 litres per lactating cow
Lactation period	7.4 months
Yield per lactation period	2 030 litres
Total cost	Rp 804 per day[a]
Gross income from milk production	Rp 2,116 per day[a]
Net income from milk production	Rp 1,312 per day[a]
Annual income from milk production	Rp 353,917
Total annual income	Rp 522,381

Source: Adapted from Krijnen (1982).
[a]For farms with at least one lactating animal; family labour and fodder not priced.

slopes. This is increasingly the case with the expansion of vegetable cultivation, for which beds must be made by hand. On *tegalan* much of the tillage activity takes place during the dry season when there are fewer other demands on labour. Thus an increasing number of farmers with small holdings may have found it not worthwhile to keep draught cattle.

Despite the profitability of dairy farming, there are numerous constraints on its development in the area. Limitations of fodder supply, family labour, and space cause low yields and prevent farmers from devoting more land and capital to dairying. Few farmers have more than three or four animals. Only a few large farmers have specialized in dairy husbandry, keeping stocks of 10 or more. The cost of hired labour for fodder collection and the cost and uncertain supply of high-quality feed would leave too small a profit margin. For large farmers, breeding has often proved more profitable.

Land, Capital, and Labour

There is little willingness and apparently little need for small farmers to part with their land. Accordingly, little land is rented in the area. In 1983 only 13 per cent of the landholdings in Pujon consisted wholly or partly of rented or sharecropped land (KSM, 1985). In adjacent Batu this figure was 40 per cent, due to the greater interest of urban investors in this more accessible area and to the greater number of non-agricultural employment opportunities.

Although capital is more readily available than it was in the 1960s, lack of it can still be a big constraint, especially for small farmers. Most of the capital used in agriculture in Pujon is generated by the farmers themselves from the sale of crops, livestock, wood, and fodder, and from wage labour. If money is borrowed at all, it is generally done within the hamlet (*dukuh*) community. In Pujon's most commercialized central part, more use is made of credit provided by the Indonesian People's Bank (Bank Rakyat Indonesia or BRI) and a few farmers borrow from outside moneylenders. Budiono (1981) suggests that the role of outside capital in crop cultivation has actually declined as outsiders have shifted to investments in dairy cattle placed with households in the area.

Most of the dairy cows, however, are owned by people living in the area, and the bulk of the increase in their numbers during the early years of the PUSP was financed through credit schemes.[9] The Pujon dairy co-operative is also an important source of credit since it provides its members with rice bran to supplement local fodder and the costs are subtracted from the monthly payments for milk delivered. Since the programme was stopped in 1983 breeding and market purchases have become the only ways of obtaining new stock.

The family provides most of the labour for crop cultivation (Table 7.6). Hired labour is used more for commercial crops, made affordable by the cash flow generated by these crops. Vegetables absorb more hired labour per hectare per cropping time than staple crops, particularly maize. The expansion of vegetable cultivation must have led

TABLE 7.6
Family Labour and Hired Labour for Various Crops in the Upper Konto Area, 1986–1987

Crop	*Total Labour Input (labour days per ha)*	*Family Labour (%)*	*Hired Labour (%)*	*Hired Labour per 100 Cropping Days per Ha*
Rice	320	69	31	66
Maize	180	83	17	29
Cassava	174	72	28	16
Potato	305	67	33	111
Cabbage	250	76	24	71
Carrot	250	70	30	83
Shallots	330	50	50	183
Chillies	310	71	29	50
Coffee	290	66	34	27

Sources: de Graaff and Kusrianto (1987); Nibbering (1986).

not only to more labour being used in crop cultivation, but also to an increase in the use of hired labour. Small farmers use hired labour as well; for instance, when tasks have to be performed quickly. Small farmers may find it cost-effective to hire labour to work on their own land while they themselves work elsewhere for wages. They may also be obliged to work for farmers who employ them regularly, and then have to hire labour to work on their own land. Since many activities in vegetable cultivation involve female labour, opportunities for off-farm agricultural labour for women have probably improved as well, despite the decline in rice cultivation in Pujon which traditionally involved female labour.

Dairy farming is also essentially a family affair. In 1982 family labour made up three-quarters of total labour input (Krijnen, 1982). If a household has several animals, fodder collecting is often done by contracted labour. Fodder collectors enter into an agreement with cattle owners to provide one *pikul* (shoulder-load) of fodder every day during one year. Payments are made in advance and varied between Rp 40,000 and Rp 70,000 in 1985. Outside labour is sometimes also used for tending cattle, usually on a profit-sharing basis or in return for the offspring of the animals tended. Large farmers may have permanent young male workers living with them (*ngenger*), often from outside the area. They look after the cattle and have various other tasks. They may eventually be rewarded with a cow. All these arrangements were practised with traditional livestock and have expanded to solve the labour (fodder collecting) constraints in dairy farming. The *ngenger* institution, however, seems to have become eroded, since cattle owners in Pujon are no longer willing to pay for their workers' circumcision or marriage expenses.

The rapid decline in draught cattle has accelerated the decline of rice cultivation which requires draught cattle for intensive puddling of the soil. A group of farmers in the central, flatter part of Pujon has adopted the use of a hand tractor which they operate collectively. In general, however, the land is tilled entirely with human labour. The steep terrain, the small holdings, the aversion to collective efforts for which Pujon farmers are known, and perhaps also social unacceptability may all have militated against mechanized land preparation.

Non-agricultural Activities and Migration

In 1983 the proportion of households in Pujon engaged in non-agricultural activities as a primary or secondary source of income was estimated at 14 per cent (*dukuh* administrations).[10] As in other upper-slope highlands in Java (Hefner, 1983; Palte, 1981: 39), non-agricultural activities play only a modest role in livelihood strategies compared to other rural areas in Java, where employment and income from non-agricultural activities may even surpass those from agricultural activities (Nibbering and Schrevel, 1982: 37–8; Rietveld, 1986). Agriculture and animal husbandry still absorb the larger part of the population in Pujon. Recent trends have reinforced this pattern. Location, natural resources, and types of crops grown offer little scope for handicrafts or cottage industries to develop.

Most non-agricultural activities are conducted by landless households or small farmers, usually in addition to agricultural work. One source of non-agricultural income is the forest, through the sale of wood and fodder to fellow villagers or at the market, although increasing employment opportunities in vegetable cultivation and dairy farming have drawn people away from these activities. Households with little or no land may still face periods of underemployment and turn to the forest for additional income, meeting an increased demand for fodder and also for wood for cooking rice bran for dairy cattle (Munneke and Vorsterman van Oyen, 1987: 54). Employment in regular forestry is small: reforestation schemes provide food, income, and employment only on a temporary basis.[11]

The second group of non-agricultural activities—construction, brickyard labour, bamboo weaving, carpentry, repairs, retailing, and some food processing—serves primarily local needs. These involved on average 14 people in each *dukuh*, and 41 people in the central *dukuh* of each village in 1983 (estimates from *dukuh* administrations). On the whole, earnings from these activities were higher than wages earned in land labour. The main constraint on their further development is demand. Shops, repair workshops, and other services in the central villages have shown some growth, partly in response to higher income levels in the area, but not much change has been recorded in the other villages.

Few production linkages exist between the non-agricultural sector and agriculture. Processing of agricultural products is minimal, with most of the produce being transported to the regional or provincial centre. Some bamboo weaving occurs in Pujon to meet the demand for packaging material for vegetables. Backward linkages in the community are also minimal: virtually all inputs for agriculture are generated at the farm (labour, manure), derived from the forest (wood, fodder) or imported (fertilizer, crop chemicals). The increase in marketable produce has led to a growth in trade and transport in the area, but it involves mostly people from outside the area.

There is also little commuting or other circular migration out of Pujon. Instead, many workers, especially men, come into the area to work as farm labourers, mostly from Ngantang but also from the poorer *kabupaten* to the south-west (for example, Blitar). Most of them work in the most commercialized central and eastern villages, where wage levels are highest. The 1980 Population Census showed for the age-group 25–49 a male : female ratio of 1.02, supporting the observation regarding male labour in-migration. Recent growth, birth, and death rates suggest a net in-migration.

TABLE 7.7
Annual Income and Productivity by Farm Size in the Chief Hamlet of Ngabab Village, Pujon, 1986 (US$1 = Rp 1,121)

	Income				
Mean Farm Size[a] (ha)	*Cropping (%)*	*Livestock (%)*	*Outside Farm (%)*	*Total (Rp '000)*	*Family Size*
0.91	70	23	8	1,429	4.4
0.52	41	40	18	1,068	5.2
0.27	36	40	24	707	4.4
0.03	6	3	91	435	2.4
Total 0.43	47	29	24	920	4.1

	Family Labour Product (Rp per labour day)				
Mean Farm Size (ha)	*Cropping*	*Livestock*	*Outside Farm*	*Total*	*Land Productivity[b] (Rp '000 per ha)*
0.91	2,274	2,439	2,707	2,339	1,095
0.52	2,123	2,445	955	1,823	865
0.27	1,710	2,419	879	1,537	982
0.03	1,555	1,091	1,097	1,118	933
Total	2,111	2,409	918	1,776	1,012

Source: Adapted from de Graaff and Kusrianto (1987).

[a]Data were derived from an agro-economic survey held among 20 households. Each class represents 25% of the sample.

[b]Crops only: fodder, firewood, and livestock production not included.

Income and Productivity

Income and productivity levels in Pujon in 1986 are illustrated in Table 7.7. In all farm-size categories incomes were above the poverty line as defined by Sajogyo (1977).[12] The income of most households has increased since the early to mid-1970s, but large inequalities continue to exist.

Crop cultivation was still the primary source of income for households with large holdings, but for those with smaller holdings animal husbandry, mainly dairy cattle, had become equally important. The category of largely landless households depended almost entirely on off-farm employment. Labour productivity in crop cultivation declined with landholding size, demonstrating, among other factors, small farmers' lack of capital, which prevents them from using sufficient capital inputs and from cultivating more lucrative crops. Labour productivity in animal husbandry was quite high, underlining its significance for small farmers. Labour productivity in activities outside one's own farm was lowest, except for farmers with the largest holdings, some of whom were engaged in trading. Although the number of family workers and labour input per family worker differed from one category to another, the income levels obtained largely reflected the land and capital resources available.

Thus, in Pujon, the expansion of vegetable cultivation for cash crops and the boom in the dairy industry, both activities for which the area is particularly well suited, have boosted income and employment conditions.

Developments in Ngantang

The Setting

Ngantang had a population of 49,000 in 1985. Its agricultural land is at an altitude ranging between 620 and 800 metres. The average temperature varies between 22 and 23 °C, depending on the altitude, and the mean annual rainfall is 2 600 millimetres, exceeding the rainfall in Pujon, although dry-season rainfall is fairly similar. Soils are more leached and less permeable, but still fertile.

Although the proportion of irrigated land is almost the same as in Pujon (Table 7.8), the water supply in the lower part of Ngantang is more abundant during the dry season because water can be tapped from the Konto River and other streams. Virtually all *sawah* here are planted with rice during the rainy season. In the dry season the area under rice is smaller and varies from year to year, depending on water supply. When water is insufficient, *palawija* crops (non-rice food crops) such as maize, shallots, and chillies are grown, or the fields are left fallow. The *tegalan* are generally cropped with maize, and shallots and tobacco are grown in suitable spots. The area under cassava, groundnuts, and soya beans is slightly larger than in Pujon, but the cultivation of these crops has

TABLE 7.8
Land Use in Ngantang, 1983

	Area (ha)	*Percentage of Agricultural Land*	*Percentage of Total Land*
Irrigated land (*sawah*)	1 138	28	–
Dry-cultivated land			
with annuals (*tegalan*)	1 216	30	–
with perennials (*kebun*)	10 172	12	–
Home lots (*pekarangan*)	680	14	–
Total agricultural land	4 051	100	27
Other[a]	399	–	3
State forest land	10 818	–	71
Total	15 194	–	101

Source: KSM, *Kabupaten Malang dalam Angka, 1983.*
[a]Selorejo reservoir, dam site, and hydroelectric plant.

declined. The area under temperate-climate vegetables is limited. Nearly half the dry-cultivated land, however, consists of perennial gardens planted largely with coffee, but also with cloves and various fruit trees. The *pekarangan* are larger than in Pujon and a variety of tree crops is grown, such as bananas, coconuts, citrus, coffee, and cloves, in combination with various annual food crops and condiments. Livestock is mostly draught cattle and goats. The State forest land is largely covered with exotic shrubs, as in Pujon. Forest plantations in Ngantang consist mainly of *Agathis* and mahogany.

Changes in Agricultural Production

Despite fluctuations, rice cultivation in Ngantang has retained its importance (Figure 7.5). Many Ngantang farmers participated in the national Bimas credit programme until it ended in 1985, and adopted HYVs developed by the International Rice Research Institute (IRRI) in Los Baños. Although performing much better than in Pujon, yields from these HYVs have not reached the same levels as in the lowlands. Around 1980 many farmers still grew HYVs because they were more resistant than local varieties to the brown planthopper which had infested rice crops throughout Java in previous years (see Chapter 6). When brown planthopper attacks subsided, many farmers shifted back to local varieties, since IRRI varieties provided disappointing yields. Although local varieties have longer growing periods than HYVs, they require less inputs, people prefer their taste, and they fetch higher prices. By 1983 only 40 per cent of rice-growing farmers still used HYVs, largely the more attractive national HYVs such as Cisadane and Krueng Aceh. In the mid-1980s yields varied between 2.5 and 4 tonnes of dry grain per

FIGURE 7.5
Harvested Areas of Various Crops in Ngantang, 1967–1986

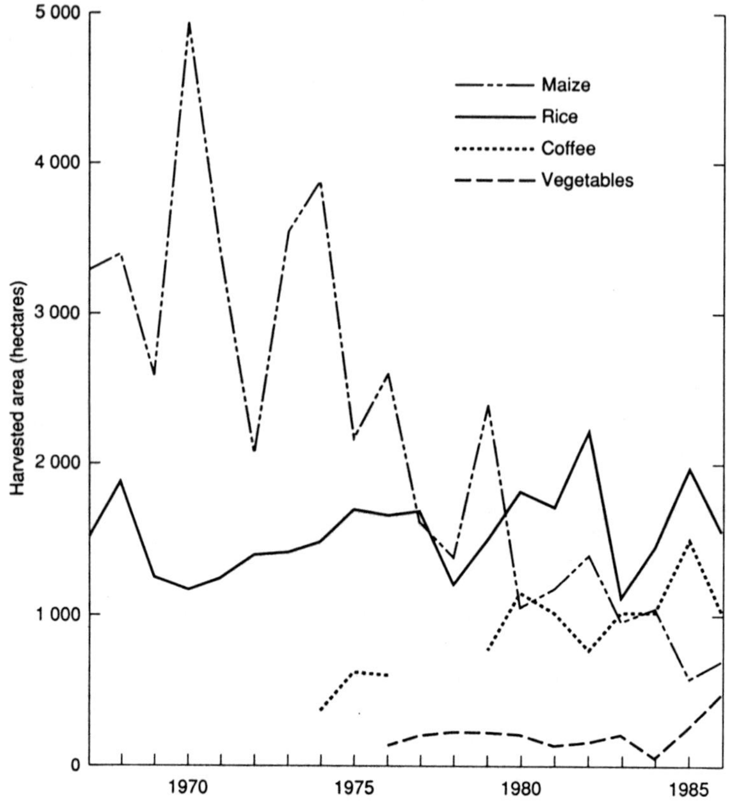

hectare. Increased yields raised production considerably, and the crop has now assumed an important commercial role in the local economy.

The cultivation of maize—essentially a subsistence crop, as in Pujon—has declined drastically. Frequently recurring natural hazards such as droughts, excessive rainfall, strong winds causing lodging, and damage inflicted by forest animals have long affected yields. Yields were also said to be decreasing due to declining soil fertility. Annual cash crops such as shallots and tobacco have replaced maize in some locations. The main change, however, has been the conversion of *tegalan* into coffee gardens.

Smallholder coffee cultivation took off in the 1970s. Rising real prices after 1968 (McStocker, 1987) and a coffee boom from 1976 to 1979 prompted the rapid expansion of the area planted with coffee across Indonesia (de Graaff, 1986: 279). In East Java, the area under smallholder coffee increased from 23 000 hectares in 1970 to 31 000 hectares in 1978 and to 39 000 hectares by 1982 (McStocker, 1987; KSJT, *Jawa Timur dalam Angka, 1982*). Coffee planting, fostered by the prospect of high income, was partly spontaneous and partly stimulated by government programmes, some offering the added incentive of certification of land title. Coffee yields in 1984 were about 400 kilograms per hectare of dry beans annually, the average for Kabupaten Malang (KSM, *Kabupaten Malang dalam Angka, 1983*).

Cloves are also grown in the area, but they have not become as important as coffee due to a high incidence of disease, a longer initial unproductive period, and higher costs. In 1986 a total area of 200 hectares was estimated to be under cloves in Ngantang (KSM, *Kabupaten Malang dalam Angka, 1986*), much of it in *pekarangan*.

Dairy husbandry, with Friesian cows, is now also promoted in Ngantang. The higher temperatures in this area are likely to restrict milk yields, since the breeds used are not well adapted to the high temperatures and humid conditions that prevail in low altitude regions in South-East Asia. As a result, milk yields are well below those in more temperate climates. Achieving worthwhile milk yields seems to require restricting the industry to altitudes above 1 000 metres (Remenyi, 1986).

Coffee Cultivation and Marketing

Ngantang farmers have specialized in coffee cultivation, in contrast to farmers with perennial gardens in other areas in Java, which usually have a mixed composition (Palte, 1984: 49). Ngantang farmers thereby expose themselves to greater risks. These risks are different from those involved in vegetable cultivation. Although capital requirements are lower and can be spread over a longer period if planting or rejuvenation is carried out gradually, farmers lose flexibility. They cannot easily revert to staple crops or other annuals if disease or low market prices affect them. They also have to forgo income during the initial unproductive stage. Theft during the much longer harvest season also becomes a risk, often forcing farmers to pick the coffee berries prematurely.

Harvesting is generally carried out by the farmers themselves and not by traders. Most of the coffee is sold depulped and dried, a way of adding value. A few households dehusk coffee by pounding the berries in a mortar. But the processing of coffee in the area is gradually being refined. Village co-operatives (*koperasi unit desa* or KUD) have begun operating depulping and hulling machines. Some farmers' groups have adopted the collective use of hulling machines. A very few large farmers own their own machines. They obtain even better prices since they can offer enough dehusked coffee to bypass local traders. The quality of coffee which is dehusked by machine is superior to pounded coffee and losses are less, again adding to the price (de Graaff and Kusrianto, 1987: 40–2). However, there are no facilities for further processing such as roasting.

Local prices closely follow trends on the world market (McStocker, 1987) but are also affected by regional fluctuations. These movements, however, are not as swift and erratic as for vegetables. Few farmers store their coffee to await better prices, for they lack the necessary storage facilities and need the money.

Farming Strategies

As in Pujon the shift from maize to cash crops has enabled farmers to purchase the same amount of food as they previously produced themselves and still leave a cash surplus. Nevertheless, farmers still keep part of their rice harvest for their own needs rather than buying rice later at much higher prices. The decrease in subsistence production resulting from the decline in maize cultivation has been partly offset by higher rice yields.

Coffee cultivation appears to be more within the reach of farmers with large holdings, particularly if they have access to some irrigated land on which they can produce food for themselves. Yet many small farmers have also planted coffee. Some farmers took to coffee cultivation because their maize-cropped *tegalan* became enclaves surrounded by new coffee gardens, and increasingly suffered from too much shade and marauding animals from the nearby forest.

Land, Capital, and Labour

Renting and sharecropping occur more often in Ngantang than in Pujon. Twenty-two per cent of the holdings involved rented or sharecropped land. This equals the average for the entire *kabupaten* (KSM, 1985). There is little capital from outside the area in agriculture or animal husbandry. Part of the capital invested may have been acquired by local inhabitants who have temporarily worked elsewhere. Ngantang farmers have enjoyed more support from the government than those in Pujon, through the Bimas rice programme and coffee rejuvenation and rehabilitation programmes executed by the Service for Estate Crops (Dinas Perkebunan or Disbun) which is particularly active in Ngantang.

The new technology for rice cultivation which has transformed labour organization in the lowlands has not been adopted widely in this area. Contrary to the practice in the lowlands, female labour has remained predominant in harvesting local varieties, which are still harvested with the traditional *ani-ani* (rice knife). Only when HYVs are harvested with sickles, as in the lowlands, do men participate. The traditional *bawon* system, which entitles harvesters to a portion of the rice, is still common, although no longer is everyone free to join in. Pre-harvest selling (*tebasan*) of rice does not occur. Farmers harvest their rice themselves and keep a large proportion for household consumption. Surplus rice is sold to retailers, assembly traders, the KUD, or private huller operators. In maize cultivation, mutual help and remuneration-in-kind for harvesters (usually relatives or neighbours) are still common practices involving both sexes.

Coffee cultivation does not require much wage labour. Harvesters are often paid in kind on the basis of their picking share, but access to harvest work is often more restricted than in maize cultivation (Schmit,

1981: 131). Both men and women participate in coffee picking. Contract labour for preparing land for coffee gardens is a new activity in the area.

Change in labour relations in Ngantang has therefore been minimal. Nor have employment opportunities in agriculture and animal husbandry for landless households or small farmers been as numerous as in Pujon.

Non-agricultural Activities and Migration

The proportion of households engaged in non-agricultural activities in 1983 was estimated at 20 per cent (*dukuh* administrations). Non-agricultural activities therefore appear to be more important than in Pujon. This may be a result partly of lower labour absorption in agriculture, but perhaps also of more marketing opportunities. Whereas Pujon has only one market centre, Ngantang has three. The number of people engaged in crafts, repair, and cottage industries (1,314) is larger than in Pujon (433). Food processing, tile-making, and brick-making are the most prominent cottage industries in Ngantang. However, as in Pujon, direct linkages with local agriculture are minimal.

The Selorejo dam has provided opportunities for non-agricultural employment. Its construction occupied many local people who, after its completion in 1970, continued to perform construction work outside the area. The area around the dam was developed as a tourist attraction and has created some local employment. About 50 households are engaged in part-time fishing.

Fodder and firewood collection offers less employment than in Pujon

TABLE 7.9
Demographic Data on the Population of the Konto Area, Kecamatan Batu, and Kabupaten Malang

	Ngantang	*Pujon*	*Batu*	*Malang*[a]
Annual growth				
1920–30	1.5	1.8	1.2	2.3
1930–61	0.9	1.6	1.5	0.8[c]
1961–71	2.1	1.7	2.7	1.9
1971–80	0.4	1.9	2.8	1.6
Net migration balance[b]				
1980–4	−0.76	0.51	0.34	−0.16
Sex ratio				
1980	0.98	1.01	0.98	0.97

Sources: CKS (1922, 1933–6); Universitas Gadjah Mada and BPS (1980); BPS (1983a); KSM, *Kabupaten Malang dalam Angka, 1984.*
[a]Capital of the *kabupaten* excluded.
[b]Annual increment = birth – death rate.
[c]Low increase due to annexation by the municipality of Malang town.

because of lower demand. There are fewer cattle in Ngantang, and fodder intake per cow for traditional cattle is smaller than for dairy cattle. A large amount of firewood is obtained from prunings of coffee and shade trees in the perennial gardens.

Many young men and women work outside the area. The largest number of these work in nearby Batu as factory workers, land labourers, domestic servants, shop assistants, and construction workers. A smaller number work in Malang and Surabaya in similar activities. A few young men are employed in Pujon as land and cattle labourers. Educational levels are higher in Ngantang than in Pujon, giving rise to aspirations for jobs with the government and business. In 1983 Ngantang had four junior and two senior secondary schools, whereas Pujon had only two junior secondary schools.

Population growth has been low in recent years (Table 7.9), largely due to out-migration which was boosted by the completion of the Selorejo dam. However, low population growth in Ngantang has probably been a much older trend, since it had already been low before the large influx of people when the Selorejo dam and its associated hydroelectric plant were built. Population growth in Pujon has been higher.

Income and Productivity

Income and productivity levels which might be considered typical of Ngantang are given in Table 7.10. In 1986 the two smallest farm-size categories had incomes around Sajogyo's (1977) poverty line. Inequalities between the various categories were larger than in Ngabab village in Pujon. Crop cultivation was the largest source of income for all but the lowest landholding category. For the intermediate categories traditional animal husbandry did not contribute to incomes to the extent that dairying did in Pujon.

As in Pujon, labour productivity in crop cultivation tended to decrease with landholding. This was also true of animal husbandry, for small farmers commonly raised goats, while large farmers raised cattle. For all farm-size categories labour productivity was lowest in off-farm activities. As in Pujon, income levels largely reflected the land and capital resources available. On average, productivity of labour and land were lower than in Ngabab village in Pujon.

Developments in Ngantang are also characterized by increasing productivity and commercialization of agriculture, although involving different products from those in Pujon. Increases in income and employment and changes in labour organization do not seem to have been as great as in Pujon. The construction of the Selorejo dam has had a significant impact on employment and migration patterns in Ngantang.

TABLE 7.10
Annual Income and Productivity by Farm Size, Gagar Hamlet of Tulungrejo Village, Kecamatan Ngantang, 1986 (US$1 = Rp 1,121)

	Income				
Mean Farm Size[a] (ha)	*Cropping (%)*	*Livestock (%)*	*Outside Farm (%)*	*Total (Rp '000)*	*Family Size*
1.40	74	25	1	1,562	4.4
0.59	57	29	15	792	5.6
0.28	56	14	31	394	5.8
0.10	19	14	67	327	4.8
Total 0.59	61	23	15	769	5.2

	Family Labour Productivity (Rp per labour day)				
Mean Farm Size (ha)	*Cropping*	*Livestock*	*Outside Farm*	*Total*	*Land Productivity[b] (Rp '000 per ha)*
1.40	2,445	2,450	615	2,374	824
0.59	1,764	2,152	991	1,657	759
0.28	2,018	675	612	1,023	785
0.10	1,319	958	676	781	620
Total	2,131	1,837	711	1,586	798

Source: Adapted from de Graaff and Kusrianto (1987).
[a]Data were derived from an agro-economic survey held among 20 households. Each class represents 25% of the sample.
[b]Crops only: fodder, firewood, and livestock production not included.

Environmental Effects

Highland environments are highly vulnerable. Certain forms of land use may not only be detrimental to the users themselves, but also have far-reaching effects on soil and forest cover, on water supply and river regimes, and thereby on economic development in the lowlands.

The forest has long been a source of timber, firewood, fodder, and other products for the local population. As landholdings become smaller and the number of landless people increases, dependence on the forest is becoming greater. With agricultural land being devoted to the cultivation of food and cash crops, little is left for the production of less valuable but essential products such as wood and fodder, which are available in the nearby forest. Home gardens, which in the lowlands are an important source of wood and fodder, are small in the highlands, and the few farmers who have room to grow wood and fodder often prefer to use all their land for annual cropping and to buy firewood and fodder. For many poorer households, commercial wood collection is still an important supplementary source of income, and large amounts of firewood and fodder are still collected for people's own needs. The very presence of the forest contributes to the viability of smallholdings. Increased production of vegetables and particularly the development of dairying have increased pressure on the forest's resources.

There is no proper management system in which the population bears responsibility for the forest or has some controlled share in its benefits. As a consequence, the forest is illegally exploited, people seizing what they require with no regard for sustainability or the interests of Perum Perhutani. Massive forest degradation and failing forest plantations have been the result. Vast stretches of forest land have been turned into mere shrubland which now covers 41 per cent of the total forest area. Most of the remaining natural forest (36 per cent of the area) has become degraded (RIN, 1984).

The forest land has a number of specific national and regional functions: securing the hydrological balance, producing timber and other tree products, generating revenue for the State treasury, and promoting local development through the provision of employment, food, wood, and fodder. The absence of proper management and the ensuing forest degradation prevent the forest area from fulfilling these functions adequately (KRP, 1985).[13]

Perum Perhutani has become increasingly aware of the environmental problems in the forest and their causes. A special plan for the area has been devised and a series of experiments involving reforestation by means of agro-forestry systems has been initiated. The population will be involved for much longer periods than in previous reforestation schemes. People will be permitted to grow perennial crops, fuel wood, and fodder for their own needs, in combination with commercial trees for which they will also be responsible. Simultaneously, measures will be taken to increase the productivity of the people's own land.

Terracing has long been practised in the Upper Konto area to facilitate cultivation and rainfall interception (Schuitemaker, 1949). While naturally permeable, soil on the terraces becomes susceptible to erosion following the formation of less permeable hardpans after continuous cultivation (Unibraw, 1984: 123). Cultivation reduces the capacity of the soil to intercept rainfall during heavy rainstorms, leading to excess water and, consequently, run-off. The erosive capacity of run-off depends partly on the slope of the terrace, which is often considerable. Erosion generally starts as rill erosion (characterized by long ripples on the soil surface). The rills are removed by tillage, but reappear and eventually result in deterioration of the terraces, which become irregular and sloping. In this condition, instead of conserving water, they tend to channel run-off and encourage the formation of new rills (Unibraw, 1984: 123–4).

Another common practice which encourages rill erosion is the construction of outward-sloping terraces with beds running parallel to the slope direction and without edge ridges to prevent water from running over the edges. This practice has become more pronounced with the increased cultivation of potatoes and shallots, which are highly sensitive to moisture in the soil. Although farmers are aware of the erosion this may cause, they continue the practice to avoid waterlogging and consequent landslides. Adequate drainage can be encouraged by the correct construction of terraces, and of an adequate drainage system to receive the water after it has left the terrace. There are no such drainage systems in the Upper Konto area. The enormous pressure to leave no land unused has led to near-vertical risers and the virtual absence of regular drainage ditches. As a result, run-off is uncontrolled and, where the slopes are long enough, gully erosion occurs. Large gullies have developed, especially in Ngantang where soils are less permeable (Zonneveld, 1988: 4). Most farmers seem unconcerned about soil erosion, given the depth of fertile soil. However, there have also been some developments which tend to hold back erosion. These include the creation of permanent vegetation cover in coffee gardens, the cultivation of grass for fodder on terrace risers, and increased intercropping and relay cropping of maize and vegetables.

In 1970 the construction of the Selorejo dam was completed and a reservoir formed with a capacity of 50 million cubic metres. Its main functions are flood and sedimentation control downstream. The reservoir also supplies irrigation water downstream to an estimated total area of 5 700 hectares (de Graaff and Kusrianto, 1987: 84). A hydroelectric power station with a capacity of 4 500 kilowatts was also built (KRP, 1985: Vol. III, 66). Siltation of the reservoir, caused by erosion, exceeds predicted levels and threatens to shorten its life, thereby jeopardizing its multipurpose functions (Fish, 1983; KRP, 1985: Vol. IV, 37).[14]

Conclusion

Development in the two subzones of the Upper Konto has followed different paths due to the different agro-ecological conditions, determined largely by climate and geomorphology. In the higher and cooler part of the area, Pujon, development has been carried by an increase in the cultivation of temperate-climate vegetables and the expansion of dairy farming. In Ngantang, where temperatures are higher and water supply is more abundant, development has taken the form of the intensification of rice cultivation and the expansion of coffee cultivation. Only Ngantang has benefited at all from the Green Revolution in rice cultivation.

Unlike in the lowlands, intensification of what were the traditional subsistence crops, maize and rice, has been limited. More importantly, farmers have taken up forms of commercial production in which the highlands have a comparative advantage. Among them, dairy husbandry and coffee cultivation have received government support.

Farm activities have become more diverse, reflecting the complementary nature of many farm activities and the variety of resources available, but also the lack of capital and the need to spread risk. Although farming has become more commercialized, subsistence production has not disappeared. Specialization has therefore seldom occurred and tension exists between the various activities as to the use of scarce resources, causing the relative underdevelopment of one activity in favour of another, not necessarily in the most economically beneficial way. This is felt most by small farmers who have the least resources. Small farmers are in a sense more commercialized than large farmers, since they sacrifice self-sufficiency in food to earn much needed cash income, whereas large farmers can produce cash crops while retaining self-sufficiency. The cultivation of cash crops has increased farm incomes, but income disparities have probably widened. A notable exception is dairy farming in Pujon, since it appears to contribute proportionally more to the income of small farmers than it does to that of farmers with larger holdings.

In Pujon the increased demand for labour in agriculture and especially in dairying has led to more opportunities for wage labour. In Ngantang the growth in labour demand seems to have been much lower. Nevertheless, even in Pujon landless households or small farmers may still experience periods of underemployment. Selling wood collected in the forest has remained a supplementary activity.

Incomes in the Upper Konto area compare very favourably with average incomes in East Java. In 1982 income per capita was estimated at Rp 189,000 in Ngantang and Rp 187,000 in Pujon (KSM, *Kabupaten Malang dalam Angka, 1983*). In East Java it was Rp 98,977 (KSJT, *Jawa Timur dalam Angka, 1982*). Higher productivity in Pujon apparently makes up for its smaller landholdings.

Diversification has been confined to the agricultural sector. There are almost no forward or backward linkages between agriculture and other sectors in the area. Most processing of agricultural products takes place outside the area. The general rise in income seems to have had little effect on the demand for local non-agricultural goods and services, because of a preference for urban-based products. Thus there has been no transformation of the local economy away from agriculture.

In a number of ways the developments in Ngantang and Pujon have differed as a result of their varying potential. The predominance of very small landholdings in Pujon attests to the viability of labour-intensive, high-value horticultural activities on fertile soil and animal husbandry with fodder resources near at hand. Non-agricultural activities, such as cottage industries and small-scale trade, prominent in many lowland areas, are rarely seen in Pujon. In Ngantang, soils are less fertile and more susceptible to erosion. Accordingly, population densities are lower and average landholdings are larger but less evenly distributed. Employment opportunities for farm labourers are fewer in Ngantang, which may account for both the larger number of people involved in non-agricultural activities and the higher levels of out-migration. Ngantang therefore takes an intermediate position between the lowlands and the higher uplands with regard to crops, landownership, and occupational structure. However, the differences between the two *kecamatan* cannot be explained only in terms of labour absorption capacities. The Selorejo dam and reservoir and probably also the higher education levels in Ngantang have had a major impact on people's livelihoods in stimulating circular migration.

Development has also brought problems, some of which already impose constraints on production and may undermine the sustainability of development. In vegetable cultivation, excessive and incorrect use of pesticides threatens the stability of cropping. Prospects for future exports seem low, since vegetables contain unacceptable levels of toxic chemicals. The uncertainties involved in vegetable marketing are also not easily overcome, but might be reduced if the losses encountered in handling and transportation could be reduced and price prediction systems developed.

The precarious food supply in the dairy industry is another serious limitation on sound development. Fodder and firewood supplies are derived largely from the forest, causing degradation and hampering regrowth. The quality of fodder is an even greater problem. High-protein feed is rarely available locally and expensive feeds have to be imported. The government has initiated the expansion of dairying in the area and has protected it by price regulations. It will have to continue to do so or else farmers will find it even harder to provide their animals with sufficient protein-rich feed for milk production. Dairy husbandry in Ngantang is not likely to thrive, since the higher temperatures there can be expected to constrain milk yields, and this will add to the difficulties of setting up a sustainable dairy industry.

In coffee cultivation it is the uncertainties of the world market which may disrupt the local economy; the more so the greater the local specialization. Farmers could overcome slumps on the world market more successfully if they were better equipped to cope with local fluctuations. Investing in depulping and hulling equipment to add value to the produce and rejuvenating old gardens earlier are two ways in which this could be done. Capital is still a tremendous brake on development, especially for small farmers.

Environmental problems are also becoming more pressing. Rapid siltation of the Selorejo reservoir is occurring as a result of the intensive cropping systems which are used in the area, often without adequate soil conservation, although the land users themselves are probably not yet much affected. Forest management has until recently paid insufficient attention to the needs of the population and has done little to promote a sense of responsibility for the forest. Rapid degradation has been the result, disturbing the hydrological balance and causing loss of revenue for Perum Perhutani and reduced potential for sustainable local development. The degradation may eventually affect the adjacent lowlands, which have to bear the costs of flooding during the rainy season and will suffer from lack of water during the dry season. This will affect agricultural, industrial, and domestic water use as well as the generation of electricity. A balanced development of East Java's highlands is a prerequisite for the sustained development of its lowlands.

1. The Agricultural Service of East Java defines 'highland' as land at an altitude of over 500 metres (Diperta, 1980: 1-2).

2. The data used for this chapter have been derived from a number of secondary sources as well as from surveys conducted in the area between 1980 and 1988 in the framework of the Proyek Kali Konto (Konto River Project (KRP), ATA 206), a development co-operative project set up by the Indonesian and Netherlands governments to develop a model for watershed management.

3. For a historical account and a discussion of developments in forest land use in the Upper Konto area, see Nibbering (1988).

4. The main competing area is the Tengger mountain complex, east of Malang (Figure 7.1). Improved accessibility since the late 1970s has caused vegetable cultivation there to increase markedly. Yields are much higher for potato and white cabbage, the major crops in Pujon which declined most during the period (Diperta, 1983).

5. Because of their supplementary role and long growing period they are usually planted on the edges of fields and terraces or in home gardens.

6. After the last decades of the nineteenth century, when the coffee leaf disease attacked coffee plantations in Java, *arabica* coffee varieties well suited to high altitudes were almost entirely replaced by *robusta* varieties. Only very recently have improved *arabica* varieties become readily available.

7. The price paid to the milk co-operatives was Rp 250 per litre of milk. The co-operatives paid Rp 210 to the farmers. The cost of producing milk powder was estimated at Rp 120. The price of recombined milk was about Rp 125 per litre (Netherlands Mission, 1982: 4–5).

8. Some schemes required collateral and stipulated that borrowers should have at least two cows of their own. Other schemes, aimed more at poorer farmers, did not have these requirements. In practice, however, cows distributed under the latter schemes were often allocated to the not-so-poor by the co-operative or the village administration (Budiono, 1981: 45; Netherlands Mission, 1982: Chapter 2).

9. The main schemes used were Kredit Investasi Kecil (KIK or Credit for Small Investments), Bankop, and Banpres.

10. All *dukuh* headmen in the two *kecamatan* (38 in Pujon; 57 in Ngantang) were approached and asked to report the number of households in their hamlets engaged in non-agricultural activities.

11. The people living near the reforestation sites can participate in site preparation and tree planting, in return for which they are allowed to grow annual crops for themselves among the newly planted trees for periods of two to three years.

12. Sajogyo (1977) has set a minimum income level (the poverty line) for rural households at 240 rice equivalents per person per year, which is the amount of money required to buy 240 kilograms of cookable rice. With a retail price of Rp 300 per kilogram, this amounts to a minimum income of Rp 360,000 per year for a household consisting of five members (without making allowances for age differences).

13. The total annual gross product from forest land in the Upper Konto area under present management was calculated at Rp 1,655 million in 1986 (Rp 220 million from Perum Perhutani and Rp 1,435 million accruing to the population in the form of wood, fodder, and crops; KRP, 1985: Vol. III, 98). Various alternatives for more productive but sustainable land use were designed and benefits calculated. The alternative emphasizing employment for the local population showed benefits with a net value of Rp 1,566 million in addition to the present product. Another alternative, emphasizing maximal added value, showed a net value of Rp 2,157 million (KRP, 1985: Vol. IV, 102).

14. Sounding surveys were conducted between 1977 and 1982, showing an annual sediment volume of 232 000 cubic metres. It has been estimated that the dead storage part of the reservoir will be completely filled by the year 2023. It would then no longer perform effectively its flood control and downstream irrigation functions and would carry out only part of its electricity supply function (de Graaff and Kusrianto, 1987: 84).

8

Plantations and Cash Crops in East Java: Changing Patterns

Jamie Mackie

Introduction

PLANTATIONS were the main source of export commodities in East Java during the last half-century of colonial rule, a period when the province was one of the major centres of estate agriculture in the Dutch colony (along with North Sumatra and West Java) and when export crops constituted the resource basis of the colony's prosperity.[1] The big Dutch estates in East Java used to produce about two-thirds of the colony's sugar, nearly all its plantation coffee, substantial amounts of high-quality cigar tobacco, and small amounts of rubber.

They still do, although they are no longer foreign-owned (and Indonesia has not been a colony for well over 40 years), having been nationalized in 1957/8. Nearly all the estates have been under the control of State enterprises since then. Yet their importance has declined dramatically in East Java and their character has changed in various ways. Meanwhile, smallholder production of those export crops, almost negligible before 1941, has increased greatly.[2] That reversal in the relative standing of plantations and smallholder agriculture is one of several interrelated changes that have occurred in this sector of the East Java economy since the 1930s. Another is the more general decline in the importance of export commodities within the provincial economy as a fraction of gross regional income (and in the national economy since the 1974 oil boom). A third is the blurring of the sharp distinction, drawn earlier by theorists of the 'dualistic economy' school such as J. H. Boeke, between export-oriented plantations and allegedly subsistence-oriented smallholders.[3] The latter are today engaged extensively in cultivation of cash crops, partly for export but largely for Indonesian domestic consumption. Any account of the plantation sector in East Java since 1945 must, therefore, be set alongside the broader set of changes taking place in the smallholder and cash-crop sectors.

East Java in the 1990s has the most complex and interesting array of plantations in all of Indonesia's provinces (Table 8.1). They are significantly different from the enclave-type rubber, tea, and oil palm

TABLE 8.1
Indonesia: Plantation Crops by Province, 1986[a]

	Sugar		*Coffee*		*Cocoa*		*Rubber*	
	Ha ('000)	%	*Ha ('000)*	%	*Ha ('000)*	%	*Ha ('000)*	%
East Java	154 320	51.0	38 247	82.5	16 480	42.0	28 776	5.7
Central Java and Yogyakarta	55 395	18.3	4 240	9.2	1 149	3.0	31 000	6.2
West Java	20 617	6.8		nil	4 761	12.0	86 045	17.1
North Sumatra	nil		42	0.1	131	0.3	215 627	43.0
Indonesia	302 972	100.0	46 337	100.0	39 351	100.0	502 370	100.0

Source: BPS (1986b).

[a]Figures refer to estate production only; smallholder production of rubber and coffee is therefore not shown. Sugar is here regarded as an estate crop, even though most of it is now cultivated by smallholders under the TRI system.

estates of North Sumatra and West Java in their structure, history, and relations with the surrounding populace. There are two distinct types in East Java, upland and lowland plantations, quite apart from the now much larger and more diversified smallholder cash-cropping sector.[4] The upland enterprises are tree-crop, enclave-type plantation systems (primarily coffee and cocoa, with some rubber and tea) which have changed relatively little in East Java since Independence. The lowland systems, sugar predominantly and tobacco to a lesser extent, are both grown in close conjunction with rice and other foodstuffs; their cultivation systems have been changed significantly since the 1950s. In both cases, the dominance of the plantations over the regions surrounding them has diminished considerably since the colonial era.

At the same time smallholder production of other cash crops, including upland tree crops like cloves, vanilla, and cashews, as well as fruit and vegetables, has increased greatly. Smallholder cultivation of coffee and rubber was never significant in East Java in Dutch times, as it was in Sumatra and Malaya; hence, the intermediate-sized rubber holdings, between 20 and 200 hectares, such as those found in Malaysia, are not found in East Java. Instead one still sees a sharp 'dualistic' division between estates and smallholdings of the kind Boeke categorized. Yet that pattern has also been changing quite radically under the New Order.

In the next section of this chapter, the main types of plantation crops in East Java and the differences between the plantation sector and smallholder cash cropping will be briefly outlined, the situation in colonial times being contrasted with that which has come about since Independence. The three principal plantation crops of the late colonial era—sugar, tobacco, and coffee—will then be surveyed in greater detail with an emphasis on the way the organizational arrangements have in each case changed since Independence, the part being played by smallholders having increased greatly. The less important tree crops, such as rubber, cocoa, tea, cloves, and coconuts, will be dealt with more briefly. Finally, the dramatic rise of commercial cultivation of fruit and vegetables by smallholders over the last 20 years will be sketched in broad outlines.

Estates and Smallholdings in East Java

The classic example of the upland tree-crop plantation in Indonesia is the modern rubber or coffee estate, owned and operated as a large, self-contained unit, with a carefully tended and regularly replanted area under close management. It requires a large labour force, generally housed on the estate, and it is usually located on what were once called 'waste lands' (unoccupied or thinly populated areas) on the fringes of the forested lower slopes of mountain ranges. In East Java such estates have relatively little direct involvement in the economic life of the surrounding population, except in cases where the labour force is drawn from nearby villages or towns.[5]

The most numerous of this type in East Java are the coffee plantations, established around the turn of the twentieth century, mainly along the slopes of the southern mountain chain extending eastwards from Madiun to Malang and Lumajang (Figure 8.1). This region, known as the Oosthoek (Eastern Corner), of which Besuki Residency became the main estate area, was then sparsely populated but attracted a stream of migratory workers until the 1930s.[6] Some of these estates have diversified into rubber and cocoa in response to favourable prices and yields, but the coffee plantations have become the most extensive.[7] A few tea estates were also set up, although they never became very important. None of these upland plantations has changed much in basic structure since the high noon of Dutch colonial rule, between 1880 and 1930, when massive capital investment occurred in estate crops of various kinds.

At the other end of the spectrum are the sugar and tobacco plantations. The former are situated in the densely populated lowland river valleys of East Java, the Brantas basin in particular, for the cultivation of sugar-cane needs abundant labour and a lot of irrigation water; they have developed what C. Geertz (1963: 56) called a 'mutualistic' relationship with wet-rice (*sawah*) cultivation and the people it supports. The tobacco plantations are concentrated between the foothills of Besuki Residency, mainly around Jember. The two crops entail very different systems of cultivation, sugar being a 14-month crop, which profoundly disrupts rice cultivation, whereas tobacco does not, for it requires the land only for about four months in the dry season. In both cases, major changes have occurred since Independence in the direction of an increased role for smallholders and a lesser role for the estates.

In the colonial period the sugar mills rented land from nearby villages on short-term leases negotiated collectively, and they organized the cultivation of the sugar-cane themselves. The tobacco estates in Besuki Residency entered into contracts with individual farmers to grow the tobacco and sell the leaf to them for processing and export. Under the latter system the farmers bore the risks of loss, and the estates had only a general supervisory role in the cultivation process in order to ensure high-quality tobacco leaf. Thus tobacco growing was in one sense a form of smallholder cultivation, although under increasingly tight estate control.

The huge sugar-mills used to be colonial enclaves of high-technology, capital-intensive enterprise (and in many respects still are, although with Indonesian officials now running them) amidst the surrounding rice-growing villages and *kampung*. They created distinctive clusters of large modern offices and staff bungalows around the factory complex, yet their relationships with the surrounding population were far more intimate and complex than those of the upland enclave plantations. In colonial times both the land they rented on 21-year leases and the labour force they needed constantly for field preparation, harvesting, and factory work had to be obtained through negotiations with the local officials in nearby villages. Since the introduction in 1975 of the TRI (Tebu

FIGURE 8.1
Map Showing Location of Main Crops

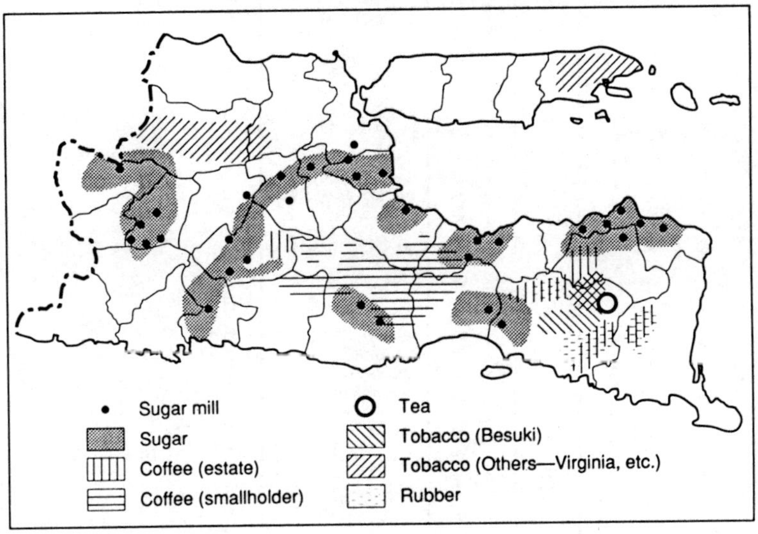

Rakyat Intensifikasi or Smallholder Sugar-cane Intensification) system the task of organizing the cultivation of cane has been transferred from the mill authorities to the farmers themselves. Even so, the mill-estate complex remains a powerful socio-economic force within the region from which it obtains its cane. Likewise, in the Besuki cigar tobacco area, far-reaching changes have occurred on the old estates, although they survive in attenuated form as part of a large State enterprise.

Sugar, tobacco, coffee, and rubber have been by far the most important plantation crops in East Java throughout the twentieth century, with small amounts of tea, cocoa and other crops also produced at times (Table 8.2). Smallholder production of those crops by local farmers, on the other hand, was relatively insignificant in East Java during the colonial era.[8] Boeke's use of the term 'dualism' was inspired mainly by the contrast he discerned between the 'dynamic', technically advanced, and efficient plantation sector and the allegedly 'stagnant', subsistence-oriented smallholder sector.[9] Yet today it is the latter which is expanding and the former which has become stagnant and inefficient. This is one of the most important structural changes that have occurred in the East Java economy since Independence.

More than any other part of Indonesia except North Sumatra, East Java experienced an extremely rapid rate of economic development between the 1880s and the 1930s Depression under the stimulus of the fast-expanding plantation sector. The sugar industry was by far the most important factor in that process, followed by the *bergculturen* (upland crops; that is, coffee and tea initially, rubber and cocoa later) and the high-quality estate tobacco produced in the foothills of Besuki Residency. The momentum of growth generated by the opening up of new lands for plantations and the big investments laid out in sugar mills,

TABLE 8.2
East Java: Plantation Crops by Area and Production, 1923–1986

	1923		*1970*		*1986*	
	Area ('000 ha)	*Production ('000 tonnes)*	*Area ('000 ha)*	*Production ('000 tonnes)*	*Area ('000 ha)*	*Production ('000 tonnes)*
Sugar	112	864	–	459	154	134[a]
Coffee	74	29	–	15	38	24
Cocoa	0.4	8.5[b]	–	–	16.5	8
Tea	3	?	–	2	3.5	5
Rubber	75	15	–	19	28.8	24

Sources: 1923: CKS (1925: Appendices AA, BB); Landbouwatlas (1926: Vol. 2, Table 5).
1970: Anon. (1971).
1986: BPS (1989b).

[a]Provisional figures, plantation production only (i.e. excluding smallholder cultivation under TRI).
[b]Provisional figures.

irrigation works, roads, railways, and port facilities was lost during the Depression. And in the disrupted, destructive years that followed in the 1940s, contraction, followed by deterioration and stagnation, afflicted the entire plantation sector. Nothing else provided a comparable impetus to the regional economy until the Green Revolution and the industrial investments of the 1970s–80s.

Instead of being one of the world's great sugar exporters, Indonesia has become a net importer since the 1960s, despite a sharp increase in sugar production, because domestic consumption of sugar has been rising even faster than output.[10] Today the value added of the entire cash-crop sector accounts for only about 3 per cent of East Java's GRP (see Chapter 2, Table 2.1), barely one-sixth of that of the main food crops. Less than 20 per cent of the contribution of this sector comes from plantations (0.6 per cent of GRP), the bulk of it being produced by smallholders.[11] Yet smallholder production, not only of export crops previously grown predominantly on plantations but also of new cash crops produced for local consumption, such as fruit and vegetables, cloves, and tobacco for the booming *kretek* industry, has become far more important than it ever was in colonial times in Java.

The Dutch-owned estates were not only the most dynamic economic force behind the rapid growth of East Java throughout the last half-century of colonial rule, but also the politically dominant one, exerting great influence over the colonial authorities in The Hague and Batavia, as well as at the provincial and lower levels. In the early years of the twentieth century their owners and managers were powerful enough to curb or obstruct smallholder cultivation of plantation crops and even to minimize the competition of rival Chinese estates to the point of virtual insignificance.

Since Independence, however, the plantation sector has been neither politically influential, nor economically dynamic. Plantations are no longer expanding vigorously and are far from profit generating as they were in the late colonial era.[12] The few privately owned plantations, mostly small and many of them in the hands of ex-military officers or former officials, are today a relatively unimportant element in the provincial economy. None of the plantations is making new investments on a large scale, or innovating with new crops or new methods of production as their predecessors did. Nor are they opening up new areas for cultivation, as was done in the Jember–Banyuwangi and Kediri–Blitar regions in the late nineteenth century. The large State-owned plantations are essentially stagnant at best; in many cases they are patently unprofitable. Nowhere are they notable for productive efficiency as their predecessors used to be.

Because of their poor performance record, the plantations have been highly vulnerable to political attack within the post-Independence political and administrative structure. Few of the owners of private estates or administrators of government estates are politically influential at either the regional level or in the national capital, certainly not to anything like the same degree as the Dutch plantation owners and managers were in the colonial period.[13]

The production of plantation crops did not collapse altogether after Independence, although it sagged badly between 1930 and the mid-1960s, before recovering in the 1970s (Mackie, 1961–2). By the early 1980s sugar production in East Java was reaching levels not far below those achieved in the peak years before the Depression; coffee and tobacco production were also doing much better than before 1965, although below 1920s levels. The total number of people involved in the production of the traditional plantation crops may even be about the same as in the peak years of the 1920s, perhaps slightly more (there are no reliable estimates for either period), although it would now be a much smaller proportion of the total work-force. Other sectors of the East Java economy have expanded far more rapidly than these crops (over the last half-century), so their relative significance has declined.

Sugar

Sugar plantations constituted the leading sector of the East Java economy during the century before World War II. Sugar-cane is still an important crop cultivated on more than 150 000 hectares of land every year and directly affecting the lives of at least 200,000 households (BPS, 1989b: Table f-1, b.2).[14] Yet it no longer has anything like its former significance in the provincial economy. The stimulus to new investment and growth in the provincial economy, generated by the rapid expansion of sugar cultivation in the late colonial period, collapsed abruptly in 1930 and has never been reactivated, despite the attempt to reconstitute the industry on a radically new basis in 1975 through the introduction of the TRI system. In 1929 there were 100 sugar mills in East Java, but since 1950 only 33. Many were closed in the Depression or destroyed during World War II and the Revolution.

About two-thirds of Indonesia's entire sugar output, approximately one million tonnes, is currently produced in East Java and yields per hectare are substantially higher there than elsewhere in Java.[15] In the late 1980s the area planted varied between 150 000 and 170 000 hectares, more than 10 per cent of the total *sawah* area of the province (although sugar is now grown increasingly on dry land as well). The average area of land planted per sugar mill has increased greatly since Independence.[16]

The sugar industry has changed in various ways since colonial times. First, it has been entirely nationalized and is now run by State enterprises whose records of profitability and efficiency have been far less impressive than those of the former Dutch sugar mills, with only rare exceptions.[17] Secondly, the switch to the TRI system in 1975 marked a historic change towards a new form of smallholder cultivation of sugar-cane, entailing the abandonment of the century-old system under which the sugar mill played a key role in organizing the cultivation of the cane, as well as in crushing it and refining the sugar content. Thirdly, the relative importance of sugar and rice in the sugar districts has been reversed. Today rice cultivation is generally far more lucrative for the farmers than sugar-cane.

The colonial system of sugar-cane cultivation was extremely efficient before World War II, when Javanese plantations had a world-wide reputation for high productivity that is almost unimaginable today, both in the cultivation of cane and in its processing (O'Malley, 1990). The very large modern mills of several thousand hectares installed in the early twentieth century by the big Dutch company, HVA (Handelsvereeniging Amsterdam), in the Jember–Lumajang and Kediri areas, with their impressive networks of irrigation canals built especially for them, were unrivalled anywhere else in the world. But the sugar plantations that survived into the post-Independence era faced an entirely new situation. Their administrators found that they could no longer rely on the support of local officials to ensure that they obtained access to the best land or the labour supply they needed at the times they wanted it, as in the past. Productivity per hectare was declining alarmingly in the 1950s, long before the nationalization of the Dutch estates in 1957–8 (Mackie, 1961–2; Mackie and O'Malley, 1988).

After the estates passed into the hands of the Indonesian government, the problems continued, for by that time inflation was becoming uncontrollable and increases in the government-controlled rents paid by the mills lagged far behind the rises in general price levels, as well as behind the returns farmers could earn from rice or other crops. Whole villages became reluctant to lease their land to the sugar mills, which now had to rely upon pressure by local administration officials to maintain minimal access to the land and water they needed. And as rice yields began to increase dramatically under the New Order rice intensification schemes, the differences between the cash returns per hectare from rice and sugar-cane cultivation widened even further. By 1967 production had declined to a point where Indonesia had become a net importer of sugar to meet the steady increase in domestic demand (Figure 8.2).

Under the Suharto regime, the local authorities in East Java immediately achieved some success in reversing the decline in production simply by strengthening the administration of the plantations. Output of refined sugar in East Java rose from 377 000 tonnes in 1966 to 460 000 tonnes in 1970 and 606 000 tonnes by 1975 (Table 8.3). That rise was accomplished more easily because farmers and labourers suspected of having been associated with the Communist Party before 1965 were now too vulnerable politically to resist the pressure upon them to grow sugar-cane.

The basic problem remained, however, that the system of compulsory leasing of land was becoming highly unpopular and increasingly unprofitable, so that fewer farmers were willing to rent their best land to the mills. Productivity was declining steadily, with yields per hectare of sucrose production falling by the early 1970s to about 30 per cent below their pre-war levels. This once highly profitable industry was more often making losses than profits, even though it was now selling the sugar not

FIGURE 8.2
East Java: Sugar Production and Area Harvested, 1923–1989

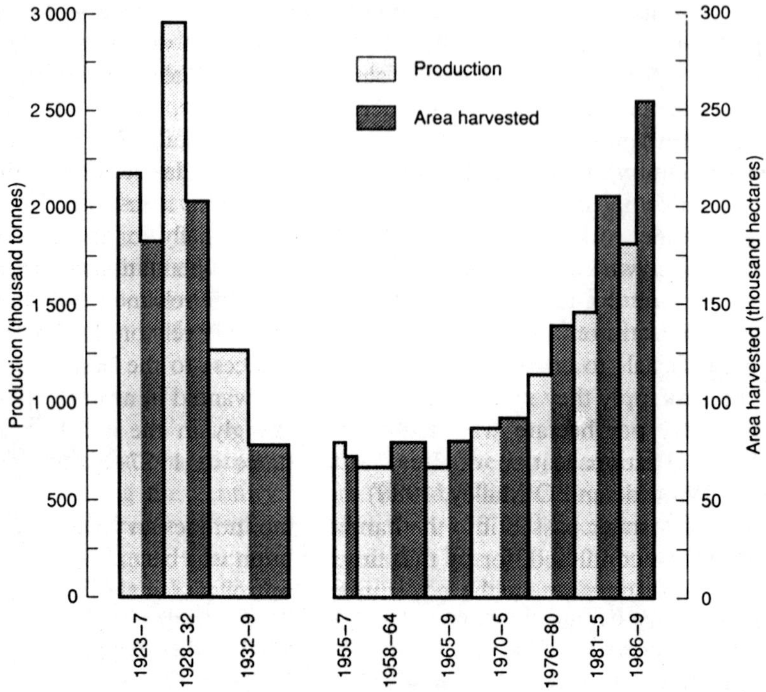

on highly competitive world markets, but to a captive local market, at regulated and often subsidized prices.

The introduction of the TRI system in 1975 was a major new initiative by the government to tackle the problem of declining productivity by transferring the task of cultivating cane from the mills to the farmers themselves, and at the same time gearing the cash payments they received to the sucrose output from the cane they deliver to the mill. It was hoped that this would give farmers an incentive to increase production and improve yields.[18] The role of the mills was reduced to the primary task of crushing the cane brought in by the farmers and secondarily, providing technical advice and 'guidance' (*bimbingan*), along with fertilizers, pesticides, and seedlings appropriate to the area.[19] In principle the TRI scheme seemed a well-conceived idea, but it went badly wrong on two counts. One was that the government determined the prices paid to farmers for cane by arbitrary decree, frequently at levels lagging far behind the inflation rate, so that cane cultivation still returned less income to them than rice in most areas. The other was that coercion of various kinds was applied by the local authorities against recalcitrant farmers to ensure that the mill's cane cultivation targets were met in each *kabupaten* (district), *kecamatan* (subdistrict), and village. Instead of having new and strong incentives to improve their cultivation practices and raise sugar yields, most farmers now plant sugar-cane reluctantly and feel little incentive to put more effort into their work beyond the minimum needed to achieve the area targets imposed upon them. A 'target mentality' among growers, State plantation officials, and local government authorities responsible for ensuring that each village or subdistrict plants the required amount of cane has replaced any incentive towards achieving higher productivity and efficiency across the industry as a whole (Mackie and O'Malley, 1988: 741–7).

The initial results of the new system were encouraging, however. Production of sugar in East Java rose rapidly to slightly over a million tonnes per annum by the early 1980s, although it has not risen much beyond that level since then (Table 8.3). But although the output figures show an impressive increase, the socio-economic consequences of the TRI system have been costly to most of the farmers concerned. Yields per hectare have declined even further, and the overall productivity, efficiency, and profitability of the sugar industry have deteriorated almost everywhere. Farmers are generally reluctant to plant sugar-cane on prime *sawah* because the cash return from rice has become so much higher; hence they plant only as much as they are compelled to, with little concern for higher productivity, usually on poor land and increasingly on dry land (*tegalan*). It is a far cry from the situation in the 1920s when the larger landowners were eager to rent their land to the sugar mills, which in turn were able to bargain for the best *sawah* (Elson, 1984: 219).

Two important technological innovations have occurred since the 1970s, however, which have radically transformed the agronomy and economics of sugar-cane cultivation. The first is that sugar-cane can now be grown successfully on *tegalan* under a wider range of soil and water conditions than before, due to the development of new strains by the Pasuruan Sugar Research Station. This marks a major structural change in the sugar industry, a most timely one since it now pays better to use prime *sawah* for rice in most cases. Sugar-cane grown on *tegalan* can often produce a higher cash return per hectare than alternative crops normally grown there, and so the farmers may benefit from it,

TABLE 8.3

East Java: Sugar-cane Production and Area Planted, 1975–1989

	Production ('000 tonnes)	*Area ('000 hectares)*
1975	609	63.7
1980	756	94.2
1985	1 031	154.7
1986	1 128	160.8
1987	1 215	153.8
1988	1 123	163.6
1989	1 071	149.8

Source: Figures supplied by Kantor Statistik Jawa Timur, based on data from Directorate-General of Plantations.

even though the mills find it less efficient from their viewpoint to crush lower quality cane. Secondly, sugar-cane is now commonly ratooned for two or three years (that is, allowed to grow again from the root stock after being harvested), a practice that was formerly rejected by the Dutch because it resulted in lower sucrose yields per hectare. Yet this method of cultivation reduces the labour costs involved in preparing the land, which suits many farmers despite the reduction in productivity. But the cumulative effect of these changes has been a further decline in sucrose yields per hectare.

These and other indications of deteriorating efficiency throughout the industry at both the technical and commercial levels suggest that the TRI system has not provided a long-term solution to the problems it was intended to resolve. The complaints of farmers about the low prices for cane set by the government, their reluctance to participate in the TRI system except under pressure, and the 'target mentality' pervading the industry at so many levels all indicate continued decline in efficiency rather than any real improvement. The mills are subsidized in various ways and many would not be able to survive if they had to face competitive markets and lower sugar prices. And because such a large part of the industry is located in East Java, the adverse effects of the combination of reduced efficiency and greater area under sugar-cane must be costing the province a great deal in terms of the opportunity costs incurred, despite the increase in output.

The overall balance of costs and benefits of the new system for the East Java economy cannot be assessed with any precision. It seems certain, however, that the increase in production of sugar-cane since the 1960s has not given rise to any commensurate increment in aggregate regional income or purchasing power, since any income gains accruing to farmers who cultivate cane willingly have to be offset against incomes forgone (from more lucrative crops) by others who do so only because they have to. (The contrast here with the gains from higher rice production and productivity is striking, for in that case rising prices accrued to virtually all farmers involved, as did higher output for the whole country.) One of the social costs of the increase in cane cultivation has been the forced diversion of much rice land to sugar, to the disadvantage of the farmers concerned in terms of the potential income forgone from rice; but the area involved cannot be estimated with any precision, beyond a crude estimate that the net amount has probably been well below 5 per cent of total *sawah* land. Conversely, some farmers must have gained from the opportunity to grow cane on *tegalan* instead of less lucrative crops.[20] The net balance of advantages therefore would be very complex to compute.

Any cost-benefit assessment would also have to take account of the wide regional variations in yields and the reasons behind them (Chapter 6, Table 6.10). Sidoarjo, in the fertile Brantas Delta, has generally had the highest sugar-cane yields (91 kilograms per hectare in 1984), mostly on *sawah*, but an area harvested of less than 7 000 hectares. At the other extreme, Malang and Pasuruan recorded less than

50 kilograms per hectare. In Malang, which had by far the largest area under sugar (over 20 000 hectares) of any *kabupaten* in East Java, the authorities had been actively promoting the shift from *sawah* to dry land. This is a historic transformation in the region whose rich *sawah* provided the basis in the 1840s for the most productive sugar-producing area in Java.[21]

The employment-creating effects of the TRI system must have been substantial, simply in terms of the increased number of man-hours of labour needed for land preparation, planting, harvesting, and transporting the cane to the mills, all of which are highly labour-intensive operations. Factory work is much less so, although the milling season now extends to about six or seven months, whereas it used to be barely half as long.

The haphazard geographical distribution of sugar-cane cultivation in East Java today, mainly in the great river valleys, is an accident of recent history, depending on where the surviving mills were after the struggle for Independence. The mills and main cultivated areas are concentrated in five main regions (Figure 8.1; see Table 6.10), although locally they are much more scattered than in earlier decades, since truck transport now makes it possible to grow cane scores of kilometres away from the mills. Malang and Kediri *kabupaten* alone account for nearly 30 per cent of the total planted area and have some of the largest and most efficient mills. But the once great sugar-growing areas of Pasuruan and Surabaya residencies have largely switched away from cane to rice on their prime *sawah* since World War II. Some of the smaller mills in Situbondo–Probolinggo and elsewhere survive more because of their local significance as a source of employment and income (their 'social function') than because they are highly productive.

Finally, some mention must also be made of a small but tenacious sector of *tebu rakyat* (peasant sugar-cane) which is produced for making *gula merah* ('brown', unrefined sugar) sold largely in village markets. It is grown mainly in southern Kediri and around Malang (van der Kolff, 1953). Although the mills are small and crude, formerly buffalo- but now diesel-powered, and crush at most a few scores of tonnes of cane a day, this branch of the industry has proved remarkably durable and adaptable to changes in demand and supply even in the face of tough competition from modern high-technology mills. The Dutch plantation managers tried without success to squeeze them out of the market altogether. Since Independence that attitude has changed, so that farmers are now free to sell their cane to whichever purchaser offers them the better deal. But this sector is unlikely to grow significantly; in fact, it is in some respects an even more anachronistic survival under the TRI system than it was before.

Tobacco

Tobacco became an important plantation crop in East Java in the second half of the nineteenth century when the legendary cigar tobacco estates in Besuki Residency, first developed by George Birnie around 1860, began producing a high-grade leaf suitable for the European cigar market. Since Independence, two major changes have occurred, apart from the nationalization of Dutch estates.[22] The most striking has been a shift from the colonial-era, estate-dominated mode of production of cigar tobacco towards one in which smallholder cultivation (and the processing of cigar tobacco leaf) is now widespread. The other has been a rise in domestic demand for lower quality tobacco from the fast-growing *kretek* (clove-flavoured) cigarette manufacturing industry, which has coincided with the decline of the international market for high-quality cigar tobacco (see Young, Chapter 13). Just as the strong export demand for cigar tobacco gave rise to the dominant position of the Besuki estates during the last years of the colonial era, now it is the rising local demand for cigarette tobacco that is resulting in the expansion of smallholder production in many parts of the province.

Tobacco has a short growing season which causes little disruption to wet-season rice cultivation, so it is very suitable for smallholder cultivation. High-quality leaf can frequently obtain a substantial premium in the market, but there is a great deal of risk attached to its cultivation (and to trading in it), since export tobacco is subject to wild price fluctuations in accordance with weather conditions and international demand.

Various types of tobacco were cultivated by farmers in many parts of East Java until the early decades of the twentieth century, most notably in the Brantas Valley (Kediri, Tulungagung, Blitar, and southern Malang), Bojonegoro, Madura, and Besuki. By far the most valuable type, however, was the high-quality cigar tobacco produced on or for Dutch 'estates' or tobacco companies in Bondowoso and Jember[23] that became famous as Besuki *Na-oogst* ('post-harvest' tobacco; that is, grown after the rice harvest, in the dry season). The processed tobacco leaf was exported to Holland for use as binder or wrapper leaf in the manufacture of cigars. A low-quality type known generically as *krosok* or *tembakau rakyat* (peasant tobacco) had long been produced by smallholders in many parts of the province. The best *krosok* leaf was exported for use as filler in cigars; the remainder was consumed locally by the fledgeling *kretek* and 'white' (that is, machine-made, Western-style) cigarette industries.

Between about 1910 and 1930, Jember and the Vorstenlanden came to dominate the export of tobacco from Java, earning extremely high returns and gradually squeezing other regions of *krosok* production, such as Kediri, Malang, and Rembang, right out of the market by raising quality and productivity to levels which smallholders simply could not match. In the last years before World War II, tobacco estates became predominant in the production of export-quality tobacco in East Java (Figure 8.3), mainly because the strict quality control they exercised in Besuki enabled them to displace the lower quality *krosok* almost completely from the export market. They thereby confined tobacco production in other parts of the province to the then limited domestic market for *kretek* and, after 1930, for Virginia tobacco for 'white' cigarettes.[24]

Besuki was then, and still is, one of the three major estate centres in Indonesia producing high-quality cigar tobacco for the lucrative European market, the others being the Deli region (in North Sumatra just outside Medan) and the principalities (Vorstenlanden) of Surakarta and Yogyakarta. The Deli tobacco estates produced a uniquely valuable variety of wrapper leaf, while Besuki (particularly Jember) and the Vorstenlanden produced lower grades of less expensive binder leaf, as well as small quantities of wrapper and large quantities of filler. The quality was generally not comparable with Deli wrapper leaf but it was sufficiently good to command higher export prices than the sometimes large amounts of *krosok* previously produced throughout Java for export as filler.

As with the sugar plantations, the Dutch tobacco planters did not actually own or rent the land (with one major exception), nor did they cultivate the tobacco themselves, but made contracts with local farmers to grow the tobacco on their own land, under estate supervision, and sell the green leaf to them at predetermined prices.[25] The Dutch companies then cured, processed, and exported it. The complex relationships that developed between planters and farmers were summarized as follows by Allen and Donnithorne (1957: 96–7):

> the planter leased land for tobacco from the villages, paid the land tax, supplied the seedlings to the natives who contracted to supply the produce, and finally purchased the crop ... the farmers or native contractors arranged to deliver the crop to the planter and to work under his guidance. Risk was thus shared between the Western firm and the native cultivator.... At first the Western planters concerned themselves solely with the preparation and marketing of the produce delivered to them. But the necessity for ensuring that the tobacco should be of good and even quality impelled the planters to take an ever-increasing interest in the actual processes of cultivation.

This account idealizes slightly the nature of the frequently strained relationships prevailing between the tobacco companies and the farmers under contract to them prior to World War II. Many farmers preferred to grow tobacco without entering into contracts with the companies, in order to sell it to 'wild' traders outside the company-controlled marketing channels. The companies fought hard to suppress that trade, ostensibly in order to maintain high-quality production of leaf for the all-important export market but also to ensure they could maintain tight control over the flow of tobacco into the lucrative (for them) export trade. The tobacco companies were engaged in a constant struggle against 'free' cultivators (that is, the smallholders not under contract to them) throughout the early twentieth century in order to enhance their hegemony over the market in Besuki (Mackie, 1985: 117–24). The various control mechanisms they exercised became increasingly tight as time passed, so that by the 1930s a small group of four large Dutch companies came to exercise virtual dominance of the cigar tobacco industry there. This battery of administrative, legal, and economic controls began

FIGURE 8.3
Estate and Smallholder Besuki *Na-oogst* Tobacco Production, 1870–1982 (annual average)

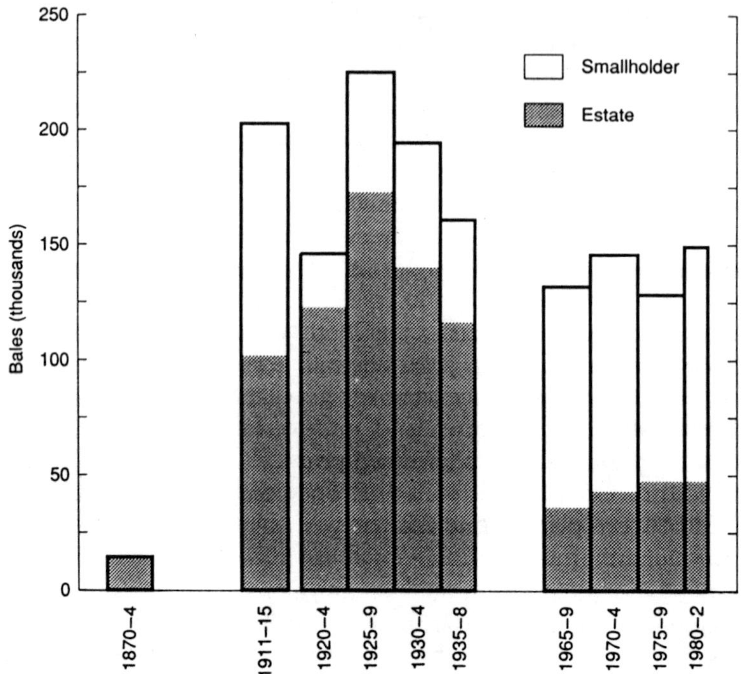

to disintegrate soon after Independence, but well before the nationalization of Dutch enterprises transformed the system of tobacco cultivation and trading in Besuki Residency.

After the Dutch estates were nationalized in 1957–8, a State-owned plantation company, now known as PTP XXVII, took over the assets of the Besuki companies and at first continued to produce and export *Na-oogst* much as before. The most spectacular consequences were an upsurge in smallholder production of *Na-oogst* and a proliferation of locally owned smokehouses and curing facilities (previously curbed by the Dutch) erected by wealthy farmers or private traders and exporters, who were for the first time able to enter the lucrative export market, albeit in competition with the State corporation.[26] The government was unwilling and unable to prevent this, despite its *étatist* economic philosophy, so that something like boom conditions prevailed in the early 1960s in and around the town of Jember, by then the centre of *Na-oogst* production. Many of the new traders eventually failed, for export price fluctuations and periodic overproduction made tobacco trading a highly risk-prone business in which only a few of the more cautious newcomers survived for long.

The important change for the farmers was that the restrictions on production and marketing which had sustained the dominant position of the Dutch companies were now abolished, so that a free market for tobacco prevailed, with numerous traders bidding for leaf from farmers everywhere. Hundreds of smokehouses were set up by the wealthier farmers who could afford the capital outlay, for there was initially big money to be made from them. Overproduction became chronic and quality declined. Some of the farmers and traders became very rich (usually after moving up-market from growing tobacco into trading), although no lasting structural changes in local society resulted from these boom conditions, such as the emergence of a new class of large-scale tobacco farmers, as might have been expected.

The quality of leaf exported deteriorated steadily over the course of the 1960s–70s, partly due to the breakdown of the close relationships formerly maintained between the tobacco companies which processed and exported the commodity and the farmers who cultivated the leaf under their supervision. While PTP XXVII attempted with some success to maintain similar relationships with its client farmers, it has encountered increasing difficulty in persuading them to enter into the old-style contracts, except in one area of long-lease lands under its control, where the farmers are dependent on it for access to the land.[27]

Since the 1960s only about 5 000 hectares have been planted under the State corporation's auspices, out of a total planted area that has fluctuated between 14 000 and 20 000 hectares in Jember. The corporation has tended to stress its role as a source of technical expertise and 'guidance' to the industry in general rather than as a mechanism for generating commercial dynamism and expansion like its forerunners. That was perhaps inevitable, since the primary need in the 1980s has been to reduce the quantity of tobacco produced while raising the quality in the face of a long-term decline in world demand for cigar tobacco and competition from new producers in Africa. The decline of the tobacco estates has been similar in outcome to that of the sugar plantations, although the two processes have had very different socio-economic dynamics.

Meanwhile, the cultivation by smallholders of other types of tobacco for domestic consumption has grown steadily in East Java to a point where it far exceeds that of Besuki *Na-oogst*. An estimated 64 000 hectares were planted with Virginia tobacco in 1979–80, mainly in the Bojonegoro region. About 40 000 hectares were under *krosok*, principally in Madura, Lumajang, and Bojonegoro, more than twice the area under Besuki *Na-oogst* (Perhepi, 1984: 384). Subsequently, production of Virginia has been declining, however, as the increasing popularity of *kretek* has reduced demand for the previously more prestigious 'white' cigarettes (Soegiyanto Padmo and Edhie Djatmiko, 1990: 215).

The consumption of tobacco by the *kretek* industry has grown steadily, more than sixfold between 1970 and 1989, and now embraces various types: Virginia, *tembakau rakyat* of various qualities, and Besuki *Voor-oogst*, an old established variety less suitable for cigars than *Na-oogst*. Although the unit value of the tobacco cultivated for the *kretek* industry is not as high as that grown for other purposes, the prices are less erratic, and so production for that market is becoming increasingly popular even in the Besuki region. Smallholder production of lower quality tobacco for the domestic market now seems to have won out decisively in East Java over high-quality export-oriented estate production.

Coffee

Coffee has become East Java's major export crop since World War II and coffee plantations are the main form of hill-country estate of the classic enclave or 'dualistic' type still surviving there. No other part of Indonesia has ever had such a large area of plantation coffee, almost 40 000 hectares in the 1980s (although that is barely half the area recorded in the 1920s), which is nearly 90 per cent of Indonesia's total area under plantation coffee.[28]

In the other provinces coffee is cultivated almost entirely by smallholders (Table 8.4). The total area under coffee in Indonesia was almost 950 000 hectares in the late 1980s (including estates), nearly three times the area planted in the 1950s. Smallholder cultivation in East Java (44 000 hectares in 1988) has expanded since the 1960s to a point where its area slightly exceeds that of the estates, although the quantity and quality of coffee produced are lower (Table 8.5).[29] This indicates a greater degree of adaptability on the part of smallholders in responding to favourable world market prices (prior to the collapse of the World Coffee Agreement in 1989) than was shown by the estates, which have achieved only a small increase in area and output since 1970.

The prominence of plantation coffee in East Java is due to the historical accident that many coffee estates were established there by Dutch companies around the turn of the twentieth century when Besuki Residency was a booming frontier region (Broersma, 1913; Tennekes, 1963). The compulsory cultivation of coffee under the Cultuurstelsel (Cultivation System)[30] was then being phased out gradually, and so there was scope for Dutch private plantations to produce coffee there, as well as tea, rubber, and (much later) cocoa. Coffee had a less dramatic impact on the development of the region than tobacco, however, by way of opening up new lands and attracting new workers, except in the large Banyuwangi estate area in the early twentieth century.

About half of East Java's estate production of coffee occurs on privately owned plantations, mostly rather small (between 200 and 300 hectares), many of them reportedly of marginal profitability in the early 1980s. But they stand out as an exceptional phenomenon in a country where privately owned plantations are now rare. Not many have undertaken much new investment or expansion of planted area, however, and in general they seem like a run-down and anachronistic legacy from a past era, like the government sugar and tobacco estates, rather than a dynamic sphere of economic activity, as they originally were, contributing substantially to new jobs and markets.

Overall, East Java ranks third among the coffee-producing provinces of Indonesia, after South Sumatra and Lampung, accounting for

TABLE 8.4
Indonesia: Coffee Production and Area Planted, 1967–1987

	Area ('000 hectares)		*Production ('000 tonnes)*	
	Estates[a]	*Smallholders*	*Estates*	*Smallholders*
1967	34	289	13	140
1970	44	351	15	170
1975	39	361	15	155
1980	44	663	19	276
1985	45	875	21	289
1987	46	896	20	333

Source: Moeljarto and Dwi Retnandari (1990: 139).
[a]Specific figures for East Java over this period are not available. But since almost 90 per cent of Indonesian estate coffee is grown in East Java, these all-Indonesia data provide some indication of the approximate levels of plantation production there at different times. The area under smallholder coffee in East Java was 34 000 hectares in 1968 and 45 000 hectares in 1988 (Anon., 1971; KSJT, *Jawa Timur dalam Angka, 1989*).

TABLE 8.5
East Java: Estate and Smallholder Production of Major Tree Crops, 1980–1988

	Area Planted ('000 hectares)			*Production ('000 tonnes)*		
	A	*B*	*C*	*A*	*B*	*C*
Coffee						
1980	36.8	19.1	16.7	11.6	11.4	7.0
1983	41.4	19.3	17.3	10.0	8.6	8.0
1988	45.5	21.6	18.3	16.0	10.1	10.0
Cloves						
1980	26.8	–	–	0.7	0.2	0.2
1983	35.7	2.3	4.2	5.5	0.5	0.2
1988	43.2	3.0	5.2	8.1	0.3	0.4
Coconuts						
1980	24.6	1.1	2.6	12.9	1.2	0.5
1983	23.4	0.9	2.7	14.8	0.6	0.3
1988	24.4	0.7	3.1	17.4	0.5	0.4
Kapok						
1980	13.2	0.6	3.5	21.2	0.6	1.6
1983	9.7	–	–	18.5	0.2	2.0
1988	9.3	0.9	3.4	22.4	0.2	–

Sources: KSJT, *Jawa Timur dalam Angka, 1981*: 256-60; *Jawa Timur dalam Angka, 1988*: 106–15.
A = Smallholders.
B = Government estates.
C = Private estates.

11.5 per cent of the nation's aggregate output and 8.8 per cent of its area in 1987 (Moeljarto and Dwi Retnandari, 1990: 100). Its coffee exports were earning the province around US$80–100 million in the late 1980s, slightly more than the total export earnings from all agricultural commodities, quite apart from sales on the domestic market. However, the overall socio-economic impact of coffee has never been as great as that of the sugar industry, nor of tobacco, which have both had greater scope for expansion in the lowland *sawah* areas, well beyond the confines of the colonial-era patterns of production. Expansion into new hill-country areas has occurred only to a small extent with smallholder coffee so far, much less than in Sumatra and Sulawesi. Moreover, measures taken by the government have inhibited the expansion of estate coffee; limitations on replanting have even been imposed on them in order to prevent overproduction (Moeljarto and Dwi Retnandari, 1990: 104). At the same time the Ministry of Agriculture in East Java has been endeavouring to upgrade the quality of smallholder as well as estate coffee. Some government estates were switching from coffee to cocoa during the 1980s, as the cash returns were much greater; others had earlier been switching from rubber to coffee for the same reason. But neither process has gone very far. The structural changes in the estate coffee sector have been marginal in comparison with those affecting sugar and tobacco, while the quantitative expansion has occurred mostly in the smallholder sector.

Other Tree Crops

The total area planted with tree crops other than coffee and fruit in East Java (rubber, cocoa, tea, cloves, vanilla, cashew nuts, cinnamon, coconuts, and kapok) amounted to almost 470 000 hectares in the late 1980s, more than half of it in smallholder coconut stands and nearly a quarter in kapok. Except for cloves, no great increase appears to be occurring in any of these crops in East Java, and their relative economic importance has declined greatly since the early years of the twentieth century. Rubber, tea, cocoa, and cinnamon are exclusively plantation crops in East Java, but they account for less than 50 000 hectares in total. Production of rubber and tea has stagnated since the 1930s and is confined primarily to a few old Jember and Banyuwangi estates. They amount to little more than relics from the colonial era, with almost static production levels.

On the other hand, cloves and various minor tree crops, like vanilla and cashew nuts, are expanding rapidly, grown largely by smallholders, and totalling around 100 000 hectares (KSJT, *Jawa Timur dalam Angka, 1987*: 106–10). Coconut production, which occurs in nearly all parts of the province, but particularly in Banyuwangi, Jember, and Blitar, was important in the early twentieth century; it then remained static for a long time, before increasing slowly in the late 1980s. Kapok production has been rising faster but is a significant source of income only in a few areas.

Clove production for the *kretek* industry has been the greatest tree-crop success story in East Java since Independence. Its cultivation was negligible there in the 1960s and even by 1980–1 production had only reached 1 140 tonnes; but it then rose rapidly to 6 392 tonnes by 1987 (KSJT, *Jawa Timur dalam Angka, 1981*: 259–60; *Jawa Timur dalam Angka, 1988*: 114). It is a risky crop because of its susceptibility to disease, although it can be extremely profitable. Smallholders grow cloves in most parts of East Java, usually in very small gardens. Malang stands out as by far the biggest producing area (with nearly 30 per cent of the provincial output in 1987), while Blitar, Ponorogo, and Jombang also recorded high levels of production. In Jombang production rose 10-fold in a steady progression between 1982 and 1987, and in the Madiun–Magetan–Nganjuk area it rose nearly fivefold. In some of these regions clove cultivation must have added quite considerably to regional incomes. Interestingly, this is one crop that has done well at times (albeit capriciously) in poorer areas like Pacitan and Trenggalek.

Fruit and Vegetables

The cash incomes generated by smallholder cultivation of fruit and vegetables have become an important part of farmers' incomes in many parts of East Java during the New Order years, since high prices can at times be earned for these crops (see Chapter 7). Rising demand for fruit and vegetables has extended more broadly into modest but widespread increases in their production throughout most of the province. Fruit and vegetables of many kinds have long been grown both commercially and for domestic consumption in nearly all parts of Indonesia, but large-scale and intensive commercial cultivation has developed vigorously in East Java only since the 1970s, stimulated mainly by the rise in urban demand associated with rising middle-class incomes. The increases in production recorded for some fruit between 1983 and 1987 have been considerable (Table 8.6); threefold or more for pineapples, some types of *jeruk* (citrus) and mangoes, as well as other minor fruit, and as much as 10-fold in the case of *jeruk siam* (tangerines).[31] The increase in commercial demand for various crops, such as pineapples and several types of *jeruk*, has led to dramatic growth in production in certain places with favourable physical conditions.

East Java ranks first among the provinces of Java in the production of pineapples (with over 90 per cent of the total), mangoes, apples, *jeruk besar* (grapefruit), and *jeruk keprok* (oranges) (with over or around 50 per cent of total production in each), although it falls behind the other provinces of Java in bananas, durians, and *jeruk siam* (BPS, 1987b).

There is a high degree of regional specialization in several of the main fruit and vegetable crops, with one or two *kabupaten* accounting for the lion's share of East Java's output of fruit in all but a few cases (Table 8.6). Kediri is prominent in many forms of fruit production (pineapples in particular, which flourish on the sandy volcanic soils of the western

TABLE 8.6
East Java: Fruit Production, 1986

	Total Production ('000 tonnes)	*Main Producing Kabupaten*	*Production ('000 tonnes)*
Avocado	19.7	Malang	5.1
		Lumajang	4.3
		Probolinggo	3.0
Mango	143.5	Probolinggo	27.3
		Kediri	22.0
		Pasuruan	16.5
Rambutan	30.6	Blitar	14.4
		Jember	7.3
		Kediri	5.7
Duku/Langsat	4.0	Kediri	1.7
		Jember	1.3
Tangerine (*jeruk siam*)	47.0	Kediri	19.8
		Tulungagung	8.4
		Lumajang	8.1
Orange (*jeruk keprok*)	38.3	Pamekasan	10.2
		Ponorogo	6.2
		Pasuruan	5.2
Grapefruit (*jeruk besar*)	12.4	Magetan	4.7
		Kediri	1.9
		Madiun	1.0
Other citrus (*jeruk lain-lain*)	3.4	Kediri	1.3
		Malang	0.6
Durian	13.8	Kediri	4.1
		Pasuruan	2.8
		Ponorogo	1.2
Guava (*jambu biji*)	16.4	Lumajang	5.3
		Bangkalan	1.9
		Blitar	1.4
Watery rose apple (*jambu air*)	14.9	Lumajang	5.3
		Kediri	2.6
		Gresik	2.0
Pawpaw (*papaya*)	89.4	Malang	26.2
		Jombang	15.1
		Blitar	8.8
Sawo	9.2	Lumajang	2.1
		Kediri	1.1
		Ponorogo	0.9
Banana (*pisang*)	334.4	Banyuwangi	54.2
		Bangkalan	41.0
		Jember	40.7
Pineapple (*nanas*)	385.9	Blitar	359.4
		Kediri	24.3
		Tulungagung	0.7
Zalaka edulis (*salak*)	6.4	Bojonegoro	4.8

Source: BPS (1987e).

TABLE 8.7
East Java: Vegetable Production, 1987

Vegetable	*Production ('000 tonnes)*	*Area ('000 ha)*	*Main Producing Kabupaten*	*Production ('000 tonnes)*
Shallots (*bawang merah*)	112.0	13.8	Probolinggo	60.9
			Kediri	15.0
			Nganjuk	14.4
Leeks (*bawang daun*)	19.9	3.8	Malang	11.6
			Probolinggo	4.0
Garlic (*bawang putih*)	9.1	2.3	Malang	5.0
Cabbage (*kubis*)	108.9	8.1	Probolinggo	49.6
			Malang	17.1
			Magetan	19.6
			Pasuruan	16.7
Chillies (*cabe*)	102.5		Gresik	17.8
			Tuban	14.4
			Jember	9.2
Potatoes (*kentang*)	51.1	5.6	Malang	19.6
			Probolinggo	17.6
			Pasuruan	9.7

Source: BPS (1987b).

slopes of Mount Kelud), as is the Pasuruan–Probolinggo–Lumajang region (on the slopes of Mount Bromo and the Tengger Range) to a lesser extent. Malang is famous for its apple-growing district around Batu, where production roughly doubled between 1983 and 1987, as well as for vegetable production. The poorer regions of the south-west and north-west are minor producers of fruit and vegetables, but it is not clear whether this is due to poor soils and water supplies or other reasons, for some of them are now producing cloves in abundance. Proximity to urban markets is also an important factor, although the spread of truck transportation has enabled some remote areas to flourish.

Regional specialization seems to be less marked in vegetable production (Table 8.7), although in some mountain areas of the Tengger Range, the Upper Konto River in Malang (Hefner, 1983; Nibbering, Chapter 7), and various districts specializing in onions, particular crops have proved extremely lucrative. Cash returns per hectare for vegetables are sometimes very high but the risks of disease and seasonal price fluctuations make them a dangerously speculative crop for small farmers, since the timing of sales can be crucial. It is almost inevitable that the rising urban demand for vegetables will continue to stimulate further production increases and probably greater specialization in particular crops.

Conclusion

The increasingly prominent role of smallholders in the production of sugar, tobacco, and coffee, as well as in the various other tree crops, fruits, and vegetables, is a trend of potentially great significance in the socio-economic development of East Java. As domestic demand increases in the years ahead, prices and farmers' incomes may be expected to rise as production increases. But the trend has been noteworthy as much for its slow rate of progress prior to the 1980s as for its extent. The various changes described above have been unfolding very gradually over the course of nearly 50 years since the collapse of Dutch colonial rule. While the old plantation structures are gradually disintegrating, they are doing so less rapidly than one might have expected in the 1950s. Institutional inertia is a formidable force. Smallholder production of sugar, cigar tobacco, and coffee has increased, but many government officials employed in the plantation companies have entrenched interests in maintaining their privileged status as long as possible.

Government policies have played some part in the shift towards smallholder production since 1945, most notably the important 1975 decision to adopt the TRI scheme in the sugar industry. At other times they have affected outcomes more by default than deliberate intent, it seems. The Suharto government has not been aiming purposefully at such a goal; in fact, it tried initially to restore and strengthen the government estates as much as the smallholders or private estates. Massive World Bank loans were obtained for the rehabilitation of sugar-milling equipment, for example, in the 1970s–80s. But a combination of economic, social, and institutional pressures of various kinds has influenced the general outcome at least as much as government policy. The result has been that structurally the plantation sector has become a curious hybrid, still surviving, but gradually declining in significance, and in the cases of sugar and cigar tobacco becoming less sharply distinguished organizationally from the smallholder cash-crop agriculture which has been expanding and diversifying alongside it. It would be going too far to assert that the latter has taken over the economic roles of the former (investment, innovation, and entrepreneurship, for instance), but it has modified them profoundly.

One point that these trends underline is that demand conditions are decisive in most spheres of commodity production, as they generally are in all countries. The dramatic increase in smallholder output of fruit, vegetables, cloves, and tobacco for domestic markets since the 1970s, in response to the growing urban markets for these commodities, provides clear evidence of that. Farmers have been quick to seize market opportunities whenever they can get access to them, although the establishment of commercial linkages can be a capricious process, while price fluctuations or plant diseases are often disastrous for smallholders in the short run.

Yet the long-term trends towards the general commercialization of agriculture are plain to see, for the more traditional food crops—rice, corn, and cassava—are now produced with as keen an eye to market demand and prices as the export crops. That was far less the case before World War II, when most food production was for home consumption and, apart from the great export staples, some rice and a few vegetables like chillies and onions, there was precious little that would sell in large quantities. As agriculture in East Java has become more commercialized, the distinction between the spheres of activity of plantations and smallholders has become increasingly blurred. Structurally, it is likely to persist for a long time to come, but the dualism noted by Boeke in the colonial era is now much less sharply drawn. And it is the smallholders rather than the plantations who are showing themselves most adaptable, dynamic, and best fitted to seize the new market opportunities that have been opening up during the New Order years.

1. The words 'plantation' and 'estate' are used interchangeably here to refer to any large-scale agricultural enterprise, most of them highly capital-intensive (especially in the case of the huge sugar mills) and technologically sophisticated. They were usually monocultures and in the colonial era they were almost always foreign-owned, either by Dutch, Chinese, or a few British planters or plantation companies; they are now owned predominantly by State enterprises. In the case of tobacco, some 'estates' were not easily distinguishable from trading and exporting companies; moreover, they were usually involved in processing and selling tobacco leaf but not in growing it.

2. The term 'smallholder' refers not only to small landowners but also to large ones, by local standards (the word 'peasant' is more than usually inappropriate here, as well as being condescending), who grow cash crops other than traditional foodstuffs, usually on small plots of less than 10 hectares.

3. While Boeke (1910, 1953) provided the classic formulation of the 'dualistic society', a more perceptive treatment of smallholder production of cash crops and the more appropriate term 'plural economy' (and society) was put forward by Furnivall (1944: 319–22, 460–4). For assessments of dualistic theories, see Higgins (1955) and Mackie (1980).

4. The upland–lowland distinction as drawn here differs slightly from the seminal idea of a swidden–*sawah* dichotomy as introduced by C. Geertz in *Agricultural Involution* (1963: 106–14), a brilliant although in several respects flawed analysis; his 'ecological' approach in that work to the influence of different cropping patterns on economic structures and social relationships was a major advance at that time and has strongly influenced the approach here.

5. 'Coolie labour' was commonly brought in from other parts of Java in the late nineteenth century, but this soon became unnecessary as population increased in the estate areas.

6. The term 'Oosthoek' was applied rather generally by the Dutch to the eastern end of Java, roughly from the Pasuruan–Malang area to Banyuwangi. Besuki Residency consisted of the modern ***kabupaten*** Situbondo, Bondowoso, Jember, and Banyuwangi.

7. The total area of plantation crops planted in 1986, apart from sugar, was less than 90 000 hectares, of which coffee made up nearly half; see Table 8.1. Smallholder cash crops of various kinds, including coconuts, kapok, cloves, cashews, tobacco, and sugar totalled well over 600 000 hectares.

8. This was unlike the situation in parts of Sumatra and Sulawesi where there were few estates but extensive smallholder cultivation of rubber, coffee, copra, and other export crops.

9. Boeke (1953: 87) remarked that 'Western plantations are typically dualistic ... almost exclusively in the form of big business', with a set of modern characteristics which differentiated them sharply from traditional peasant agriculture.

10. Indonesia's exports of sugar reached nearly 3 million tonnes per annum in the late 1920s, but fell to around 600 000 tonnes in the mid-1950s, then declined steadily to zero by 1967, when the country had to import sugar to meet the rising domestic consumption. In some years it still has to import sugar, but the quantities have not greatly exceeded a quarter of a million tonnes since 1975.

11. By contrast, it is noteworthy that in the 1920s, the overall cash value of the tobacco grown on plantations in the uniquely fertile Jember region was approximately the same as that of the rice crops grown there (Mackie, 1985: 138).

12. The profitability of the State plantation enterprises is a topic on which reliable information is almost impossible to obtain, although press reports indicate that many are incurring losses. Private plantations were also reported to be in difficulties in the early 1980s. The reasons for this are too complex to go into here.

13. The officials in charge of the State plantation enterprises are usually rotated at roughly five-year intervals, which militates against any tendency for them to become strongly committed to the long-term success of a single plantation or area. While not unimportant figures among the local authorities in *kabupaten* capitals like Kediri or Jember, they exercise nothing like the same political clout their Dutch predecessors were able to exert in their dealings with the local Resident or Controleur (both of them Dutch), let alone the subordinate 'native' officials.

14. This figure is for sugar-cane cultivation only; it excludes harvesting (and factory work) and is taken from BPS (1986b: Table F-1, 26).

15. Sugar yields by province (Perhepi, 1984: 107):

	Cane (tonnes/ha)	*Rendement (%)*	*Sugar (kw/ha)*
East Java	79	9.73	7.6
Central Java	72	9.41	6.8
West Java	63	8.42	5.3
DI Yokyakarta	56	8.85	5.0
Java average	75	9.53	7.1

16. Most pre-war estates were in the 500–800-hectare range and the very large new mills of over 2 000 hectares at Jatiroto and Semboro in the Lumajang–Jember region were quite exceptional. In the 1980s many mills were drawing their cane from areas of more than double that size.

17. The two sugar plantations formerly owned by the famous Chinese tycoon, Oei Tiong Ham—Krebet and Kebonagung—were nationalized in 1961, but instead of being put under the same State enterprise as the Dutch estates they have been run under Finance Ministry auspices by a special agency, PT Rajawali, which has achieved a reputation for higher efficiency than the other State enterprises, having retained many of the original pre-nationalization technicians and managers.

18. Informative accounts of the TRI system have been given by Mubyarto (1977) and Brown (1982); for a fuller discussion of the reasons for productivity decline under the new system, see Mackie and O'Malley (1988). Statistical data on the sugar industry in the 1970s and 1980s are given in Perhepi (1984).

19. The word *bimbingan* has strongly paternalistic connotations in Indonesian, meaning literally 'to lead [a child] by the hand'.

20. Officials assert that the net cash returns from cane grown on *sawah* can be more attractive to farmers than the comparable return on rice and other crops, although this seems to be the case only in unusual circumstances, and generally turns out to refer in fact to cases of *tegalan* cultivation (which was less than 40 per cent of the area planted in the mid-1980s). The shift from planting cane on *sawah* to *tegalan* is due, in any case, not only to this technological innovation which represents an improvement for some, but also to the farmers' efforts to avoid utilizing their best land for cane while formally meeting the targets set for them.

21. The original Pasuruan Residency, incorporating what later became the Malang and Probolinggo residencies, ranked first in East Java in the 1830s–40s in terms of area planted with cane and as late as 1929, with over 29 000 hectares planted, was exceeded only slightly by Surabaya Residency (O'Malley, 1990: Tables 7.1 and 7.6). Its yields were initially the highest in Java. The history of the Pasuruan sugar industry by Elson (1984) gives an unrivalled account of the region's economic and social dynamics up to 1930. Today, the area planted in the *kabupaten* of Pasuruan is only 2 000–3 000 hectares.

22. Recent accounts of the Indonesian tobacco industry generally can be found in Soegiyanto Padmo and Edhie Djatmiko (1990) and for the Besuki region in Mackie (1985); for earlier accounts of tobacco in East Java and elsewhere, see Allen and Donnithorne (1957), Fruin (1926), Jaeggi (1946), and van der Broek (1946).

23. Use of the terms 'estate' or 'plantation' is slightly arbitrary here, for this was not a classical 'plantation' system, except in so far as the Dutch companies exercised considerable control over the labour and produce of the farmers. The 'estate complex' of smokehouses and curing sheds was the first link in the chain of operations they conducted in processing and exporting the tobacco leaf they obtained from the farmers.

24. The cultivation of Virginia had been introduced in the 1930s to meet the need for suitable tobacco for the newly established British American Tobacco factory producing 'white' cigarettes, consumption of which increased steadily between World War II and the 1980s, particularly in the 1970s, when production of Virginia more than doubled. It subsequently declined in the following decade as popular demand shifted dramatically towards *kretek*.

25. The exception was a large *erfpacht* (long-lease) concession held by LMOD (Landbouw Mij. Oud Djember), the major tobacco estate, founded by Birnie, now in the hands of the State-owned company, PTP XXVIII, which rented the lands it held on a concession from the government to the villagers who lived on it and planted tobacco for it; thus the company had a powerful instrument of control over them. An agrarian rights conflict that erupted there in 1980, known as the 'Jenggawa episode', had its origins in these unusual arrangements.

26. A medium-sized smokehouse might cost about US$2,000–3,000 in the early 1980s and usually lasted only one or two seasons before needing substantial repairs. Many wealthy farmers invested in them in the 1960s, when big profits could be made from them. Traders (whose main business consisted of purchasing smoked leaf tobacco for sale to the processing establishments which sorted and fermented it) sometimes owned smokehouses or fermenting sheds, although the latter are now generally in the hands of the tobacco exporters who both process and export cigar tobacco. For fuller details on these steps in the chain of processing and marketing cigar tobacco, see Mackie (1985: 116–17).

27. Again the exception has been the former LMOD *erfpacht* estate south-west of Jember: see note 25 above.

28. The statistical material used here has been taken from KSJT, *Jawa Timur dalam Angka* (1981 and 1988) and BPS (1989b) while accounts of the Indonesian coffee industry are from McStocker (1987) and Moeljarto and Dwi Retnandari (1990).

29. The area of smallholder coffee in East Java was less than 7 000 hectares in 1955, far less than the figure for Central Java; it increased rapidly to 26 000 hectares in 1960 and then rose gradually to 34 000 hectares by 1968 and 45 000 hectares by 1988 (McStocker, 1987: 46). But that was less than half the area of smallholder coffee in Lampung and barely a quarter of South Sumatra's area.

30. See Chapter 12 for further explanation and references on Cultuurstelsel.

31. These figures may in part reflect a statistical aberration, due to the fact that effective compilation of production figures for fruit and vegetables has been introduced only recently and the earliest estimates were probably too low. How can banana production be reliably assessed when they are grown in so many millions of tiny gardens or chilli production, when chillies are grown along *sawah* edges nearly everywhere?

9
The Working of Rural Co-operatives (KUD) in Malang, 1970–1984

Amir Santoso

Introduction

In the implementation of any government policy there are frequently great differences between the officially declared aims, as laid down by the national leadership, and the ways in which the policy is actually implemented at the grass-roots level. In Indonesia the few existing studies of the implementation of public policies suggest that what happens at lower levels may bear little relationship to the intentions of the government, or that it may do so in only a formalistic way (Grindle, 1980; Santoso, 1986). The circumstances prevailing in society in each region can strongly influence policy implementation, as can the relationship between lower level officials and local community leaders. The nature of these grass-roots relationships is revealed in this chapter, which deals with the implementation of rural development policies in one part of East Java.

The chapter arises out of an investigation carried out in 1983/4 into the ways in which the policies of the Suharto government to increase rice production and to promote rural development in Indonesia have been implemented at the level of the *kecamatan* (subdistrict) in Kabupaten Malang in East Java. The study throws light on the political relationships between central government officials and the village élites involved in the rural co-operatives (*koperasi unit desa* or KUD) in five *kecamatan* in Malang.

Rice in Kabupaten Malang

Malang is one of the major rice-producing regions of East Java, one of eight *kabupaten* (districts) which in 1983 produced in the order of 400 000 tonnes of rice (Santoso, 1986). It is a large and mountainous area containing in 1983 57 167 hectares of irrigated rice fields (*sawah*) and 126 773 hectares of dry-cultivated fields (*tegalan*) on which traditional annual food crops other than rice (*palawija*) and tree crops were grown.

TABLE 9.1
Malang: Selected Production Statistics for Rice, 1970–1983

	Area Harvested (ha)	*Production (tonnes)*	*Production Average (kg per ha)*
1970	69 117	187 034	2 653
1971	64 924	233 103	3 520
1972	67 837	274 215	3 963
1973	71 550	302 153	4 141
1974	74 423	277 107	3 602
1975	79 244	335 682	4 153
1976	77 058	335 068	4 263
1977	71 460	319 837	4 388
1978	72 435	352 637	4 773
1979	71 726	380 144	5 196
1980	73 313	384 165	5 137
1981	78 273	423 238	5 301
1982	72 166	391 739	5 322
1983	70 884	397 722	5 501

Source: Diperta Malang.

Rice production in Malang increased between 1970 and 1983 at an average rate of 8 per cent per annum (Table 9.1), higher than the increase for East Java as a whole despite decreased production in several years due to pest attacks. Production peaked at 423 238 tonnes in 1981.

The Impact of the Rice Intensification Programme

The increase in rice production in Malang in the 1970s resulted largely from the government's rice intensification programme, which comprised a number of policies designed to assist farmers to increase their rice production. First came the introduction of new rice-cultivation technology, generally referred to as 'Panca Usaha Tani' (Five Principles of Good Farming), involving new planting and harvesting methods developed especially for the new high-yielding varieties of rice (HYVs) being introduced at the time (see Chapter 6). Secondly, various government schemes—Bimas (Bimbingan Massal or Mass Guidance), Inmas (Intensifikasi Massal or Mass Intensification), and Insus (Intensifikasi Khusus or Special Intensification)—were introduced, under which farmers were encouraged to use the new HYVs in conjunction with a package of inputs such as fertilizers, pesticides, and rat control measures. Thirdly, the government pursued a price stabilization scheme, carried out by the State Logistics Board (Badan Urusan Logistik or Bulog), which fixed the floor price for rice. Fourthly, the government promoted the development of rural co-operatives—known initially as *badan usaha unit desa* (BUUD), and later as KUD—as a means to channel subsidized credit and fertilizer to the villages and to assist in the collection of harvested rice for purchase by Bulog.

Particularly after 1974 the impetus for the increase in production came largely from the farmers themselves, as they increasingly saw the benefits of planting HYVs and applying the Panca Usaha Tani methods as demonstrated by the officers of the Agricultural Extension Service (Penyuluh Pertanian Lapangan or PPL).

The Bimas programme succeeded in extending the use of HYVs in all five *kecamatan*. According to the district officers (*camat*), the PPL, and interviews conducted with farmers, most of them had shifted away from local varieties to HYVs by 1983/4. The government has also succeeded in securing the availability and accessibility of production inputs such as fertilizers and pesticides. Because the market was favourable for rice, most farmers preferred it to other crops. Many sugar-cane planters in rice-producing villages returned to rice, especially since there were problems with the government's Smallholder Sugar-cane Intensification Programme (Tebu Rakyat Intensifikasi or TRI).

The increase in production per hectare also shows that farmers generally accepted the Panca Usaha Tani method. However, a small number of farmers (especially large farmers with more than 2 hectares) refused to plant the types of seeds recommended by the PPL or their own farmers' groups. Some did not plant rice at all but planted *palawija* crops instead. There were usually economic reasons for their non-compliance. Since the number refusing to participate was small, their actions did not have serious implications for the overall implementation of the rice programme.

The Effects of Bimas on Per Capita Income

According to the *kabupaten* office, average per capita incomes in Malang increased between 1976 and 1982 by 19.4 per cent per annum on a current price basis and by 6 per cent per annum based on constant prices. How much farmers actually benefited from this is hard to gauge. A study conducted in villages in East and West Java during the period 1976–83 found that the increase in farmers' incomes on a constant price basis was between 41 and 78 per cent in highland areas and between 13 and 73 per cent in lowland areas (Yusuf Saefuddin and Yuni Marisa, 1984). According to a study by Edmundson (1977) in a rice-producing village in Malang, the standard of living of most of the population improved between 1971 and 1976. However, there was also a concentration of wealth in the hands of large farmers over the period.

From interviews conducted in various villages it became apparent that, for most large farmers, life was better than before the introduction of Bimas. The scheme enabled large farmers to restore houses, buy radio and television sets, buy more land, or even build rice-milling units. However, among small farmers, some felt that their conditions of life were better while others felt that they were neither worse nor better. The small farmers who felt that their life was better usually said that although the Bimas programme had increased the production of their *sawah*, most of their added income actually came from other economic activities or from those of their children.

The number of farm households owning less than 0.5 hectare of land increased by 19 per cent between 1973 and 1980. During the same period there was a slight decrease (1.4 per cent) in the number of households owning the land they cultivated, and the number of landless labourers increased by 5.8 per cent (KSM, 1982). How much of this can be attributed to the effects of the Bimas programme and the introduction of technology based on HYVs of rice, and how much to an increase in population is unclear.

The Working of Rice Policies at the Local Level

Although the agricultural statistics reveal a doubling of both rice production and yields per hectare in Malang between 1970 and 1983, it became clear from enquiries in various parts of the *kabupaten* that the implementation of government policies left a lot to be desired. One almost has to ask whether rice production increased because of the government's policies or in spite of them. Perhaps the answer is a little of each. The extension services, which were originally regarded as a crucially important part of the Panca Usaha Tani programme, reached only a small part of the rural population in the survey area. There were not enough PPL to service all the farmers' groups through which information should have been passed on to farmers about new rice varieties and agricultural technology. The PPL were supposed to keep in touch with one or more contact farmers (*kontak tani*) in each group who would then provide guidance to the other villagers. In practice this system worked poorly. It was difficult for the PPL to reach the farmers since many of the former lacked transport and lived in larger towns away from their work areas, and because the farmers' groups themselves were often unenthusiastic about the programme. For example, meetings between the *kontak tani* and the farmers were frequently poorly attended.

There were also problems for the farmers. The PPL in many cases paid only a token monthly visit to the *kontak tani*, particularly in the more remote parts of their work areas, ostensibly to provide information and guidance but often just to get the signatures to show that they had made the visit. Farmers often lacked support from village officials for PPL activities. This support depended on the nature of the relationship between the PPL or *kontak tani* and the leading villagers who ran the village administration. Where these relations were strained, the PPL found it hard to reach the farmers. Where they were close and cordial, the system worked well. Active involvement in a farmers' group was likely to be greater if the participants' economic situations were roughly similar. Much depended, too, on their experiences with government programmes. One farmers' group had collapsed because the Insus premium due to be paid to them by the *kabupaten* authorities had not reached them. All these elements affected the nature of the relationship between the villagers and the lower level government officials, who had a critical effect on the success of the government's overall policies in the area.

The decline in farmers' participation in the Bimas programme from the late 1970s is often regarded as an indication of its failure. While it is true that the number of participants in the Bimas programme declined continuously from 1976, participation in the Inmas and Insus programmes increased. The larger farmers, those working 0.5 hectare or more, had the capacity by then to finance new rice varieties without subsidized credit from the Bimas credit package. Seeds and other inputs became available through the Inmas scheme which did not supply credit.

There were other reasons why farmers became unwilling to participate in the Bimas programme. In some cases complaints were made that local Bimas officials applied pressure on farmers to repay the loans when they had been exempted from their repayment obligations because of harvest losses during the brown planthopper attacks of 1976/7. In other cases farmers were cheated by staff of their village unit bank and no action was taken to remedy the matter. Delays in the distribution of fertilizer were often extended by Bimas officials to force farmers to pay premium prices on the open market in order to obtain supplies in time for the planting season. All these abuses gave the Bimas scheme a bad reputation, even though it had been successful in achieving its primary aim of increasing rice production in the 1970s. What finally made it redundant was simply the fact that private distribution made fertilizer and pesticides readily available on the open market. It was not only more convenient and reliable but even cheaper in many cases, after transport costs had been taken into account.

The problem of Bimas credit arrears also became a matter of some controversy in the early 1980s, adding to the scheme's bad reputation. The *kabupaten* office in Malang reported that in 1983, Bimas credit arrears amounted to Rp 1,024 million and involved over 33,000 defaulters (Santoso, 1986). Significantly, village officials were the main offenders—presumably because they were confident that no severe action would be taken against them. It is certainly true that a team set up by the *kabupaten* office to recover the debts was not very active. Most of its work was delegated to the *kecamatan* offices, where the officials were likely to have close personal contacts with the village officials concerned. In 1984 almost Rp 200 million was still outstanding in the five *kecamatan* surveyed, which suggests that only a small proportion of the arrears had been collected. The common view was that the authorities were not showing much determination in the matter and that co-ordination between the various agencies involved was poor. Relations between the *camat* and the police or village unit banks were often strained by their conflicting interests in pursuing claims. Much was being said about debt recovery at the national level, but at the local level officials had no strong motivation to remedy the situation.

The Development of the KUD in Malang

Eleven years after their establishment in 1973, the KUD in Malang still faced serious difficulties, and with few exceptions were not serving the interests of all the farmers. There was a formalistic quality about them, most vividly seen in the fact that all 33 KUD in Kabupaten Malang (not including those in the municipality of Malang) were classified by the government as model KUD, even though they did not always fulfil all the necessary criteria.

One of the criteria was the ability to recruit a minimum of 5,000 members. In Malang there were only four KUD with more than this number in 1983. Most of them had around 2,000 members, and one had only 230 (BPS, 1986b). But even those with 2,000 members represented only a small proportion of the *kecamatan* population (that is, around 400 households per *kecamatan* or less than 3 per cent of the average population (KSM, 1982)). The designation of all 33 KUD in Malang as model KUD, based on the instructions of the *bupati* (*kabupaten* head), was done simply to present the local government in the best light to provincial government officials. It was little more than a formal gesture.

A central government regulation stipulated that a KUD should be run by the farmers themselves and should serve their interests. A KUD is supposed to be managed by a board chosen by members at an annual general meeting. At this meeting a supervisory body is also elected which has the task of supervising the management of the co-operative. A manager is appointed by the board to run the business activities of the KUD. The regulation also stated that the profits of the business were to be distributed to its members, that the welfare of the members should be given high priority and that there should be open management. At the *kabupaten* level a co-operative office is responsible for developing the KUD under the co-ordination of the *bupati*, while the *camat* supervises its development at the *kecamatan* level.

The KUD in the five *kecamatan* surveyed did not function as effective instruments for advancing the major aims of the government rice policy. While generally they were successful in their rice procurement and business activities, they failed to serve the interests of farmers and were dominated by a few members of the élite in each *kecamatan*.

The KUD of Tamping[1]

From the very beginning the KUD of the rice-rich Tamping area was dominated by a few members of the *kecamatan* élite: local government officials and a few wealthy villagers. By 1984 it had become an arena for political groups competing to dominate the organization, the leaders manipulating support from their own groups to maintain their leadership. The purpose of the leaders was to tap the financial resources provided by the government for their own personal use.

Members of the KUD board included government officials, ex-servicemen, and rich farmers who owned more than 0.5 hectare of *sawah* and also pursued other business activities. Representatives of all three political parties—Golongan Karya (Golkar), Partai Demokrasi Indonesia (PDI), and Partai Persatuan Pembangunan (PPP)—were on the board. However, unlike other KUD in Malang, the Tamping KUD had been dominated by Golkar since it was established as a BUUD in 1973. Golkar had been successful in eliminating the influence of the PDI which previously had strong support in Tamping. Moreover, after 1981 the KUD was dominated by rich farmers from one village, all of whom were members of Golkar.

In August 1973, when the first BUUD was established in Tamping, all the members of the former agricultural co-operative board (who were mostly members of Golkar) were appointed to the BUUD board. An election to choose a new board was held in 1974 in accordance with a new BUUD regulation, and Golkar members retained a majority.

In 1975 the intervention of Pepabri (Persatuan Purnawirawan Angkatan Bersenjata Republik Indonesia or Association of Retired Army Members, closely linked with Golkar) in the BUUD began when a retired army lieutenant was elected as the new chairperson. At that time Golkar had three members on the board, PDI had two and PPP one. By 1978 the PDI and Golkar had four members each on the board and PPP had two. PDI influence increased when it created a new position on the board during 1978, occupied by one of its members.

On 9 April 1979 the BUUD became a KUD. The day marked the beginning of an increase in PPP activity in the KUD and a decline in PDI influence. On that day the PPP successfully manoeuvred two of its members on to the supervisory body of the KUD, at the expense of a PDI member. However, PPP efforts to take over the position of first secretary, occupied by Golkar, were unsuccessful.

At the annual general meeting of the KUD in 1981 a young teacher, who was also a farmer and a member of the National Committee of Indonesian Youth (Komite Nasional Pemuda Indonesia or KNPI, a Golkar-backed youth organization), was elected chairperson of the KUD. This move maintained the power of Golkar and was the beginning of the domination of the KUD by rich farmers from one village.

In 1983 the business manager of the KUD in Tamping was accused of financial corruption involving Rp 14 million. Neither the chairperson of the KUD nor the *camat* took any action, either to charge the manager before a court or to examine the KUD books. The only result was the replacement of the manager with a friend from the same village. The person who had made the report, a member of the supervisory body, resigned in protest.

This case points to the powerlessness of KUD supervisory bodies to prevent or to address corruption effectively. There is little they can achieve unless they gain the support of the *camat*. There seem to be three reasons for this. First, the supervisory body generally has insufficient authority to take any action to remedy corruption, especially if this would counter the authority of the *camat*. Similar cases can be found in other KUD. Secondly, because some members of the KUD board and the supervisory body come from the same village or political group, interpersonal relationships and a feeling of *esprit de corps* have prevented the necessary action being taken if mismanagement occurs. Thirdly, most of the members of the supervisory body have insufficient knowledge of management, accounting, and bookkeeping to monitor the management of KUD.

The rich farmers who dominated the co-operative in Tamping used it for personal gain. For example, the new business manager was accused of buying rice from the farmers at below the floor price, and later selling it to the KUD at a higher price. The PPP used this rumour in an appeal to discharge the new manager. The appeal was successful and at the next annual general meeting he was replaced by a member of PPP.

At this meeting the *camat* sponsored as the new chairperson a retired deputy *bupati* (district head) who was not a member of the KUD. This contravened the KUD regulation that a nominee for the board must be a member of the co-operative. The *camat* simply bypassed the regulation, confident that the *bupati* would support him.

Despite the intergroup competition, the KUD made some progress in its business activities. These included purchasing food stocks, rice milling, and distribution of Bimas and other small-scale credit. However, only those who attended the annual general meetings actually knew the full amount of the profit and other financial benefits; and those who enjoyed the benefits were perhaps only the *camat*, district council officials, and KUD staff. Most of the KUD budget was spent on staff salaries. Furthermore, the *camat* always asked for 5 per cent of the profit from each KUD project for the *kecamatan* budget, and even used KUD finances for personal purposes.

The KUD also encountered problems in its food stock activities. First, it usually had no ready capital to purchase rice, so that many farmers sold their rice not to the KUD but to the agents of private rice mills, even though the price at the KUD was sometimes higher. Most farmers needed cash urgently and the KUD usually had no capacity to pay cash at the time of harvest. Credit for the KUD to purchase rice was often delayed by complicated administrative procedures and came only after the harvest, when much of the rice had been sold to traders, often at below the floor price. Although the KUD reported this problem, no action was ever taken to remedy it.

Secondly, the local operational logistics unit, the Sub-Dolog (Sub-Depot Logistik), sometimes refused to accept rice from the KUD because it was considered to be of inferior quality. This resulted in financial losses for the KUD. Consequently, in order to minimize risk, the KUD decided to deal with local rice traders in preference to the Sub-Dolog. Similar situations were found in other KUD.

Farmers in Tamping also complained about delays in fertilizer distribution, caused not only by delays in shipment from the services centre for co-operatives but also by regulations in the Bimas programme, for example, about the way credit was to be distributed. The KUD lacked the facilities to act as a distributor of government credit, it lacked the staff to cope with credit repayments from farmers, and its facilities for the long-term storage of fertilizer were inadequate.

The KUD board, on the other hand, complained about the farmers' refusal to buy production inputs at the KUD kiosks, while at the same time recognizing that the location of the kiosks, far from the villages, was inappropriate. This was due to difficulty in finding land near the villages. In fact most of the kiosks were never opened. The KUD claimed that they had insufficient staff to manage them.

The KUD of Jambang

The KUD in the much poorer *kecamatan* of Jambang was also dominated by members of the *kecamatan* élite. But, whereas the Tamping KUD had been controlled by Golkar, the KUD of Jambang was dominated by the PPP chair. Jambang is an example of the government's lack of attention to the development of KUD in non-rice-producing areas.

The first members of the BUUD board, in 1973, appointed by the *camat*, were former members of a farmers' co-operative board established in 1956. In 1973 the leader was a member of PDI, but all other members of the board were from PPP. In 1974 a member of PPP and former head of the supervisory body of the BUUD (Haji M) was appointed chairperson. This marked the beginning of Haji M's domination of the BUUD/KUD which continued until 1983, explaining why it came to be regarded widely in Jambang as his family firm. The majority of members of the KUD board were from PPP and were friends of Haji M, many from his own village. This closed system meant that many members of the KUD did not know how it was managed since they never received any account of the board's operations. Moreover, the board rarely conducted annual general meetings. These factors gave rise to suspicions that some of the board members were involved in financial corruption.

During this period the KUD was badly managed. For example, it had no list of members and no registration of profits. During his time as chairperson, Haji M successfully prevented any intervention by the *camat* or the *kabupaten* co-operative office in the management of the KUD. No annual general meetings were held until 1979, and the 1979 meeting was merely a ceremony to strengthen the position of Haji M and his supporters. From 1979 to 1983 again no annual general meetings were held. In 1981 the secretary of the KUD board absconded from Jambang with around Rp 2 million of the co-operative's funds.

The fact that Haji M managed to avoid having annual general meetings is evidence of the powerlessness of the *camat* and the co-operative office to intervene in KUD management. This was due to three factors. In the first place, the *camat* and some staff members of the co-operative office had themselves been involved in the financial scandals of the KUD. Secondly, *kabupaten* officials seemed to have no interest in the development of the KUD in Jambang. Since Jambang was not potentially a rich rice-growing area, its contribution to food stocks was small and hence the development of the KUD in Jambang tended to be disregarded.

Thirdly, it seems that the lack of attention from officials was also part of a deliberate attempt to weaken an organization in which Golkar had a lesser role than other parties. The head of the co-operative office in Malang categorized the KUD in which PPP or PDI members had a majority of positions on the board as trouble spots. The implication was that the KUD was in the wrong hands and efforts to replace its board members should be made.

In 1983 the position of chairperson was taken from Haji M and given to the chairperson of Pepabri. On the new board, the number of Golkar members was greater but the majority of positions were still in the hands of PPP. Yet there was no improvement in the management of the KUD: it still had no list of members and no registration of profits.

The domination of the KUD by one person associated with a particular political party meant that most farmers in Jambang received no benefit from the KUD. Even the farmers in Haji M's own village appeared to be cynical about benefits they had obtained.

The KUD of Kajen

The KUD of Kajen was also dominated by one person, in this case a retired army officer, a member of Pepabri who was strongly backed by Golkar. The majority of the members of the KUD board belonged to both Golkar and Pepabri, most of them being public servants or ex-soldiers. None of them had been a farmer.

The BUUD of Kajen was established on 2 February 1973 and became a KUD on 1 January 1980. The first board was appointed by the *camat*, as in other *kecamatan*. During the years 1973–5 there were no annual general meetings. In 1976 the first annual general meeting was held, after strong demands for the replacement of the business manager on the grounds of his alleged involvement in financial corruption. At this meeting, a retired lieutenant-colonel and member of Pepabri (to be named S) was appointed as the new chairperson, a position he still retained in 1984. Although five annual general meetings were held after 1976, no significant changes occurred in the membership of the board. Some members occupied their positions for many years and the majority were still members of Golkar.

S's domination of the KUD, and particularly his interventionist attitude towards its operations, created difficulties with some of his KUD colleagues. S was powerful enough to avoid control by the supervisory body, the *camat*, and the co-operative office. Various informants in Kajen reported that before 1982 money belonging to the KUD was often borrowed by S or other staff members without any receipts being given and this was frequently not repaid. However, nobody dared to publicize this malpractice at the time.

In 1982 a new member of the supervisory board (also a member of Pepabri), discovered financial corruption in the KUD which he reported to the co-operative office. He got no response. Rumours then arose that the lack of response was due to the fact that Rp 200,000 had been given by S to the co-operative office to protect his position. The member who had reported the matter withdrew from the supervisory body in protest.

The KUD of Kajen was not accepted widely by the farmers as their own organization. Many of them said they had received no benefits from the KUD. As in other KUD, meetings were held to which only the *kontak tani* were invited, each representing 10 farmers. Yet it was considered widely that they did not represent the opinions of farmers. Information about the profits or losses of the KUD generally was not made available to the majority of the members. In all the five KUD investigated, it was commonly said that the annual general meetings were mere formalities, held simply to comply with the regulations.

Most of the rice in Kajen was collected not from farmers within the Kajen area, but from other areas, through co-operation with traders. This occurred regularly from 1973 for several reasons. First, the KUD lacked the experience, staff, and facilities to compete with the rice traders. However, the co-operative was able to profit from collecting the transportation fees reimbursed for the distance between Kajen and the Sub-Dolog warehouse. The amount of the reimbursement increased with the distance between a KUD and the warehouse. As a result some KUD managers, like the manager in Kajen, speculated in rice procurement, even if the KUD was not located in a rice-producing *kecamatan*. These managers made deals with traders in rice-producing *kecamatan*, particularly those located near the Sub-Dolog warehouses, to deliver rice to the warehouse on their behalf. Meanwhile the rice traders also benefited from their transactions with local farmers through buying rice below the floor price.

Secondly, the relationship between the Kajen KUD and the traders was tacitly approved by the government in that the latter ignored the problem of the sources of rice handled through the KUD. The government's primary concern was that the KUD should provide its set quota for the national rice stock. The KUD's function in contributing to the welfare of the farmers was quite secondary to this.

Thirdly, the Sub-Dolog often refused to accept local rice from the KUD in Kajen, on the grounds that it was below Sub-Dolog standards. Testing was carried out without supervision of KUD staff but it was suspected that the results of the tests were manipulated. These suspicions were enhanced by the fact that a cash payment or 'sweetener' had to be given to the Sub-Dolog staff before they would approve rice for purchase. The KUD thus preferred to sell its rice to private rice traders who were adept at negotiating the 'sweetener'. This reduced the risk of losses to the KUD if a consignment were refused and meant less work for KUD staff.

The KUD of Sumbersari II

There were two KUD in Sumbersari, to cover the *kecamatan*'s large area. They have been named Sumbersari I and Sumbersari II. This study focused on Sumbersari II because of unusual problems which arose there, especially in the years 1982–4.

The KUD in Sumbersari II was dominated up to 1984 by a small élite group of villagers. The Pepabri was able to penetrate the KUD only after an internal conflict in 1983 which broke the control of the dominant group, Haji R and three colleagues, S, F, and P. This conflict provided the local government with the opportunity to intervene and eventually to take control of the management, making it the only KUD in Malang officially run by local government officials.

The domination of the KUD by a local élite excluded most farmers from participating in the organization and also from enjoying its benefits. Moreover, these élite members were able to use the KUD for their own enrichment rather than for the benefit of the ordinary farmers. This could be seen from their involvement in business contracts with the co-operative which, although not prohibited by law or by the co-operative's regulations, provided personal profits for some members of the KUD board.

As in other KUD, the *kecamatan* officials also withdrew funds for their own purposes. In the TRI programme, for example, the KUD of Sumbersari II was expected to provide a contribution to the *kecamatan* office at the rate of Rp 1 per 100 kilograms of sugar. In 1982, when production of sugar was over 21 million kilograms, this meant a contribution of over Rp 200,000 to *kecamatan* officials.

The conflict which broke the control of the small group of villagers headed by Haji R arose when Haji R (first chairperson of the KUD) reversed a decision taken by F to discharge four KUD staff members and an official seconded from the co-operative office in Malang to handle TRI matters in Sumbersari. F had received a report from a member of the supervisory body that the Malang official and some board members had misappropriated Rp 130 million of TRI funds. However, P, the chairperson of the supervisory body, did not endorse the report and this soon divided the board into two groups: the Haji R group and the F group.

The conflict between F and Haji R had both a personal and a political dimension. For some years F had suspected that Haji R was collaborating with KUD staff to use the funds of the TRI programme improperly, but he had no proof. When the report of the corruption within the KUD was received, F took measures against the alleged collaborators in order to teach them a lesson. Haji R felt that F had acted too harshly, particularly, he claimed, since he had not been consulted.

However, informants in Sumbersari II felt that the reversal of F's decision by Haji R was made in order to protect two of the four KUD staff members, who were Haji R's relatives.

The affair was reported in the local newspaper. Pepabri, which had always been prevented by F from moving into the KUD, then used the opportunity to topple F from his position by proposing that the whole KUD board be replaced. Pepabri also circulated a rumour that F was a member or a supporter of the Indonesian Socialist Party (Partai Sosialis Indonesia or PSI) which had been banned by Sukarno in the early 1960s. The Pepabri campaign was successful and their own nominee was placed on the KUD board. In order to resolve the leadership dispute and settle the internal conflict, the *bupati* ordered the deputy *bupati* in Sumbersari to take over the management of the KUD. He then established a new board with himself as chairperson. The new board comprised mainly local government leaders of Sumbersari.

The story of this KUD has several interesting features. First, no action was taken by the village unit bank or the extension workers of the plantation office to prevent the corruption, although they must have known about it. Hence, there was the suspicion that the chairperson of the village unit bank and the extension workers were also involved in the scandal.

Secondly, it is significant that the *camat* rarely made any check on the management of the KUD, although he was officially a supervisor and as such was responsible for its development. He intervened in the case only when it was publicized in the newspaper. Either he had received no prior information about the TRI mismanagement or he knew of it but took no action until it became unavoidable.

Thirdly, it is clear that the farmers generally had no voice with regard to the problems that arose in the co-operative, although it is often declared that the KUD is a farmers' organization. Thus it is not surprising that the farmers have generally stood outside the co-operative and have allowed the problems to be solved (or otherwise) by the management.

Finally, the story shows that people who served the organization well would not necessarily be rewarded and might even suffer penalties if their actions did not reflect the interests of the local authorities. The person who reported the corruption was discharged from the supervisory body on the charge that he had given an interview to the local newspaper. The result of this was that the affair became public throughout East Java and was said to have brought shame to the *kecamatan*. F, apart from being discharged from the board of the KUD, was also removed from the position of chairperson of the co-ordinating body of the KUD (*badan kontak organisasi* or BKO). On the other hand, no action was taken against the official from Malang who was at the centre of the controversy: he was allowed to return to the co-operative office in Malang.

The KUD of Paraji

The KUD of Paraji was also dominated by the *kecamatan* élite. In this case the dominant leader was the business manager, and the board comprised government civil servants and retired army officers. As in Kajen they were non-farmers. The group conflict in Paraji was between Golkar and PDI.

From 1973 until 1981 the BUUD/KUD was dominated by its manager, W, from PDI. His strong influence meant that there was inadequate monitoring of the KUD management. W and his colleagues were reportedly involved in various financial scandals. At the end of 1981 some KUD members, particularly those from Pepabri, reported their suspicions to the *bupati*, since the *camat* and the co-operative office had failed to take action. The *bupati* ordered an annual general meeting and then persuaded the meeting to discharge W. The meeting was conducted under the tight control of army and police officers and was also attended by members of the PDI and PPP.

H, a civilian and also chairperson of an army co-operative organization, was appointed as the new chairperson. In fact, most members of the KUD did not support his nomination, but the *bupati* and the *camat* gave their strong support to Pepabri and Golkar, which secured H's appointment. This marked the beginning of military intervention in the KUD. In March 1984 H was replaced by the chairperson of the supervisory body. This appointment gave rise to the rumour that the KUD of Paraji had simply held a symbolic election by choosing someone from the internal circle of the KUD.

Many farmers in Paraji who were registered as members of the KUD knew nothing of its benefits and had never received any distribution of funds. As in other KUDs, they were never invited to attend annual general meetings, except for a small number selected by the KUD board.

Conclusion

Undoubtedly some success has been achieved by the KUD in these five *kecamatan*. In fact, all five KUDs indicated some measure of progress in their business activities and recorded profits from them. They were successful, for example, in handling the sugar intensification programme, in rice milling, and in chicken breeding, all of which were backed by government programmes. However, the farmers and the majority of the KUD members themselves did not obtain any direct benefits from the co-operatives.

The central government's success in promoting an increase in rice production was due largely to its ability to induce local government officials to work in accordance with its directions, including the use of coercion to compel farmers to accept new rice-planting technology, particularly in the early years of the Bimas programme.

In implementing its rice policy, it seems that the government gave attention primarily to increasing rice production. This was probably due to the government's need to ensure the loyalty of the groups supporting the regime: the armed forces, the civil servants, and various urban groups, especially the technocrats and the students. It was important for the government to meet the demands of these groups for a reasonable rice price, hence the need for adequate stocks to prevent unexpected shortages which might force up the price. Thus, as long as the production targets were achieved, the central government tended to give only secondary consideration to the views and needs of the farmers themselves, and to disregard some of the administrative problems which arose in the course of implementing rice policy. The local officials themselves, because their careers depended on their superiors, also tended to ignore the interests of farmers.

There was also the problem of the accountability of local officials. They tended to report whatever would make their superiors happy and to conceal the truth if that would create difficulties for them or discontent among their superiors. Hence the phenomenon of the 'Laporan ABS' (Laporan Asal Bapak Senang or As-long-as-the-boss-is-happy Report) arose. Such reports inform superior officers only about what they want to hear and are intended primarily to secure the careers of local officials. The delays in fertilizer distribution and the various financial scandals in the KUD illustrate the results of the ABS spirit.

The implementation of the Bimas and KUD programmes has also demonstrated the lack of serious supervision by the responsible superior officers. Even worse was the inability of the government to address the corruption that was associated widely with the programmes. This corruption not only compromised the performance and authority of the officials but also made the farmers less eager to join the programmes.

In the implementation of rice policy, the regional heads, the *bupati* and the *camat* seemed to have difficulty in co-ordinating the various central government agencies and offices at the local level. This provides further evidence that to implement policy effectively the regional heads, although they have been designated as the sole administrators of their regions, cannot exercise their authority merely on the basis of the formal decisions made by the central government.

In the area of personnel and training, the government endeavoured to recruit more staff in the local government offices involved in the Bimas and KUD programmes and carried out training programmes to increase their skills. However, these efforts were not sufficient to cope with the demands for more personnel and a more efficient bureaucracy. Programme implementation also disregarded the need for adequate rewards and incentives and for sanctions for local officials implementing policy. On the one hand, many were hampered in obtaining promotions by bureaucratic red tape; on the other hand, penalties for those who broke the rules and became involved in corruption were rarely carried out firmly.

The implementation of the Bimas and particularly the KUD programmes suffered from lack of popular participation. Participation by the farmers is important in ensuring adequate supervision of officials and board members of the KUD. It is also essential if the objective of growth with equity, which seems often to be ignored, is to be achieved. To increase the level of farmers' participation, the government should allow them more freedom of choice in rice-planting methods and rice varieties. The government should also give the farmers the opportunity to set up and manage the KUD themselves. The public as a whole should be encouraged to participate and assist in monitoring the programme. This monitoring role could be shared by the press. In this context the government should give real encouragement to the press to report the process of programme implementation and to investigate any malpractices or deviations that might occur.

1. The names used for the five *kecamatan* studied are fictitious.

10
Manufacturing*

Howard Dick

Introduction

INDUSTRIALIZATION is often regarded as the very essence of economic development. Because of East Java's concentration of sugar milling, railways and tramways, and shipbuilding and ship repair, the province in fact led the incipient industrialization of Indonesia up to the Great Depression of the 1930s. Then, at just the time when the colonial government embraced industrialization as a deliberate aim of policy and imposed protective tariffs and quotas, East Java's economy was crippled by the collapse of the sugar industry and left in hiatus for several decades. When industrialization again became a national priority under the New Order's Second Five-Year Development Plan (Repelita II, 1974/5–1978/9) with an acceleration of import substitution, East Java continued to lag behind the Jakarta–West Java complex.

According to gross regional product (GRP) figures, as late as 1984 East Java was still by a narrow margin Indonesia's most industrialized province, with the manufacturing sector accounting for almost 15 per cent of GRP compared with 13 per cent for Jakarta–West Java and about 12 per cent for Central Java–Yogyakarta Special Region (Daerah Istimewa Yogyakarta or DIY) (Table 10.1). By other indicators its manufacturing sector was rather less advanced. The Economic Census of 1986 showed that in the base year of 1985 manufacturing value added in East Java was only two-thirds the size of that in Jakarta–West Java (see Table 10.3).[1] Moreover, reflecting a much narrower manufacturing base, East Java's Food, Drink, and Tobacco (FDT) sector was still disproportionately large.[2] Finally, East Java lagged well behind Jakarta–West Java in penetration of international markets for manufactures.

*This chapter is a product of research carried out with funding from the Industrialization Project in the Research School of Pacific Studies at the ANU and under the sponsorship of the Lembaga Ilmu Pengetahuan Indonesia (LIPI) and the Faculty of Social Sciences (FISIP) at Airlangga University, Surabaya. The Central Bureau of Statistics (BPS) kindly allowed access to unpublished data from tapes of the Economic Census, 1986. The author is indebted to Loene Doube for all the data processing and to Jane Lindsay and Robin Grau for preparation of the computer maps. This final version has benefited from the comments of various colleagues, especially Heinz Arndt, Hal Hill, and Jamie Mackie, and the careful editing of Loene Doube.

TABLE 10.1
Java: Gross Regional Product, 1984[a] (per cent)

	East Java	*Jakarta–West Java*	*Central Java–DIY*
Agriculture	34.1	13.6	34.4
Mining	0.4	8.9	0.5
Manufacturing	14.8	12.9	12.3
Utilities	1.0	2.0	0.6
Construction	0.9	5.6	5.6
Trade, Restaurants, and Hotels	25.5	22.0	19.4
Transport and Communications	7.9	7.8	4.5
Financial Services	4.3	14.1	6.0
Community Services	11.0	13.2	16.8
Total	100	100.1	100.1
Rp billion	12.3	20.6	9.1

Source: BPS (1988b).
[a]Sector shares at market prices.

Nevertheless, since the mid-1970s the growth of East Java's manufacturing sector has been rapid and sustained; it has also diversified and, since the mid-1980s, it has begun to show rapid growth in exports.

The leading edge of the industrialization process is the Large- and Medium-scale (L and M) sector of manufacturing (factories having 20 or more workers), which roughly corresponds with the modern sector. In 1985 the L and M sector accounted for a little over one-third of employment in manufacturing in East Java but probably about 90 per cent of value added (Table 10.2). Although half of East Java's employment in manufacturing was still in the Household sector (establishments having less than 5 workers), that sector's contribution to value added and productivity growth was small. The same is true of the Small-scale sector (5–19 workers), which provided 15 per cent of manufacturing employment but probably no more than 5 per cent of value added. Moreover, this last sector was concentrated in a very narrow range of industries, most notably rice milling, prawn crackers, tailoring, furniture, printing, lime, brick and tiles, and simple agricultural tools (BPS, unpublished census tapes). Despite the importance of the Household and Small-scale sectors in labour absorption, there is as yet little evidence of direct stimulus from and linkages with the growth of L and M industries. Employment trends are difficult to identify because of an apparent overestimate of Household-sector employment in the 1974 Industry Census. At face value, however, the figures suggest that employment growth has been concentrated in the L and M sector but that the Small-scale sector has also grown strongly, while employment in the Household sector has remained much the same (Table 10.2).

After a historical overview of the industrial development of East Java, this chapter examines the changing structure of L and M industries

TABLE 10.2
East Java: Manufacturing Employment and Value Added, 1985

	Employment			Value Added[a]	
	1974 ('000)	*1985 ('000)*	%	*1985 (Rp billion)*	%
Large and Medium	206.0	412.5	36	1,764	88[b]
Small	71.2	165.9	15	132	7[b]
Household	569.0	556.9	49	n.a.	5[b]
Total	846.1	1,135.2	100	2,000[b]	100

Sources: BPS (1978a; 1989c; unpublished census tapes).
[a]At market prices.
[b]Estimate only.

between 1963 and 1985. Discussion of the ownership pattern in 1985 is followed by analysis of the spatial distribution of L and M industries across the province. These three sections draw on the very good database, based on surveys done in 1985, on the L and M and the Small-scale sectors which is now available from the 1986 Economic Census.[3] The final section considers the orientation of East Java's recent industrial development towards both the international and the domestic markets.

Historical Overview

East Java was the first part of Indonesia where the Industrial Revolution made an impact. From the outset its modern industry was oriented not towards the production of consumer goods such as textiles but to the processing of agricultural crops, most notably sugar, and to heavy engineering. The town of Surabaya, blessed with a natural harbour and linked by river to a fertile hinterland, had in the 1830s become the focus for an expanding sugar industry. In the 1860s the application of steam to the milling and boiling up of sugar gave rise not only to much larger sugar factories but also to a metal-working and engineering industry to service them. Meanwhile, the commencement in the 1850s of regular steamship services within the Archipelago and the establishment in Surabaya of the Naval Base led to a large ship-repair industry. The third strand in the development of heavy industry was the opening in the later decades of the nineteenth century of railways and tramways with associated engineering workshops.[4] This phase of incipient industrialization ended with the Great Depression of the 1930s, which forced the closure of many sugar mills and undermined the purchasing power of the local market in East Java.

The period between the two world wars was marked by some diversification into consumer goods industries. Surabaya and some smaller towns had long sustained local manufacturing of bread, soft drinks, ice, and bricks and tiles. During the 1920s East Java attracted several important new consumer goods industries which were oriented to a growing domestic market of affluent Europeans. The main examples were factories making European-style ('white') cigarettes (in Surabaya and Malang) and a brewery (in Surabaya). After 1934 the imposition by the Netherlands Indies government of protectionist tariffs and quotas fostered other import substituting industries.[5] The much greater relative decline of purchasing power in East Java, as well as the growing power of the central government bureaucracy, however, meant that this development was now heavily biased towards Jakarta, which by the 1920s was overtaking Surabaya–East Java as the modern industrial centre of the Archipelago.

Independence increased the tendency of new manufacturing investment to cluster in Jakarta–West Java. As the capital of a unitary state, Jakarta became more and more the locus of bureaucratic decision-making, public expenditure, and the emerging middle class. The trend was only partly offset by the commissioning in East Java in the 1950s and 1960s of some large government projects such as the Waru soda-ash plant, the Gresik cement works, the Leces and Banyuwangi paper mills, and the Patal Grati spinning mill (near Pasuruan). After 1967, when foreign investment was liberalized, import-substituting industries proliferated in and around Jakarta (Hill, 1988) but East Java was almost ignored. By the early 1970s it seemed in East Java that these centripetal forces were irresistible.

Given its long-established industrial base and, once rehabilitated, fairly good infrastructure, the puzzle is why East Java was unable to attract a more substantial share of the industrial investment pouring into Indonesia. It had the big advantage that the port of Surabaya was under-used and did not have the acute congestion suffered in Tanjung Priok (Jakarta). Many foreign companies looking for a factory site were attracted initially to Surabaya but eventually decided upon Jakarta. The explanation lay partly on the side of demand and partly on that of supply. On the demand side, real disposable income per capita was much lower in East Java than in Jakarta–West Java and was growing much more slowly. A large proportion of the increase in real disposable per-capita income in East Java in the early years of the New Order was probably being allocated to food, clothing, and housing. On the supply side, East Java suffered two main disadvantages. First, Jakarta offered the benefits of economies of agglomeration: the necessary inputs of goods and services were on hand. Secondly, firms needed to locate close to the central government in order to negotiate the maze of bureaucratic regulations and to secure government orders.

The same line of analysis nevertheless helps to explain why Surabaya became a more attractive site for investment after the mid-1970s. On the demand side, East Java's success in agricultural development (see Chapters 6 and 8) meant a steady rise in mass purchasing power. Increasingly, East Java was becoming an important market in its own right. On the supply side, several factors can be adduced. First, the provincial government, aided by central government funds, made rapid progress in rehabilitating infrastructure, especially roads and power supplies. Specifically, the central, provincial, and Surabaya municipal governments together invested in a fully serviced industrial estate of some 245 hectares at Rungkut, to the south-east of the city. Its opening in 1975 as SIER (Surabaya Industrial Estate Rungkut) coincided auspiciously with the surge in oil prices and public expenditures. Secondly, improved communications, such as the introduction of hourly shuttle flights between Jakarta and Surabaya and an efficient interprovincial telephone service, made it possible for entrepreneurs based in Surabaya to carry out their business in Jakarta and fly back the same day, or indeed to avoid going to Jakarta at all.

These demand and supply factors to some extent interacted. Expansion of the East Java market created the opportunity for new entrants to secure a competitive advantage by locating in East Java rather than competing for a share of the national market from an already crowded Jakarta. As part of a competitive strategy to retain control of the market, some firms which already had a factory in Jakarta, like Kedaung Subur glassware, set up branch factories in East Java. Secondly, the soaring land costs and traffic congestion in and around Jakarta made the cheaper land in East Java, close to good highway and port facilities, more attractive to firms which, in an increasingly competitive environment, had to be more cost-conscious. A further attraction was the availability from rural areas of an increasingly well-educated work-force. Eventually, there was a snowball effect. The opening of the Rungkut industrial estate may well have acted as a catalyst by helping to focus attention on Surabaya but, as the industrial base expanded and

TABLE 10.3
Indonesia: Large and Medium Manufacturing by Number of Establishments, Value Added, and Employment, 1985

	Number of Establishments	Value Added[a]		Employment	
		Rp billion	*%*	*Number ('000)*	*%*
Jakarta	1,798	1,340	18.3	231.9	13.8
West Java	3,134	1,922	26.3	392.5	23.3
Jakarta–West Java	4,932	3,262	44.6	624.4	37.1
Central Java	2,373	709	9.7	287.7	17.1
East Java	3,038	1,519	20.8	412.5	24.5
Java	10,343	5,490	75.0	1,324.7	79.0
Outer Islands	2,566	1,829	25.0	360.1	21.0
Indonesia	12,909	7,319	100.0	1,684.7	100.0

Source: BPS (unpublished census tapes).
[a]At factor cost.

diversified, Surabaya began itself to generate economies of agglomeration, especially in the supply of services.

Over the period since the mid-1970s, East Java has therefore consolidated its position as the second heartland in Indonesia for the L and M sector of manufacturing. The predominance of Jakarta–West Java is still marked, with no less than 45 per cent of *national* value added in 1985, double that for East Java, which in turn is double that for Central Java–Yogyakarta (Table 10.3). In terms of employment, the L and M sector in East Java also ranks well behind Jakarta–West Java but ahead of Central Java–Yogyakarta.

Industrial Structure

The earliest survey of L and M manufacturing after Independence is the 1963 Industrial Census. It reveals an industrial structure which, after a century of industrial development, was still primitive. Reflecting the historic importance of sugar milling and, more recently, clove cigarettes (*kretek*), no less than 74 per cent of employment in the L and M sector was in the light industrial FDT sector and another 13 per cent in Textiles, Clothing, and Footwear (TCF) (Table 10.4). Heavy industry, namely the Chemicals and Metals and Machinery sectors, accounted for only 5 per cent of employment. This picture is consistent with qualitative evidence of stagnation in the industrial base because of the successive blows of the Great Depression, the Japanese Occupation, the Revolution, Independence, and the nationalizations of 1958.

Identification of trends in industrial employment since 1963 is by no means straightforward. The apparent decline of about one-fifth in total

TABLE 10.4
East Java: Large and Medium Manufacturing Employment by Industry Group, 1963, 1974, and 1985 (per cent)

Sector	*1963*	*1974*	*1985*
Food and Drink	38	28	23
Tobacco	36	38	34
Textiles, Clothing, and Footwear	13	14	9
Wood and Furniture	1	1	4
Paper and Printing	2	2	3
Chemicals	2	4	9
Rubber	3	3	3
Non-metals	2.5	3	4.5
Metals and Machinery	3	6	10
Other	0.5	2	0.5
Total	101[a]	101[a]	100
Number	251,100	205,900	412,500

Sources: BPS (1970; 1978a; unpublished census tapes).
[a]Rounding error.

L and M employment between 1963 and 1974 is surprising and could be attributed to changing definitions. Whereas in the 1963 Industry Census the lower bound for the medium category was factories with five or more employees using power-driven machines or ten or more employees not using machines, in the 1974 Economic Census the lower bound was raised to factories with 20 employees (with or without machines). In Table 10.4 this has been accommodated by ignoring the two lowest categories of the 1974 Census, thereby raising the minimum size to 25. Thus the 1963 figures quoted in Table 10.4 are, if anything, an underestimate, so that the decline would also be understated. A more likely reason for the apparent drop in L and M employment is that the agricultural work-force on sugar and tobacco plantations was counted as engaged in manufacturing in 1963 but not in 1974. Unfortunately a disaggregation of the 1963 figures to a five-digit industry code (International Standard Industry Classification or ISIC) is not available to test this hypothesis.[6]

What stands out from Table 10.4 is the steady broadening of East Java's industrial base. The main trends in the changing composition of industry between 1963 and 1974 were maintained between 1974 and 1985. The employment share of the light industrial sectors FDT and TCF fell from 87 per cent in 1963 to 80 per cent in 1974 and 66 per cent in 1985. This decline was offset partly by the rising share of the heavy industrial sectors of Chemicals and Metals and Machinery. Together with a growing role from other categories such as Wood and Furniture and Non-metals, this suggests that the doubling of L and M employment between 1974 and 1985 was accompanied by marked broadening of the industrial base and the emergence of a more sophisticated industrial sector.

Although no reliable figures are available from the Economic Census on realized capital investment, power consumption in kilowatt hours can be used as a crude indicator of capital intensity. However, figures on power usage need to be interpreted with some caution. In 1963 many large plants such as sugar mills were still using steam power. Although by the 1970s electricity was the main source of power, the State Electricity Corporation (Perusahaan Listrik Negara or PLN) grid covered such a small area of the province and, even in the vicinity of Surabaya, was so unreliable that most industrial firms continued to install 'captive' generators (see Chapter 11). Consumption is therefore likely to be understated for 1963 and 1974. Subject to these qualifications, Table 10.5 suggests that the consumption share of the Food and Drink sector fell from around 40 per cent in 1963 and 1974 to 26 per cent in 1985. By contrast, the share of power used by Paper, Chemicals, and Metals and Machinery increased sharply from 8 per cent in 1963 to about 45 per cent in 1985. Trends in power consumption reveal the shift towards heavy industry more dramatically than trends in employment. Moreover, while L and M employment doubled between 1963 and 1985, recorded power consumption soared almost 20-fold (Table 10.5).

TABLE 10.5
East Java: Large and Medium Manufacturing Power Use by Industry Group, 1963, 1974, and 1985 (per cent)

Sector	*1963*	*1974*	*1985*
Food and Drink	39.3	43.8	26.4
Tobacco	1.8	2.9	3.0
Textiles, Clothing, and Footwear	7.1	12.0	7.7
Wood and Furniture	1.2	0.3	2.4
Paper	0.5	6.5	12.2
Printing	0.7	0.3	0.2
Chemicals	4.0	3.5	24.7
Rubber	2.0	n.a.	0.7
Non-metals	38.7	2.8	13.8
Metals and Machinery	3.6	7.0	8.7
Other	1.2	21.0	0.1
Total	100.0	100.0	100.0
Kwh	134	535	2 529

Sources: As for Table 10.4.

Figures on value added (at factor cost) reveal similar trends (Table 10.6). While these figures are available only for 1974 and 1985, they are not, like those on employment and power usage, biased by the labour or capital intensity of an industry. Between 1974 and 1985 the Food and Drink sector's share of value added fell by almost half, from 40 to 22 per cent. The tobacco industry, however, markedly increased its share from 30 to 37 per cent. The establishment of two large plywood factories and increased production of wooden and rattan furniture resulted in a much more prominent Wood and Furniture sector. In heavy industry, the share of value added provided by the Chemicals and Paper industries increased from 4.5 to 18 per cent. The share of the Metals and Machinery sector, however, rose only marginally.

Nevertheless, the shift from light to heavy industry has been much less marked in East Java than in Jakarta–West Java. The great difference in the relative importance of light and heavy industries shows up from a two-digit breakdown of industry structure by value added for the three main provinces of Java (Table 10.7). In East Java in 1985 the single category of FDT still accounted for 59 per cent of manufacturing value added, compared with less than 10 per cent in Jakarta–West Java, where the sugar and clove cigarette industries were of little importance. In fact FDT was the only sector where in rupiah terms the value added in East Java—and even in Central Java—exceeded that in Jakarta–West Java. The two main light industry sectors of FDT and TCF together accounted for almost two-thirds of value added in East Java but much less than one-third in Jakarta–West Java. Conversely, and despite East Java's historical lead in this sector, Metals and Machinery contributed less than 10 per cent of value added in East Java compared with

TABLE 10.6
East Java: Large and Medium Manufacturing Value Added by Industry Group, 1974 and 1985[a] (per cent)

Sector	*1974*	*1985*
Food and Drink	39.7	22.2
Sugar	(29.5)[b]	(9.8)[b]
Tobacco	30.5	36.8
Kretek	(15.8)[b]	(34.5)[b]
Textiles, Clothing, and Footwear	6.4	5.4
Wood and Furniture	0.2	3.3
Paper	1.4	4.3
Printing	0.6	0.4
Chemicals	3.1	13.5
Plastic	0.2	1.3
Rubber	1.8	0.6
Non-metals	1.7	2.5
Metals and Machinery (including Iron and Steel)	8.4	9.6
Other	6.0	0.1
Total	100.0	100.0

Sources: As for Table 10.4.
[a]Value added at factor cost.
[b]Provisional figures.

37 per cent in Jakarta–West Java. These features of East Java's industrial structure are summarized in the last column of Table 10.7, which by sector expresses value added in East Java as a proportion of the total for all Java. Overall East Java accounted for 28 per cent of value added, but the contribution of individual sectors varied widely. FDT accounted for more than double the average, while TCF, Non-metals, and Metals and Machinery fell well below it.

On the whole, the industry structure of East Java therefore resembles the smaller and more backward one of Central Java rather than the larger and more sophisticated one of Jakarta–West Java. Both East and Central Java have large FDT and small Metals and Machinery sectors. The main differences between these two provinces is that Central Java has retained its historical importance as a centre of textile production, most notably in batik. Value added in the TCF sector in East Java is only half that in Central Java, even though by this measure its L and M manufacturing sector is more than twice as large (Table 10.7).

The marked contrast between the manufacturing sectors of East Java and Jakarta–West Java is not, however, a phenomenon only of the New Order. It was already apparent by 1963, although figures from the Industrial Census of that year unfortunately are available only for employment and not for value added (Table 10.8). According to the initial census registration, for which the L and M sector was more broadly defined than in the final census, East Java had almost four times the proportion of FDT workers as Jakarta–West Java but only 40 per cent the

TABLE 10.7
Java: Large and Medium Manufacturing Value Added by Industry Group, 1985[a] (per cent)

Sector	*East Java*	*Jakarta–West Java*	*Central Java–DIY (%)*	*East Java as Percentage of Java*
Food, Drink, and Tobacco	59.0	9.6	45.3	58.6
Textiles, Clothing, and Footwear	5.4	19.8	24.9	9.1
Wood and Furniture	3.3	2.4	8.3	26.7
Paper and Printing	4.8	3.8	1.8	34.5
Chemicals	15.4	18.0	7.9	26.7
Non-metals	2.5	9.0	5.1	10.4
Metals and Machinery	8.9	23.2	6.1	14.5
Iron and Steel	0.7	13.6	0.3	2.2
Other	*	0.6	0.3	2.6
Total	100.0	100.0	100.0	27.7
Rp billion	1,519	3,262	709	–

Source: As for Table 10.3.
[a]Value added at factor cost.
* = Insignificant.

proportion of TCF workers. Despite the long history of the Metals and Machinery sector in East Java, by 1963 that sector's share of employment was only half that in Jakarta–West Java. This could be explained by the weak demand of the sugar industry in East Java after the contraction which began in the 1930s, and also the greater ability of the Metals and Machinery sector in Jakarta–West Java to take advantage of the changing pattern of demand.

Under the New Order the Metals and Machinery sector in Jakarta–West Java has been boosted by the emergence of new industries, most notably steel, high-rise construction, automobile assembly, component manufacture, electronics, and even aircraft. Between 1974 and 1985 the Metals and Machinery sector (including basic iron and steel) in Jakarta–West Java increased its share of the booming L and M sector of manufacturing from 26 to 37 per cent of value added. This was attributable entirely to developments in West Java, most notably the establishment of the Krakatau iron and steel complex and the spillover from Jakarta of metals and machinery enterprises. East Java benefited little from all this. It was never in contention as a site for the steel complex, which was built on the tip of West Java to gain deepwater access from Sunda Strait. More surprisingly, despite some pioneering vehicle assembly plants dating from the 1950s and 1960s, East Java failed to develop as a centre of the heavily protected automobile industry, though in the vicinity of Malang and near Nganjuk a lively body-building industry fits out local public transport vehicles. The province did, however,

TABLE 10.8
Java: Large and Medium Manufacturing Employment by Industry Group, 1963 (per cent)

Sector	*East Java*	*Jakarta–West Java*	*Central Java–DIY*
Food and Drink	34.1	16.2	18.6
Tobacco	27.5	*	19.8
Textiles, Clothing, and Footwear	17.2	41.9	45.6
Wood and Furniture	3.7	1.8	1.8
Paper and Printing	2.3	5.5	2.5
Chemicals	3.0	3.5	1.5
Rubber	1.5	11.1	3.3
Non-metals	2.9	5.9	2.4
Metals and Machinery	6.8	12.6	3.7
Other	1.2	1.3	0.8
Total	100.0	99.8	100.0

Source: BPS (1970).
* = Insignificant.

become the site of one high-technology project of the Ministry of Research and Technology, namely the former naval dockyard (PAL), now converted to the construction of civilian and naval ships and boasting a work-force of about 6,000 people.

An important aspect of the changing structure of the manufacturing sector in East Java is the decline in the relative importance of plantation-based industries. Unfortunately these cannot be identified from the two-digit data of the 1963 Industry Census but five-digit figures are available for the corresponding 1974 and 1985 censuses. In East Java the main complex of plantation-based industries consists of sugar milling, tobacco drying, rubber curing, and coffee preparation. In some rural districts these remain the dominant industries. In the *kabupaten* of Jember and Lumajang, which together account for more than a quarter of provincial value added by plantation-based industry, this complex of industries represents about 95 per cent of value added in L and M manufacturing. Very high proportions are also recorded for the *kabupaten* of Bondowoso, Situbondo, Jombang, Nganjuk, Madium, Magetan, Bojonegoro, Lamongan, and Sumenep—in the last three very poor districts tobacco drying is the main L and M activity. Over the province as a whole, however, the relative importance of these industries has declined considerably. Between 1974 and 1985 their combined share of total employment in East Java declined from 36 to 28 per cent; in terms of value added it fell dramatically from 33 to 11 per cent.

The declining importance in East Java of plantation-based industries can be seen most clearly in the case of sugar milling. As late as 1974 it still accounted for 59 per cent of employment, 75 per cent of power consumption, and 74 per cent of value added in the dominant Food and

Drink sector (BPS, 1978a). Measured by value added, the sugar industry had ranked ahead of *kretek* as the leading industry of the province (Table 10.6). By 1985, when value added by the Food and Drink sector had itself fallen to about half its former share, the share of sugar milling in that sector had fallen to 39 per cent of employment, 40 per cent of power consumption, and 44 per cent of value added. The stagnation of the sugar industry is discussed in Chapter 8.

Ownership

A striking feature of East Java's manufacturing sector is the minor role played by direct foreign investment. In 1985 only 2 per cent of the number of L and M manufacturing establishments were classified as having foreign investment status under the Foreign Investment Law (1967), meaning that half of the equity was controlled by non-Indonesians. Because foreign investments are usually on a large scale, the corresponding shares of employment (6 per cent), value added (10 per cent), and power consumption (16 per cent) were greater than this but still only a small proportion of the total (Table 10.9). Domestic investments, mostly by Indonesians of Chinese origin, fell into two categories. By number, 20 per cent of establishments were classified as domestic investments in the sense of enjoying tax privileges under the Domestic Investment Law (1968). The remaining 78 per cent of establishments, classified as 'Other', are also domestic investments but enjoy no special status. Establishments in this last category are typically small and labour-intensive and account for only one-quarter of value added and power consumption. In terms of value added, investments classified as 'domestic' under the Domestic Investment Law are dominant.

Foreign investment has not always been so unimportant. Until 1958 the L and M sector, both plantation-based and non-plantation industries, was dominated by foreign (mainly Dutch) investment. In this respect, East Java was no different from much of the rest of Indonesia, where the Dutch had retained a 'neo-colonial' economic dominance. In

TABLE 10.9
East Java: Investment Status of Large and Medium Manufacturing Establishments, 1985 (per cent)

Investment Status	*Number of Establishments*	*Employment*	*Value Added*[a]	*Power*
Foreign	2	6	10	16
Domestic	20	46	64	58
Other	78	48	26	26
Total	100	100	100	100

Source: As for Table 10.3.
[a]At factor cost.

1958 Dutch business was seized and incorporated into the public sector. The remaining foreign firms—British, Belgian, German, Swiss, and US—were taken under government control in 1964/5. At the beginning of the New Order this latter group reverted to foreign control under the new Foreign Investment Law (1967), with the owners financing rehabilitation. In East Java this applied to the Bir Bintang brewery, British–American Tobacco (cigarettes), Philips-Ralin (lamps), Unilever, Proctor & Gamble, and Prodenta (toiletries), all located in Surabaya, the Faroka cigarette plant in Malang, and the Inbritex textile mill near Pasuruan. However, for some years after 1967 East Java attracted few new foreign investment projects in manufacturing. This was in marked contrast to the situation in Jakarta–West Java. One of the few fields which did attract some early foreign investment was the processing of cassava chips, maize, and copra cake for export as cattle feed.

However, foreign inputs have played a more significant role in the recent industrialization of East Java than the above figures suggest. What seems to have happened is that by the mid-1970s, when investment began to flow to East Java, the constraints of foreign investment status had become apparent. Many manufacturing ventures established by local entrepreneurs still needed to obtain foreign technology and capital but found it more convenient to obtain them under the status of domestic investments (*penanaman modal dalam negeri* or PMDN) by means of joint ventures, licensing agreements, equipment loans, and technical assistance.[7]

The legal status of L and M establishments is of interest for the very high proportion which are legally unincorporated. In 1985 almost two-thirds of establishments had no legal status separate from their owner(s), while another 7 per cent were incorporated but had no limited liability (Table 10.10). Not surprisingly, these establishments are typically small. Although limited liability companies and State enterprises numbered only one-quarter of L and M manufacturing establishments, they

TABLE 10.10
East Java: Legal Status of Large and Medium Manufacturing Establishments, 1985 (per cent)

Type of Investment	*Number of Establishments*	*Employment*	*Value Added*[a]	*Power*
State enterprise	4	13	30	14
Limited liability	23	62	64	78
Unlimited liability	7	5	2	2
Unincorporated	63	19	3	5
Other	3	1	1	1
Total	100	100	100	100

Source: As for Table 10.3.
[a]At factor cost.

accounted for about three-quarters of employment and no less than 92 per cent of value added and 94 per cent of power consumption in 1985. State enterprises are prominent in the plantation sector (sugar, coffee, rubber, and tobacco), a hangover from the nationalizations of 1958, but include some very large manufacturing enterprises: cement (Semen Gresik), fertilizer (Petrokimia), paper (at Leces and Banyuwangi), metal and engineering (PAL, Barata, Boma Bisma Indra, Dok Surabaya), and spinning (Patal Grati).[8] The capital intensity of the large-scale State enterprises is shown by their share of total L and M power consumption (30 per cent in 1985), double their share of L and M value added. There is also a wide variety of provincial government enterprises, mostly nationalized ex-Dutch enterprises operating with outmoded equipment and little prospect of financial viability.

Spatial Distribution

While manufacturing employment is spread right across East Java, employment in the L and M sector is quite heavily concentrated. Table 10.11 ranks the 37 *kabupaten* and *kotamadya* according to total employment in manufacturing in 1985. Although none employed less than 5,000 workers in manufacturing, in many *kabupaten/kotamadya* most of these were in small-scale or household industries. Counting L and M sector employment only, 13 *kabupaten/kotamadya* had less than 5,000 jobs and only 8 had more than 10,000. The spatial distribution is illustrated clearly in Figure 10.1 (*kotamadya* are counted as part of their surrounding *kabupaten*) which shows that L and M employment is concentrated along the Surabaya–Malang corridor, with secondary concentrations to the east in Jember (mainly plantation-based processing such as smokehouses and fermenting) and to the west in Kediri (mainly

FIGURE 10.1
East Java: Employment in Large and Medium Manufacturing Industries, 1985

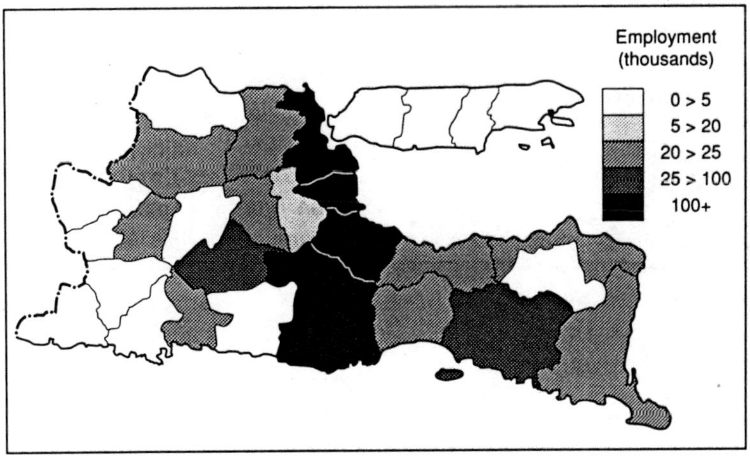

TABLE 10.11
East Java: Rank Order of *Kabupaten/Kotamadya* by Employment in Manufacturing Industries, 1985

Kabupaten/ Kotamadya	*Employment*			
	All Sectors	*Rank*	*L and M*	*Rank*
Surabaya	108,230	1	72,829	1
Jember	83,552	2	49,185	2
Sidoarjo	61,557	3	41,910	4
Malang	54,453	4	18,165	8
Pasuruan	47,321	5	19,693	7
KM Kediri	47,297	6	43,626	3
Tulungagung	46,889	7	9,327	
Blitar	46,542	8	619	
Gresik	44,987	9	25,735	6
KM Malang	43,175	10	32,192	5
Banyuwangi	39,486	11	9,503	
Sumenep	39,883	12	1,272	
Lamongan	39,257	13	5,166	
Probolinggo	34,741	14	4,733	
Kediri	31,062	15	4,695	
Magetan	27,431	16	2,247	
Bojonegoro	28,084	17	7,889	
Jombang	25,526	18	6,464	
Mojokerto	24,445	19	6,208	
Ponorogo	24,167	20	2,122	
Nganjuk	24,062	21	3,686	
Trenggalek	22,000	22	212	
Lumajang	21,930	23	7,572	
Tuban	17,879	24	3,517	
Ngawi	17,648	25	2,723	
Pacitan	15,547	26	46	
Bondowoso	14,489	27	3,832	
Bangkalan	14,195	28	606	
Situbondo	13,589	29	5,578	
Madiun	13,578	30	3,739	
Sampang	11,509	31	1,771	
KM Pasuruan	10,138	32	3,367	
Pamekasan	7,579	33	126	
KM Madiun	6,595	34	4,081	
KM Mojokerto	5,728	35	2,774	
KM Blitar	5,102	36	1,883	
KM Probolinggo	5,117	37	3,451	

Source: As for Table 10.3.

TABLE 10.12
East Java: Spatial Distribution of Large and Medium Manufacturing Establishments by Employment and Value Added, 1985

Region	Employment		Value Added[a]	
	Number	%	Rp billion	%
Surabaya (*kotamadya*)	72,829	18	294	19
Susisik	140,474	34	601	40
Surabaya–Malang corridor	213,891	52	757	50
Surabaya–Malang and Kediri	257,517	62	1,233	81
Other *kabupaten* (non-plantation)	56,344	14	126	8
Other *kabupaten* (plantation)	98,639	24	160	11
East Java	412,500		1,519	

Source: As for Table 10.3.
[a]At factor cost.

kretek cigarettes). Elsewhere, apart from sugar mills there is little L and M manufacturing except for the paper mills at Leces and Banyuwangi. Table 10.12 provides a more detailed breakdown of L and M employment within this corridor. Kotamadya Surabaya has the single largest concentration of industry, which over recent decades has spilled over into the adjacent *kabupaten* of Sidoarjo and Gresik. These three *kabupaten/kotamadya*, which may be identified by the acronym SUSISIK, accounted in 1985 for one-third of all L and M employment. If the corridor is extended to include Pasuruan and Malang, this proportion rises to more than half. With the further addition of the *kotamadya* of Kediri, the centre of the huge Gudang Garam tobacco complex (see Chapter 13), almost two-thirds of the L and M work-force is accounted for.

In terms of value added (at factor cost) the concentration of L and M manufacturing industries is even more striking (Figure 10.2). The Susisik area itself accounts for two-fifths of L and M value added and the whole Surabaya–Malang corridor accounts for about half (Table 10.12). Another third, consisting almost entirely of the tobacco industry, is contributed just by the *kotamadya* of Kediri. The rest of the province contributes only one-fifth of value added, largely through *in situ* processing of agricultural commodities—rice, coffee, sugar, tobacco, and rubber. Were this commodity processing excluded, less than 10 per cent of L and M industrial value added would be located outside the Surabaya–Malang corridor and the *kotamadya* of Kediri.

Within the Surabaya–Malang corridor, manufacturing also has a distinctive spatial pattern. Figures 10.3–10.5 disaggregate the location of L and M manufacturing along this corridor to the *kecamatan* level, showing the spatial distribution of value added, employment, and power use respectively. Apart from the tobacco complex in Kediri which constitutes the largest single component of value added, the core of the

FIGURE 10.2
East Java: Value Added at Factor Cost in Large and Medium Manufacturing Industries, 1985

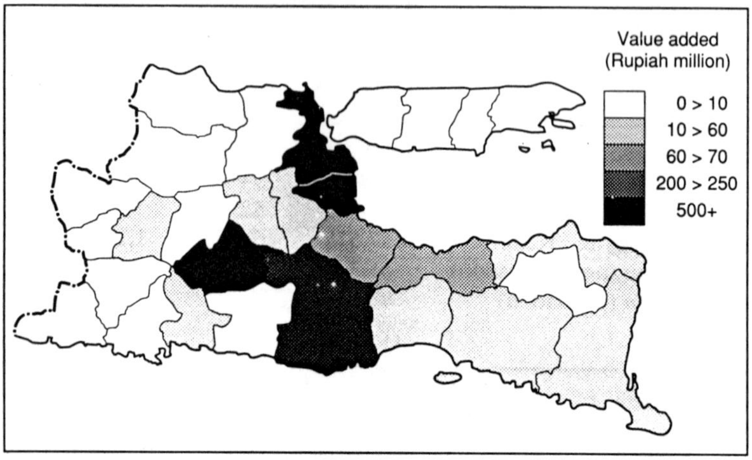

FIGURE 10.3
Value Added at Market Prices in Large and Medium Manufacturing Industries in the Surabaya–Malang Corridor, 1985

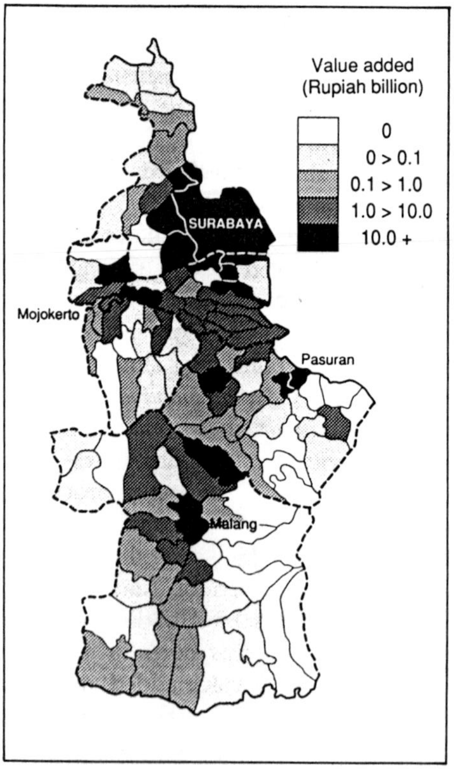

FIGURE 10.4
Employment in Large and Medium Manufacturing Industries in the Surabaya–Malang Corridor, 1985

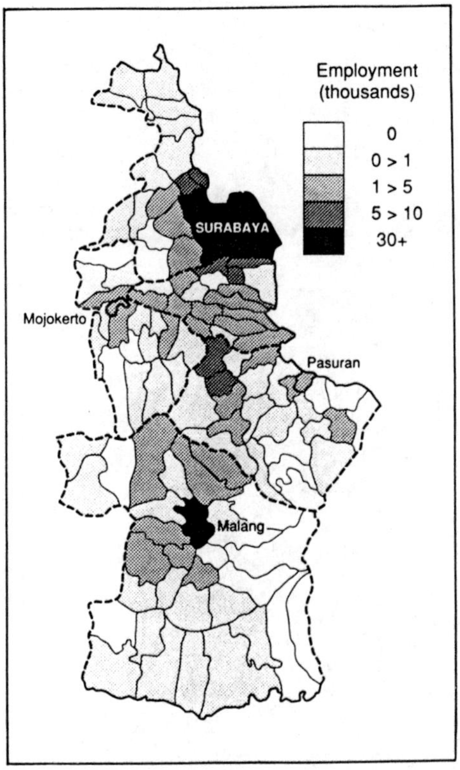

industrial zone is the *kotamadya* of Surabaya, where the focal point is the Rungkut industrial estate which, like a magnet, has drawn the city to it. By 1985 the estate was already full and is now being extended across the border into the *kabupaten* of Sidoarjo. Industry has also spilled over the western boundary of the *kotamadya* into Gresik. This process began in 1957 with the opening behind the town of the State-owned cement plant (Semen Gresik). In the mid-1960s construction began of a State-owned fertilizer and petrochemical complex (Petrokimia). Having the advantage of deep-water access, Gresik has been transformed from a sleepy backwater surrounded by salt-ponds to a centre of heavy industry. This trend was encouraged by the Surabaya Master Plan, which zoned heavy and polluting factories away from the *kotamadya*. Completion in 1987 of the toll-road from Gempol to the port of Tanjung Perak has made the coastal belt between the port and Gresik much more accessible and a feeder toll-road is to be built to link with Gresik. Most of the remaining salt-ponds between Surabaya and Gresik are likely in time to be occupied for warehousing or industry.

Hitherto the main migration of industry has not been westward from Surabaya, however, but southward in the form of ribbon development along the main highways (see Figure 1.1). One fork has been south-west

FIGURE 10.5
Power Use in Large and Medium Manufacturing Industries in the Surabaya–Malang Corridor, 1985

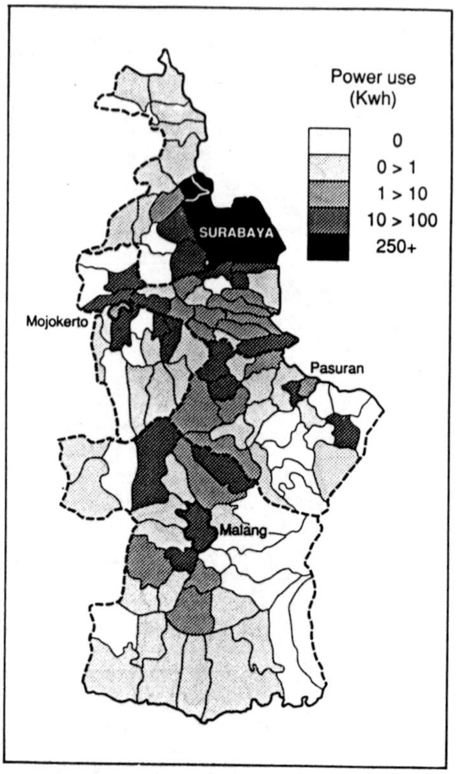

along both sides of the Brantas River towards Mojokerto. The other has been due south through Sidoarjo towards the city of Malang. This latter migration is not a recent phenomenon. As early as the 1930s textile plants were being located in the foothills beyond Surabaya to gain the benefit of an abundant supply of cheap labour released by the declining sugar industry, cheap land, and fresh water. Until the industrial boom of the 1970s, such decentralization involved only a handful of plants. There was then something of a rush for land along the main highways, especially that through Sidoarjo into the foothills around Pandaan, about half way between Surabaya and Malang (see Chapter 12). This ribbon of development has nevertheless been a very thin one: few factories have yet been located at any distance back from the main highways.

Comparison of the industrial agglomeration along the Surabaya–Malang corridor with that of the Greater Jakarta area (Jabotabek: Jakarta, Bogor, Tangerang, and Bekasi) reveals a contrast in relative size. L and M employment in the Surabaya–Malang corridor was in 1985 a little over half the size of that in the Greater Jakarta area (Table 10.13). In terms of value added the proportion was only one-third. However, the Greater Jakarta region accounts for some two-thirds of employment and value added in L and M manufacturing in Jakarta–West Java,

TABLE 10.13
Industrial Centres of East and West Java: Employment in Large and Medium Industries, 1985

Region	*East Java (n)*		*West Java (n)*
Susisik Region	140,474	Jakarta	231,910
Surabaya	72,829		
Sidoarjo	41,910		
Gresik	25,735		
Malang–Pasuruan Region	73,417	Botabek	167,656
KM Malang	32,192		
Kabupaten Malang	18,165		
KM Pasuruan	3,367		
Kabupaten Pasuruan	19,693		
Total			
Surabaya–Malang corridor	213,891	Jabotabek	399,566
Percentage of whole province	52		64

Source: As for Table 10.3.

whereas the Surabaya–Malang corridor (without the outlying *kotamadya* of Kediri) accounts for just half the corresponding total in East Java (Table 10.13 and BPS, unpublished census tapes).

Markets

Until the Great Depression of the 1930s East Java was a very open economy whose exports were dominated by plantation crops (see Chapter 8). In fact East Java ranked second only to North Sumatra in the value of export crops. Sugar was the staple: in 1929 sugar accounted for 58 per cent of the value of East Java's exports and, together with rubber and coffee, around three-quarters. Sugar exports from East Java reached a peak of 1.8 million tonnes in the late 1920s but by the mid-1930s had fallen away to about one-third this amount and in the best subsequent year (1939) were little more than half the 1920s peak. After Independence, sugar exports from East Java rarely exceeded 0.1 million tonnes and in 1966 ceased altogether. The collapse of one export staple was not offset by the rise of others. Almost by default, coffee and rubber became the province's two leading exports by value, together accounting for half the total in 1969. By 1986 coffee was still the leading commodity export with 18 per cent of value of non-oil exports, attributable both to growth in tonnage and to good prices, but rubber production had stagnated and now accounted for only 3 per cent (Table 10.14). With tobacco, these plantation crops accounted for one-quarter of the value of exports.

Since 1978 successive devaluations and policies to promote non-oil exports have helped East Java to diversify its export base. This has involved the emergence of some new primary produce exports, such as

TABLE 10.14
East Java and Jakarta–West Java: Value and Composition of Exports, 1986

Sector	*East Java*		*Jakarta–West Java*	
	US$ (million)	*Percentage of Non-oil Exports*	*US$ (million)*	*Percentage of Non-oil Exports*
Total Manufactures	348.5	42.0	1,019	81.0
Food, Drink, and Tobacco	11.1	1.3	15	1.2
Textiles, Clothing, and Footwear	152.5	18.3	627	49.8
Plywood and Wood Products	63.9	7.7	30	2.4
Rattan Goods	13.9	1.7	3	0.2
Paper and Printing	7.1	0.9	24	1.9
Chemicals	35.3	4.2	59	4.7
Plastics	7.3	0.9	2	0.1
Cassettes (unrecorded)	38.0	4.5	5	0.4
Rubber	–	–	11	0.9
Cement	–	–	25	2.0
Non-metals	0.9	0.1	13	1.0
Metals and Machinery	13.6	1.6	139	11.0
Jewellery	3.3	0.4	52	4.1
Other	1.6	0.2	14	1.1

Total Commodities	485.5	58.0	241	19.0
Coffee	146.4	17.6	–	–
Tobacco	40.0	4.8	–	–
Rubber	24.4	2.9	–	–
Prawns	55.1	6.6	–	–
Rattan	33.5	4.0	–	–
Other	186.1	22.3	–	–
Total Non-oil	834	100.0	1,260	100.0
Oil and Liquefied Natural Gas	23		750	
Total Exports	857		2,010	

Scurce: BPS (1987d).

frozen prawns which were in 1986 by value the province's second commodity export, and some minor exports such as frogs' legs and cashew nuts. All other commodity exports could be described as 'traditional'. The main development has been the growth of manufactured exports, which by 1986 accounted for 42 per cent of total non-oil export value (Table 10.14). Only Textiles, Clothing, and Footwear, however, made a large contribution in its own right, contributing about the same share to total exports as coffee. The next biggest item, plywood and wood products was little above the contribution of frozen prawns. The broad category of chemicals (Chemicals, Plastics, and Cassettes) contributed 10 per cent, of which almost half was blank cassettes. The whole Metals and Machinery sector, however, contributed just 1.6 per cent, while the huge *kretek* cigarette industry exported only a minute share of its total output.

East Java's modest achievement in the development of non-oil exports can be seen in perspective by comparison with Jakarta–West Java. Although accounting for twice as much value added in L and M manufacturing as East Java, in 1986 Jakarta–West Java exported three times the value of manufactures. The difference was attributable primarily to the TCF sector. Jakarta–West Java exported four times the value of Textiles, Clothing, and Footwear as East Java, this category accounting for almost two-thirds of its manufactured exports. The explanation for this difference is straightforward: as the centre of the Indonesian textile industry, Jakarta–West Java was better placed to exploit international demand than East Java. Yet the Metals and Machinery sector also made a significant contribution to the exports of Jakarta–West Java, being the second main component of exported manufactures and having an absolute value 10 times that of East Java. In short, while Jakarta–West Java has penetrated international markets for both light and heavy manufactures, East Java appears still to be struggling to secure market penetration for manufactures with potential for rapid growth. Since the 1980 ban on log exports, the notable expansion has been plywood exports, which between 1986 and 1988 almost trebled in value and became the province's leading export (17 per cent of the total) (KSJT, *Jawa Timur dalam Angka, 1988*). Further growth, however, is likely to be constrained by the emerging shortage of logs. Perhaps the best prospect is the export of rattan goods, which by 1988 had risen to 8 per cent of the total exports (KSJT, *Jawa Timur dalam Angka, 1988*). Coinciding with the recent ban on the export of raw rattan, East Java has been designated as the national centre for the manufacture of rattan products which, together with wooden furniture and other wood products, can make a big contribution to labour absorption. Whether international demand and the unit value are high enough to make a large contribution to export earnings remains to be seen.

Manufacturing in East Java therefore remains heavily oriented towards Indonesia's domestic market, which is split between Java and the Outer Islands. On Java the trend is towards bifurcation of the market into a western part oriented towards Jakarta and an eastern part oriented towards Surabaya. While the north coast and south-west of Central Java are supplied mainly from Jakarta and Bandung, the valley of the Solo River as far as Yogyakarta has become part of the marketing area of Surabaya. Indeed, the commercial links between Solo and Surabaya have always been strong.

A bifurcation is also apparent in trade with the Outer Islands. While Jakarta–West Java has well-developed commercial links with Sumatra, Riau, and West Kalimantan, the domestic trade of East Java is oriented towards South and East Kalimantan, Sulawesi, and Maluku and, of course, Bali, Lombok, and the rest of Nusa Tenggara. East Java conducts some trade with Sumatra, shipping out a large tonnage of sugar (of which West Java has no surplus) and *kretek* cigarettes, and bringing back shrimp paste and fertilizer (urea) which are not available locally or in the east of the Archipelago, but such items are notable exceptions in the general trading pattern. Similarly, Jakarta–West Java has made only minor inroads into the east of the Archipelago except for Irian Jaya and East Timor, which has always been under tight control from Jakarta.

East Java's trade with the Outer Islands secures a double benefit. First, it enables local manufacturers to increase the size of their market beyond what is available in Java. This increment to the market may well facilitate access to economies of scale and improve plant utilization, thereby reducing unit costs. Secondly, because the value of East Java's exports to the Outer Islands is much greater than the raw materials it imports, there is a surplus in trade with the rest of the Archipelago which probably more than offsets East Java's trade deficit with the rest of the world. In other words, exports to the Outer Islands help to finance foreign imports. From this perspective it would be misleading to accept, on the basis of foreign trade figures alone, that East Java's manufacturing development has been 'inward looking'.

Conclusion

Industrialization means not just rapid growth of the manufacturing sector but also a structural shift in the economy from the primary sector (mainly agriculture) to secondary industry. The doubling of the L and M manufacturing work-force between 1974 and 1985, the fivefold increase in power consumption by L and M manufacturing and the broadening of the industrial base are clear indicators of a renewed phase of industrial development in East Java, but need to be set in the context of trends in the composition of gross regional product (GRP). Fairly reliable provincial GRP figures are available only from 1978 to 1986 but they reveal a significant increase in the share of manufacturing (Table 10.15). Including utilities, the manufacturing sector rose four percentage points from 14 per cent in 1978 to 18 per cent in 1986. Nevertheless, this shift accounted for less than two-fifths of the decline in the share of agriculture, which fell from 41 per cent in 1978 to 30 per cent in 1986.

TABLE 10.15
East Java: Composition of Gross Regional Product at Current Prices, 1978 and 1986 (per cent)

Sector	*1978*	*1986*
Primary	41.2	29.9
Manufacturing	13.3	17.3
Utilities	0.5	0.9
Construction	0.7	4.5
Trade, Restaurants, and Hotels	22.2	21.7
Transport and Communications	6.0	6.7
Financial Services	3.4	2.3
Dwellings		1.9
Public Administration and Defence	12.7	9.4
Other Services		5.4
Total	100.0	100.0

Source: KSJT, *Jawa Timur dalam Angka, 1988*: 19.

A better understanding of the industrialization process can be gained from focusing not upon the provincial economy, which is to some extent an artificial construct, but upon identifiable geographic areas. As shown above, L and M manufacturing divides into the geographically dispersed processing of agricultural commodities, such as sugar, coffee, tobacco, and rubber, and industrial manufacturing, which is heavily concentrated within the Surabaya–Malang corridor. Much of the growth in industrial manufacturing has occurred within the *kotamadya* of Surabaya, which has long been the industrial centre of East Java. In proportional terms, however, manufacturing has done little more than hold its share of the city's GRP. Even within the enlarged boundaries of 1965, the city itself has not become more industrialized. It is the hinterland of Surabaya that has been industrializing. The former salt-ponds and the dry limestone hills of Gresik, the rich well-irrigated flood-plain of Sidoarjo, formerly dominated by the sugar industry, and, to a lesser extent, the foothills around the town of Pandaan, and the highlands around the city of Malang are the districts where the shift out of agriculture into industry has been most apparent.[9] Land and labour are available in abundance to sustain this expansion. As East Java's industries benefit increasingly from economies of agglomeration and improve their access to international markets, there are strong grounds for confidence that the province is at last beginning to fulfil the potential for industrialization that already existed by the late colonial period.

1. Value added refers to the gross value of output, excluding the cost of inputs of goods and services, and is therefore equivalent to factor incomes (wages, interest, profit, and rent). Value added at factor cost (as opposed to market prices) allows also for the deduction of net indirect taxes.

2. In this chapter census categories will be given initial upper-case letters, for example the Food, Drink, and Tobacco industry and the Large- and Medium-scale manufacturing sector.

3. Data on the Household sector are still being processed. It should be noted that the census data exclude oil refining (ISIC code 353).

4. Details of the early industrial history of Surabaya can be found in von Faber (1931, 1934).

5. On this first phase of protection, see Segers (1988, especially pp. 27–38).

6. The Economic Census disaggregated industries according to the ISIC code. A five-digit code represents the highest and a two-digit code the lowest level of disaggregation.

7. See Hill (1988: 45–7) for elaboration of this point.

8. See Hill (1988: 25–6) on the role of State enterprise at the national level.

9. In 1986 manufacturing and utilities accounted for 49 per cent of GRP in Kabupaten Gresik, 38 per cent in Sidoarjo, and 19 per cent in Kotamadya Surabaya, averaging out at 27 per cent for the whole Susisik region; in the *kabupaten/kotamadya* of Malang, Mojokerto, and Pasuruan the corresponding figures were 18, 18, and 15 per cent (figures calculated from Bappeda, 1989).

11
Electricity Supply*

Imron Husin

Introduction

ONE of the biggest advantages East Java has had over other provinces of Indonesia in achieving a balanced pattern of development has been a well-established electricity supply system dating back to the early twentieth century. For many years production of electricity was concentrated in Surabaya and a few plantation districts, and the distribution grid was confined to the Surabaya–Malang–Kediri–Probolinggo region, which remains the economic heartland of the province.

After Independence, however, this advantage did not translate into development. Although wartime damage was repaired, neglect of maintenance caused the power supply to become both inadequate and unreliable, even in the cities. Most commercial premises had to install 'captive plants' in order to survive.

Under the New Order, the power-generating capacity in East Java has increased dramatically. In the 1970s the building of the Karangkates hydroelectric power complex, a series of multi-purpose dams on the Brantas River between Malang and Blitar, boosted East Java's generating capacity as much as did the Jatiluhur hydroelectric system for the Jakarta–West Java region. A further boost was the establishment of two large oil-fuelled thermal generators, in Surabaya and Gresik. The total power supply available in East Java more than tripled between 1974 and 1984. By the mid-1980s the grid had been extended to cover most of the province and link with the rest of Java.

While the development of East Java's electricity supply system has made an important contribution to regional economic development, it has done so at a cost. First, the power industry was not a leading sector. The extension of the grid tended to follow pre-existing industrial development and merely enabled plants to obtain power more cheaply than they could do from captive diesel generators. Secondly, the impact of electrification may have been, at least initially, to widen regional and social disparities, since much of the increase in power generation went to a few large industries.

*Material for this chapter is derived from Husin (1989).

East Java has a less impressive record of rural electrification than have Central and West Java. Although in many rural areas electricity is now available to increasing numbers of consumers, it will be many years before the distribution system provides access to power for everyone in the province.

The Electricity Industry and Economic Growth: The Early Years

The supply of electricity in East Java entered the modern era in 1909 with the establishment of the private power company Algemeene Nederlandsche Indische Electriciteit Maatschappij (ANIEM or General Netherlands Indies Electricity Company), which had its head office in Surabaya. The new company rapidly developed power stations and distribution systems in major towns in Java and Kalimantan. The largest power station, at Surabaya, was driven by steam turbines with what today would be a very small total capacity of about 13.5 megawatts (MW).[1] By the end of the first quarter of the twentieth century there were seven public utilities in East Java supplying electricity. Most of the power was generated by ANIEM, which served the densely populated Surabaya–Malang–Kediri triangle where the bulk of the modern-sector economic activities in the province were concentrated. Outside this area electricity was provided by several small electric companies.[2]

These electric companies were established mainly to supply manufacturing and service industries in Surabaya, the plantations in the eastern part of the province (mainly the tobacco and coffee plantations in Probolinggo and Besuki), the government railways workshop in Madiun, and other Dutch facilities such as offices, schools, settlement areas, and tourist resorts. In other words, the pattern of growth during this period was determined by the interests of foreign enterprises producing export commodities. The growth of power generation was concentrated around these industries and in the areas of Dutch settlement, where the demand for electricity was high enough for its supply to be profitable. Even in the towns, few Indonesians could afford the luxury of electricity.

Between about 1920 and 1940 most of the growth in power capacity came from hydroelectric generators. The first hydroelectric plant in East Java was Giringan (with an installed capacity of 1.4 MW), near Madiun. Built by the government to supply the railway workshops in Madiun, it was in operation as early as 1917. Next to be established was the Mendalan station (16.5 MW) near Malang in 1928. This plant, which before World War II delivered most of the electricity in East Java, from the south (Malang and nearby) to Surabaya in the north, was owned by Nederlandsche Indische Waterkracht en Electriciteit Maatschappij (NIWEM or Netherlands Indies Hydropower and Electricity Company), a joint venture between the Dutch government and ANIEM. Mendalan was intended to be the basis for a grid which could supply Surabaya, Pasuruan, and other nearby towns. A transmission line was laid from Mendalan to Surabaya.

Not all the power generated in these early years came from large plants. In areas remote from the main supply lines, Dutch plantations (mainly sugar, coffee, and tobacco) generated their own electricity for domestic or factory needs, using small, private hydroelectric generators. By 1939 these small generators had a total capacity of 5.7 MW. A few indigenous or Chinese-owned rice or cassava-tapioca mills also established hydroelectric power stations.[3]

The concentration of major power generators in or near Surabaya, Madiun, and Malang was both a cause and an effect of the growth of economic activities along the corridors between Surabaya–Malang and Madiun–Kediri–Surabaya. In 1930, 81 per cent of the consumers of electric power in East Java were located in the area between Surabaya, Pasuruan, Malang, and Kediri, and they consumed 89 per cent of the power generated. These figures mirror the concentration of industrial activities in that area, particularly in Surabaya, which was becoming a significant manufacturing centre. By 1930 there were more consumers of electricity in East Java than in any other area in the colony: 37 per cent of all consumers of power in Java and 32 per cent of the total number in the Netherlands East Indies.

The development of Surabaya as a centre of manufacturing industry in the early years of the twentieth century, particularly of machine shops to service the sugar mills and the shipping industry, also contributed to the demand for electric power in East Java. Neither Semarang nor Jakarta had such a concentration of heavy industry at that time. On the basis of this early industrial growth, Surabaya has continued to be a centre for metal and machine industries (see Chapter 15). Because of the unreliability of the grid system until recently, most industries established their own power generating capacity. The potential demand for electricity has therefore been high in and around Surabaya (including the Gresik industrial complex), and the association between industrial development and electric power generation has been a close one.

Power Supply and Regional Development after Independence

Because of the damage done to ANIEM installations during World War II and the subsequent struggle for Independence, major rehabilitation had to be carried out when ANIEM resumed operations in 1947. The Mendalan hydroelectric plant was not brought back into operation until the mid-1950s, when NIWEM was able again to supply ANIEM. Although the government of the new Republic of Indonesia established the Djawatan Gas dan Listrik (Department of Gas and Electricity) soon after the Declaration of Independence in 1945, it was not until November 1954 that ANIEM and NIWEM were nationalized and their plant and equipment brought under the control of the national government.[4] After nationalization the bureaucracy expanded rapidly, and became increasingly complex with the subsequent regionalization of the electricity service. The facilities and overhead capital of these enterprises later became the basis for reorganizing the power industry under the new national electric power authority, the State Electricity Corporation (Perusahaan Listrik Negara or PLN).[5]

Until the 1960s power generation on Java was largely hydroelectric. However, as demand for electricity increased it became necessary to establish new power stations quickly, cheaply and close to the urban centres where the demand was. Thermal power generation fulfilled these criteria, even though the operating costs of hydroelectric plants were lower, and eventually became the major source of power in East Java (Table 11.1). In 1965 the old ANIEM plant in Surabaya was replaced by the Tanjung Perak thermal plant, with a capacity of 50 MW. This was increased to 150 MW in 1978. Hydroelectric power was boosted in 1973 when the first stage of the Karangkates (now Sutami) hydroelectric project, financed by Japanese war reparation funds, began operation with a capacity of 70 MW. However, even after the completion of later stages this development did not outweigh the concentration of power facilities in the Surabaya and Gresik areas.[6] By 1986 about two-thirds of the total power generated in East Java was provided by the thermal and gas plants in Surabaya and Gresik.[7]

During the First Five-Year Development Plan (Repelita I, 1969/70–1973/4), the industrial sector in East Java grew very rapidly. In 1969 there were 7,261 industrial plants, mainly chemical, textiles, and small industries, but by 1974 there were 10,083, despite a decline in the number of textile mills. Because all forms of infrastructure, including electricity, were more readily available in Surabaya and its surrounding areas, manufacturing was concentrated initially in and around the city.

The agglomeration of industry in Surabaya, Gresik, and Sidoarjo is reflected in the fact that 61 per cent of all foreign investment projects in East Java between 1967 and 1984 were located in this area, accounting for 75 per cent of the total foreign investment of US$711 million

TABLE 11.1
East Java: Installed Capacity by Prime-mover Power Source, 1954–1986 (MW)

Year	*Diesel*	*Thermal (oil)*	*Hydroelectric*	*Gas*	*Total*	*Percentage of All Indonesia*
1954	29.2		15.3	–	44.6	20
1964	32.8		51.5	–	84.3	20
1969	19.9	50.0	45.4	–	115.3	21
1974	19.5	50.0	116.4	–	185.9	20
1979	23.8	150.0	205.5	67.5	446.8	18
1984	27.9	350.0	210.0	67.5	655.5	14
1985	25.4	350.0	210.0	67.5	652.9	n.a.
1986	26.4	350.0	210.7	89.0	676.2	n.a.

Sources: 1954–79: BPS, *Statistical Pocketbook of Indonesia*, relevant years.
1984–6: PLN (1986).

(KSJT, *Jawa Timur dalam Angka, 1985*). Similarly, 66 per cent of domestic investment projects, representing 47 per cent of the total domestic investment of Rp 1,262 billion were made in the area.[8] These developments have been the major reasons for the construction of high-capacity units for thermal and gas power generation in Surabaya and Gresik. The location was also convenient because the supply of oil and spare parts for the power stations could be maintained easily through the port.

The sixfold increase in the generating capacity of the PLN power plants in East Java between 1967 and 1985 enabled it to service more customers and to increase the average amount of power consumed per customer. In 1967 the level of power consumption per customer was 1 247 kilowatt-hour (kWh); by 1985 it had doubled to 2 479 kWh. This is a clear indication of economic development, with much of the increased consumption due to manufacturing industry (see Table 11.3).

The figures supplied by the PLN, however, understate the level of electricity consumption in East Java. In 1983 the industrial sector generated 867 874 megawatt-hour (MWh) from its own generators ('captive' power), and purchased only 505 019 MWh from other sources, mainly the PLN (KSJT, *Jawa Timur dalam Angka, 1985*: Table vi.1.13). Furthermore, a survey conducted by the Biro Pusat Statistik (BPS or Central Bureau of Statistics) in 1983 found that 72 per cent of rural households using electricity obtained it from non-PLN sources, while only 26 per cent were serviced by PLN (BPS, 1985: Table 1.7). Clearly there was still considerable demand for electricity in East Java which PLN was unable to satisfy, both in the industrial sector and in rural areas.

Transmission

PLN's failure to cover a wider area and a greater number of consumers was due not only to the limitations of its generating capacity but also to problems involved in rehabilitating and expanding the transmission and distribution systems. These services are crucial for channelling to consumers the additional power produced by the increased generation capacity, but their cost is high. In constructing an electricity system, the capital costs of generation, transmission, and distribution are in the ratio of 1 : 2 : 3 (Direktorat Djendral Tenaga dan Listrik, n.d.). The increasing demand for electricity cannot be met by PLN despite its greater capacity to generate power, since many of the old power distribution lines and transformer stations are inadequate. Major improvements have been achieved so far only in and around the Surabaya–Malang–Kediri triangle.

Until 1974 public electricity generation in East Java consisted of five separate generation and distribution systems:

1. the Kali Konto system, using power from the Mendalan, Siman, and Selorejo hydroelectric plants (29 MW);
2. the Karangkates hydroelectric plant (70 MW);

3. the thermal power plant at Tanjung Perak (Surabaya) (50 MW);
4. the small Madiun system (6.5 MW), deriving its power mainly from the Golang, Giringan, and Ngebel hydroelectric plants;
5. the small Jember and Banyuwangi systems.

There were also scattered diesel power plants with a total capacity of 12.1 MW. The transmission lines were very limited, not only in length but also in the number of high-voltage—150 kilovolts (kV)—lines.

Since 1974 the East Java grid has undergone substantial changes (Figure 11.1). By 1986/7 all electricity systems in Java had been connected to a single grid. More extra-high-voltage lines (500 kV) are now

FIGURE 11.1
East Java: Power Concentration, Distribution, and Major Networks, 1974 and 1986

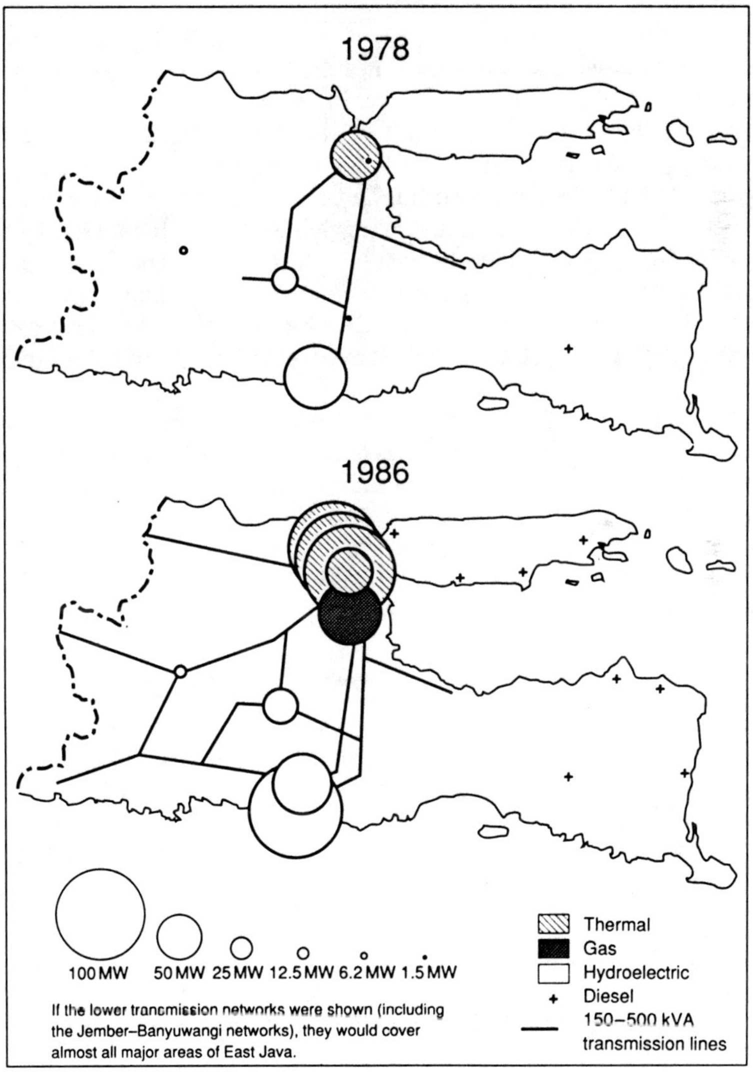

being used and lines of less than 30 kV are gradually being replaced. In 1988 an underwater cable (150 kV) connected Madura to the grid. A 500 kV direct line to Paiton (Probolinggo), where a coal thermal generator will be built, is planned. When this plant is established, the composition of prime-mover power sources in East Java will be dominated by cheaper energy resources such as hydroelectric and coal power, rather than the more expensive oil.

Industrial Growth and Power Consumption

In Java the distribution of electric power capacity is dominated by the Jakarta Raya and Tangerang distribution systems: in 1984/5 about 43 per cent of electricity sold by PLN in Java was consumed in this area, compared with 24 per cent in East Java, 21 per cent in West Java, and 12 per cent in Central Java. This can be seen clearly in the per-capita kWh sales in each distribution area (Table 11.2). The per-capita kWh sales in Jakarta were about eight times the East Java sales, an imbalance which did not change over the 10-year period.

Jakarta is by far the main source of revenue for PLN, with East Java second. The concentration of a large population in a small area, as occurs in Jakarta, reduces distribution costs. Jakarta and its surrounding districts are also the main industrial agglomeration in Indonesia, leading to high power consumption. In East Java, a similar situation exists in and around Surabaya. Large industries which consume huge amounts of electric power are cement (Semen Gresik), petrochemicals (Petrokimia Gresik), engineering (Barata and Boma Bisma Indra), and shipbuilding (PAL).

The proportion of PLN electric power in East Java which is used in industry has been growing steadily, from 16 per cent in 1967 to 52 per cent in 1985. The increase in the industrial use of electric power was

TABLE 11.2
PLN Electricity Sales, 1975–1985 (kWh per capita)

Year	*Indonesia*	*Outer Islands*	*Jakarta*	*West Java*	*Central Java*	*East Java*
1975/6	21	11	175	22	10	20
1976/7	23	12	193	22	11	20
1977/8	26	14	216	27	12	21
1978/9	31	16	251	31	14	36
1979/80	37	20	291	35	17	36
1980/1	44	26	342	42	20	40
1981/2	52	29	403	47	24	50
1982/3	59	31	449	50	28	61
1983/4	63	34	472	53	32	64
1984/5	68	36	498	59	36	67

Source: PLN (1986: Table 3.3.2).

TABLE 11.3
East Java: Distribution of Power Sold by PLN to Various Types of Customers, 1980/1 and 1984/5 (per cent)

	1980/1			*1984/5*		
Type of Customer	*East Java*	*Jakarta*	*Java*	*East Java*	*Jakarta*	*Java*
Households	39	45	42	34	41	39
Commercial	8	15	11	5	14	9
Industry	41	22	32	52	30	40
Government buildings/offices	10	17	13	7	14	11
Street lighting	2	1	2	2	1	1
Total (million kWh)	1 161	2 222	5 112	2 088	3 785	8 771

Source: Calculated from PLN (1986: Tables 2.1.3–2.1.7).

larger in East Java than in Jakarta and Java as a whole, as the figures for 1980/1 and 1984/5 show (Table 11.3). This trend also reflects the rapid growth of manufacturing in the province, especially in the vicinity of Surabaya where the infrastructure needed to stimulate the growth of industries is better established than elsewhere in East Java. There is a better road network to the hinterland, good seaport and airport facilities and a higher level of available technical training than elsewhere in the province. Most important of all is Surabaya's long experience as an industrial and service centre, which has enabled the continuing growth of several established industries, such as textiles, shipbuilding, ship-repair, and heavy engineering, as well as the development of new industries such as cement, fertilizer, and plywood.

The medium- and large-scale industries in East Java consume a high proportion of the electric power sold by PLN. Almost 50 per cent of the power sold in 1984/5 was channelled through medium- and high-tension distribution lines (PLN, 1986: Table 2.3.2), which can be connected

TABLE 11.4
East Java: Industry Share of Electric Power, 1967–1984/5

Year	*Power Sold ('000 MWh)*	*Industry Share (%)*	*Total Customers ('000)*	*Industry Share (%)*
1967	248	15.7	199	0.4
1971	355	18.3	211	0.8
1980/1	1 161	40.7	483	0.5
1984/5	2 088	51.5	842	0.4

Sources: 1967 and 1971: KSJT, *Jawa Timur dalam Angka*, relevant years
1980/1–84/5: PLN (1986).

only to large establishments. Furthermore, 52 per cent of power used for industrial purposes was consumed by only 3,128 industrial customers (0.4 per cent of the total customers of PLN) (Table 11.4). The increase in power channelled through the medium- and high-tension distribution lines, from 37 per cent in 1980/1 to 50 per cent in 1984/5, also means that the number of large consumers (industries or businesses) supplied by PLN has gradually increased. Hence, the high cost of investment in 'captive' power plants by the industrial sector can now be avoided by establishments obtaining their power directly from PLN.

Rural Electrification

The electrification of rural areas is a fairly new phenomenon in Indonesia, although the idea has been under discussion for many years. In a few areas villages were connected to facilities established in colonial times, but these were exceptions. The idea of rural electrification came to the fore in the 1970s as part of the government's programme to reduce socio-economic inequalities. The rapid improvement of electricity supply in the towns underlined the need to make greater provision in rural areas.

In East Java various attempts have been made since 1972 to bring more electric power to rural areas. The provincial government has promoted the idea as a means of improving the standard of living of rural people. Several surveys of possible sources of hydroelectric power have been initiated since the early 1970s. One survey, of small-scale hydroelectric power in seven villages, brought together officials and experts from PLN, the Surabaya Institute of Technology, the Rural Development Office, and the Irrigation Office, as well as staff from local government. The survey increased awareness of the need to stimulate the participation of the local community and organizations in any attempt to provide electricity to rural areas. The result was the so-called *gotong royong* (mutual self-help) programme of rural electrification, in which villagers, under the direction of provincial technical supervisors, contributed their labour and the necessary materials for electricity distribution in their villages, with the provincial government and PLN providing the basic infrastructure.

Although the provincial government formulated a policy for rural electrification and mobilized funds from various sources, it could not develop its own targets, since the planning of overall electricity development remained the responsibility of PLN. Hence any additional effort must take account of PLN procedures and plans. Moreover, PLN decision-making is highly centralized, and it is difficult to adjust lower level initiatives to the rules and regulations of the higher bureaucracy. Consequently, the *gotong royong* projects have been confined mainly to isolated diesel power plants and small hydroelectric projects in remote areas and other places where PLN systems are not expected for many years. The first outcome of the early initiatives in village electrification in

East Java was a small-scale hydroelectric power plant in Bajang village (Blitar) in 1974, with a capacity of 25 kilowatts (kW). This was followed by a similar plant of 75 kW in Tirtomulyo village (Malang) which began operating in 1975/6.

The results achieved in village electrification have been disappointing in comparison with those of Central and West Java. In March 1986 rural electrification under PLN auspices had reached only 1,731 out of 8,359 villages in East Java, with about 376,000 customers. In Central Java, 2,383 villages were electrified, with about 435,000 customers,[9] while in West Java 588,000 customers had been connected, in 1,442 villages (PLN, 1986). One limitation in East Java was the policy of PLN and the local authorities to provide 450-watt (W) power connections as a minimum; many poor villagers would like 200 W or less, for lighting only. Low-wattage connections with low connection costs and a flexible term of payment are no longer available through the rural electrification programme. Many poor people cannot afford the 450-W house connection and are thus unable to gain access to electricity.

In 1986 villages in rural areas were far less well provided with electricity supply facilities than those in urban areas (Table 11.5). Barely 25 per cent of villages in the rural areas were connected to the power grid, compared with 80 per cent in urban areas. Even within rural areas, higher priority has generally been given to the provision of electricity to *kecamatan* (subdistrict) centres than to the rural villages themselves. This practice makes it easier for PLN to reach a large number of customers in a compact area, particularly in towns close to the grid. Moreover, it makes it possible for the government to claim that more and more *kecamatan* have been supplied with electricity, even though only the urbanized villages have been connected. In fact, the proportion of rural households connected to the PLN electricity supply system is far lower than the proportion of *kecamatan* connected. The more *kecamatan* electrified the easier it will be for the government to convince rural people that it is really concerned to increase their standard of living. At the lower level of government structure, the centre of the *kecamatan* is highly likely to represent the political power of the *kecamatan* as a whole.

Although the total number of villages electrified had increased markedly by the end of 1986, the provision of electric power was concentrated in three types of areas: those located close to the power generation centres, those near the major centres of economic activity, and those adjacent to the main towns in *kabupaten* (districts) or *kotamadya* (municipalities). Areas located elsewhere had received few services from PLN (Figure 11.2). Thus electric power is distributed extensively in Madiun and the surrounding areas, in the Surabaya–Malang–Kediri area, in Banyuwangi, and a few other scattered areas. On the other hand, the provincial government's aim to electrify all *kecamatan* centres has resulted in an increase in the number of isolated PLTD (*pembangkit listrik tenaga diesel* or diesel-generating plant) services, which are usually

TABLE 11.5
East Java: Percentage of Villages Electrified in *Kabupaten* and *Kotamadya*, November 1986[a]

	Villages Electrified in the Main Town	*Villages Electrified outside the Main Town*
Kabupaten		
Sidoarjo	100.0	62.1
Malang	–	47.7
Banyuwangi	100.0	41.5
Situbondo	100.0	39.5
Pasuruan	–	35.6
Mojokerto	–	33.8
Madiun	–	33.6
Magetan	76.0	32.8
Nganjuk	40.0	32.1
Blitar	–	31.8
Jember	85.0	25.5
Probolinggo	–	25.1
Bondowoso	54.5	24.8
Gresik	86.9	23.9
Kediri	–	23.8
Jombang	90.0	21.6
Tulungagung	35.7	21.4
Trenggalek	30.7	20.1
Pamekasan	66.7	19.9
Bojonegoro	57.7	17.3
Ponorogo	100.0	14.7
Lumajang	29.4	11.9
Tuban	82.3	10.9
Lamongan	65.0	10.1
Bangkalan	54.5	9.3
Sumenep	73.9	9.1
Ngawi	56.2	9.0
Sampang	38.9	7.1
Pacitan	72.0	2.9
Total *kabupaten*	69.4	24.7
Kotamadya		
Surabaya	99.3	–
Malang	100.0	–
Pasuruan	82.3	–
Probolinggo	96.5	–
Kediri	80.4	–
Blitar	95.0	–
Madiun	65.0	–
Mojokerto	94.4	–
Total *kotamadya*	91.6	–
Total	80.4	24.7

Source: PLN Distributors, East Java.
[a]'Villages electrified' means that the area has an electricity service (mostly from PLN) even though only a few households or only parts of a village might receive the service.

FIGURE 11.2
East Java: Electrified *Kecamatan* by Number of Customers, 1978 and 1986

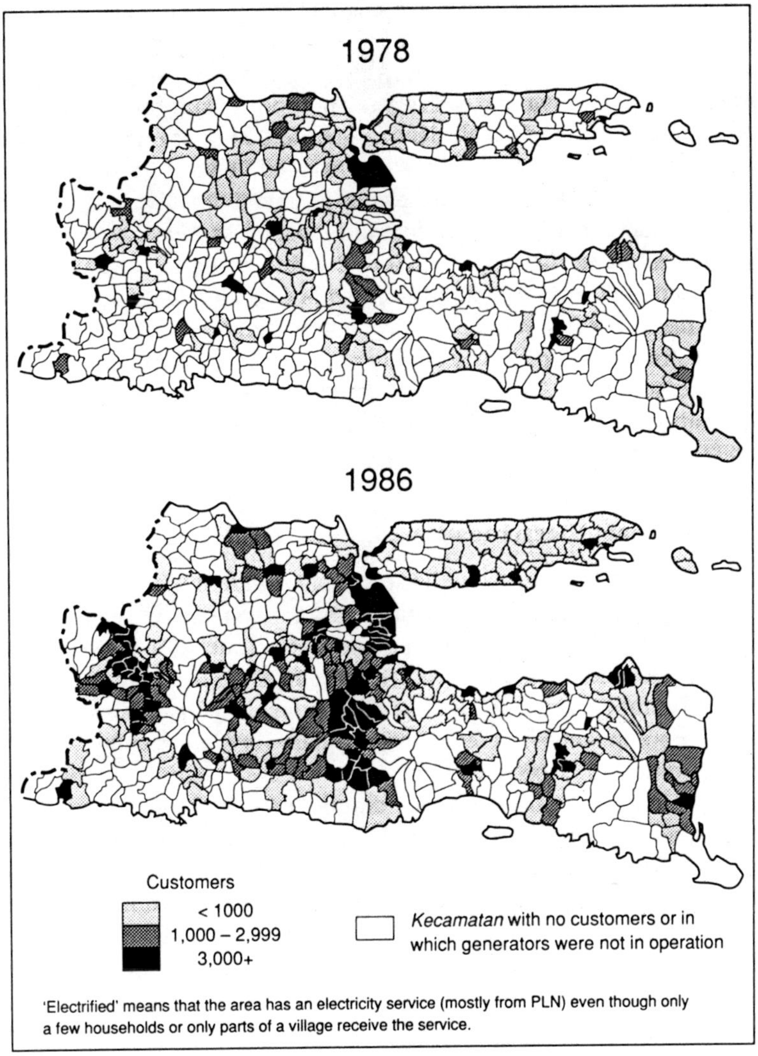

constructed under the *gotong royong* scheme. These are found in Madura and in a number of remote areas of the mainland. Consequently, East Java accounts for about 60 per cent of all PLN diesel power generators in Java. These isolated PLTDs are run at a loss due to high operating costs, so that they have adversely affected the commercial performance of PLN in the province as a whole. The cost per kWh of electricity in East Java in 1984/5 was Rp 90, while the sale price was Rp 84.

The uneven distribution of electric power in East Java has also resulted in the growth of small, privately owned generators. Their use spread in the early 1970s and had the effect of introducing electricity to people in rural areas where the PLN power network did not reach. Machines with capacities of 2–5 kW were operated by private owners, with small amounts of power often being distributed to neighbours for a monthly payment. Even at the end of the 1980s many isolated villages still had their own generators, sometimes using bamboo poles for power lines. In a 1985 survey of non-PLN electricity undertakings in 20 provinces, East Java had the highest number of such businesses, with 21 per cent of all non-PLN electrical undertakings in Indonesia, producing 22 per cent of the total kWh produced (BPS, 1986c). Even in the areas where PLN services are available, many small, private electricity supply businesses still find a demand for their services. They usually offer their customers a supply of 10 to 20 watts per house, at a charge of between Rp 1,000 and Rp 2,000 per month (about US$1), operating only at night for between 6 and 10 hours. In a few cases local co-operatives run diesel plants of a higher capacity, but such operations are risky in remote areas, and servicing the machines is difficult. Moreover, higher capacity, larger generators are less mobile than small ones, which can be moved elsewhere when the PLN service is brought into the area.

Rural Electrification and the Rural Economy

The introduction of electricity has so far had little impact on rural production and productivity. The main effect has usually been a large increase in the number of consumer durables such as televisions and radio/tape recorders. Santoso (n.d.), for example, in his summary of the impact of rural electrification in 10 villages in East Java, has shown that leisure-time appliances increased in number very significantly after the introduction of an electricity service to the areas concerned. Only in the villages which had better economic conditions did electric power stimulate new industrial and productive activities such as ice-making, battery charging, poultry breeding, *tahu* and *tempe* production, workshops, and services. Elsewhere, electricity was used only for illumination and recreational purposes.

The impact of the rural electrification programme in East Java was explored in a study made by the author in Kecamatan Pare and Kecamatan Pandaan (Husin, 1989). Although both areas have had access to the grid since the first quarter of the twentieth century, the availability of electric power has not had a significant impact on either agricultural production or local enterprises.

Pandaan is now a well-known industrial area, due to the establishment since the early 1970s of many new manufacturing industries (see Chapter 12). This development, however, has been the result mainly of the overspill effects of the rapid economic and industrial expansion of Surabaya, and not because the local industries or economy were growing significantly. Almost all the capital investment in the area has come from foreign sources or Surabaya capitalists.

Initially, many industries in Pandaan generated their own electric power. Until 1981 the PLN's delivered output was insufficient to meet their demand, and in any case the PLN service was unreliable. However, by 1986 nearly 80 per cent of PLN electricity sold in the area went to 30 industrial establishments, the average power consumption of which was more than 55 000 kWh per month (Table 11.6). Most of these were large- and medium-scale manufacturing plants, all established during the New Order.

The rapid development of industries and the high consumption of electric power in Pandaan have nothing to do with the rural electrification programme. Development has had little effect on the local economy except through spillover effects such as employment for the local people. Moreover, it is not because of the availability of electric power in the area that industrialization has occurred, so much as the town's proximity to Surabaya, cheaper land, and a good transportation network (see Chapter 12).

Kecamatan Pare is different in that it is part of one of the most important rice baskets in the province. An electricity service has been provided in Pare town since the Dutch period, initially to serve the sugar plantations and industries as well as Dutch facilities in the town. Few of the old plantations and industries still remain, so that electricity consumption in the area is now overwhelmingly residential. In 1986 most of the electric power (90 per cent) consumed in Pare was for domestic purposes (Table 11.7). Industrial consumers represented only 0.2 per cent of all customers and consumed only 5 per cent of the power sold by PLN in the area. The average power consumption in those industries (2 300 kWh per month) was much lower than that of their counterparts in Pandaan and reflects the limited scope of industrial activities in Pare. The power contracted by each of the 14 industrial customers in October 1986 was less than 61 kWh, and most of them had been connected to the service only since 1980.

The growth of industries in Pare thus owes nothing to the length of time that electricity has been available. On the contrary, there has been

TABLE 11.6
Customers and kWh Sold through the Pandaan Branch of the PLN, August 1986

Type of Customer	*Customers*		*Power Consumed*		*Average per Customer (kWh)*
	Number	*%*	*kWh*	*%*	
Residential	5,726	94.7	354 863	17.1	62
Commercial	184	3.0	36 001	1.7	196
Industry	30	0.5	1 655 939	79.8	55 198
Government	104	1.7	28 166	1.4	271
Total	6,044	99.9	2 074 969	100.0	343

Source: PLN, Pandaan Branch.

TABLE 11.7
Customers and kWh Sold through the Pare Branch of the PLN, October 1986[a]

Type of Customer	Customers		Power Consumed		Average per Customer (kWh)
	Number	%	kWh	%	
Residential	6,953	90.0	442 601	68.7	64
Commercial	551	7.1	79 680	12.4	145
Industry	14	0.2	31 907	4.9	2 279
Government	211	2.7	90 158	14.0	427
Total	7,729	100.0	644 346	100.0	83

Source: Calculated from the October 1986 report of PLN, Pare Branch.
[a]The Pare branch of PLN also covers the *kecamatan* of Ploso (2 villages), Wates, Plemahan (4 villages), and Gurah.

little stimulation to industrial growth there, even less than in Pandaan, and the area has lost its old sugar mills and a spinning mill. The present industries in Pare are very small compared with those of Pandaan: most are food processing industries which need little electric power. There has been a small increase in electricity consumption in several villages engaged in raising chickens and small-scale food processing.

In both Pandaan and Pare the average household power consumption appears to have been nearly twice as high as it is in most rural areas which have been brought under the rural electrification programme: about 63 kWh per month as against the usual 30–40 kWh. It may be that people in these two areas have been accustomed to the use of electricity for much longer and have come to rely upon it more. But it is noteworthy that only to a very small extent has electric power been put to productive or commercial use by ordinary households.

Conclusion

Development of the electric power industry in East Java has been linked with the growth of the more modernized sectors of the provincial economy since the early decades of the twentieth century. The pattern of distribution and the types of power-generating facilities have been influenced largely by the concentration of industrial demand for power in and around Surabaya. The basic distribution network, initially established in the last decades of colonial rule, tended to supply the main plantation areas and urban centres where the Dutch population was concentrated. The rural areas were neglected then, and mostly still are, despite the rural electrification scheme.

The impact of electrification in stimulating economic activity in East Java is still difficult to measure. Cheap power may have boosted manufacturing in the period 1920–40, although the textile industry that flourished in Central and West Java with the ready availability of power did not develop as strongly in East Java.

Most of the big industrial users of electricity have had to rely on their own power generators for much of the post-Independence era, largely because the frequency of power failures necessitated the purchase of standby generators for emergency use. This has probably meant that the much increased electricity supply since the late 1970s has not greatly affected the rate of industrial development. The big increase in industrial development in East Java actually occurred before then. Some diversification of medium- and small-scale industrial, commercial, and service activities may have resulted from the greater availability of electric power in the 1980s, but evidence to confirm this hypothesis is not yet available.

1. When referring to the installed capacity of a generating system, the unit of power used is the kilowatt (kW) or megawatt (MW). The kilowatt-hour (kWh) or megawatt-hour (MWh) measures amounts of 'electrical energy' and is a unit of output.

2. These small companies were Gemeente Electriciteit Bedrijf Madioen, which supplied Madiun from the Giringan hydroelectric plant, Banjoewangi Electriciteit, supplying the Bondowoso and Jember areas, Lawangsche Electriciteit in Lawang, and the small Electra in Tulungagung. In 1928 the Probolinggo, Besuki, and Lawang companies were taken over by ANIEM.

3. These stations were small, in the main producing less than 75 kW. See also McCawley (1971: Part I, Chapter 1, and Appendix 3).

4. After nationalization these companies were controlled by the Surabaya Administration Board for Electricity and Gas Enterprises.

5. In 1954 electricity in East Java was organized under PLN Djawa Tengah/Djawa Timur (the State Electricity Corporation for Central Java and East Java). In 1961 the name was changed to PLN Daerah Eksploitasi IX (PLN Regional Exploitation IX), with an area of operation covering the whole of East Java and Nusa Tenggara. In 1963 the area covered was limited to the East Java region only, minus the *kabupaten* of Bojonegoro and Tuban.

6. The hydroelectric capacity was boosted further during Repelita II (1974/5–1978/9) by the expansion of Karangkates (Sutami) to 105 MW and the operation of the Wlingi plant (54 MW). During Repelita III (1979/80–1983/4) a second large thermal plant, in Gresik (200 MW), began operation.

7. Surabaya (Perak) provided 27.5 MW and Gresik 61.5 MW of power generated by gas.

8. There were 72 foreign investment projects and 329 domestic investment projects established in East Java between 1967 and the end of 1984 (KSJT, *Jawa Timur dalam Angka, 1985*).

9. By October 1985 there were 470 villages in Central Java, with about 75,000 customers, connected to electric power under USAID (United Stages Agency for International Development) projects.

12
Industrial Expansion into a Rural Subdistrict: Pandaan, East Java

Patrick Guinness and Imron Husin

Introduction

IN East Java, industrial development has centred on the capital, Surabaya, but has spread to the neighbouring *kabupaten* of Gresik and Mojokerto, and along the highway to the second largest urban centre, Malang (see Chapter 10). This highway passes through the rapidly industrializing *kabupaten* of Sidoarjo and then the *kecamatan* of Gempol and Pandaan in Kabupaten Pasuruan. Since the beginning of the First Five-Year Development Plan (Repelita I, 1969/70–1973/4), these *kecamatan* have experienced rapid development of large and medium industries. The required capital has come from outside the area, much of it international. Land has been purchased and local labour employed for the construction and operation of factories. Yet this capital-intensive industry is still marginal to the local economy, which remains highly dependent on agriculture. Manufacturing has developed along a ribbon of land adjacent to the highway, with little impact on villages and hamlets at any distance from it. This chapter will describe the industrial expansion into Pandaan and then discuss in detail some of its impacts throughout the *kecamatan*.[1]

Kecamatan Pandaan before 1970

Industry is not new to Pandaan. The Ardirejo (also called Pandaan) sugar mill in Kutorejo village on the outskirts of Pandaan town was in operation as early as 1834.[2] Large areas of wet rice land (*sawah*) close to the factory were planted with sugar-cane, and many peasants, particularly the landless, were recruited from surrounding villages to work in the fields and the factories. For the smallholders and landless, the sugar industry provided an alternative source of income and security to that traditionally provided by rice farming. One result of this early industrial activity was an increasing monetization of village life; wealthier landholders were able to pay others to work and harvest their cane.

Disparities in wealth increased and political power was consolidated in the hands of the village élite.

The early 1920s witnessed increased unionization of factory workers and agitation for higher wages and improved working conditions. Elson (1984: 201) reports at least two strikes in the Pandaan sugar factory in 1920. Improved conditions were gained, partly as a result of government intervention, but the benefits were short-lived. The sugar industry collapsed in the 1930s and the Ardirejo mill was closed.[3] Workers were forced to return to village occupations, a process which Elson (1984: 248) describes as an 'eerie sort of retraditionalisation'.

While it can be assumed that several of the villages in Pandaan were affected directly by the sugar mill, it may have had little impact on the small town of Pandaan. Elson (1984: 181) concluded that during the sugar period local towns remained for the most part 'sleepy enclaves'. Most of the industry's requirements for machines and technology were supplied from Surabaya. The town of Pandaan was probably confined in the nineteenth century to the one village administrative unit (*desa*) of Pandaan. It was, however, an administrative centre. In 1856 Pandaan was listed as a district (*kawedanan*) capital, within the *kabupaten* of Bangil in the Residency of Pasuruan. In 1920 the District of Pandaan included the subdistricts (*onderdistricten*) of Pandaan, Prigen in the mountains west of Pandaan, and Sukorejo, south along the Malang road.

The presence of a sugar mill in Pandaan prompted other developments. One was the construction in 1898/9 of a private steam-tram line (*Modjokerto Stoomtram Maatschappij*) linking Pandaan with Bangil in one direction and Porong and Mojokerto in the other. The steam-trams provided a passenger service as well as sugar transportation.[4]

In the early decades of the twentieth century the availability of fresh water in Pandaan gave rise to some other pioneer industries. In 1903 a pipeline was installed from the Kasri spring above Pandaan to Surabaya, to supplement that town's drinking water supply. Then in 1927 an ice factory was established in Kasri, using the same water source.

In about 1920 an electricity substation was installed in Pandaan along the route of the Bangil–Malang electricity power lines. Initially power was used mostly for house lighting and the only industry using electric power was the sugar mill. Power was also supplied from this substation to the nearby hill resort of Tretes. In the mid-1930s, however, a large textile mill (Kasri) opened near the ice factory, attracted in part by the availability of cheap labour as a result of the closure of the sugar mill.[5]

By 1969 the industrial activities of Pandaan were still dominated by the Kasri weaving mill, the Kasri ice factory, and the processing of kapok in the hill villages west of Pandaan town (Table 12.1). The 1970 Industry Survey (BPS, 1971) noted seven kapok processing plants, six of medium size and one large.[6] The other industries were all of medium size. The period 1967–70 was marked by impressive new industrial investment in East Java.[7]

TABLE 12.1
Pandaan: Industrial Establishments, 1970

Type	*Large*	*Medium*
Ice	1	–
Kapok	1	6
Weaving	1	2
Rice processing	0	9
Peanut oil	0	3
Cigarettes	0	2
Battery plates	0	1
Cardboard	0	1
Total	3	24

Sources: BPS (1971); KSJT, *Jawa Timur dalam Angka, 1970.*

Despite the early industrial developments, Kecamatan Pandaan experienced declining rates of population growth from 1920 to 1961, and the annual rate of growth was considerably below that for East Java as a whole (Table 12.2). Only the growth during the 1920s in foreign population, especially among Chinese and Arabs, indicated Pandaan's continued importance as an industrial, trading, and administrative centre. But by the late 1960s, when there was new growth in manufacturing industry in Pandaan, the rate of population growth exceeded that of East Java.

TABLE 12.2
Kecamatan Pandaan: Population, 1920–1971

	1920	*1930*	*1961*	*1971*
All population	25,175	29,248	39,880	48,121
Europeans	95	114		
Chinese	166	221	190[a]	
Arabs	7	44		

	1920–30	*1930–6*	*1961–71*
Annual growth (per cent)			
Pandaan	1.50	1.00	1.88
East Java	1.85	1.20	1.58

Sources: Volkstelling (1922, 1933–6); BPS (1963, 1972).
[a]All foreigners.

Developments in Pandaan after 1970

Growth of Industry

Industrial development in Pandaan after 1970 built on its existing industrial base. In 1970 Pandaan was officially designated an 'industrial town'. Industrial expansion in Pandaan was marked by a plan to expand the old Kasri textile factory. Domestic and foreign investment soon followed, including Indonesia–Japan Tobacco Ltd., the Tristate textile mill, with 70 per cent Hong Kong equity, the British pharmaceutical company ICI, and domestic investments in Mercu Buana Chemicals and Berlina, a manufacturer of plastic bottles. By 1975 four pharmaceutical factories, three textile mills, the plastic bottle factory, and an agricultural machinery plant were all in operation. Investment continued into the 1980s, and several factories still were under construction in 1986. In that year there were 10 large- and 18 medium-scale establishments in Pandaan, comprising 37 per cent and 17 per cent respectively of all large and medium establishments in Kabupaten Pasuruan (KSP, 1986). These accounted for 33 per cent and 22 per cent of industrial employment in the *kabupaten* (Table 12.3).[8] The *kecamatan* of Gempol and

TABLE 12.3
Kabupaten Pasuruan: Industrial Employment by *Kecamatan* and Size of Firm, 1986 (per cent)

	Proportion of Workers		
Subdistrict[a]	*Large*	*Medium*	*All firms*[b] *(n = 39,350)*
Gempol	32.0	17.6	16.8
Pandaan	32.7	22.1	15.8
Bangil	–	12.8	10.7
Rembang	3.6	–	9.5
Sukorejo	3.2	7.7	8.9
Beji	0.8	3.8	6.8
Grati	16.2	0.8	6.4
Purwodadi	2.5	5.8	4.0
Purwosari	1.7	6.8	3.5
Pohjentrek	6.4	1.5	3.0
Prigen	0.9	7.8	1.6
Others	–	13.3	13.0
Total	100.0	100.0	100.0
Percentage of all labour	32.6	9.3	100.0

Source: KSP (1986).

[a]The top ten subdistricts, plus Prigen, ranked by total number of workers. There are 24 *kecamatan* in Pasuruan. Prigen is included as the adjacent *kecamatan* that includes Tretes tourist resort.

[b]Including small and home industries.

Pandaan provided most of the employment in large and medium firms in 1986.

Due to the heavy concentration of industries in Surabaya and Sidoarjo, industrial investors moved further south to Gempol and Pandaan, where they could take advantage of cheap land, cheap labour, and good transportation and communication facilities. In the case of Pandaan the attraction may also have included a plentiful water supply and the proximity of the resort of Tretes, where managerial staff could be housed in comfort. In Pandaan that investment was concentrated in the industrial sectors of food and drink, textiles, and chemicals and plastics (Table 12.4).

The increase in the number of large establishments from 3 in 1970 to 10 in 1985 meant a substantial increase in industrial employment. The largest employers in Pandaan were the three textile mills, accounting in 1986 for about 2,500 workers. Located in three different villages on the urban periphery, they favoured the employment on low wages of young women from nearby villages. Employment in each reached a peak of 1,000 or more workers in the early 1980s, but in two plants had declined by the mid-1980s, when one-quarter of the labour force had been laid off. Two of these mills were owned by Indonesian residents with industrial interests elsewhere in Java, while the third represented the investment of Japanese and Hong Kong companies.

Chemical industries were also well represented. In 1986 there were five pharmaceutical plants and one plastic bottle manufacturer in

TABLE 12.4

Pandaan: Industrial Establishments by Sector, 1985 and 1986

	1985		*1986*
	Large[a]	*Medium*[b]	*Large and Medium*
Food, drink, and tobacco	3	7	8
Textiles and clothing	3	2	5
Wood and furniture	0	1	1
Chemicals and plastics	2	1	6
Cement	0	0	1
Metals and machinery	1	1	2
Others	1	6	2
Total	10	18	25[c]

Sources: 1985: KSP, *Kabupaten Pasuruan dalam Angka, 1985.*
1986: KSP (1986).

[a]'Large' refers to firms employing one hundred or more workers.

[b]'Medium' refers to firms employing 20–99 workers.

[c]The 1986 total figure of 25 establishments given here is different from preliminary figures of 28 establishments provided by *kabupaten* staff from the Economic Census. The differences between the 1985 and 1986 figures may result partly from inconsistencies in data gathering by *kabupaten* and Census officers.

Kecamatan Pandaan. The plastic bottle factory, under Chinese–Indonesian ownership, was probably the largest employer in this group, with 800 employees. Most of the pharmaceutical plants were established with foreign capital, including British, US, and German investment. Between 100 and 300 people were employed in each, with some showing preference for young village women, and others tending to employ men. Two United States firms, for example, reportedly paid high wages and recruited only high-school graduates or above. Town-based men who refused work in other factories where wages were lower were prepared to work there.[9] These factories also attracted workers from other towns and *kecamatan*.

The other prominent industrial sector in Pandaan comprised manufacturers of food and drink, and included bottled and canned drink factories, a milk treatment plant, vegetable oil production, a bakery, and a poultry processing firm. At least three of these employed between 100 and 300 workers, while seven others were of medium size, with domestic, US, and Taiwanese capital involved. At least two plants, Coca-Cola and Aqua (mineral water), were part of a network of factories in Indonesia supplying the local market.

Although located in Pandaan, most of the medium and large manufacturers were controlled by people whose interests centred in the metropolitan capitals of Indonesia or overseas. In 1986 at least 10 manufacturing concerns in Pandaan were dominated by foreign investments, with the United States and Japan—the prominent investors—involved in three each. Of the Indonesian-owned manufacturers, several were part of an industrial network that included firms elsewhere in Indonesia. Senior management in these firms was more likely to be located in the capital cities of Surabaya or Jakarta, or even overseas, with the senior staff in Pandaan responsible for just technical operations. The lack of senior management resident or even active within Pandaan contributed to the continuing impression of the town as a 'sleepy enclave', in many respects divorced from the bustle of industry on its periphery.

The size of the labour force employed in large-scale manufacturing industries in Pandaan is difficult to determine. The 1986 Economic Census listed 4,195 workers in large establishments in Pandaan, 812 in medium, 291 in small establishments, and 923 in home industries. However, the official Kantor Statistik Pasuruan yearbook, *Kabupaten Pasuruan dalam Angka 1985*, noted 5,068 workers in mechanized firms in 1982, 6,065 workers in large and medium firms in 1983, and 7,083 workers in small establishments in 1985. The apparent drop in industrial employment between 1985 and 1986 was partly confirmed by the reported laying-off of workers in several large firms, including textile mills and pharmaceutical plants, that occurred in 1985 as a result of nation-wide economic recession.

While Pandaan is becoming an important centre for large and medium industries, there has been no growth in small-scale and home industries (industries employing less than 20 people). In both these categories, less than 5 per cent of firms in Pasuruan were situated in

Pandaan at the time of the 1986 Economic Census (KSP, 1986). The growth of large-scale industry does not seem to have stimulated small downstream industrial enterprises among local residents, although these abounded in the longer established centres of Gempol (12 per cent of all small industries in Pasuruan), Bangil (16 per cent), and Sukorejo (16 per cent), all situated on the old highway between Surabaya and Malang. The modern large-scale industries, with most of their specialist marketing and technical services supplied from within or by contractors from the major cities, provided little stimulus to the growth of local small and home industries.

Population Growth and Movement into Pandaan

The administrative status of Pandaan as *kawedanan* and *kecamatan* capital remained unaltered after 1970. Police Sector (Polis Sektor or Polsek) and Military Area Command (Koramil) headquarters were also located in the town. The *kecamatan* contained eight junior secondary and five senior secondary schools, most of which were found in the town or on its periphery. The government personnel who staffed these offices and schools, as in earlier days had the managerial staff of the sugar mill, represented a thin layer of a 'metropolitan' society and culture in the town.[10]

Pandaan is at the junction of the Malang–Surabaya highway and a road that snakes up to the tourist resort of Tretes, 11 kilometres away. Originally a hill resort to which Dutch civil servants in Surabaya sent their families during the more humid months of the year, it has in recent years attracted many Indonesians from Surabaya, and even from Jakarta, who have built large homes into the steep hillsides. Firms have constructed villas for use by their staff, and the resort abounds with hotels and guesthouses. The development of Tretes as a tourist resort has generated traffic through Pandaan, leading to the recent establishment of restaurants, art shops, and fruit stalls around the junction of the two roads. The market in Pandaan services the Tretes area and some of the foodstuffs sold there, like imported fruits, cater to the wealthy clientele from the mountain resort.

Particularly during the 1970s the population of Kecamatan Pandaan grew rapidly, much more rapidly than in the *kabupaten* as a whole and slightly more than in the *kotamadya* of Pasuruan (Table 12.5).

The rapid increase in population points to a high rate of migration into the area, no doubt associated with developments in manufacturing industry. The improvement of the Malang–Surabaya highway, which led to an increasing number of people commuting between the two centres, encouraged a rapid increase in public and private transport passing through Pandaan. However, the small number of passengers boarding or disembarking from public transport in the town in 1986, and the quietness of the local bus station, suggested that daily commuting into or out of the *kecamatan* was uncommon. In fact the growing industrial employment in the *kecamatan* itself may have stemmed the

TABLE 12.5

Pandaan, Pasuruan, and East Java: Population Growth, 1961–1990

	1961	*1971*	*1980*	*1990*[a]	*1961–71*	*1971–80*	*1980–90*
	Persons ('000)				%		
Kecamatan Pandaan	40	48	61	(65)[b]	1.9	2.6	1.2
Kotamadya Pasuruan	729	872	1,034	1,106	1.8	2.0	0.7
Kabupaten Pasuruan	63	87	119	134	1.7	2.4	1.2
East Java	21,823	25,527	29,189	32,504	1.6	1.5	1.1

Sources: BPS (1963, 1972, 1982); Pasuruan Statistical Office, unpublished data.

[a]EPS, unpublished data from 1990 Census.

[b]1986 estimate; later figure not available.

flow of population, both commuters and migrants, to the metropolitan centres. The only available statistical evidence, the 1983 and 1985 *kabupaten* statistics (KSP, *Kabupaten Pasuruan dalam Angka*, 1983 and 1985), indicated that immigration into Kecamatan Pandaan exceeded emigration. In 1983 there were 445 arrivals and 363 departures; in 1985, 866 arrivals and 665 departures.

The Spatial Impact of Industrial Development in Pandaan

Population data (Table 12.6) allow us to differentiate four types of villages within the *kecamatan*: four 'urban villages', officially designated as such since 1974 and characterized by high population densities and, in three of the four, rapid population expansion since 1961; four rural 'industrial villages', the sites of most of the modern industry constructed since 1970, with population densities higher than other rural villages and rapid population growth during the 1961–80 period; and the 'central agricultural' and 'remote agricultural' villages, distinguished by their location and by lower population growth and density (Figure 12.1). The industrial and central agricultural villages are clustered around the urban centre but the remote agricultural villages are, as their classification implies, well away from the urban centre.

The population expansion in the industrial villages is related both to the establishment of industry in or near the villages and to their location near town and highway. The central agricultural villages are also situated near the town, but have poorer access to the Surabaya–Malang highway and have grown less rapidly. Other statistics confirm these impressions of differential development. The Community Development Office (CDO) collects statistical information annually from village officials and presents it as measures of development in education, productivity, employment, community activities, village institutions, and public facil-

TABLE 12.6
Kecamatan Pandaan: Size and Population of Villages, 1961, 1980, and 1986

Type of Village	*Area (sq km)*	*Population*		*Population Increase (%), 1961–80*	*Population Density (per sq km), 1980*
		1961	*1986*		
Urban	4.14	10,174	18,431	70	4,176
Industrial	11.34	10,363	18,714	70	1,550
Central agricultural	10.57	7,778	12,319	46	1,073
Remote agricultural	15.62	11,565	15,323	26	934
Total	41.65	39,880	64,787	52	

Sources: Area and Population, 1986: Directorate-General of Community Development. Population, 1961 and 1980: BPS (1963, 1982).

FIGURE 12.1
Kecamatan Pandaan

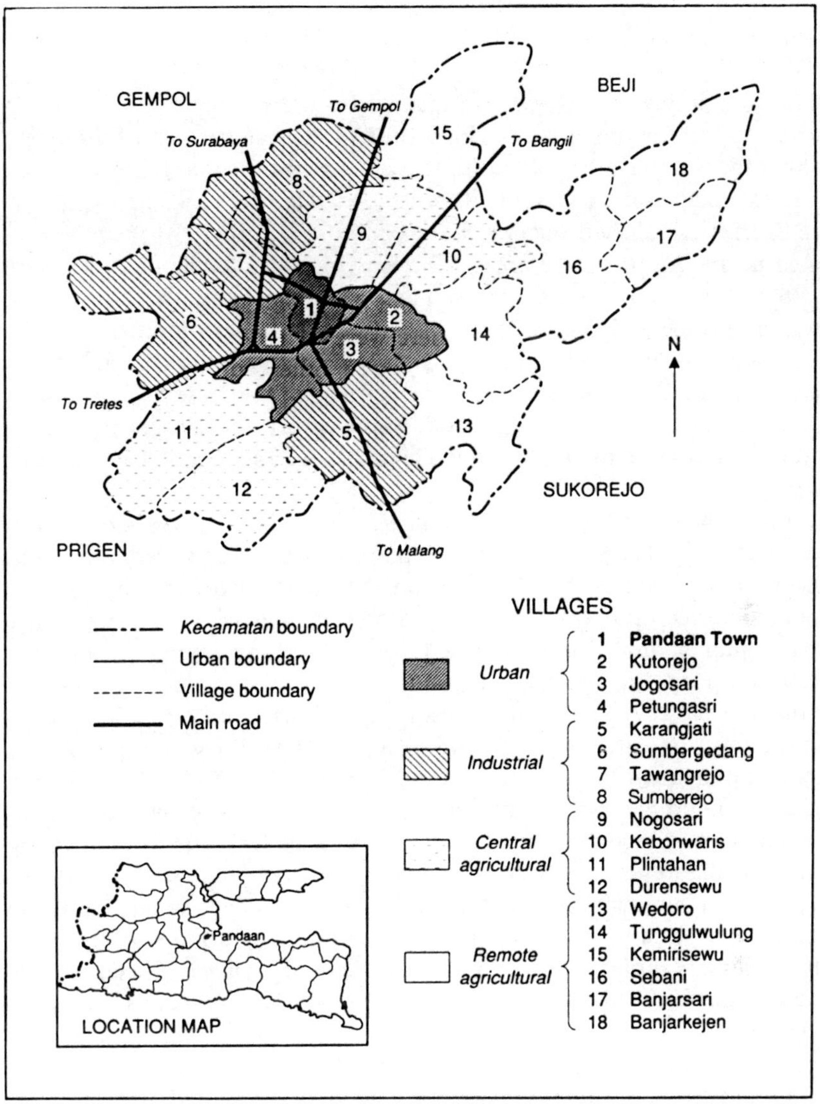

ities. These measures are aggregated to enable the CDO to categorize each village as 'subsistence' (*swadaya*), 'developing' (*swakarya*), or 'developed' (*swasembada*). The results (Appendix Table A12.2) support these distinctions.

In 1972 there was no clear distinction between the village categories, the majority being labelled as *swakarya*. By 1980, however, all villages except the remote agricultural ones were classified as *swasembada*. Urban and industrial villages were the only ones listed as dominated by tertiary employment, and only they had over 60 per cent of the population with primary school education.[11] By 1986 only the remote villages were not classified as *swasembada*: scoring maximum points in the CDO's assessment of educational achievements, employment classification, and overall development.

Industrial Villages

The four industrial villages are located on the periphery of the urban centre along the major roads (Figure 12.1): Tawangrejo and Sumberejo along the Surabaya highway, Sumbergedang just off that highway at the Tretes road junction, and Karangjati along the Malang highway. Industries established outside the urban core before 1970 were all located in these four village areas. The Kasri ice and textile factories were in the Tawangrejo–Sumberejo area and the large kapok-processing plant was in Sumbergedang. In 1986 there were 21 modern industries in the Tawangrejo–Sumberejo area (with three others under construction), seven in Sumbergedang, and 17 in Karangjati.[12] These factories were constructed on former village land. Some displaced villagers purchased land further from the highway, while others became dependent on wage labour.

Many factories employed local village labour, in some cases on a preferential basis. Village youth more often than their elders were employed in the new factories, both because of the young people's reluctance to pursue agricultural employment and factory management's preference for young and/or better educated workers. Many young people had grown up to expect salaried employment in government or factory offices.[13] However, the more prestigious factories often required references from potential workers, and villagers claimed it was impossible to gain employment there without 'inside contacts'. In this process the village head and *kecamatan* officials played a vital part in providing recommendations to factories for a few privileged local workers. Among young men unable to get industrial employment and reluctant to work in agriculture, unemployment was therefore high, as instanced in one hamlet in Sumberejo where young men provided the bulk of workers in the 1986 flood control project initiated by government and village officials. While young men worked on this project for Rp 700 a day, older men in the village preferred to hoe, earning Rp 1,000 a day, or plough, for Rp 2,500 a day.

Employment in industry was not limited to households with little or no access to land. Some of those in the Kasri ice factory, for example, had been employed there for twenty years but retained their farming land and intended to return to farming once they retired. Agricultural field officers in Pandaan noted the neglect of farms in some industrial villages, as farmers moonlighted in factories. The capacity of households to combine agricultural and non-agricultural employment was documented in a study (Kabul, 1977) in Sumberejo in 1976, where the first modern factories in Pandaan were built. In a survey of all 918 households in the village, Kabul found that in 42 per cent of households all

TABLE 12.7

Sumberejo: Sources of Income of Agricultural Households, March–October 1976 (per cent)

Size of Farm[a] *(ha)*	*No. of Households*	*Mean Household Income (Rp)*	*Agricultural Product*	*Agricultural Wages*	*Non-agricultural Wages*
0 (farm labour)	23	61,964	0	76	24
0.1–0.25	13	121,285	64	9	27
0.25–0.5	37	154,429	67	2	31
0.5–1.0	47	154,754	73	2	25
>1.0	5	256,302	83	0	17

Source: Kabul (1977).

[a]Categories are taken directly from Kabul (1977).

members were engaged solely in agriculture, as farmers and/or farm labourers. The other households had members employed in industrial labour, petty trade, and small enterprise.

In terms of income, however, agriculture remained the most important occupation, with 74 per cent of households obtaining at least some of their income from farming or farm labour. These are referred to as 'agricultural households'. Industrial employment was rarely the sole source of household income. Only 13 per cent of households earned all their income from industrial labour, while another 26 per cent earned income from industrial labour and agriculture. Table 12.7 indicates the importance for agricultural households of non-agricultural sources of income, of which 84 per cent is income from industrial labour and the rest from petty trade.

While the contribution of agricultural wages was small and declined as farm size grew, the contribution of income from non-agricultural employment remained similar in relation both to farm size and the nature of farm tenure (not shown). Only among households farming over 1 hectare was there a decline in the proportion of households obtaining income from non-agricultural employment, though not in its actual size. It is clear that households of all economic levels relied significantly on industrial labour. After an analysis of hours spent in various activities, Kabul concluded that people employed in agriculture had a very low level of employment compared with people employed in non-agricultural activities, implying that there were few possibilities for expansion of employment opportunities in agriculture. Additional employment had to come from the non-agricultural sector (Kabul, 1977: 42). Thus, even in the early days of modern industrialization in Pandaan, an interdependence had emerged between agricultural and industrial employment. Industrial employment by itself was not enough to lift a family to material well-being, though it helped.[14]

The comments of the village head of Sumberejo in 1986 were indicative of the impact of industry in that village a decade later. When asked about changes in the village during the industrial period, he claimed that there had been little improvement for people generally. Only those who had been rich before had benefited. Employment in industry was limited to those who had the right contacts or family connections. His comments support the findings of Kabul that large landowners were benefiting from industrial employment, while those households relying entirely on industrial labour and/or agricultural labour remained poor.

Urban Villages

One-third of the industries noted in the 1970 industrial survey (see Table 12.1) were located in Kutorejo, Jogosari, and Petungsari, which at that time were classed as rural, not urban, villages. The high proportion of industrial firms in these villages on the outskirts of the 'town' (at that time defined as the one 'urban' village of Pandaan) indicates the tendency of industry to locate just beyond town limits where urban facilities are still available but land prices are considerably lower than in the urban area. The official absorption of these villages into the urban area during the 1970s recognized their largely non-agricultural nature, reflected in higher population densities, industrial employment, and administrative and commercial premises. The industries in these villages in 1970 were linked closely with the agricultural production of the area or with servicing the local population. As such they may have spawned subsidiary businesses and small industries that contributed to the urban transformation of the village population. This is much less likely in the industrial villages of the 1980s, where firms are oriented to remote city or international markets. Since 1980 industrial development within the urban villages has been limited to a workshop providing spare parts for the textile factories and an industrial plant making ladies' shoes, household equipment, and furniture components.

Until 1931 Kutorejo was the site of the sugar factory, staff houses, railway station, and the Dutch colonial army depot. In 1986, however, it was the least densely settled of the four urban villages, and included 85 hectares of rice-land. The 80 owners of agricultural land were mostly non-farmers who rented the land to landless people or small landowners. This testifies to another trend within industrial society, the aggregation of land by non-farmers who reap the benefits of higher and steadier incomes from government service and commerce and invest their savings in farm-land. All but seven of the landowners in Kutorejo were outsiders who had moved there and invested in rice-land. In a population of about 600 households, only 120 (20 per cent) controlled farming land.[15] The rest of the economically active population were traders, entrepreneurs, government officials, teachers, and factory employees. The village head claimed in 1986 that every major island of Indonesia was represented among the population of the village.

The rapid population expansion since 1970 in the urban villages was partly the result of the industrial development occurring just beyond the urban boundaries. Much of this increase was due to migration, particularly of factory staff, into Kecamatan Pandaan, which created a demand for accommodation, food, household goods, and other services within the town itself. The urban villages provided accommodation not only for government employees but also for industrial workers. In 1986 small rooms with very basic facilities in the town were fetching up to Rp 20,000 a month, a considerable rent. However, there was little better accommodation, reflecting the lack of demand by more senior factory staff.[16] All indications were that Pandaan town had become a population centre feeding the manufacturing industries on its periphery but failing to attract a wealthier, 'metropolitan' population.

Market trade and retailing dominated the economy of the urban villages. The town was the centre for a large number of mostly local, petty traders and artisans, many of whom worked in or around the market. The most permanent of these rented space, for which an initial payment and a monthly rental were charged. They sold food, clothing, watches, radios, hardware, and other household needs, making a daily profit of

Rp 5,000–10,000. A second category of market traders set up temporary stalls outside closed or unoccupied stall sites, thus escaping stall rental charges but still paying a market fee. A third category walked around the market with goods like watches, shirts, or medicines displayed on their arms. These were the poorer traders who tried to avoid the market fee. In 1986 the District Office recognized an increase in market activity by constructing a new market on the eastern edge of town in Kutorejo. There was little indication, however, of luxury goods flooding into the market as a result of industrial developments in the *kecamatan*. Rather, the market and the town shops catered mostly for a poorer, predominantly rural clientele. The shops, for example, did not stock larger items of household furniture and appliances, nor were there bookshops or clothing shops that catered for 'metropolitan' tastes.

In trade and services, several successful entrepreneurs had emerged. Kecamatan Pandaan in 1986 had 16 suppliers of building materials, by far the largest number for any *kecamatan* in Kabupaten Pasuruan (KSP, 1986). These suppliers had set up premises in the urban area to meet the demand for permanent materials for housing throughout the town and adjacent villages. Several more luxurious two-storey homes had been constructed, reportedly owned by the town's commercial entrepreneurs (mostly Chinese). A prominent indigenous businessman owned a fleet of over 20 minibuses which he hired out on a daily basis to drivers who plied mainly the Pandaan–Tretes road carrying passengers and goods.

Nevertheless, the town did not display commercial prosperity or the urban sophistication to match the industrial investment taking place on its periphery. The reasons, as in the earlier sugar period, lay in the propensity of large industry to be managed from the main metropolitan areas, for their staff to commute to factories from those cities or, in the case of Pandaan, from the nearby resort of Tretes, and for most servicing and supply functions to these factories to be met from Surabaya or Malang. It appears that the developments noted above, such as the emergence of entrepreneurs in service sectors, growth in the construction industry, and development of market facilities were less a consequence of industrial development than of Pandaan town's strategic location as the gateway to a large tourist resort. Any commercial growth Pandaan was experiencing was linked not with the dramatic emergence of manufacturing activities in the 1970s but with the development of the town as an administrative centre and as a service point for the nearby tourist resort.

Central Agricultural Villages

Four villages were categorized as 'central agricultural'. They were characterized by moderate population growth and density, employment predominantly in the tertiary sector, relatively high incomes, and good education (Table 12.6 and Appendix Table A12.2). All four villages were located on the periphery of town, with fairly good access to it along sealed roads. They experienced growth under the colonial administration but then declined, since their distance from the Surabaya–Malang highway resulted in industrial development passing them by.

Nogosari and Kebonwaris were the only villages in the *kecamatan* labelled as 'developed' in the 1972 CDO report (Appendix Table A12.2). In that year they were rated highly on education, productivity, and infrastructure. Their position on the main roads linking Pandaan with the former *kabupaten* capital of Bangil probably secured them some advantage in commerce and infrastructure development. During the nineteenth century and the first part of the twentieth century their well-irrigated fields were planted with sugar-cane to supply the nearby factory in Kutorejo, and the sugar industry probably provided many of their residents with employment and other income opportunities. In the 1970s many residents were attracted into industrial employment in the nearby industrial villages of Tawangrejo, Sumberejo, and Karangjati. In the 1970 industrial survey (BPS, 1971), two medium-scale textile mills and two rice mills were noted in Nogosari and Kebonwaris. The Tristate textile mill was also built at Nogosari in 1975, and the construction of at least one other large factory was begun. This factory was never finished (its walls were the only remaining structure in 1986) and the textile mill suffered severe cutbacks in production and staff in the 1980s. The village head of Kebonwaris stressed in 1986 that his village had not benefited from industrial development. He emphasized the poverty of its residents, due to fragmentation of land and the failure of irrigation. Only 25 per cent of families ate three meals a day, he said, and he had advised many to register for transmigration. This slump in the fortunes of Kebonwaris occurred despite its having won a 'best village' award in the early 1960s.

Despite their proximity to the *kecamatan* centre and their early favourable introduction to industrial development, none of these four agricultural villages experienced the industrial expansion noted in neighbouring industrial villages. Durensewu and Plintahan, above Pandaan, also showed early promise of industrial development. Both were kapok-growing areas, and Plintahan was the site in the 1980s of a cigarette factory with Japanese investment, plus large-scale poultry farms. However none of these villages consolidated its earlier industrial development. The explanation would seem to lie in the importance of the Surabaya–Malang highway and the Tretes road as sites of large industrial concerns. Industrial expansion transformed a ribbon of land along the main highways through the *kecamatan*, leaving other areas relatively worse off.

Remote Agricultural Villages

Finally, there was a group of six villages identified as 'remote'. These were characterized by low population density and growth, probably indicating a high incidence of out-migration. Income and education levels were low and the majority of the economically active population worked in either the primary or the secondary sector. Even in 1980, when all other villages had well-developed infrastructures, these villages were poorly endowed with public works. None of them was linked by sealed roads to the town, and in many cases bridges were in disrepair. With the exception of Kemirisewu to the north-east, all these villages are situated in the eastern corner of the *kecamatan,* an area with poor irrigation. In 1986 most houses were constructed of bamboo rather than brick, with primitive facilities and no electricity. School buildings appeared to be in poor repair. Government-backed organizations of any sort were reportedly difficult to initiate. Agricultural fieldworkers expressed difficulty in dealing with these villages, particularly in introducing new ideas, because of the traditional authority of religious leaders.[17]

The poverty of the remote village also illustrates the narrow impact of industrial development and the uneven spread of government services. Some factories recruited workers from the more accessible areas of these villages and provided transport by truck. Yet the more remote areas were cut off by the poor state of roads and bridges, making impossible any truck or minibus service. Thus these villages were cut off from industrial employment and government services. In these cases it was not surprising to find very low population growth as people left the area to find jobs.

Conclusion

Pandaan is a *kecamatan* noted for its industrial growth under the New Order. This growth has taken place as a result of the investment of capital from outside the subdistrict. It has not generated much downstream industrial activity of service industries, small-scale manufacturing, or petty commodity producers. Neither has the town's commercial sector witnessed any large injections of capital commensurate with the industrial development on the town periphery. Pandaan has served as an administrative centre and supplied cheap land, cheap labour, and improved infrastructure but it has not developed into a major town.

At the level of the village, industrial expansion has augmented rather than transformed employment opportunities. Farming continues to be the mainstay of the village economy but its capacity to support households financially is diminishing. The population is increasingly dependent on employment in the industrial sector. Employment there, however, is at the whim of management making decisions in remote offices and with other than local concerns in mind. Factory wages are low, especially for unmarried women, and surplus labour is laid off in times of economic recession. The rural sector therefore bears the reproduction costs of this labour. The parallel with the earlier sugar industry is striking. As in that earlier period, Pandaan is vulnerable to the decline of its industrial heavyweights as the world economy and far-away company directives dictate the closure or relocation of manufacturing activities in the subdistrict. The area experienced large lay-offs of factory personnel and go-slow approaches in the construction of new factories in the mid-1980s. In such a situation, village labour is forced to revert to traditional activities or migrate to the cities.

Within the villages one impact of modern manufacturing industry has been the widening of wealth differentials. Landowners benefited from the high prices paid for land by industrial firms. The village élite secured jobs for themselves and their children within these firms by virtue of 'connections'. Non-farmers purchased farming land as an investment, giving rise to a substantial landlord group within urban and peri-urban villages. At the same time others experienced a drop in fortunes and income, and poverty characterized many households.

Titus et al. (1986) examined the role of small urban centres in the Serayu Valley region of Central Java. They noted that planners envisaged all kinds of development tasks for small towns, as regional facility centres, stimulators of agricultural modernization, and as counterweights for primate city dominance (Titus et al., 1986: 269).[18] Their own conclusions were not as optimistic. In only two cases in the Serayu Valley had small towns developed into manufacturing service centres, and these only by virtue of their location in the most commercialized farming areas of the region. The small town itself was not seen as a catalyst for industry.

Pandaan is a clear case of industrial expansion in terms of ribbon development. The interest of investors is with accessibility not to the town but to the highway linking the hinterland with Surabaya. With almost all industrial sites strung along this highway the benefits of industrial employment have been biased towards those hamlets within easy access. The more remote agricultural villages have gained little or nothing, being penalized not just by their distance from the big factories, but also by the loss of population to employment centres and their relative neglect by *kecamatan* and *kabupaten* governments under pressure to service the industrial firms. Although the industrial development of Pandaan appears to have restricted migration out of the area, it has done little for the long-term livelihood of much of the *kecamatan* population. Despite their size and dramatic emergence, the industrial developments in Kecamatan Pandaan are benefiting only a small proportion of its population.

Appendix Tables

TABLE A12.1
'Modern' Pandaan Industries[a]

Industrial Firm	*Year of Opening*	*Ownership*	*Labour Force*
Food and Drink			
Amputraco	1975	Soegiarto	
Aqua	1985	Dwi Satrya Utama Group	
Coca-Cola (bottling)	1985	(US)	300
Dennys (Danish bakery)	1984		
Kasri (ice)	1927	Dwi Satrya Utama Group	70
Merbacal (cooking oil)	1973	Mercu Buana (Probosutejo)	
		(Taiwan)	158
Oksi Milk Treatment	1982		
Tobacco			
Janger Bali 'Diamond'	1979		
Indonesia Japan Tobacco	1971	Dai Nipon & Caichi Bushho	
		Henry Jonosiswojo	103
Textiles			
Easterntex	1974	Toray Industries	
		(Japan, Hong Kong)	800–900
Kamajaya Tekstil	1981		
Kasrie	1934	Dwi Satrya Utama Group	700–800
Tristate	1975	Jam Darmadi Group	
		Honyah (Hong Kong)	
		Dwi Satrya Utama Group	
		Ruffino Utama	1,069
Wood			
Jaslim	1980	(Denpasar)	

Pharmaceuticals/Chemicals			
Berlina (plastic bottles)	1973	Dwi Satrya Utama Group	
		Tjiptobiantoro family	700–900
Central Sari (medical)	1979		200
Essex Indonesia	1975	Schering Plough (US)	
ICI	1970	(UK)	144
Johnson & Johnson	1973	(US)	
PIM			238
Widatra Bhakti (infusion)	1986	Fresenius (W. Germany)	
		(Gen. Sumitro, Chairman)	100
Tonggorejo			
Rubber			
Indonesia Rubber			
Vima Rubber			
Metals			
Yammar Machinery	1974	P.T. Pioneer (Japan)	135
Cement			
Ubin Surabaya Permai			

[a]This is not a complete list of the industrial establishments in Pandaan. The details on ownership and labour force may not be up to date but are a compilation of facts that could be gleaned from secondary sources and field observations.

TABLE A12.2

Kecamatan Pandaan: Community Development Data

Village	*Developing Category*[a]			*Industrial Sector*[b]			*Education*[c] *(%)*		
	1972	*1979*	*1986*	*1972*	*1979*	*1986*	*1972*	*1979*	*1986*
Urban									
Pandaan	D	S	S	P	T	T	<30	>60	>60
Petungasri	K	S	S	P	T	T	<30	>60	>60
Jogosari	K	S	S	P	T	T	<30	>60	>60
Kutorejo	K	S	S	P	T	T	<30	>60	>60
Industrial									
Tawangrejo	K	S	S	P	T	T	<30	>60	>60
Sumbergedang	K	S	S	P	T	T	<30	>60	>60
Karangjati	K	S	S	P	T	T	<30	>60	>60
Sumberejo	K	S	S	P	T	T	30–60	>60	>60

Central agriculture									
Nogosari	S	S	S	P	S	T	>60	30–60	>60
Kebonwaris	S	S	S	P	S	T	>60	30–60	>60
Plintahan	K	S	S	P	S	T	30–60	30–60	>60
Durensewu	K	S	S	P	S	T	<30	>60	>60
Remote agriculture									
T'wulung	K	K	S	P	P	T	<30	30–60	30–60
Wedoro	K	K	S	P	S	S	30–60	30–60	>60
Kemirisewu	D	K	K	P	S	S	<30	30–60	30–60
Sebani	K	K	S	P	S	T	30–60	30–60	>60
Banjarsari	K	K	S	P	S	T	<30	<30	>60
Banjarkejn	K	K	K	P	P	S	<30	30–60	30–60

Sources: Directorate-General of Community Development (1972, 1979, 1986b).

[a]D = *swadaya* (subsistence), K = *swakarya* (developing), S = *swasembada* (developed); this classification is based on an aggregate of a wide range of development indicators, including education, industrial sector, village gross product, village institutions, and infrastructure.

[b]Industrial sector (P = Primary, S = Secondary, T = Tertiary) refers to the sector in which 55% or more of the economically active population earn their livelihood.

[c]Education refers to the percentage of the population who have completed at least primary school.

1. The data for this chapter came mainly from secondary sources. Imron Husin conducted fieldwork in Pandaan in 1986, but his interests focused on rural electrification rather than manufacturing industry. Patrick Guinness visited the *kecamatan* in 1986.

2. 'Pandaan', in earlier spelling Pandakan, refers to the *kecamatan*, but also to the town centre of the *kecamatan*, and to the smaller administrative village (*desa*) from which the town developed. The text will make clear to which of these units the discussion refers.

3. NV Modjokerto Stoom Tram Maatschappij recorded minimal output of freight from Ardirejo mill in 1935 and none at all by 1939.

4. See Elson (1984: 171–3) for similar comments on the Malang steam-tram company. The Pandaan–Porong line carried 15,416 passengers in its initial year (1898) and grew from that to a peak of 294,820 in 1920, thence declining to 44,210 in 1939. The Pandaan–Bangil line carried a peak of 251,103 passengers in 1920, but by 1935 had been closed down. Freight in and out of Pandaan town and sugar factory reached 15 149 tonnes in 1910 and 31 467 tonnes in 1920, then declined to 3 183 tonnes in 1935.

5. The Dutch East Indies official industrial monthly report for December 1935 reported that Kasri was one of four large weaving factories in East Java.

6. 'Medium' referred to firms without mechanization employing 10–99 workers and with mechanization 5 – 49. 'Large' referred to firms without mechanization employing 100 or more workers, or with mechanization 50 or more.

7. During 1967–70 foreign investment in the industrial sector increased from 3 to 32 projects, with total investment rising from US$230,000 to US$32.13 million. This growth was due to the government policy announced in 1967 that freed up the procedures for foreign investment and gradually created a favourable climate for capital investment. Similar changes occurred in domestic investment.

8. Kecamatan Pandaan represented only 6 per cent of the *kabupaten* population.

9. They claimed that women could take the lower paid jobs and wages because they were not supporting a family.

10. H. Geertz (1963: 36) describes this 'metropolitan superculture' in some detail. Its adherents are those oriented towards the national and provincial capitals and the 'national' culture being nurtured there. This culture includes the colloquial everyday use of the Indonesian language, the acquisition of higher education, wide travel experience, and the proliferation of voluntary associations.

11. Tertiary-sector occupations included trade, medical services, public services, and employment in the private sector, including factory employment. Secondary-sector occupations included small and home industries and artisans.

12. The term 'modern' refers to large and medium factories. The authors were not able to differentiate between large, medium, and small factories on the basis of their information. It is noted that the authors' figures differ from those of the 1986 Economic Census.

13. Hotman Siahaan et al. (1983) report similar trends among village youth on the outskirts of Surabaya. With the youth refusing to work on the farms, landowners had little alternative but to sell their land to factories. They also reported that the youth would not work either in Chinese-owned factories or in factories within their own villages, for fear of losing prestige. Village youth therefore go to work in similar factories elsewhere, while migrant factory workers rent rooms or houses in the village.

14. In a study of female factory workers in Sidoarjo, Yerita (1985) concluded that 65 per cent of their households were 'poor', although 92 per cent had been 'poor' before the women began employment.

15. In Sumberejo in 1977, 31 per cent of households controlled farming land (Kabul, 1977).

16. These were often accommodated at Tretes.

17. The local urban explanation for the lack of development in these villages was that their populations contained a large proportion of migrants from Madura. Banjarsari and Banjarkejen were predominantly Madurese, and Sebani and Tunggulwulung contained

substantial Madurese populations. In the 1930 Census, the last which gave ethnic affiliations, 22.2 per cent of the population of the District of Pandaan were enumerated as Madurese.

18. Hariri Hadi, Deputy Head of the National Planning Development Board (Badan Perencanaan Pembangunan Nasional or Bappenas), encouraged the building up of agriculture-linked, small capital industry in small towns, particularly *kecamatan* towns, to stem the flow of population to metropolitan centres (Hariri Hadi, 1984).

13
Kediri and Gudang Garam: An Industrial Enclave in a Rural Setting

Kenneth Young

Introduction

EXCEPT for the giant Gudang Garam *kretek*[1] cigarette factory, Kediri is an unremarkable town. Located on the banks of the Brantas River, in the flat, flood-prone southwestern corner of a broad, fertile river valley, just below the eastern foothills of Mount Wilis, it was the Residency capital in late colonial times and the centre of an important plantation area. The plantations have since lost much of their importance and parts of Kabupaten Kediri seem to have stagnated over the last 50 years. Nevertheless, with a population at the 1990 Census of 250,000 people, Kediri is still the third largest city in East Java (BPS, *Statistik Indonesia, 1990*: 37) and is said to contribute nearly 30 per cent of all manufacturing value added in the province (see Chapter 10). Cigarette production accounts for practically all of this.

The Gudang Garam factory is the only big manufacturing enterprise in the *kabupaten*. By the 1980s it had become by far the largest of the 'Big Four' Javanese *kretek* manufacturers in Indonesia.[2] Indeed, by 1989 the company had become the fourth largest conglomerate in Indonesia, with total assets similar to those of the giant Sinar Mas palm-oil empire. Its contribution to the economy of Kediri town and its hinterland is therefore a matter of considerable significance.

Kretek manufacturing is by far the largest industry in Indonesia (Hill, 1989: 24) and has been growing rapidly since the 1960s as the purchasing power of Indonesians has increased. Production more than trebled between 1975 and 1986. It seems that everyone in Indonesia smokes (or at least most men, although far fewer women)—and while that is no doubt an exaggeration, the proportion of men who smoke must be far higher than in countries like Australia or Europe where anti-smoking lobbies have had a powerful influence. In Indonesia they barely exist. *Krétek* smoking used to be predominantly a lower-class addiction: the educated middle classes tended to prefer 'white' (Virginia) cigarettes. But that has changed since 1970 as massive advertising campaigns and sophisticated promotion have created a huge market for *kretek* amongst the urban middle classes also. By the 1980s, *kretek* production far exceeded that of 'white' cigarettes, and the main beneficiaries of that change were the 'Big Four' *kretek* manufacturers, of which Gudang Garam was the largest.

This chapter begins with a brief review of the history of tobacco cultivation and *kretek* production in Java and then examines the rise of the Gudang Garam enterprise. In the third section the impact of Gudang Garam on Kediri is discussed, suggesting that the factory has so far remained very much an enclave.

Tobacco, *Kretek*, and Kediri

The pratice of mixing cloves with tobacco to make *kretek* cigarettes had its origins in Java in the late seventeenth century, but not until about 1870 did it become a popular item of consumption and trade (Castles, 1967: 33). *Kretek* was one of the few manufacturing industries in which indigenous businessmen were preponderant in the early twentieth century, most notably in Kudus, in the north of Central Java, which became the main centre of production. As the industry spread into the main Brantas Valley towns in East Java, however, it was dominated by Chinese from the start. In the late 1920s when the price of cloves increased, producers in the Brantas Valley were able to expand at the expense of the Kudus producers, who 'lost their reputation for quality', and over the next 30 years saw their share of the East Java market slip from nearly 50 per cent to about 28 per cent (Castles, 1967: 35). Over the same period production declined in Kediri Residency, which includes several centres apart from Kediri town, while it increased in the new production centres of Malang, Surabaya, and Madiun (Table 13.1). As late as 1961 most of the country's 941 *kretek* producers were still very small, each having a small but loyal circle of customers attracted by the brand name and/or its flavour (*rasa*). Many producers did not sell outside their own district.[3]

Kediri's prominence as a centre for *kretek* production may be related to its earlier prominence as a tobacco producing region. In the 1870s Kediri produced around 40 per cent of all high-quality leaf tobacco (*bladtabak*) in Java and 60–80 per cent of the filler (*krosok*). By 1910–14, the new estate production systems in Besuki and Vorstenlanden (Surakarta–Yogyakarta) had almost completely taken over the production of *bladtabak*, although Kediri was still a major producer of *krosok*. In the 1920s Kediri ceased to be a major tobacco-producing area and produced no *bladtabak* at all (van der Broek, 1946: 550–1). Although in the 1930s the cultivation of Virginia tobacco for the domestic 'white' cigarette industry began to increase rapidly in the Rembang–Bojonegoro region, not far to the north of Kediri, relatively little of the new crop was grown in Kediri.

TABLE 13.1
Kretek in East and Central Java, 1934 and 1961

Residency	*Production of Kretek (million)* 1934	*Production of Kretek (million)* 1961	*Number of Enterprises (1961)*
East Java			
Kediri	3,715	3,148	131
Surabaya[a]	395	1,427	112
Malang	105	3,020	134
Madiun	208	1,340	83
Bojonegoro	125	204	31
Central Java			
Japara–Rembang	5,300	5,755	209
Semarang	510	2,116	38
Kedu	400	306	51
Pekalongan	317	277	15
Yogyakarta–Solo	310	893	67
West Java	n.a.	70	29
Total Java	11,468	18,613	909

Source: Castles (1967: 139, 144).
[a]Includes Madura and Besuki.

Any locational connection between tobacco cultivation and the development of the *kretek* industry is a tenuous one. There is no compelling reason why *kretek* production should be concentrated in areas of tobacco cultivation, for it is labour costs rather than transport costs which are critical in determining the location of a *kretek* industry. *Kretek* production could be expected to develop most vigorously in regions with few alternative employment opportunities and therefore abundant surplus labour, especially female labour. Since tobacco cultivation involves a high demand for female labour, it may be no coincidence that *kretek* production began to develop in Kediri around the time that the cultivation of tobacco was collapsing.

The Rise of Gudang Garam

In 1961, several years after it was founded, Gudang Garam was one of 131 *kretek* enterprises in the Residency of Kediri (Castles, 1967: 139). Since then it has gradually displaced or taken over all its small- and medium-sized rivals in the Kediri region. Output and employment began to expand early in the New Order. Output soared from 9.1 billion cigarettes in 1979 to nearly 23 billion in 1981 and employment increased from 28,000 to 37,000 over the same period (Figure 13.1). After a hiatus between 1981 and 1985, a period of difficulty for the firm,

FIGURE 13.1
Gudang Garam: Production and Employment, 1968–1987

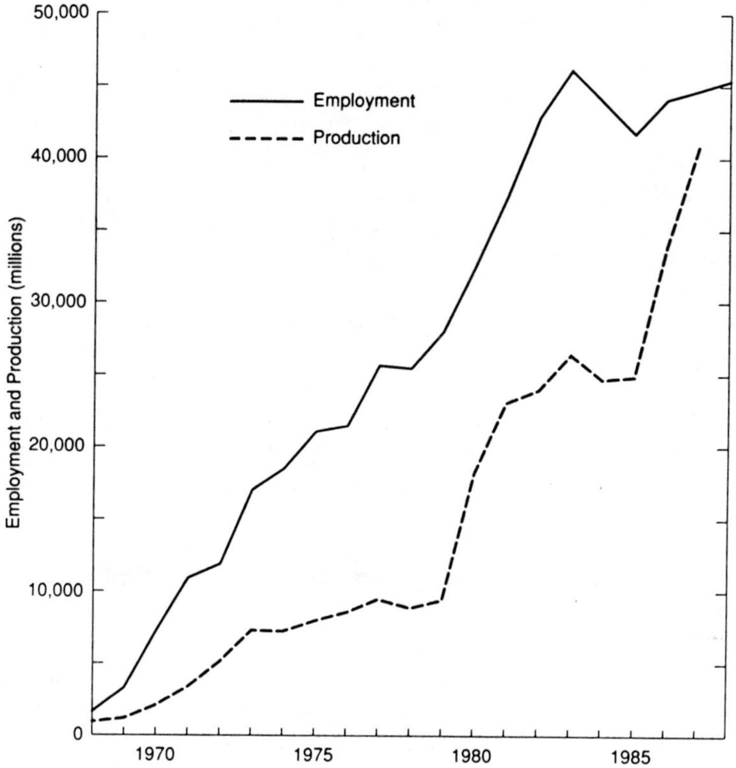

output almost doubled again to around 40 billion in 1988/9. By the late 1980s the industry was dominated by the four huge mechanized firms, although there were still another 260 small producers.[4] The industry had become markedly dualistic, with hardly any firms of medium size (Simandjantuk and Widiyanto, 1983: 73, 76). In Kediri town only Gudang Garam remained: the others had all collapsed or been bought up.

The founder of Gudang Garam, Surya Wonowijojo (Tjoa Ing Hwie), was born in Fujian, China, in 1926. In 1929 his family established itself in Indonesia, at Kota Sampang, Madura. They were poor—his father was a petty trader in tins and metals. When Ing Hwie was still young, his father died and he began to work to support his mother and family. He came to Kediri looking for work in the early 1950s. His uncle, Tjoa Kok Tjiang, owned a factory in Kediri, one of the larger *kretek* firms in East Java. Ing Hwie worked in his uncle's factory for five years, during which time he acquired the considerable skills of blending tobaccos and concocting the distinctive clove *saus* (sauce) of *kretek* cigarettes.

In 1956 Ing Hwie left his uncle's factory after a row and gradually established himself as a dealer in tobacco and cloves. The buying skills he learnt in these difficult years were probably as important to his later success as was his expertise in production and marketing. In June 1958 he started his own modest cigarette factory. Enticing some 50 workers from his uncle's factory, he set up production on the site near the Brantas River where 'unit (or factory) one' of Gudang Garam still functions today. The business grew steadily but slowly, until in 1962 Ing Hwie (or Surya, to use his Indonesian name) released his Gudang Garam Kuning—the famous 'yellow pack'.[5] It was a great success (Figure 13.1). Envious rivals put around the story that the Kuning blend contained cannabis. Surya agreed that the taste, due to his specially blended clove *saus*, was the secret of the yellow pack's popular appeal, but vehemently denied the gossip about cannabis. More substantially, his skills in buying and marketing contributed to the firm's expanding sales of the yellow pack.

Local informants identify two turning points in the developing prosperity of Gudang Garam which coincide with key national decisions on industry policy in Indonesia.[6] First, in 1968 the new innovation of hand-rolled *kretek* cigarettes with filters, pioneered by firms in Kudus and Solo, enabled *kretek* to make inroads into the market share of 'white' cigarettes. In the same year the government, under the new Domestic Investment Law, issued mechanization licences to just four firms, one of which was Gudang Garam. The concentration of production occurred quickly after this. As national marketing and distribution became more important, this also led to the polarization of the industry between a handful of highly profitable large firms and numerous small ones with very low margins. In Central Java there were 389 firms in 1961, 75 in 1970, and just 58 by 1975 (Simandjantuk and Widiyanto, 1983: 73, Table 6).

The second turning point, in 1978, marked a surge of investment in the hand-rolled Taman Sriwedari cigarette, just before the government set a mandatory production ratio of 1 : 2 between machine and hand-rolled *kretek*. The impact of this edict was reinforced by a 50 per cent devaluation of the Indonesian rupiah in November 1978, which suddenly doubled the price of cloves and tobacco. Small producers had no choice but to raise their prices, while Gudang Garam and the other large firms were able to hold their prices down (Simandjantuk and Widiyanto, 1983: 67).

Gudang Garam had formidable strengths in what was then a highly competitive industry, quite apart from any favours it may have had from the government. The company complex in Kediri includes some huge warehouses, testimony to the firm's ability to buy and store raw materials. Company buyers were spread throughout Indonesia and beyond, buying the best materials, in large quantities and often direct from producers. It had a network of warehouses and trucks to ensure efficient storage and movement of inputs. Surya's buying skill and the ability to buy in bulk at an opportune time, perhaps even ahead of the price movements resulting from devaluation, meant that Gudang Garam was in front of its small rivals even before the manufacturing process began.

Production was partly mechanized and partly manual but on a large scale and efficiently managed. Surya took a constant and personal interest in monitoring quality. He continually tested tobacco types and blends from around the world and personally tested the crucial clove *saus* for his various *kretek* brands. He was conscious from the beginning of the importance of taste and marketing. Gudang Garam maintains its own large-scale direct distribution network, while its smaller competitors must work through wholesale companies and distributors. The numerous company vehicles, which can be seen in towns and cities all over Java, carry the firm's striking and distinctive advertising. These marketing and distribution strategies gave the Kediri giant an edge in the market-place that few could match.

There are other signs that Surya's business connections with important figures within the State were well developed. In the mid-1980s Gudang Garam moved to reduce its dependence on imported paper by setting up its own production of quality cigarette paper (with the possibility of sales to the other giants). Surya set up a substantial joint venture company, Surya Zig-Zag, in partnership with President Suharto's brother, Probosutejo.

In 1980 Surya, in failing health, retired in favour of his sons. In 1982 sales fell by 16 per cent and in 1983 by 10 per cent (Figure 13.1). At the same time Gudang Garam's major rivals increased their turnover—in 1983, the firm Djarum's sales increased by 53 per cent (*Tempo*, 29 June 1985). The slump in Gudang Garam's business was so serious that Surya came back in 1984 to try to arrest the decline. The Surya Zig-Zag joint venture was one of his new initiatives, as was the release in 1985 of a new brand, 'Surya'. Unfortunately, he was in no condition to run the business. In 1975 he had been treated in New Zealand for a heart condition and had been told to give up smoking. He persisted in testing new tobaccos and the daily testing of his clove *saus* but he managed to 'cut down to one pack per day' (*Kompas*, 1 October 1985). His health was too poor to sustain the stress of running the firm. In August 1985 he was admitted to hospital in Surabaya and soon after was taken to New Zealand, where he died on 29 August 1985. His body was returned to Surabaya where the plane was met with great ceremony by the governor of East Java. At his funeral there were wreaths and condolences from many influential people, including President Suharto and his wife, Probosutejo, and Kyai Machrus Ali, the nationally influential leader of the Lirboyo *pesantren* (an Islamic school) in Kediri. Without its founder, the business now faces serious challenges from the other oligopolistic firms, businesses which have moved faster in marketing and in identifying the tastes of the 1980s.

The Impact of Gudang Garam on Kediri

The Gudang Garam factory site is large. In 1985 there were six factories on the 150-hectare site at Kediri. New factories, warehouses and the paper manufacturing plant were under construction. On the site or in nearby streets other buildings abound—warehouses, offices, garages, maintenance workshops, a generating plant, and a medical clinic. There are recreational facilities on the site (tennis courts and a swimming pool) and the company provides hostel (guest house) accommodation for female employees from distant areas. A large, walled residential estate where executive employees can purchase houses at a subsidized rate had recently been constructed between the factory and the Brantas River. Most of the executives of the company were housed there in 1985.

Production in 1985 was about 25 billion cigarettes (see Figure 13.1), about half of them hand-rolled and half machine-made. Raw materials were consumed on an impressive scale: up to 80 tonnes of tobacco and 40 tonnes of cloves were used daily, according to local informants in 1985. All raw materials, except the 2 tonnes of glue used daily to seal cigarette papers, were imported from outside the district. Production consisted almost entirely of the various brands of *kretek* cigarettes, but machine production included a number of 'white' cigarette brands made under licence.

Despite the size and extent of the complex, a casual visitor to Kediri before about 1980 might well have concluded that the Gudang Garam manufacturing complex had had little impact on the economic life of the town. Despite the large amount of employment in the factory, there were few signs of brisk commercial turnover or new investment in the main shopping streets, and almost no new hotels or restaurants. In fact there was little to be seen except the huge factory complex itself and a handful of adjacent food stalls (*warung*), a small testimony to the enhanced purchasing power of the town-dwellers. Kediri still seemed rather a sleepy town, outwardly little changed since colonial times. As late as 1983 only one bank in the town would cash a traveller's cheque. Although the wages being pumped into the town's economy must have boosted demand for basic commodities such as foodstuffs, clothing, and accommodation, demand for obviously middle-class consumer goods was much less apparent than in the bustling towns of Malang and Jember.

By the mid-1980s, however, changes had become apparent. Several new hotels were being built and there were a few more restaurants. New housing was being built around the outer edges of the town, as well as a university complex, largely funded by Gudang Garam, on the lower slopes of Mount Wilis at the western end of the town. The need to provide for an increased flow of commercial travellers—though still few tourists—was leading to the sort of hotels, restaurants, and more middle-class goods and services that were already available in most of Java's larger towns.

Yet all the activity taking place in and around the Gudang Garam factory complex seems to have generated little development of other industrial enterprises in Kediri. The only other businesses in the town of even medium size were a tyre retreading business, a wood products plant, and a factory at nearby Pare which manufactured gunny sacks. Company policy at Gudang Garam seems to have aimed for the highest degree of self-sufficiency. This has left little scope for subcontracting in fields where opportunities for supplying services or extra capacity (for example, vehicle repairs and maintenance) to the factory might be expected.

On the other hand, there is a fair spread of informal-sector business activity which is sustained by the purchasing power of Gudang Garam's more than 40,000 employees. Accommodation and other services needed by the workers are provided by these small-scale businesses. The clean but strictly disciplined guest houses (there is a 9.00 p.m. curfew) operate at about 60 per cent of capacity: most workers from out of town prefer to live in private accommodation or with families nearby. There are numerous household operations preparing soya bean curd (*tahu*), soya bean cake (*tempe*), and other foodstuffs around the factory and throughout the town.

The most important gain for the local economy is the steady flow of wage incomes to workers in the factory. Most of the work-force employed in Kediri in 1985 were either people paid daily (14 per cent) or piece workers paid three times a week (78 per cent), with women making up 90 per cent of their number (Table 13.2). What the table does not show is something a visitor to the factory very soon notices—that the workers are not only predominantly female but also very young. This pattern matches trends in light industrial employment elsewhere in Java (Mather, 1983; Wolf, 1984). However, unlike Mather's study, in particular, the earnings of these young women appeared to be above the norm. The other two categories of employees were the construction labourers paid at a daily rate and employees on monthly salaries, both predominantly male.

The majority of Gudang Garam employees were well paid. The day labourers were paid at or a little above the prevailing market rate. The basis of the piece-rate system was Rp 460 for the first thousand hand-rolled cigarettes as a daily base rate: above that, incentive rates applied. The most adept workers could roll three to four thousand cigarettes a day and could earn Rp 2,000–3,000. Many earned in the range Rp 1,500–2,000. A worker of average skill would earn Rp 1,000 per day, well above the average for the cigarette industry at the time (Rp 650 per day) and also well above wage rates in other employment in the district. In 1985 the average daily wage for agricultural labourers in the Kediri area was Rp 1,300 for men and Rp 800 for women. Factory work paid less: around Rp 900 per day for men and Rp 600 for women (wages at the Kediri wood factory, for example, were in the Rp 400–600 range).

The stratification of the work-force was more complex than what Table 13.2 suggests, for the first three categories of Kediri employees were further subdivided according to which factory they worked in and which stages of processing they were involved in (rolling, wrapping, or packing, for example). As in most large-scale manufacturing industries in Java, the wages paid were generally well above those in small industries or informal-sector activities. The salaries of the people on monthly wages were in another league, some receiving hundreds of thousands of rupiah per month, and they did not include the top executives. These were people who were also assisted to buy company houses on generous loan terms.

Conditions in the workplace were marked above all by tight, almost stern discipline, much more so than in other, smaller cigarette enterprises. The factories were clean, orderly, and well lit. Hours were regular, as were breaks for eating and religious observances. There were further benefits, such as the use of the clinic and the dormitory-style guest house for those who needed it.

With pay and conditions such as these, jobs in the Gudang Garam factory were much sought after. It is clear that Surya, living in a region where Chinese businesses were vulnerable to popular resentments, took considerable pains to build up good relations with the local community. Providing above-average pay and conditions for his workers was one aspect of his public relations. Since for hand-rolled cigarettes the cost of labour then represented a very small fraction of the sales value of the final product (only 3.4 per cent, according to Castles (1967)), and since the company gained economies of scale through its large-scale buying, storage, and distribution networks, the additional margin of costs on the wage bill was more than compensated by much larger gains elsewhere.

Nevertheless, if around 40,000 workers are earning roughly Rp 1,000 per day, at least Rp 40 million is being pumped into the local economy daily. It is hard to explain why there has been so little new economic activity. C. Geertz (1988: 47) observed, after returning to Kediri in 1986, over 30 years since he was first there: '... the factory doesn't have much to do with the town ... almost the entire labour force is non-local—they're all girls from other parts of East Java.'

In fact, there are many young women employed at Gudang Garam who live in villages around Kediri, up to 20 kilometres from the town. A drive through Kediri at the factory's change-of-shift time will reveal a seemingly endless torrent of young women on bicycles, three or four

TABLE 13.2
Gudang Garam's Kediri Work-force, 1985

	Men	*Women*	*Total*
Monthly wage workers	1,526	290	1,816
Daily wage workers	3,722	2,274	5,996
Piece workers	115	32,481	32,596
Day labourers	1,407	–	1,407
Total in Kediri	6,770	35,045	41,815
Total work-force	n.a.	n.a.	47,000[a]

Source: Data supplied by P.T. Gudang Garam.
[a]This figure is not exactly the same as the one in Pariwara, Suplemen Khusus (Figure 13.1), but is of the same order of magnitude.

abreast, flooding the roads to rural villages around the town. The torrent of bicycles does not entirely contradict C. Geertz's observation about the sources of the factory's workers, but does suggest that a large part of the work-force must be from within or close to the town itself.

One might expect that the earnings of these workers would amount to a substantial addition to the purchasing power of their families in the surrounding villages. Despite this increment to normal agricultural incomes, it was difficult to discern any impact on the economy of the surrounding areas. Earnings from the factory must often have been a significant contribution to households, making them capable of building up savings during the period the job lasted. These savings were frequently controlled by male heads of household, who in some cases used the money to buy or rent land and in others to break away from farming altogether. In the latter case, the money was sometimes used to invest in the town, setting up the family in petty enterprises providing services for Gudang Garam employees, or seeking wage work at Gudang Garam itself.

If the wages generated by the Gudang Garam factory are being spread across such a wide area and are not being channelled directly into the urban economy in the form of highly liquid purchasing power, it is perhaps not surprising that they have not had a more obvious impact on the town's prosperity. Similarly, because of the relatively few direct linkages with the other industrial activities or services in the town, very little derived investment has yet occurred. As time passes that may change. In the third decade of Gudang Garam's dominant position, the factory may have a more diverse impact on the local economy. Its philanthropic contributions to various local causes are widely acknowledged: a road resurfaced here, a new building there, schools and the new regional university. Kediri is gradually becoming a more diversified economy, although apparently at nothing like the same speed as Malang, Jember, or even nearby Jombang.

Conclusion

How is the dramatic expansion of Gudang Garam to be explained? (Its production increased 10-fold in the 1970s alone and by 1980 the firm was producing almost as many *kretek* cigarettes as the entire country had produced in 1961.) While many contributory factors can be identified, there is no simple answer to the question. The popularity of the brand on account of its flavour was an important factor in its early years (and perhaps until well into the 1980s, to judge from the sharp fall in demand when Surya withdrew because of ill-health in 1982/3, coupled with the recovery when he returned). So also was the introduction of filters in *kretek* in 1968. Equally important was the switch to mechanization at about that same time—and the firm's good fortune in obtaining one of only four licences to mechanize, which brought major advantages of scale.

It is surely significant that the companies which obtained licences to mechanize in 1968 are the giants in the 'Big Four' today, whereas three other large firms of that period which did not get licences have fallen far behind since then. Inevitably, questions arise about the extent to which political connections were influential in such a fateful decision, but there is no evidence to support a firm conclusion either way on that crucial matter. It is perhaps significant that Surya later joined forces with Probosutedjo, President Suharto's half-brother, in the establishment of his Surya Zig-Zag cigarette paper enterprise, but it is not clear how far back that association extended, nor whether it was significant in the early expansion of the firm. (Surya was careful to maintain a good reputation and image for Gudang Garam in Kediri by contributing funds widely to local welfare and educational organizations—and presumably to key officials also, although he was not generally regarded as one of the more notoriously 'political' tycoons of the 1980s.) And one of the other essentially non-political factors contributing to the early success of the company was its successful use of advertising to tap the expanding market of urban middle-class consumers in the 1970s, along with a very efficient and wide-ranging distribution system. It also set up a nationwide purchasing network for obtaining tobacco and cloves, which gave the firm a competitive edge over its rivals. But other companies could have done likewise and in the 1980s several of Gudang Garam's rivals began to do so, thereby providing stiff competition for market share.

Financial constraints appear not to have been a major constraint upon Gudang Garam's expansion, and Surya's access to copious funds from the state banks is frequently mentioned by his rivals and critics as one of the indications that political connections have been important. It is noteworthy that the firm embarked on a major investment programme around 1978 which slightly preceded the announcement of a mandatory production ratio of 1 : 2 between machine-made and hand-rolled *kretek*. Rivals complained that this severely constrained them but worked to the advantage of Gudang Garam. But it was generally agreed that Surya's managerial skill and lucky timing (which is perhaps a part of that skill) were important elements in the success of the firm. Since his death, his sons have been able to maintain the firm's place at the head of the 'Big Four', but the rate of expansion slowed down in the 1980s.

In the late 1980s, the new managers of the firm were starting to diversify into other activities beyond the *kretek* industry and beyond Kediri, including a bank in Surabaya and urban property development, like most of the other big conglomerates. It is too early to gauge how successful this new strategy will be. It runs counter to Surya's single-minded concentration on *kretek* production and marketing, which paid off handsomely during the phase of rapid expansion.

The secret of entrepreneurial success is never easy to identify, but it is undeniable that Surya possessed it. His story is a remarkable one, even in an era of many outstandingly successful Sino-Indonesian tycoons. But it is hard to discern any aspect of it that is directly attributable to the location of Gudang Garam in Kediri—or even in East Java—rather than any other place. If Surya had grown up in another town, or another province, his enterprise might have flourished there equally successfully. But regardless of such hypothetical speculations, there can be no doubt that East Java, as also Kediri, has benefited considerably from the demand for goods and services and labour generated by Gudang Garam. Its impact on the lungs and general health of the millions of smokers of its product is another story, of course, but this is not the place to open up that controversial question.

1. *Kretek* cigarettes are filled with a mixture of tobacco and cloves. The blending of the clove 'sauce' (*saus*) for each brand requires special skills. The recipes are jealously guarded, since consumer brand loyalties depend to an important degree on taste.

2. The other firms in the 'Big Four'—Bentoel, Jarum, and Sampurna—are located in Malang, Kudus (Central Java), and Surabaya respectively.

3. The author is indebted to Dr W. A. I. M. Segers for information about the *kretek* industry in the colonial period: see Segers (1988) and his doctoral dissertation cited therein.

4. Some small firms survive by specializing in the production of a distinctive *kretek* with a flavour, quality, or price that appeals to an established clientele or segment of the market; these are now usually confined to smokers who are too poor to afford the Rp 300 packs made by the larger companies. One such is the Kabayak enterprise in nearby Ngancar, which produced about 10.5 million *kretek* and millions of the cruder *klobot* cigarettes in 1981. It is clearly much more than a mere backyard operation.

5. 'Gudang Garam' means 'the salt warehouse'. Surya is said to have had an auspicious dream in which an old salt warehouse located close to his original workplace figured prominently; so he was advised to use its picture on every packet of his cigarettes to ensure good fortune. The emblem has been retained, even after the packaging has been redesigned and modernized.

6. The author is grateful to Pak A. Basoeki, head of the Dinas Perindustrian of Kabupaten Kediri, who was most helpful in providing information and comments which expanded on the data gathered directly from Gudang Garam.

14
Regional Finance in Indonesia: An East Java Case-study

Anne Booth

Introduction

THE Indonesian fiscal system has long been highly centralized. For such a large country, the system has provided few incentives or instruments for subnational levels of government to increase efforts to raise revenues. Persuasive evidence that this continues to be the case was provided in the 1988 *World Development Report*, which presented data on revenues and expenditures of subnational governments in 18 developing countries. The proportion of total expenditures covered by locally raised revenue for the years 1974 to 1986 was lower in Indonesia than in any other country examined (World Bank, 1988: 156). Furthermore, the percentage of total government expenditures accounted for by subnational and local governments was also much lower in Indonesia than in other large developing countries such as Brazil or India.

The oil boom of the 1970s accelerated the trend towards fiscal centralization. During this decade the government made a determined effort to spread the benefits of the oil bonanza across the archipelago through an ambitious programme of central government development grants to provincial, *kabupaten* (district), and *desa* (village) governments. These grants (usually known by the acronym Inpres [Instruksi Presiden or Presidential Instruction]) were given both for general infrastructure rehabilitation and extension, and for specific purposes including implementing reforestation programmes, supplying drinking water, and building health clinics, markets, roads, and primary schools.

The Inpres programmes implemented through the 1970s helped to rehabilitate existing infrastructure and to provide new facilities such as schools and health clinics in many areas where they had never existed before. During the 1980s, however, the value of Inpres grants fell, both in absolute terms and relative to total government expenditure and to gross domestic product (GDP).[1] This was part of the budgetary retrenchment made necessary by the fall in world oil prices and the growth in foreign debt-servicing obligations. Realization that the central government will not continue to carry the burden of financing development projects has forced subnational levels of government to look for ways to intensify their own revenue efforts.

East Java provides an excellent case-study, both of the potential for provinces, *kabupaten*, and *desa* in Indonesia to increase their own revenue efforts and of the problems they face. East Java was ranked eleventh among the 27 provinces of Indonesia in 1986 in terms of per capita income. In 1986, its per capita income of about US$400 was about the same as Sri Lanka's, although East Java's population was almost twice as large. Sri Lanka's total government revenues in 1986 have been estimated to be 21 per cent of GDP (World Bank, 1988: 268). There is no obvious reason why East Java's total revenue effort should not be as high. In fact, as will be argued below, it is probably less than half this amount, although the province has, by Indonesian standards, a sophisticated administrative structure and an obvious need to improve its revenue performance as a way of compensating for falling central government subsidies.

A review of East Java's regional financial system is thus useful both as a way of exploring deficiencies in the structure of central–local financial relations in Indonesia and in order to answer crucial questions about the future course of economic development in East Java such as:

1. What are the impediments to provincial and subprovincial levels of government raising more revenues?
2. Are they denied lucrative 'tax handles' by the central government or do they fail to exploit fully those taxes they do control?
3. How carefully monitored are regional expenditures?
4. Is there any persuasive evidence that the reliance on central funding has impeded East Java's development effort in the past, and to what extent will failure to develop the local revenue base impede development in the future?

These issues are examined in the following sections.

Sources of Revenue

Four levels of government in Indonesia are empowered to raise revenue and implement expenditure: the central government, the province, the *kabupaten*, and the *desa*. At the provincial level, the two sources of revenue are funds from the centre and revenues raised within the province. Not all revenues raised within the province are at the disposal of the provincial government. Those collected through central government taxes, such as income tax, value added tax, and import duties, accrue directly to the central government. Those raised through taxes assigned to the *kabupaten* stay at that level. The province receives only those revenues (such as taxes and 'retributions'—usually user charges) which are collected within the provincial borders and assigned to the province.

East Java relies more on the central government than do Indonesian

TABLE 14.1
East Java and All Provinces: Percentage Breakdown of Provincial Revenues by Source, 1979/80–1986/7[a]

	Own Revenues	Central Grants: Routine	Central Grants: Development	Other	Total
East Java					
1979/80	15.5	77.6	6.9	0.0	100
1980/1	18.3	76.3	5.3	0.1	100
1981/2	22.9	71.8	5.3	0.0	100
1982/3	19.6	73.6	4.5	2.3	100
1983/4	13.2	81.4	3.9	1.5	100
1984/5	17.0	79.2	3.3	0.5	100
1985/6	15.6	77.9	3.2	3.3	100
1986/7	17.9	75.5	3.0	3.6	100
All Indonesia[b]					
1979/80	19.1	59.0	9.4	12.5	100
1980/1	19.8	58.2	13.2	8.8	100
1981/2	19.7	58.6	11.5	10.2	100
1982/3	16.6	59.2	13.5	10.7	100
1983/4	16.3	62.4	13.1	8.2	100
1984/5	17.3	60.9	11.3	10.5	100
1985/6	18.0	59.7	11.6	10.7	100
1986/7	20.1	61.4	10.9	7.6	100

Sources: BPS, *Statistik Keuangan Pemerintah Daerah Tingkat I*, various issues; KSJT, *Jawa Timur dalam Angka*, various years.

[a]In this and subsequent tables routine grants refer to those given for payment of wages and salaries and other recurrent expenditures; development grants refer to those given to finance specific development projects.

[b]Average for all provinces excluding East Timor.

provinces on average. In 1985/6, 81.1 per cent of provincial revenues in East Java were derived from central subsidies, compared with just over 70 per cent for all provinces (Table 14.1). As in most other provinces, by far the most important taxes collected within and assigned to the province are those derived from the registration and change of ownership of motor vehicles (Table 14.2). This has accounted for over 80 per cent of all revenues raised from provincial taxes, levies and charges for most of the 10 years up to 1986/7. These *pendapatan asli daerah* (revenues raised within the region) in turn have amounted to about 0.5 per cent of gross regional product (GRP) over the same period. Table 14.2 shows just how small provincial own revenues have been compared with central government grants, especially those given for routine purposes. In most years, central grants have comprised at least 80 per cent of total revenues accruing to the provincial government.

Total revenues accruing to all *kotamadya* (municipalities) and *kabupaten* in East Java have been consistently less than those accruing to the province. In 1985–6 they amounted to only half as much (Table 14.3).

TABLE 14.2

East Java: Provincial Revenues, 1976/7–1986/7 (Rp billion)

	Motor Vehicle Taxes	Total Own Revenues[a]	Total Own Revenues as Percentage of GRP	Central Grants[b]		Total Revenues	Central Grants (Routine and Development) as Percentage of Total Revenues
				Routine	Development		
1976/7	6.0	10.7	0.5	47.3	6.7	67.4	80.1
1977/8	8.7	10.9	0.4	73.4	8.2	95.2	85.7
1978/9	13.1	15.4	0.5	82.1	8.8	109.2	83.2
1979/80	15.7	18.4	0.4	108.8	9.6	140.2	84.5
1980/1	25.1	29.5	0.5	157.4	11.0	206.3	81.6
1981/2	32.6	41.8	0.6	187.3	13.8	261.0	77.0
1982/3	34.7	54.5	0.6	204.9	12.4	278.6	78.0
1983/4	33.9	41.6	0.4	256.7	11.7	315.4	85.1
1984/5	48.8	64.0	0.5	286.0	12.1	361.2	82.5
1985/6	52.6	64.1	0.5	321.1	13.0	412.1	81.1
1986/7	68.1	80.3	0.5	340.8	13.7	451.2	78.6

Sources: As for Table 14.1.

[a]Refers to all revenues from provincial taxes, user charges, etc.

[b]See Table 14.1 for definition of routine and development revenues.

TABLE 14.3

East Java: Routine and Development Revenues of *Kabupaten*, 1979/80–1985/6 (Rp billion)

	Local Taxes	Retribution	Total Own Revenue[a]	Routine Grants		Ipeda/PBB	Other Development Revenue	Development Grants		Total[b]
				Centre	Province			Centre	Province	
1979/80	3.7	7.2	26.4	9.7	12.0	13.2	7.3	9.6	2.8	81.1
1980/1	4.7	9.0	30.3	22.4	15.9	14.8	15.6	13.2	2.8	116.3
1981/2	4.8	10.9	28.3	37.0	19.8	16.6	8.5	19.1	3.6	134.2
1982/3	5.1	12.4	33.8	32.6	21.0	17.9	15.6	28.8	4.4	158.3
1983/4	6.6	15.6	39.8	37.5	26.0	21.6	8.2	13.0[c]	4.3	156.3
1984/5	7.9	19.6	40.7	44.6	16.1	23.5	4.7	3.3[c]	5.0	147.5
1985/6	9.7	24.1	60.7	69.0	15.9	20.0	13.6	6.4[c]	5.8	205.5

Source: BPS, *Statistik Keuangan Pemerintah Daerah Tingkat II*, various issues.

[a]Refers to all revenues raised from provincial taxes, user charges, etc.

[b]Total includes loans and carry-over from previous years.

[c]Figures appear to be understated compared with those in Table 14.5.

TABLE 14.4

East Java: Rural Village Revenues, 1976/7–1985/6[a] (Rp billion)

	Routine		Development				
				Of Which Grants from			
	Total	Of Which Subsidies from Higher Levels	Total	Centre	Province/ Kabupaten	Swadaya Masyarakat[b]	Total Routine and Development
1976/7	11.6	0.6	13.8	5.6	0.9	6.1	25.4
1977/8	14.0	0.8	13.9	5.7	0.9	6.2	27.9
1978/9	14.8	0.9	15.1	5.9	1.1	6.2	29.9
1979/80	18.8	1.0	16.0	4.5	1.1	8.9	34.8
1980/1	22.2	1.3	17.3	6.5	0.8	8.2	39.5
1981/2	28.5	1.4	20.8	8.0	1.4	9.5	49.3
1982/3	34.1	1.4	22.8	9.6	1.0	9.8	56.9
1983/4	36.8	1.8	25.7	9.2	1.2	12.0	62.5
1984/5	42.4	1.9	29.4	9.5	0.8	16.1	71.8
1985/6	45.8	2.0	33.4	11.8	1.3	17.4	79.2
1986/7	46.6	2.1	33.4	10.6	1.0	18.3	80.0

Sources: BPS, *Statistik Keuangan Desa: Jawa dan Madura*, various issues.

[a]Data refer to rural *kelurahan* only.

[b]Refers to voluntary contributions in cash and kind by the village populations.

However, *kotamadya* and *kabupaten* appear to be less dependent on subsidies from higher levels of government. In 1985/6 about 47 per cent of their revenue was derived from subsidies, compared with 81 per cent for the province. But the data on central development subsidies to the *kabupaten* for 1983/4 onwards appear to be rather understated, so that the reliance of the *kabupaten* on the centre may well be higher than is shown in Table 14.3.

Revenues accruing to *kelurahan* (rural villages) in East Java are, not surprisingly, small compared with those accruing to either *kabupaten/kotamadya* or to the province itself. However, the *kelurahan* are in fact less dependent on subsidies than either of the two higher levels. In 1985/6 subsidies from the centre, province, and *kabupaten* amounted to less than 20 per cent of all revenues accruing to rural villages. Routine revenues (derived mainly from village land, including the *tanah bengkok*, use of which is assigned to village officials in lieu of salary) accounted for 58 per cent (Table 14.4). Voluntary contributions in labour and kind (*swadaya masyarakat*) accounted for most of the balance.

Since the mid-1980s central government development grants to the three levels of government have been stagnant in nominal terms and therefore declining in real terms. Moreover, East Java's share in total central development grants has been declining since the First Five-Year Development Plan (Repelita I: 1969/70–1973/4); East Java's share of grants to the provinces has fallen from 10.7 per cent in the Repelita II (1974/5–1978/9) period to only 4.2 per cent in 1987/8 (Table 14.5). The main reason for this decline is that since Repelita III (1979/80–1983/4) the central government development grants to the provinces have been given on a lump-sum basis, with very little variation according to population size. Indeed in 1988/9 each province received an identical grant. As the country's most populous province, East Java has thereby been disadvantaged. East Java's share of the total grants to *kabupaten/kotamadya* and villages has fallen less rapidly, since these are

TABLE 14.5
Percentage Accruing to East Java of Total Central Government Grants to Regions, Repelita I to Repelita IV[a]

Five-Year Development Plans	*Central Grants Accruing to*		
	Province	*Kabupaten*	*Desa*
Repelita I (1969/70–1973/4)	n.a.[b]	21.6	16.8
Repelita II (1974/5–1978/9)	10.7	20.5	13.9
Repelita III (1979/80–1983/4)	4.9	19.0	12.6
Repelita IV (1984/5–1988/9)	4.2	18.5	12.5

Sources: Department of Information (1985, 1989).
[a]These data refer to provincial, *kabupaten*, and *desa* Inpres grants. They exclude sectoral Inpres grants for schools, health clinics, reforestation, and the like.
[b]Provincial development grants began in 1974.

much more dependent on population. In this case the fall in East Java's share reflects only its declining share in Indonesia's population.

Revenue Performance

Given that revenues from oil and gas are almost certain to continue to fall relative to GDP, and that non-oil revenues will grow only slowly, it seems clear that central government development grants to the regions, as a proportion of GDP, are unlikely to return to the level they reached in the early 1980s. It is thus useful to estimate provincial own-revenue effort in East Java. Data on own-revenue collection at the provincial, *kabupaten/kotamadya* and *desa* levels are available; the only missing information is the province's share of central government taxes. The central government has not published a breakdown of central taxes by province of origin since the late 1960s. Probably the best estimate can be achieved by assuming that the ratio of central taxes to GRP in East Java is the same as the ratio of non-oil domestic revenues to non-oil GDP for the country as a whole. This is probably an overestimate, since a high proportion of non-oil domestic revenues is in fact collected in Jakarta. Nevertheless, on this basis the ratio of central taxes to GRP in East Java in 1985/6 was 8.6. Revenues accruing to provinces, *kotamadya/kabupaten*, and *desa* (excluding grants from higher levels of government) amounted to a further 1.7 per cent of GRP. Thus total provincial revenue effort in 1985/6 was about 10.3 per cent of GRP. This is hardly an impressive result, especially compared with a country like Sri Lanka, where, with the same per capita income level as East Java, taxes are more than 20 per cent of GDP (World Bank, 1988).

One frequently cited reason for the very low ratio of 'local' taxes (that is, those raised by the province, *kabupaten*, and *desa*) to GRP concerns the inelasticity of taxes with respect to the revenue base. It is argued that the taxes given to the provincial and sub-provincial levels of government in Indonesia are often insensitive (or 'inelastic' in the jargon of economics) to rising incomes, so that revenue collection tends to lag behind income. In fact the evidence on the income elasticity of provincial, *kabupaten*, and *desa* revenues in East Java is very mixed (Table 14.6). Provincial own revenues over the decade from 1976/7 to 1986/7 have increased in step with rising provincial income. Undoubtedly this is due largely to the role of motor vehicle taxes as the largest single source of provincial revenues (Table 14.2); these would have grown with motor vehicle registrations, which have risen rapidly in East Java in recent years.

Taxes at *kabupaten* level have been much less responsive to GRP. In East Java as in most other provinces the two most important *kabupaten* taxes have been the entertainment tax and the hotel and restaurant tax. Devas (1988) has argued that revenues from the entertainment tax (primarily a tax on cinema attendance) may have been affected by the growth of television and video ownership, while the hotel and restaurant trade may have been affected by slower economic growth in the 1980s.

TABLE 14.6

East Java: Time-series Estimates of Elasticity of Revenue with Respect to Gross Regional Product and Components, 1976/7–1985/6

Type of Revenue	*Explanatory Variable*	*Years*	*Elasticity Estimate*[a]
Provincial own revenue[b]	GRP	1976/7–1986/7	1.05
Kabupaten taxes	GRP	1979/80–1985/6	0.78
Kabupaten retributions	GRP	1979/80–1985/6	1.02
Total *kabupaten* revenues[c]	GRP	1979/80–1985/6	0.60
Desa routine revenues	Agricultural GRP	1976/7–1985/6	0.89
Desa swadaya revenues	Agricultural GRP	1976/7–1985/6	0.63
Rural-sector Ipeda[d]	Agricultural GRP	1980–1986	0.57
Estates-sector Ipeda[d]	Estates GRP	1980–1986	1.66
Urban-sector Ipeda[d]	Non-agricultural GRP	1980–1986	1.33

Sources: As for Tables 14.1, 14.3, and 14.4.
Kabupaten income: KSJT (1987).

[a]Derived by fitting a simple log linear regression to time series data as indicated. Results significant at 5% unless otherwise stated.

[b]Own revenues as shown in Table 14.1.

[c]Own revenues as shown in Table 14.3.

[d]Data refer to land-tax assessments (*pokok murni*). For further details on the assessment and collection of the Ipeda see Booth (1974).

TABLE 14.7
East Java: Ipeda/PBB Assessments as a Percentage of Gross Regional Product, 1969–1986[a]

	Rural/ Agricultural GRP	*Estate/ Estate GRP*[a]	*Urban/ Non-agricultural GRP*	*Total/ GRP*
1969	0.8	0.9	0.1	0.5
1974	0.9	n.a.	0.2	0.6
1980	0.4	3.8	0.2	0.3
1981	0.4	2.8	0.2	0.2
1982	0.4	2.6	0.2	0.2
1983	0.3	2.5	0.2	0.2
1984	0.3	3.6	0.2	0.2
1985	0.3	4.3	0.2	0.2
1986	0.4	4.1	0.4	0.3

Sources: Ipeda (PBB) data: Ipeda Directorate, Department of Finance and provincial sources.
GRP data: KSJT, *Jawa Timur dalam Angka*, various years.
[a]GRP broken down into agricultural subsector is not available for the years 1972–4.

Whatever the reasons, *kabupaten* taxes and total revenues have grown much more slowly than GRP in the 1980s. Retributions (mainly user charges for facilities such as markets) by contrast have grown at the same rate as GRP. At the village level neither routine revenues (derived mainly from the village lands) nor *swadaya* contributions have grown as rapidly as agricultural GRP. This might reflect an increasing reluctance on the part of rural communities to pay taxes in labour and kind for infrastructure which may not benefit them directly.

Assessments of land tax (Ipeda; known as PBB or Pajak Bumi dan Bangunan since 1985) in rural areas did not grow as rapidly as agricultural GRP between 1980 and 1986 in East Java, but the reverse was true for estate and urban sector Ipeda (Tables 14.6 and 14.7). Apparently this reflects a conscious decision to intensify PBB assessments outside the rural sector.[2] This tendency is even more clear if Ipeda/PBB assessments (relative to the appropriate component of GRP) in the 1980s are compared with the years from 1969 to 1974 (Table 14.7). While both the estate and the urban-sector assessments have risen markedly (more than fivefold in the case of urban assessments) relative to GRP, rural-sector assessments have fallen to about half the 1969 proportion of agricultural GRP.

There is also evidence that the intensity of collection of *kabupaten* taxes (including the PBB) declines across *kabupaten* and *kotamadya* as total income rises, so that the cross-sectional elasticity of revenues is well under unity. Taken together, the various types of *kabupaten* revenues (taxes, retributions, and PBB) comprise a much higher proportion of *kabupaten* GRP in the *kabupaten* and *kotamadya* with smaller GRP than

TABLE 14.8
East Java: *Kabupaten*[a] Taxes, Retributions, and PBB[b] Revenue as a Percentage of Gross Regional Product, 1985

1	KM Surabaya[c]	0.53	20	Blitar	0.38
2	Malang	0.26	21	Bojonegoro	0.45
3	Jember	0.46	22	Sumenep	0.27
4	KM Kediri	0.16	23	Magetan	0.30
5	Sidoarjo	0.58	24	Ngawi	0.53
6	Banyuwangi	0.51	25	Bondowoso	0.50
7	Gresik	0.30	26	Situbondo	0.57
8	KM Malang	0.53	27	Madiun	0.32
9	Pasuruan	0.34	28	Bangkalan	0.37
10	Kediri	0.56	29	Sampang	0.23
11	Lumajang	0.55	30	Pacitan	0.25
12	Jombang	0.45	31	Trenggalek	0.45
13	Probolinggo	0.44	32	Pamekasan	0.45
14	Mojokerto	0.32	33	KM Probolinggo	0.78
15	Lamongan	0.32	34	KM Madiun	0.80
16	Tuban	0.30	35	KM Pasuruan	0.71
17	Ponorogo	0.37	36	KM Mojokerto	1.19
18	Nganjuk	0.47	37	KM Blitar	1.06
19	Tulungagung	0.42			

Elasticity of *kabupaten* revenues with respect to income = 0.73.

Sources: As for Table 14.7.
[a]*Kabupaten* and *kotamadya* ranked in terms of GRP, 1985.
[b]Data on taxes and retributions refer to fiscal year 1985/6. Ipeda collections refer to rural, urban, and estate sectors.
[c]KM = Kotamadya.

TABLE 14.9
East Java and Indonesia: Own Revenues at Provincial and *Kabupaten* Levels, 1984/5 and 1987/8

	East Java (Rp billion)	*As Percentage of GRP*	*Indonesia (Rp billion)*	*As Percentage of GDP*
Province				
1984/5	61.3	0.5	489.5	0.6
1987/8	98.5	0.6	707.1	0.7
Kabupaten				
1984/5	32.4	0.3	413.2	0.5
1987/8	61.2	0.3	604.0	0.6

Source: Department of Finance as reported in Bawazier (1989).

in those with the largest GRP, such as Surabaya, Malang, Jember, and the city of Kediri (Table 14.8).

East Java's revenue performance at a provincial level is very similar to that of other provinces. At the provincial level the ratio of revenues to GRP in East Java was about 0.6 in 1987/8, which was much the same as the national average (Table 14.9). With the exception of the Daerah Khusus Ibukota (DKI or Special Capital Region) Jakarta, no province's tax receipts exceeded 1 per cent of GDP, and so East Java's performance was in no way exceptional. But at the *kabupaten* level East Java's performance was significantly worse than the national average (Table 14.9). Although *kabupaten* revenues grew more rapidly in East Java than in the country as a whole between 1984/5 and 1987/8, the ratio of *kabupaten* revenue collections to GRP was only 0.3 in 1987/8 compared with the national average of 0.6.

Growth in Expenditure

Just as it is difficult to determine the proportion of central government revenue raised in East Java, so it is difficult to determine central government expenditure in each province. Figures are available on the provincial allocation of the central government's development expenditures, but they indicate that about half the total central development budget is being spent in Jakarta (Bawazier, 1989). This is mainly because the government departments executing the development budget, and many large construction companies, State and private, are located in Jakarta. Disbursements to them show up as expenditures in Jakarta, although in many cases the expenditures actually relate to development projects in various parts of the Archipelago. For what they are worth, these data show that East Java has received about 5 per cent of total central government development expenditures during the 1980s, and about

TABLE 14.10
East Java: Development Expenditures as a Percentage of Gross Regional Product, 1976/7–1986/7

	Source of Development Expenditures				
	Centre[a]	*Province*	*Kabupaten*	*Desa*	*Total*
1976/7	n.a.	0.6	0.7	0.7	n.a.
1982/3	2.4	0.6	0.8	0.3	4.1
1983/4	3.4	0.5	0.3	1.1	4.5
1984/5	5.1	0.3	0.3	0.3	6.0
1985/6	3.7	0.3	0.4	0.3	4.7
1986/7	2.4	0.3	0.3	0.2	3.2

Sources: Centre: Bawazier (1989).
Province and subprovincial levels: As for Table 14.6.
[a]Share of central government development budget allocated to East Java.

TABLE 14.11
East Java: Breakdown of Provincial and *Kabupaten* Development Expenditures by Type of Project, 1979/80–1985/6 (Rp billion)

	Economic Infrastructure[a]					
	Heavy Repair	*New*	*Capital Equipment*	*Transfers*[b]	*Other*[c]	*Total*
Province						
1979/80	6.2	3.3	0.6	3.0	8.0	21.1
1982/3	5.9	15.1	3.3	7.1	14.8	46.2
1985/6	9.6	3.4	4.0	9.4	20.3	46.7
Kabupaten						
1979/80	6.2	6.4	2.5	0.9	13.4	29.4
1982/3	8.5	14.4	5.5	3.5	35.8	67.7
1985/6	11.9	16.9	6.6	1.6	23.4	60.4

Sources: As for Tables 14.1 and 14.3.
[a]Roads, bridges, and irrigation.
[b]To lower levels of government.
[c]Social services, government buildings, etc.

12 per cent of expenditures excluding those made in Jakarta. As a proportion of GRP East Java's share of the central development budget has fluctuated between 2.4 and 5.1 per cent between 1982/3 and 1986/7 (Table 14.10). This ratio is lower than that for all provinces taken together (excluding DKI Jakarta), suggesting that East Java has not been favoured in the allocation of central government development revenues.

The central government makes large block grants to the provinces to cover routine expenditures at provincial and *kabupaten*/*kotamadya* levels. It also makes development grants to the province, *kabupaten*, and *desa* through the various Inpres programmes. We have seen that East Java's share of these grants has been declining since the mid-1970s

TABLE 14.12
East Java: Rural Village Development Expenditures by Type of Expenditure, 1982/3–1986/7 (Rp billion)

	1982/3	*1983/4*	*1984/5*	*1985/6*	*1986/7*
Residential buildings	0.3	0.2	0.2	0.6	0.1
Other buildings	7.6	9.3	11.2	13.8	14.4
Infrastructure	9.1	9.7	10.8	11.8	11.1
Land improvement	3.2	3.5	3.5	3.4	2.5
Other machinery	0.3	0.4	0.5	0.2	0.6
Livestock	0.5	0.5	0.3	0.4	0.2
Other	2.1	2.4	3.2	3.6	4.3
Total	23.1	26.0	29.7	33.8	33.2

Sources: As for Table 14.4.

TABLE 14.13

East Java: Percentage Breakdown of Province, *Kabupaten*, and *Desa* Expenditures, 1976/7–1986/7

	Province		*Kabupaten*		*Desa*		
	Routine	*Development*	*Routine*	*Development*	*Routine*	*Development*	*Total*
1976/7	37.5	10.9	19.4	11.9	9.2	11.1	100
1982/3	46.7	9.5	17.0	14.1	7.4	5.4	100
1986/7	53.6	7.6	19.9	6.3	7.2	5.4	100

Sources: As for Tables 14.1, 14.3, and 14.4.

(Table 14.5). These grants have also been falling in real terms in the country as a whole during Repelita IV, as a result of the budget cuts forced on the government by declining oil revenues. Thus, as far as the Inpres allocations are concerned, East Java has been receiving a declining share of a shrinking pie. As a result of this and of sluggish own-revenue performance, East Java's provincial, *kabupaten*, and *desa* development expenditures have tended to fall relative to GRP (Table 14.10): together they were less than 1 per cent of GRP in 1986/7 compared with 2 per cent in 1976/7.

The overall decline in development expenditures has not been accompanied by any marked change in the nature of the expenditure. Expenditures in both the province and its *kabupaten* have concentrated on construction and maintenance of infrastructure and government facilities, including new buildings (Table 14.11). At the village level there has been some decline in the proportion of funds spent on infrastructure and land development projects, and some increase in the proportion spent on buildings (including maintenance) (Table 14.12).

The decline in development expenditures in East Java has occurred not just as a proportion of GRP but also as a proportion of routine administrative expenditures at each level of government (Table 14.13). Whereas in 1976/7 routine expenditures accounted for 66.1 per cent of all expenditures in East Java by the three subnational levels of government, a decade later the routine share had increased to more than 80 per cent. However, *desa* still spent more on development projects relative to routine expenditures than either the province or the *kabupaten*. This could indicate more popular pressure to use available funds for productive purposes in the *desa* compared with the higher government levels. Whatever the reason, in both 1976/7 and 1986/7 the villages of East Java spent almost as much on development projects as did *kabupaten/kotamadya* and province, although this was not so in most of the intervening years.

Policy Implications

The main trends revealed by this survey of East Java's regional finances are not encouraging. While the provincial and subprovincial levels of government in East Java, as in other provinces of Indonesia, lack lucrative tax handles, there is also evidence that they fail to make full use of those taxes which they do control. This is particularly the case with the *kabupaten* and *desa*, where *kabupaten* taxes and *desa swadaya* revenues have not kept up with GRP since the early 1970s. Rural-sector Ipeda/PBB revenues, which were slightly less than 1 per cent of agricultural GRP in the early 1970s, were only 0.4 per cent by 1986. In urban areas, by contrast, Ipeda/PBB revenues have grown more rapidly than GRP during the 1980s.

These problems are by no means unique to East Java; they apply to all the provinces of Indonesia.[3] The evidence available indicates that at the provincial level East Java's tax effort is about the same as the national average, although at the *kabupaten* level, tax effort appears to be below average. Several explanations can be advanced for poor revenue performance in the *kabupaten* and *desa.* One concerns the equity considerations which came to the fore in the 1970s as a result of growing concern about rural–urban income differences and rural poverty. The rural areas of Indonesia were then taxed (relative to income) more heavily than urban areas,[4] and makers of policy tended not to push collection of taxes in *kabupaten* and *desa*, which were predominantly rural, especially in a province such as East Java where, in the late 1960s and early 1970s, a high proportion of the rural poor were located. The rapid growth in oil revenues, which accrued to the central government, allowed a rapid growth in grants to lower levels of government for both routine and development purposes, and a consequent diminution in incentives to intensify own-revenue effort.

A further possible reason for the poor revenue performance at the lower levels of government in East Java is the lack of an immediate link between tax payments and expenditure, especially in the villages. For example, with the exception of the collection fee retained by village officials, the Ipeda/PBB taxes go to the *kabupaten.* There they are frequently used for purposes such as new official buildings, which have no obvious benefit for rural taxpayers, who are predominantly farmers. If more PBB revenue were used for village purposes (such as irrigation or road maintenance), compliance would probably be higher and arrears lower. Although this problem is not unique to East Java, it was certainly more pronounced there in the early 1970s than in other parts of the country, because PBB collections were larger.

To what extent does East Java's poor revenue-raising record really matter? The province has performed well in terms of a number of development indicators since about 1970, in spite of its lack-lustre performance as far as local government finance is concerned. Foodcrop production has grown rapidly, the economic base has become far more diversified, and the number of people in poverty has fallen rapidly. Even if East Java has not been favoured in terms of central government development funds, clearly it has been able to make good use of the funds it has received. Why should it not continue to do so in the future?

In addressing this question it must be borne in mind that, in spite of the obvious progress made in the last two decades, East Java is still a poor and undeveloped part of the world. If it were a separate nation, it would be classified as 'low-income' by the World Bank. It has a long way to go even to reach the standard of development of West Malaysia, let alone Singapore or Australia. In the late 1960s much of its infrastructure, such as roads and irrigation, was in need of rehabilitation, and much of the investment funds received from the centre through the 1970s were used for rehabilitating existing infrastructure. This produced a high payoff in terms of accelerated growth but investment in rehabilitating existing infrastructure is a finite process. In the future it is probable that more investment funds will be needed to sustain the rates of growth achieved in the 1970s. Investment in directly productive activities in both agriculture and manufacturing will have to come from private sources, but government funds will continue to be needed for economic and social infrastructure in sectors such as transport, public utilities, and education.

At the same time as the demand for publicly funded infrastructure projects in East Java will continue to grow, development funds from the centre are likely to continue to decline. Increasingly East Java will be viewed by the centre as one of the most developed parts of the country, with a diversified economic base, a sophisticated administrative structure, and a declining poverty problem. There will be growing pressure to devote a higher share of the central government development budget to the poorer, more remote provinces outside Java, where infrastructure is poor, population growth rates are higher, and the poverty problem is becoming more acute. In order to sustain the development momentum in East Java, the provincial government will have little option but to diversify its revenue base and increase collections of those taxes and charges which enter the provincial and subprovincial budgets.

Clearly East Java cannot effect the necessary changes alone. There is now a pressing need to tackle the problem of fiscal decentralization in Indonesia at the national level. The three most important policy initiatives are

1. a system of revenue sharing which permits more tax revenues to stay where they are collected, regardless of the legal status of the particular tax instrument;
2. a system of matching grants which tie central government subsidies through the Inpres programmes more directly to regional tax effort; and
3. a system of grant allocation which considers the revenue capacity of *kabupaten/kotamadya* and *desa* and allocates more central and provincial grants to poor areas, bearing in mind the need to stimulate their own-revenue efforts.

The first initiative would involve a general 'levelling down' of tax revenues so that revenues from central government taxes stayed in the province, provincial taxes stayed in the *kabupaten*, and *kabupaten* taxes stayed in the villages. The second would involve tying the Inpres *kabupaten* grants to own-revenue effort so that those *kabupaten* and *kotamadya* with relatively high revenue-to-GRP ratios (above, say, 0.5) (Table 14.8) would receive an extra allocation from the central Inpres allocations. The third would involve allocating a relatively higher proportion of the Inpres *kabupaten* and *desa* funds to those *kabupaten/kotamadya* where per-capita GRP is lowest.

East Java could obviously do more to intensify own-revenue collection, even with the taxes it currently has at its disposal. As we have seen, East Java is a province characterized by quite high disparities in income per capita and in revenue effort. In fact the eight richest *kabupaten* and *kotamadya* account for 51 per cent of the province's GRP. If these regions could increase their tax effort to 1 per cent of their GRP, revenues accruing from the taxes referred to in Table 14.8 could increase by 132 per cent. Since the two smallest *kotamadya* (in GRP terms) in the province were already realizing revenues above 1 per cent of their

GRP in 1985, it should not be too much to expect the richest eight regions to do the same. The most effective way to encourage these regions to take their own-revenue potential more seriously would be to tie their central grants more tightly to their revenue performance.

1. In 1983/4, the final year of Repelita III (the Third Five-Year Development Plan), total Inpres expenditures were Rp 1,315 billion. This had declined in nominal terms to Rp 1,147 billion by 1988/9. As a proportion of total budgetary expenditures, Inpres expenditures declined from 7.2 per cent in 1983/4 to 3.5 per cent in 1988/9. A substantial increase in nominal Inpres expenditures was announced in the 1990/1 budget to Rp 2,332 billion, but this was still only 5.4 per cent of total expenditures.

2. For details of the assessment and collection of the Ipeda in the early 1970s, see Booth (1974). In rural areas, assessment and collection procedures do not appear to have changed markedly after the change to the PBB in 1985. One reason for the slow growth of rural-sector Ipeda assessments relative to incomes since the early 1970s may be a concern for equity. Whatever the reasons, officials of the PBB Directorate apparently feel that the rural sector in Java offers little potential for further revenue growth: increased assessments will come mainly from the urban sector. For a full discussion of PBB assessment in the wake of the 1985 tax legislation, see Soemitro (1986).

3. For a comprehensive recent review of issues relating to regional finance in Indonesia, see Devas (1989).

4. For a discussion of this issue at the national level, see Booth (1981).

15
The Economic Role of Surabaya

Howard Dick

Introduction

SURABAYA is one of the great cities of South-East Asia. It is not just the capital of East Java and its main centre of population, economic activity, and communications, but also the second largest city in Indonesia. It dominates the trade of most of eastern Indonesia and its commercial networks extend to Singapore and East Asia. This opening to a much wider world distinguishes East Java from most other provinces of Indonesia. The dynamism of East Java's recent development owes much to Surabaya.[1]

Like other port cities, Surabaya is an interface between frontiers. It is at the intersection between the most fertile and densely populated 'rice basket' in East Java, the Lower Brantas Valley, and the industrial zone of the Gresik–Surabaya–Sidoarjo–Pasuruan–Malang corridor, and it looks across the Java Sea to the Outer Islands—especially the eastern part of the Archipelago—and the world beyond.

This chapter explores Surabaya's relationship with its hinterland, the fertile and populous interior of East Java, and with its foreland, the Outer Islands of the Archipelago. The first section compares Surabaya's degree of primacy in East Java, in terms of population size, with those of the leading port cities in Central and West Java. The second section reviews the evolution of the transport systems which link Surabaya and the areas around it, in both a physical and an economic sense. The subsequent three sections consider Surabaya's economic importance and its economic relationship with its foreland and its hinterland.

The Urban Hierarchy

At the time of the 1905 Population Census Surabaya was still the largest city in the Netherlands Indies. The three main port cities on the north coast of Java, however, had populations of much the same order of size: Jakarta (then known as Batavia) had 92 per cent and Semarang (Central Java) 64 per cent of the population size of Surabaya (Table 15.1). Since then the urban hierarchy has become much more differentiated. Between 1905 and 1920, Surabaya grew much more

TABLE 15.1
Population of Main Javanese Cities, 1905–1980

City	*1905*	*1920*	*1930*	*1961*	*1971*	*1980*	*Multiple Increase to 1980* >*1920*	>*1930*
Jakarta	138,500	306,300	533,000	2,973,050	4,084,950	6,071,750	20	11
Surabaya	150,200	192,200	343,700	1,007,950	1,308,600	1,737,000	9	5
Percentage of Jakarta	108	63	64	34	32	29		
Semarang	96,700	158,000	217,800	503,150	566,400	820,140	5	4
Percentage of Surabaya	64	82	64	50	43	47		
Bandung	47,400	94,800	166,800	972,550	1,310,910	1,744,800	18	10
Malang	30,000	43,000	86,650	341,450	365,280	491,500	11	6
Magelang	n.a.	36,200	52,950	96,500	126,800	153,000	4	3

Source: Hugo et al. (1987: 52, 101–2).

slowly than either of its two sister cities. The population of Batavia surpassed that of Surabaya around 1910 and by the 1920 Population Census was 50 per cent larger. Between 1920 and 1930 the population of both cities grew at about the same rate. However, between the 1930 and 1961 censuses the population of Jakarta grew twice as fast as Surabaya's. In the 1930s this reflected the blow to East Java's economy of the collapse of sugar exports; after Independence it reflected the centralization of government and the concentration of job opportunities in Jakarta. Though still the second largest city, by 1961 Surabaya was only one-third the size of Jakarta, after which there was a slight downward trend to 29 per cent in 1980. Since 1961 Surabaya has remained twice as large as Semarang. The difference in size between the largest and the smallest of these three cities has widened from about 55 per cent in 1905 to 640 per cent in 1980.

Another twentieth-century trend has been the emergence of large cities in the highlands of Java. By 1961 Surabaya had almost been overtaken in population size by the highland city of Bandung (West Java), which had already well surpassed the population of Semarang. Although in 1920 Bandung had yet to reach a population of 100,000, over the next 60 years its growth rate almost matched that of Jakarta. This rapid growth was stimulated by a pre-war decentralization of government departments and then sustained after the 1930s when, because of its favourable climate, the city became the centre for a new domestic cotton textile industry. By 1971 Bandung's recorded population exceeded that of Surabaya. However, given that the extended boundaries of the Bandung *kotamadya* (municipality) encompass a large rural population, the difference may be artificial. Malang, the equivalent highland centre in East Java, has grown much more slowly than Bandung. From a population in 1920 of less than 50,000, by 1980 Malang had almost reached half a million, and was little more than one-quarter the size of Bandung and still smaller than Semarang.

The emergence of Bandung—but not Malang—as a major city suggests that what has been happening to Java's urban hierarchy is more complicated than just the development of Jakarta as a primate city. Within each province, the main port city and the adjacent highland centre have had similar population growth rates. Over the period 1920 to 1980, in West Java Jakarta grew 20-fold and Bandung 18-fold, in East Java Surabaya grew 9-fold and Malang 11-fold; and, in Central Java Semarang grew 5-fold and the inland centres of Solo, Yogyakarta, and Magelang all 4- or 5-fold (Table 15.1). These figures point to differential rates of economic growth across the three provinces with a tendency towards the bifurcation of economic activity between West and East Java. However, they are no more than suggestive. For example, the pattern for smaller towns in West and Central Java is not at all consistent.[2] Nevertheless, the pattern is an intriguing one.

Another perspective on urban size can be provided by comparing levels of urbanization between the three main provinces in Java. By 1980

West Java had an urban population and level of urbanization about twice that of both East and Central Java (Table 15.2). A comparison for each province of the population in the main city with both the total and the urban populations gives a measure of primacy (Table 15.2). On both measures Jakarta/West Java had the highest degree of primacy and Central Java (including the Special Region of Yogyakarta, DIY) the lowest. Another measure of primacy is given by comparing the population size of the main city with those of the second and third largest in each province. On this measure East Java had a high degree of primacy with a remarkably similar pattern to that of West Java: in both cases the population of the second largest city was about 30 per cent of that of the main city and that of the third largest city about 10 per cent. Central Java, by contrast, showed a rather even distribution: nine other cities had populations larger than 100,000 and ranked in size between 14 per cent and 66 per cent of that of the main city (Semarang). This pattern is consistent with the fact that Central Java was lagging behind the other provinces in economic development. In other words, economic development and accompanying urbanization have tended to increase the differentiation of the urban hierarchy.

For East Java, levels of urbanization and urban hierarchies can be compared between the 1930 and 1980 population censuses. Over this period the total population almost doubled, while the urban population increased more than five times, raising the degree of urbanization from 7 per cent in 1930 to 20 per cent in 1980. Over the same period Surabaya increased its share of the provincial population from 2.3 per cent to 6 per cent, though its share of the urban population remained almost unchanged at around 30 per cent. The urban hierarchy was also stable. The second largest town, Malang, marginally gained in relative size from 25 per cent to 28 per cent of the population of Surabaya while

TABLE 15.2
Java: Indicators of Urbanization, 1980

Indicator	*Jakarta–West Java*	*East Java*	*Central Java*[a]
Urban population ('000)	11,843	5,720	5,363
Urbanization (%)	35	20	19
No. of cities with population > 100,000	10	5	10
Main city: Percentage of total population	18	6	3
Main city: Percentage of urban population	51	30	15
No. 2: Main city (%)	29	28	66
No. 3: Main city (%)	9	10	56

Source: Based upon figures in Hugo et al. (1987: 94, 101–2).
[a]Includes the Special Region of Yogyakarta (DIY).

the third and fourth largest towns, Kediri and Madiun, fell back from 14 and 12 per cent respectively to 10 per cent.

Such figures suggest that in East Java a marked urbanization of the population over the 50-year period between 1930 and 1980 was accommodated without fundamental change in the urban hierarchy. Given the simultaneous reorientation of Surabaya's trade from international to domestic markets, this stability is at first sight surprising, but several factors probably contribute to it. First, the urban-based administrative hierarchy of provincial and district government has remained very similar to that of the late colonial period. Secondly, despite the rapid growth of road and air traffic, the layout of the transport network and therefore the pattern of production and trade has undergone no significant alteration. Thirdly, Surabaya's economic role in its hinterland has perhaps undergone no fundamental change since the colonial period.

Transport Systems

The physical basis for the economic interaction between Surabaya, its hinterland, and the rest of the world is the transport system of which it is the hub. Along these pathways of roads and railways, connecting with sealanes and airlanes, flow the goods and people that articulate the spatial dimensions of the regional economy.

The transport system has evolved in a way that reflects the constraints of topography. Like the rest of the island, East Java consists of huge volcanic blocks separated by river valleys which naturally became the foci of settlement. Before the application of steam and the internal combustion engine, water provided the only cheap means of inland transport. Surabaya's location was doubly strategic because it was both the only natural harbour on the north coast of Java and it was located at the mouths of the island's two main rivers, the Bengawan Solo and the Brantas. The Bengawan Solo rises in Central Java beyond Solo, joins with the Bengawan Madiun at Ngawi, flows through the northern limestone hills and, since diversion works in the nineteenth century, debouches into the Java Sea to the north of Gresik (see Figure 1.1). The Brantas rises in the mountains to the south-west of Malang, makes a wide loop through Kediri and Mojokerto and then widens out into a delta which, after 1830, became one of the centres of the sugar industry in East Java. The Kali Mas, which flows through the city of Surabaya, is a tributary.

Until the construction of railways in the last quarter of the nineteenth century, the Bengawan Solo and the Brantas supported a lively river traffic. The railways followed the river valleys, where settlement and trade were concentrated, and also converged on Surabaya. Today highways carry the main share of both passengers and cargo but they also tend to run parallel with the rail system. In this way, modern transport systems have reinforced Surabaya's original locational advantage.

Four main road and rail corridors link Surabaya with the rest of the province. The busiest runs due south to the highland city of Malang, with the section as far as Gempol now a toll-road. Gempol is also the junction for the main highway east along the north coast to Pasuruan and Probolinggo and eventually on to the plantation centres of Lumajang, Jember, and Banyuwangi and to the vehicular ferry to Bali. The third corridor branches to the south-west near the southern boundary of the city and follows the Brantas River in the direction of Mojokerto, later forking south to Kediri, Tulungagung, and Blitar, while the main highway carries on to Madiun and Solo. The fourth corridor runs west from Gresik to Lamongan and Bojonegoro and thence on to Kudus and Semarang.[3]

A good highway system has been a major factor in the economic integration of the province under the New Order. At the beginning of the New Order the once very good highway system of East Java was in a deplorable state. Even the journey between Surabaya and Malang took several hours because of the need to weave through the potholes. On his appointment as governor in 1967, Mohd. Noer made the rehabilitation of roads a top priority, so that by the mid-1970s East Java probably enjoyed some overcapacity in its highway system. Through the Inpres (Instruksi Presiden) scheme where development grants are given for infrastructure works, attention was then turned to the improvement of feeder roads in rural areas. In the 1980s, when two-lane highways were no longer adequate for the rapidly increasing volume of traffic, especially of buses and trucks, construction began of the first toll-road between Surabaya and Gempol, where the highway along the north coast to Pasuruan branches from that to Malang. In 1987 this toll-road was connected to as far as the harbour of Tanjung Perak; in the early 1990s it will be extended to the adjacent industrial town of Gresik.

The way in which railways and highways have strengthened the dominance of Surabaya is illustrated by the relationship between Surabaya and that part of East Java known to the Dutch as the Oosthoek (Eastern Corner), which lies to the east of an imaginary line between Surabaya and Malang. Before the advent of railways, Surabaya's links with the Oosthoek were much more tenuous than with the river valleys to the west. The highlands around Malang were served not from Surabaya but from Pasuruan which, along with other north coast ports such as Probolinggo, Panarukan, and Banyuwangi, shipped out most of the sugar, coffee, and tobacco produced in the Oosthoek. As ports, they were just open roadsteads, relying upon lighters for towage from tidal creeks to ships anchored well offshore. Throughout the period between the two world wars these ports continued to export significant tonnages from their immediate hinterlands but importing was done almost entirely through Surabaya.

Since Independence Surabaya has come to dominate export trade as well. This is due mainly to the improvement in the speed, reliability, and cost of road transport. At the same time, little care has been taken to prevent the silting up of the lighterage creeks in the regional ports, and the trend towards much larger and more sophisticated ships rendered the use of such outports uneconomic. Another trend has been the shift from rail to road of passenger and freight movement to and from Malang. This enables direct communication between Surabaya and Malang, bypassing Pasuruan. Nowadays Pasuruan is a sleepy town with many fine old colonial buildings to attest to its faded importance.

Economic Importance

Population figures give some insight into the nature of the urban hierarchy but are not necessarily a good indicator of relative economic size. It is therefore helpful that estimates of gross regional product (GRP) are now compiled at provincial and even *kabupaten* and *kotamadya* levels, although their accuracy cannot be vouchsafed. For the year 1984 it is possible to compare the GRP of Kotamadya Surabaya with that of East Java, and the GRP of Jakarta with that of West Java (Table 15.3). The results are revealing. In total Surabaya contributed 14 per cent of provincial GRP. The province of Jakarta, by contrast, accounted for almost half of the combined GRP of Jakarta and West Java. In other words, the national capital has an economy not much smaller than that of the entire province which surrounds it. Were manufacturing located in the adjacent *kabupaten* of Bekasi, Bogor, and Tangerang included in a Greater Jakarta region, the dominance of Jakarta would be even more dramatic.

While Surabaya plays a leading role in the economy of East Java, it does not overshadow the rest of the province as Jakarta overshadows West Java. This is confirmed by analysis of Surabaya's sectoral contribution to the provincial economy (Table 15.3). The exercise should be treated with some scepticism, because sectoral value added is subject to a larger margin of error than total *kabupaten/kotamadya* GRP. Surabaya being mostly urban, it is hardly surprising that it has no significant primary sector, even allowing for fishing. More surprising is that the city's 9 per cent share of the trade, hotels and restaurants sector is so low. Nor does Surabaya stand out as a manufacturing centre. The share of manufacturing in the city's own GRP is only 17 per cent. Furthermore, the city's contribution to the manufacturing sector of the whole province is only 15 per cent, which is only slightly above the contribution of Surabaya to overall provincial GRP.[4] By contrast, Jakarta's manufacturing sector contributes 59 per cent of the combined manufacturing sector of Jakarta–West Java. The modest contribution of Surabaya to East Java's manufacturing sector in part reflects the zoning policy of municipal and provincial governments to locate heavy and polluting industries away from urban Surabaya (see Chapter 10).

Surabaya has remained primarily a service centre. It is in the tertiary sector that Surabaya accounts for a large share of provincial output: government and community services (43 per cent), financial services (39 per cent), and the small construction sector (32 per cent). These three sectors together represent almost half the city's GRP. The importance of the public sector is readily explained by Surabaya's being the seat of the provincial government: it contains not only large provincial

TABLE 15.3

Java: Gross Regional Product, 1984 (current prices: Rp billion)

Sector	*Surabaya*	*East Java*	*Surabaya/ East Java (%)*	*Jakarta*	*Jakarta– West Java*	*Jakarta/ Jakarta–West Java (%)*
Primary	97	4,251	2	120	4,639[a]	3
Manufacturing[b]	296	1,946	15	1,801	3,054	59
Construction	35	110	32	290	1,161	25
Trade, hotels, and restaurants	280	3,139	9	2,073	4,532	46
Transport and communications	209	975	21	1,014	1,614	63
Financial services	209	534	39	2,515	2,916	86
Government and community	588	1,357	43	1,229	2,719	45
Total	1,715	12,312	14	9,042	20,635	44

Sources: Figures supplied by BPS, Jakarta, and Bappeda, Surabaya.
[a]Includes oil-LNG.
[b]Includes utilities.

and local government bureaucracies but also the staff of the regional offices of central government departments. It is also a centre for higher education and advanced medical facilities, much of which are also in the public domain. Indeed, Surabaya's share of the provincial total for the sector of government and community services is almost the same as Jakarta's share of that sector in Jakarta–West Java.

Financial services (including insurance, property rentals, and business services) tend to cluster near the peak of the urban hierarchy where foreign trade and the management of large firms are concentrated. In East Java, Surabaya has always been the main port of foreign trade, as well as the gateway to the Outer Islands. Consequently, in Surabaya reside the big wholesalers who borrow, speculate, and pass credit down the marketing chain to the producer. There are also the offices and agents of the plantations, once foreign- but now State-owned. The manufacturing companies with plants in the hinterland of Surabaya also place their financial and marketing executives in Surabaya, if not in Jakarta.

Surabaya has therefore long been a banking centre, though its role has been in large-scale branch banking. It has never been the location for the headquarters of large banks, which in the colonial period were based overseas with local head offices in Jakarta and now are almost entirely Jakarta-based. In mid-1986, according to figures supplied by Bank Indonesia, only seven banks (small, private ones) had their headquarters in Surabaya out of a total of 81 (State and private banks) in Indonesia. Nevertheless, Surabaya has been the conduit for the flow of funds into and out of the province. For all banks the Surabaya area (including the city's immediate hinterland) accounted in August 1986 for about three-quarters of both deposits and loans for the whole province (Table 15.4), though the proportion is much higher for private banks, many of which do not have branches outside Surabaya. In all economic sectors the Surabaya area accounted for a high proportion of provincial bank loans in May 1986 (Table 15.5). Even for agriculture the figure was more than half; for manufacturing and trade it was almost 70 per cent, for transport and construction 85–86 per cent, and for services no less than 91 per cent.

Yet despite its dominance within East Java as the financial and business centre, Surabaya is unambiguously subordinate to Jakarta in terms of control over capital. The fact that so few banks have their headquarters in Surabaya is one indication. Another is that the managers of branches in Surabaya have strict limits as to the size of loans which they can approve without authority from Jakarta. In any case, business people seeking large loans often prefer to negotiate with top managers in Jakarta. Moreover, many of the principals of factories, hotels, and other businesses in Surabaya and its hinterland are themselves located in Jakarta. As mentioned in Chapter 10 ('Manufacturing'), since the mid-1970s competition has driven many firms based in Jakarta to establish branch operations in East Java. Consequently, although Surabaya is the domicile of some very rich and successful business executives, some

TABLE 15.4
Bank Deposits and Loans, 1986 (Rp billion)

	Deposits			*Loans*		
Banks	*Surabaya*	*East Java*	*Surabaya/East Java (%)*	*Surabaya*	*East Java*	*Surabaya/East Java (%)*
State banks	465	673	69	1,480	2,271	65
Private banks	569	689	83	470	524	90
Total	1,034	1,362	76	1,950	2,795	70

Source: Bank Indonesia, Surabaya office.

TABLE 15.5
Bank Loans by Sector, May 1986 (Rp billion)

Sector	*Surabaya*		*East Java*		*Surabaya as Percentage of East Java*
	Rp billion	*%*	*Rp billion*	*%*	
Agriculture	199	10	373	13	53
Other	21	1	37	1	57
Manufacturing	791	41	1,170	42	68
Trade	491	25	716	26	69
Transport	28	1	331	1	85
Construction	59	3	69	3	86
Services	361	19	395	14	91
Total	1,950	100	2,795	100	70

Source: Bank Indonesia, Surabaya office.

industrialists, some real estate developers, and some traders, as a business community it is very much dependent on Jakarta. No longer, as until the Great Depression of the 1930s, does it vie with Jakarta as a business centre and entrepôt in its own right. Its dependent status in the business world corresponds with its provincial status in the administrative hierarchy. Whether this situation will change following the opening in 1988 of the Surabaya Stock Exchange and the lifting of restrictions on branch banking by foreign banks remains to be seen.

Surabaya and Its Foreland

Shipping and trade have always been the life-blood of Surabaya. The port is still the city's *raison d'être* and the rationale for its location. The only natural harbour on the north coast of Java, it used to be a typical roadstead port. Between 1910 and the mid-1920s, in the heyday of the sugar industry, it was upgraded into perhaps the most sophisticated port in South-East Asia. Because of the stagnation of the port's foreign trade after 1930, the existing infrastructure sufficed until very recently. Under the New Order there has been rehabilitation, the addition of some bulk-handling facilities and, in the 1980s, some extension of the quay length, provision of container-stacking facilities and the opening of a new passenger terminal. However, with the exception of new bulk-handling berths to serve the heavy-industrial complex at Gresik, these have been incremental investments within the capacity constraints of the original harbour basin. Work on a new harbour basin to provide modern container-handling facilities began in the late 1980s.[5] This new phase of investment coincides with the revival in the 1980s of Surabaya's export trade after the long hiatus since the Great Depression (see Chapter 10).

In the 1980s the pattern of international shipping was transformed. Surabaya—like Tanjung Priok (Jakarta), Port Klang (Kuala Lumpur), Penang, and Bangkok—ceased to be a main port of call for liners on the main trade routes to Europe and North America. For the huge container ships (3,000-unit capacity) serving Europe and North America, Singapore is the only port of call in South-East Asia. Along with the other second-order ports, Surabaya is linked to the rest of the world primarily by feeder vessels (typically about 200 units capacity) offering daily services to Singapore. Only in the trades to East Asia and Australia are direct calls still important. Meanwhile, the amount of non-liner tonnage, such as bulk carriers and tankers, increases steadily in line with the province's industrial development. So also does the volume of inter-island shipping.

The one respect in which the business community of Surabaya retains a high degree of autonomy is in its network of trading links with the Outer Islands of the Archipelago. Surabaya has long been the focal point for the domestic trade of the eastern part of Archipelago (that is, to the east of West Kalimantan). Historically, its closest links have been with Banjarmasin (South Kalimantan), Samarinda (East Kalimantan), and, to the east, with the islands of Bali, Lombok, and the rest of

Nusa Tenggara. With the post-war decline of Makassar as an international port, Sulawesi and Maluku were also incorporated into Surabaya's trading network. The only parts of eastern Indonesia whose trade is not focused upon Surabaya are the provinces of Irian Jaya and East Timor, which for special reasons have always had close links with Jakarta. Ujung Pandang, which retains some role as a local distribution centre for South and South-east Sulawesi, Maluku, and Irian, also draws a good deal of trade from Jakarta. Surabaya's trade links with the west of the Archipelago, namely Kalimantan, Riau, and Sumatra, remain fairly tenuous except for a few bulk commodities: sugar outwards and palm oil (from North Sumatra), urea fertilizer (from Palembang), and oil products inwards. The only port in this sphere with which Surabaya conducts any lively general cargo trade is Belawan (North Sumatra), which is the distribution centre in the west of the Archipelago.

This bifurcation of the Archipelago between Jakarta and Surabaya is illustrated in Table 15.6, which for several commodity groups shows the ratio of tonnage shipped from Surabaya–East Java to that shipped from Jakarta–West Java to regions of Indonesia from west to east. Subject to some qualifications,[6] the pattern is striking: except for tobacco products from East Java to North Sumatra, the trade of the western part is dominated by Jakarta–West Java while that of the eastern part is dominated by East Java. That the pattern is less pronounced for machinery and electrical goods reflects the concentration of those industries in Jakarta–West Java.

A similar pattern stands out from the network of domestic air routes. Surabaya has East Java's one major civilian airport and is the hub for flights to eastern Indonesia. Indeed, the speed of domestic air travel, together with the introduction by satellite of efficient telephone links with the Outer Islands, have reinforced Surabaya's position as the commercial capital of eastern Indonesia. Nevertheless, the busiest route out of Surabaya is still that to Jakarta, which Garuda now operates as an hourly shuttle service. Moreover, not until 1989 did Surabaya gain limited access to direct international flights.

This polarization of the Archipelago can be seen also in the economic partitioning of Central Java. While the convention of calculating economic aggregates according to provincial boundaries implies that Central Java is a viable, integrated economy in its own right, in reality the province is largely absorbed into the economic spheres of West and East Java. Semarang, once the East India Company's stronghold on the north coast, has during the twentieth century steadily declined in relative economic importance. Unlike Jakarta or Surabaya, it does not serve as the economic centre of the province, a fact underlined by the figures on urban hierarchies (Table 15.1). Reflecting the interrelationships of topography, transport systems, and politics, Central Java is carved up by three axes. The first runs along the north coast, bringing some trade to Semarang but also drawing off trade to Jakarta and Surabaya. The second is the valley of the Bengawan Solo River, which links the former

TABLE 15.6
Percentage Ratio of East Java Share to Jakarta–West Java Share of Inter-island Trade by Tonnage, 1983

Region	*Textiles*	*Tobacco*	*Machinery Electrical*	*Construction Steel*
North Sumatra/Aceh	8	76	5	42
West Sumatra/Bengkulu	5	2	30	2
Riau	0	1	6	2
Jambi/South Sumatra	0	5	2	3
Lampung	0	0	1	0
West Kalimantan	0	0	2	5
Central Kalimantan	95	98	29	94
South Kalimantan	92	100	73	73
East Kalimantan	95	100	60	54
Bali	100	100	99	100
Nusa Tenggara	98	100	94	91
Ujung Pandang	62	100	42	84
Sulawesi	87	99	67	64
Maluku	87	97	73	72
Irian	83	87	31	12
Total	64	77	34	40

Source: Based on BPS (1984b).

court cities of Yogyakarta and Solo closely with Surabaya. The third follows the railway and highway from the highlands around Bandung to the southern port of Cilacap and the south-western part of the province, Cilacap being not much further from Bandung than from Yogyakarta. Along the second axis, Surabaya annexes a significant part of the market of Central Java.

Surabaya and Its Hinterland

The relationship between a city and its hinterland can be depicted in terms of three simple models. The first, which is a limiting case, is when the city is an enclave, sustained by the international economy but turning its back upon its hinterland. The second is where the city forms a parasitic relationship with its hinterland, drawing off its economic surplus but returning little in exchange. In this case urbanization is not part of any wider development process. This resembles the cases referred to by McGee (1969) as 'pseudo-urbanization' and by Lipton (1977) as 'urban bias', both statements of the argument that the growth processes of the Industrial Revolution, which had transformed Europe and North America, were not working in the Third World. The third and opposite case is where the city serves as a 'growth pole' for development of the hinterland, transmitting a demand for the production of goods and services in the hinterland and boosting labour absorption. This benign case is what economists envisage by their advocacy of an open economy with specialization according to comparative advantage: access to a wider market permits specialization, higher productivity, and higher real incomes.

Over the course of the twentieth century Surabaya has revealed elements of all three models as it has adapted to changed circumstances and thereby demonstrated its resilience. In the 1940s Surabaya was for some years reduced to being a virtual enclave (Frederick, 1989). Late in the Japanese occupation the city was all but cut off from the international economy because of the acute lack of shipping caused by the presence of Allied submarines. After the forcible reoccupation by the British Army in November 1945 and the subsequent brief restoration of Dutch rule, the city was then isolated from its hinterland, which was controlled by the Indonesian nationalist forces. Even the hydroelectricity and water supplies were cut off. Although the Dutch eventually reoccupied most of the province, much of the productive infrastructure, especially plantations, was damaged or destroyed in worsening guerrilla warfare.

After Independence Surabaya began to show signs of 'pseudo-urbanization'. Admittedly the population grew more slowly in the 1950s and 1960s than in the more prosperous 1920s. In terms of the pre-war dynamics of development, however, the population ought to have grown very little at all. In fact, as Steele (1980) has shown, Surabaya experienced a typical flow of migration into informal-sector activity. Undoubtedly there was an element of 'urban bias': public sector jobs with rations in kind were easier to obtain in the city, and per capita there was much more money in circulation than in the hinterland. Yet the continuing population growth of the 1950s and 1960s can probably best be understood as a process of long-term adjustment to disequilibrium. After the relaxation of colonial authority, the city became much more porous. The prosperous and mainly Dutch middle class was no longer isolated in suburban comfort from the poverty of the rest of the city and its hinterland. The walls cracked that had maintained this artificial dualism. The invasion by *becak* (a three-wheeled pedicab), the 'illegal' occupation by squatters of fire access lanes, river banks, and other vacant land, the proliferation of street hawkers, and the boom in prostitution were all part of a social revolution which, after 1958, was rather erratically encouraged by a communist-controlled municipal government.[7]

Despite the criticism of 'pseudo-urbanization' and 'urban bias', this process probably did little harm to the city's hinterland. It was a means of absorbing part of an underemployed and increasingly poorly fed population. Had the very limited amount of public expenditure in Surabaya been redistributed throughout the province it would probably have made little impact upon poverty. Until the late 1960s the basic problem was not so much the uneven distribution of investment and public expenditure as its pitifully small amount.

The third model, of the city as a 'growth pole', better fits Surabaya before the Great Depression of the 1930s and since the early 1970s. Until the 1930s the city was a classic entrepôt, exporting plantation crops such as sugar, coffee, rubber, and tobacco in exchange for imported consumer and capital goods. Both city and hinterland seemed to benefit from buoyant international demand for plantation crops. In the early 1970s, when the economy of Indonesia began to pick up and with it that of East Java, there began a beneficial interaction between rural and urban economies. First, the Green Revolution, which took hold early in East Java (see Chapter 6), helped both to offset the effects of displacement of labour from tasks such as harvesting and rice milling and to provide increased purchasing power to sustain non-agricultural employment. Secondly, industrial development quickly spread beyond the *kotamadya* boundaries of Surabaya into the Surabaya–Malang corridor (see Chapter 10). This also boosted off-farm employment. The interaction between agricultural and industrial development was facilitated by the revolution in mobility brought about by the proliferation of small-scale motorized urban transport and by the policy of both central and provincial governments in underwriting the provision of rural infrastructure (Dick and Forbes, 1992).

While Surabaya seems to have acted as a 'growth pole' in the development of its hinterland, this has not been associated with disproportionate growth of the city. As shown above by figures on urbanization and GRP, Surabaya dominates its hinterland far less than Jakarta. This impression is supported by figures on population growth. Given the experience of the previous decade of prosperity, namely the 1920s, when the population of Surabaya seems almost to have doubled, population growth could have been expected to accelerate in the 1970s. In fact, the city's rate of growth declined, from 4.4 per cent in the 1960s to 3.2 per cent in the 1970s (Hugo et al., 1987: 101). In contrast, the population growth rate of Jakarta was maintained in the 1970s at 4.5 per cent, almost the same as the rate of 4.6 per cent in the 1960s. These population growth figures are consistent with the impression that, under the New Order, urban bias has been much less marked in East Java than in Jakarta–West Java. It is intriguing to reflect whether the outcome would have been much different if the city of Surabaya had, like Jakarta, enjoyed provincial status independent of its hinterland.

Conclusion

In the course of the twentieth century Surabaya has suffered some loss of status. Having once been the largest city in Indonesia, with an international orientation, it is now the second largest city in a distinctly provincial mould. In various ways the city has become much more inward-looking. The decline was initiated by the collapse of international demand for sugar in the 1930s and reinforced by the damage to East Java's productive infrastructure in the 1940s. Political factors also came into play. In 1950 Surabaya became part of the administrative and urban hierarchy of a highly centralized, unitary state dominated by Jakarta. Increasingly remote from the centre of national life, Surabaya began to lose its cultural and intellectual dynamism. The vigorous intellectual and literary activity which made the city a birthplace of Indonesian nationalism has evaporated; its once distinctive popular culture has been overwhelmed by the modern national culture of Jakarta and television. By the early 1970s the rundown but still essentially colonial cityscape was a kind of fossilized testimony to how little investment there had been since Independence and even since the onset of the Great Depression.

Since the economic upswing of the 1970s, however, the city has gradually regained some of the vibrancy and self-assurance that seemed to have been lost in the 1930s. The relationship of Surabaya to its hinterland can again be described as that of a 'growth pole', transmitting the impulses of development to its hinterland rather than internalizing the linkages as Jakarta seems to have done. In the 1980s the depreciation of the exchange rate and other policies to promote non-oil exports have meant that access through Surabaya to world markets has again become important to East Java's development.

Although for much of the New Order period there has been concern with the perceived increasing primacy of Jakarta, the pattern which now seems to be emerging is one of bipolarity. Being the capital, Jakarta is certainly the dominant city in Indonesia. Nevertheless, after some lag, Surabaya has begun to display a degree of economic autonomy. The old commercial pattern whereby Jakarta played the leading role in the west and Surabaya a similar role in the east of the Archipelago is now being reinforced by industrialization. As between Tokyo and Osaka as the two leading cities in Japan, the consequence seems to be a growing synergy between Jakarta and Surabaya as the two leading cities in Indonesia.

1. This chapter presents an overview of research carried out under the Industrialisation Project in the Research School of Pacific Studies at the Australian National University into the economic history of Surabaya in the twentieth century.

2. These figures also reflect the vagaries of intercensal boundary changes, although the 1971 and 1981 figures have been adjusted by the NUDS Project to reflect functional urban boundaries.

3. The more northerly road that follows the old post road along the north coast is less direct, in poor condition, and little used.

4. While more recent estimates of manufacturing value added suggest that the sectoral contribution of manufacturing had been undervalued, this conclusion would not be invalidated unless the undervaluation were much greater in Surabaya than across the province as a whole.

5. The long-term problem with the port of Surabaya is that ships are limited to a draught of 12 metres and even this can be maintained only by continuous dredging. Long-range planning is for a deepwater port offshore from Madura Island, which in the 1990s will be linked by bridge to the mainland.

6. The table excludes so-called basic commodities such as rice, fertilizer, flour, and cement whose distribution is centrally directed. Secondly, the port of shipment is not necessarily the port of origin. Thus the tobacco products shipped from Jakarta would consist largely of *kretek* manufactured in Central or East Java, while textiles shipped from Surabaya would include production from West Java. Freight moving from East Java across the Strait to Bali would include goods shipped by truck from West Java, while that moving by ferry across Sunda Strait to Lampung would include goods from East Java.

7. Actually the process was not much different in Jakarta under a Nationalist administration (see Jellinek, 1990).

Bibliography

Adelman, I. (1984), 'Beyond Export-led Industrialization', *World Development*, 29(9): 937–49.

Affandy, M. (1987–8), *Analisis Migrasi Penduduk Berdasarkan Data Supas 1985: Propinsi Jawa Timur* [Analysis of Migration Based on 1985 Supas Data: East Java Province], Yogyakarta: Universitas Gadjah Mada, Pusat Penelitian Kependudukan.

Allen, G. C. and Donnithorne, A. (1957), *Western Enterprise in Indonesia and Malaya*, London: Allen & Unwin.

Altona, T. (1914), 'Rapport Wegens het Voorloopig Hydrologisch Onderzoek van het Brantasgebied' [Report on a Preliminary Hydrological Study of the Brantas Area], *Tectona*, 7: 245–67, 317–47, 418–33.

Anon. (1971), 'An Economic Survey of East Java', *Bulletin of Indonesian Economic Studies*, 7(2): 19–37.

Anon. (1988), 'Maha Raja Termuda dari Kediri' [The Newest Maharaja from Kediri], *Pariwara*, 2 July.

Azis, Iwan Jaya (1989), 'Key Issues in Indonesian Regional Development', in Hal Hill (ed.), *Unity and Diversity: Regional Economic Development in Indonesia since 1970*, Singapore: Oxford University Press.

Bakir, Z. and Manning, C. (eds.) (1984), *Angkatan Kerja di Indonesia*, Jakarta: C. V. Rajawali.

Bandiyono, Suko (1987), *Migrasi Permanen di Jawa Timur* [Permanent Migration in East Java], Jakarta: Pusat Penelitian dan Pengembangan Tenaga Kerja dan Kependudukan, Lembaga Ilmu Pengetahuan Indonesia.

Bappeda (1989), *Produk Domestic Regional Bruto: Propinsi dan Kabupaten/Kotamadya se Jawa Timur* [Gross Regional Domestic Product: Provinces and Regency/Municipality in East Java], Surabaya: Bappeda/Kantor Statistik Jawa Timur.

Barlow, Colin and Thee Kian Wie (1989), 'North Sumatra: Growth with Unbalanced Development', in Hal Hill (ed.), *Unity and Diversity: Regional Economic Development in Indonesia since 1970*, Singapore: Oxford University Press.

Bawazier, F. (1989), 'Keuangan Daerah' [Regional Finance], Paper presented to the Conference on Regional Economic Development: Processes and Policies, University of Indonesia, Jakarta.

Bernsten, R. H.; Siwi, B. H.; and Beachell, H. M. (1982), *The Development and Diffusion of Rice Varieties in Indonesia*, IRRI Research Paper Series, No. 71, Los Baños.

Boeke, J. H. (1910), 'Tropisch-koloniale Staathuiskunde: Het Probleem', doctoral dissertation, University of Leiden.

____ (1953), *Economics and Economic Policies in Dual Societies*, Amsterdam: Tjeenk Willinck.

Booth, A. (1974), 'Ipeda: Indonesia's Land Tax', *Bulletin of Indonesian Economic Studies*, 10(1): 55–81.

____ (1981), 'Taxation of Agriculture in Indonesia and Thailand', *Southeast Asian Economic Review*, 2(3): 261–89.

____ (ed.) (1992), *The Oil Boom and After: Indonesia's Economic Performance in the Soeharto Era*, Singapore: Oxford University Press.

Booth, A. and Sundrum, R. (1984), *Labour Absorption in Agriculture*, New Delhi: Oxford University Press.

BPP Ngantang (1983), *Rancangan Program Penyuluhan Pertanian Tahun Anggaran, 1983–84* [Agricultural Extension Programme for the 1983–84 Financial Year], Ngantang: Balai Penyuluhan Pertanian.

BPS (Biro Pusat Statistik) (annual), *Produksi Tanaman Bahan Makanan* [Food Crop Production], Jakarta.

____ (annual), *Statistik Indonesia* [Indonesian Statistics], Jakarta.

____ (annual), *Statistical Pocketbook of Indonesia*, Jakarta.

____ (annual), *Statistik Keuangan Desa: Jawa dan Madura* [Financial Statistics for Village Governments: Java and Madura], Jakarta.

____ (annual), *Statistik Keuangan Pemerintah Daerah Tingkat I* [Financial Statistics for Provincial Governments], Jakarta.

____ (annual), *Statistik Keuangan Pemerintah Daerah Tingkat II* [Financial Statistics for *Kabupaten* Governments], Jakarta.

____ (1963), *Population Census, 1961: Republic of Indonesia*, Jakarta.

____ (1970), *Sensus Perindustrian, 1964: Hasil Pengolahan Sektor Industri Besar dan Sedang, Jawa Timur* [Industry Sensus 1964: Large and Medium Establishments, East Java], Jakarta.

____ (1971), *Survey Perusahaan Industri, Tahun 1970* [Survey of Industrial Firms, 1970], Jakarta.

____ (1972), *Population Census, 1971: Republic of Indonesia*, Jakarta.

____ (1974), *Population Census, 1971*, Series E, Jakarta.

____ (1978a), *Sensus Industri, 1974–75: Jawa Timur* [Industry Census, 1974–75: East Java], 2 vols., Jakarta.

____ (1978b), *Indonesian Fertility Survey, 1976*, Supas III, Jakarta.

____ (1981), *Penduduk Indonesia, 1980, Menurut Propinsi dan Kabupaten/Kotamadya* [1980 Population of Indonesia by Province and Regency/Municipality], Jakarta.

____ (1982), *Population Census, 1980: Republic of Indonesia*, Jakarta.

____ (1983a), *Population of East Java: Results of the 1980 Population Census*, Series S, No. 15, Jakarta.

____ (1983b), *Population of Indonesia: Results of the 1980 Population Census*, Series S, No. 12, Jakarta.

____ (1983c), *Peta Konsumsi Pangan di Indonesia, 1981* [Patterns of Food Consumption in Indonesia, 1981], Jakarta.

____ (1984a), *Proyeksi Penduduk Indonesia per Propinsi, 1980–2000* [Indonesian Population Projections by Province, 1980–2000], Jakarta.

____ (1984b), *Lalu Lintas Angkutan antar Pulau, 1983* [Inter-island Cargo Traffic, 1983], Jakarta.

____ (1985), *Dampak Listrik Masuk Desa dan Perusahaan Listrik Non-PLN: Propinsi Jawa Barat, DI Yogyakarta dan Jawa Timur, 1983* [Impact of Rural Electrification and Non-PLN Power Companies: West Java, DI Yogyakarta, and East Java, 1983], Jakarta.

—— (1986a), *Penduduk Indonesia, 1985, Menurut Propinsi* [Population of Indonesia, 1985, by Province], Series No. 3, Jakarta.

—— (1986b), *Survei Pertanian*, 1983 [Agricultural Survey, 1983], Jakarta.

—— (1986c), *Statistik Listrik Non-PLN, 1985* [Statistics of Non-PLN Power, 1985], Jakarta.

—— (1987a), *Population of East Java: Results of the 1985 Intercensal Population Survey*, Series No. 18, Jakarta.

—— (1987b), *Survei Pertanian, 1986: Produksi Sayuran di Jawa* [Agricultural Survey, 1986: Vegetable Production in Java], Jakarta.

—— (1987c), *Population of Indonesia: Results of the 1985 Intercensal Population Survey*, Series No. 5, Jakarta.

—— (1987d), *Statistik Ekspor, 1986* [Export Statistics, 1986], Jakarta.

—— (1987e), *Survei Pertanian, 1986: Produksi Buah-buahan di Jawa* [Agricultural Survey, 1986: Fruit Production in Java], Jakarta.

—— (1988a), *National Indonesian Contraceptive Prevalence Survey, 1987: Preliminary Report*, Jakarta: Central Bureau of Statistics, National Family Planning Co-ordinating Board, and Westinghouse Institute for Resource Development.

—— (1988b), *Pendapatan Regional Propinsi-propinsi di Indonesia, 1980–84* [Regional Income by Province in Indonesia, 1980–84], Jakarta.

—— (1988c), *Proyeksi Penduduk Indonesia per Propinsi, 1985–1995* [Indonesian Population Projections by Province, 1985–1995], Series No. 34, Jakarta.

—— (1989a), *National Indonesian Contraceptive Prevalence Survey, 1987: Final Report*, Jakarta: Central Bureau of Statistics, National Family Planning Co-ordinating Board, and Westinghouse Institute for Resource Development.

—— (1989b), *Statistik Perkebunan Besar, 1986* [Large Plantation Statistics, 1986], Jakarta.

—— (1989c), *Sensus Ekonomi, 1986: Statistik Industri/Kerajinan Rumahtangga* [Economic Census, 1986: Home Industry Statistics], Jakarta.

—— (unpublished census tapes), 'Sensus Ekonomi, 1986' [Economic Census, 1986], Jakarta.

Broersma, R. (1913), *Besoeki, Een Gewest in Opkomst* [Besoeki, A Region Emergent], Amsterdam: Scheltema and Holkema's Boekhandel.

Brown, C. (1982), 'The Intensified Smallholder Cane Programme: The First Five Years', *Bulletin of Indonesian Economic Studies*, 18(1): 39–60.

Bryant, N. A. (1974), 'Village Migration and the Rural Economy of Central Java', Paper presented at the Conference on Indonesian Agriculture, University of Wisconsin, Madison.

Budiono, M. (1981), *Pola-pola Penguasaan Sapi Perah di Pedesaan: Study Kasus di Desa Pandesari* [Patterns of Control of Dairy Cattle in Rural Areas: A Case-study in Pandesari Village], Bogor: Lembaga Penelitian Sosiologi Pedesaan dan Institut Pertanian Bogor.

Castles, L. (1967), *Religion, Politics and Economic Behaviour in Java: The Kudus Cigarette Industry*, Yale University Southeast Asia Studies, Cultural Report Series, No. 15, New Haven.

—— (1989), 'Jakarta: The Growing Centre', in Hal Hill (ed.), *Unity and Diversity: Regional Economic Development in Indonesia since 1970*, Singapore: Oxford University Press.

Chang, T. T. (1979), 'Genetics and Evolution of the Green Revolution', in R. de Vincente (ed.), *Replies from Biological Research*, Madrid: Consejo Superior de Investigaciones Cientificas, pp. 187–209.

Cho, Lee-Jay; Suharto, S.; McNicoll, G.; and Mamas, S. G. M. (1976), *Estimates of Fertility and Mortality in Indonesia Based on the 1971 Population Census*, Jakarta: Central Bureau of Statistics.

CKS (Centraal Kantoor voor de Statistiek) (1922), *Volkstelling, 1920* [Population Census, 1920], 2 vols., Batavia.

____ (1925), *Indisch Verslag, 1924*, Batavia: Landsdrukkerij.

____ (1933–6), *Volkstelling, 1930*, [Population Census, 1930], Batavia.

Coedès, G. (1975), *The Indianized States of Southeast Asia*, translated by S. B. Cowing, Canberra: Australian National University Press.

Colclough, C. (1982), 'The Impact of Primary Schooling on Economic Development: A Review of the Evidence', *World Development*, 10(3): 167–85.

Collier, W. L. (1981), 'Agricultural Evolution in Java', in G. E. Hansen (ed.), *Agricultural and Rural Development in Indonesia*, Boulder: Westview Press.

de Graaff, J. (1986), *The Economics of Coffee*, Wageningen: PUDOC.

de Graaff, J. and Kusrianto Dwiwarsito (1987), *Economic Impact of Watershed Development Activities: Report on 1986–87 Implementation Activities in the Konto River Watershed*, Konto River Project, ATA 206, Phase III, Working Paper No. 16, Malang.

Demographic Institute (1974), *Indonesian Fertility–Mortality Survey, 1973, East Java, Preliminary Report*, Jakarta.

Department of Information (1985 and 1989), *Lampiran Pidato Kenegaraan* [Appendix to the President's Speech], Jakarta.

Devas, N. (1987), *Produk Domestik Regional Bruto: Kabupaten dan Kotamadya se Jawa Timur, 1980–85* [Gross Regional Domestic Product: Regency and Municipality in East Java, 1980–85], Surabaya: Bappeda/Kantor Statistik Jawa Timur.

____ (1988), 'Local Taxation in Indonesia: Opportunities for Reform', *Bulletin of Indonesian Economic Studies*, 24(2): 58–86.

____ (ed.) (1989), *Financing Local Government in Indonesia*, Ohio University Monographs in International Studies, Southeast Asia Series, No. 84, Athens.

Dick, H. W. (1987), *The Indonesian Interisland Shipping Industry*, Singapore: Institute of Southeast Asian Studies.

____ (1990), 'Inter-island Trade, Economic Integration and the Emergence of the National Economy', in A. Booth, W. O'Malley, and A. Weidemann (eds.), *Indonesian Economic History in the Dutch Colonial Era*, Yale University Southeast Asia Studies, Monograph Series, No. 35, New Haven.

Dick, H. W. and Forbes, D. (1992), 'Transport and Communications: A Quiet Revolution', in A. Booth (ed.), *The Oil Boom and After: Indonesian Economic Policy and Performance in the Soeharto Era*, Singapore: Oxford University Press.

Diperta Jawa Timur (annual), *Laporan Tahunan* [Annual Report], Surabaya.

Diperta Malang (1977), *Monografi Dinas Pertanian Kabupaten Malang* [Agricultural Service Monography of Malang District], Malang.

____ (1980), *Anjuran Pola Usaha Tani di Wilayah Pengembangan Pertanian A1* [Farming Recommendations for A1 Agricultural Development Regions], Malang.

____ (1983), *Hasil Survey Tanaman Sayuran Dataran Tinggi dan Pengembangannya di Jawa Timur* [Results of the Survey on Highland Vegetable Cultivation and Its Development in East Java], Bedali/Lawang.

Directorate-General of Community Development (1972), *Potensi Desa Kabupaten Pasuruan, Type-type Desa dan Tahap Perkembangannya, Tahun 1972* [Village Potential in Pasuruan Regency: Types of Villages and Their Level of Development, 1972], Jakarta: Departemen Dalam Negeri.

____ (1979), *Rekapitulasi dan Analisa Tipe dan Klasifikasi Perkembangan Desa, Tahun 1978/79* [Recapitulation and Analysis of the Type and Development Classification of Villages, 1978/79], Jakarta: Departemen Dalam Negeri.

____ (1980), *Daftar Isian/Pertanyaan Mengenai Potensi Desa* [Questionnaire Regarding Village Potential], Jakarta: Departemen Dalam Negeri (for various villages and for years 1979–80).

____ (1986a), *Daftar Isian/Pertanyaan Mengenai Potensi Desa* [Questionnaire Regarding Village Potential], Jakarta: Departemen Dalam Negeri.

____ (1986b), *Type-type Desa dan Tingkat Perkembangan Desa, Tahun 1985–86* [Village Types and Their Level of Development, 1985–86], Pasuruan: Departemen Dalam Negeri.

Direktorat Djendral Tenaga dan Listrik (Directorate-General of Power and Electricity) (n.d.).

Dyck, V. A. and Thomas, B. (1979), 'The Brown Planthopper Problem', in *Brown Planthopper: Threat to Rice Production in Asia*, Los Baños: IRRI, pp. 3–17.

Edmundson, W. C. (1977), 'Two Villages in Contrast, 1971–76', *Bulletin of Indonesian Economic Studies*, (8)1: 100–1.

Edmundson, W. C. and Edmundson, S. A. (1983), 'A Decade of Village Development in East Java', *Bulletin of Indonesian Economic Studies*, 19(2): 46–59.

Ehrlich, P. (1968 and 1972), *The Population Bomb*, London: Pan/Ballantine.

Elson, R. E. (1984), *Javanese Peasants and the Colonial Sugar Industry: Impact and Change in an East Java Residency, 1830–1940*, Singapore: Oxford University Press/ASAA.

Faber, G. H. von (1931), *Oud Soerabaia* [Old Surabaya], Surabaya: Gemeente Soerabaia.

____ (*c.*1934), *Nieuw Soerabaia* [New Surabaya], Surabaya: Gemeente Soerabaia.

Falcon, Walter et al. (1984), *The Cassava Economy of Java*, Stanford: Stanford University Press.

Fei, J. and Ranis, G. (1961), 'A Theory of Economic Development', *American Economic Review*, 51(3): 533–65.

Fish, I. L. (1983), *Reservoir Sedimentation Study, Selorejo, East Java*, Hydrologics Research Station Report No. OD 51, Wallingford, England.

Fontein, J. (1990), *The Sculpture of Indonesia*, Washington: National Gallery of Art.

Fox, J. J. (1988), 'Village and State: Indonesia's "Bantuan Pembangunan Desa" Program', Paper presented at the Conference on the State and Civil Society in Contemporary Indonesia, Monash University, Clayton, 25–7 November 1988.

____ (1991), 'Managing the Ecology of Rice Production in Indonesia', in J. Hardjono (ed.), *Indonesia: Resources, Ecology, and Environment*, Singapore: Oxford University Press, pp. 61–84.

Fox, J. J. and Gardiner, P. (1983), 'Distribution of Javanese Speakers in Indonesia', Addenda Sheet 1 in S. A. Wurm and Shiro Hattori (eds.), *Language Atlas of the Pacific Area, Part II*, Canberra: Pacific Linguistics, Australian National University.

Frederick, W. H. (1989), *Visions and Heat: The Making of the Indonesian Revolution*, Athens: Ohio University Press.

Fruin, Th. A. (1926), 'Tabakskultur en Tabaksproducten van Nederlandsch Indie' [Tobacco Cultivation and Tobacco Products in the Netherlands Indies], *Koloniale Studien*, 10(1): 417–35.

Furnivall, J. S. (1944), *Netherlands India: A Study of Plural Economy*, New York: Macmillan.

Gardiner, P. (1985), *Provincial Population Projections: Requirements, Methodology, Results*, NUDS Report T1.4/C3, Jakarta: National Urban Development Strategy, Department of Public Works, and UNDP.

Geertz, C. (1963), *Agricultural Involution: The Process of Ecological Change in Indonesia*, Berkeley: University of California Press.

____ (1988), 'Recollections of an Itinerant Career', *Bulletin of Indonesian Economic Studies*, 24(3): 31–52.

Geertz, H. (1961), *The Javanese Family: A Study of Kinship and Socialization*, Glencoe, Ill.: The Free Press.

_____ (1963), 'Indonesian Cultures and Communities', in R. McVey (ed.), *Indonesia*, Yale University South East Asian Studies, New Haven.

Grindle, M. S. (ed.) (1980), *Politics and Policy Implementation in the Third World*, Princeton: Princeton University Press.

Groeneveldt, W. P. (1880), 'Notes on the Malay Archipelago and Malacca Compiled from Chinese Sources', *Verhandelingen van het Bataviaasch Genootschap van Kunsten en Wetenschappen*, 39(1): 1–144.

Hamim Washsulfallah; Ma'ruf Qoribun; Gerd Ramm; Eddy Sulistyono; and Bambang Wijono (1979), *Establishment of a Price Information Service for Vegetables, Step I: Survey Report on the Establishment of a Price Information Service for Vegetables*, Indonesian–German Technical Cooperation Project ATA 85/86-GTZ 74.2183.7, Agricultural Market Information Service Publication No. 11, Jakarta.

Harahap, Z.; Susanto, T.; Soetjipto, K.; and Siregar, H. (1984), 'Krueng Aceh: Varietas Unggul Padi dengan Rasa Nasi Enak' [Krueng Aceh: A Superior Rice Variety with Good Taste Qualities], *Pemberitaan Penelitian Puslitbangtan*, 5: 27–32.

Hardjono, J. (1988), *Land, Labour and Livelihood in a West Java Village*, Yogyakarta: Gadjah Mada University Press.

____ (1989), 'West Java: Population Pressure and Regional Diversity', in Hal Hill (ed.), *Unity and Diversity: Regional Economic Development in Indonesia since 1970*, Singapore: Oxford University Press.

Hargrove, T. R.; Coffman, W. R.; and Cabanilla, V. L. (1979), *Genetic Interrelationships of Improved Rice Varieties in Asia*, IRRI Research Paper Series, No. 23, Los Baños.

Hariri Hadi (1984), '*Kecamatan* Towns Can Stem the Invasion of Large Cities', *Prisma*, 32: 50–4.

Hefner, R. F. (1983), 'The Problem of Preference: Ritual and Economic Change in Highland Java', *Man*, New Series, 18: 669–89.

____ (1985), *Hindu Javanese: Tengger Tradition and Islam*, Princeton: Princeton University Press.

____ (1990), *The Political Economy of Mountain Java*, Berkeley: University of California Press.

Higgins, B. (1955), 'The "Dualistic Theory" of Underdeveloped Areas', *Ekonomi dan Keuangan Indonesia*, 5(2): 58–78.

Hill, H. (1985), *Export-oriented Industrialisation: The ASEAN Experience*, Sydney: Allen & Unwin.

____ (1987), 'Concentration in Indonesian Manufacturing', *Bulletin of Indonesian Economic Studies*, 23(2): 71–100.

____ (1988), *Foreign Investment and Industrialization in Indonesia*, Singapore: Oxford University Press.

—— (ed.) (1989), *Unity and Diversity: Regional Economic Development in Indonesia since 1970*, Singapore: Oxford University Press.

Hill, H. and Williams, C. (1989), 'The Economic and Social Dimensions of Regional Development in Indonesia', *Ekonomi dan Keuangan Indonesia*, 37(2): 191–218.

Hotman Siahaan; Siti Norma; Wirawan, I. B.; and Subekti (1983), *Pergeseran Okupasi Penduduk di Daerah Pinggiran Selatan Kota Surabaya* [Occupational Change among People on the Southern Fringe of the City of Surabaya], Surabaya: Lembaga Penelitian Universitas Airlangga.

Hughes, H. (1988), *Achieving Industrialization in East Asia*, Cambridge: Cambridge University Press.

Hugo, G. J. (1978), *Population Mobility in West Java*, Yogyakarta: Gadjah Mada University Press.

Hugo, G. J.; Hull, T. H.; Hull, V. J.; and Jones, G. W. (1987), *The Demographic Dimension in Indonesian Development*, Singapore: Oxford University Press.

Hull, T. H. and Dasvarma, G. L. (1988), 'Fertility Trends in Indonesia: 1967–85', *Bulletin of Indonesian Economic Studies*, 24(1): 115–22.

Hull, T. H. and Hull, V. J. (1987), 'Changing Marriage Behavior in Java: The Role of Timing of Consummation', *Southeast Asian Journal of Social Science*, 15(1): 104–19.

Hull, T. H. and Tukiran (1976), 'Regional Variations in the Prevalence of Childlessness in Indonesia', *Indonesian Journal of Geography*, 6(32): 1–25.

Husin, Imron (1989), 'Rural Electrification in Indonesia: Policy Implementation in Theory and Practice', Ph.D. thesis, Australian National University.

Ingleson, J. (1979), *Road to Exile: The Indonesian Nationalist Movement, 1927–1934*, Singapore: Heinemann/ASAA.

—— (1986), *In Search of Justice: Workers and Unions in Colonial Java, 1908–26*, Singapore: Oxford University Press/ASAA.

Iskandar, N. (1970), *Some Monographic Studies on the Population in Indonesia*, Jakarta: Department of Demography, University of Indonesia.

Jaeggi, A. C. (1946), 'De Tabakscultuur in de Residentie Besoeki' [Tobacco Cultivation in Besoeki Residency], in C. C. J. Hall and C. van der Koppel (eds.), *De Landbouw in den Indischen Archipel*, Vol. II B, The Hague: van Hoeve.

Jellinek, L. (1990), *The Wheel of Fortune*, Sydney: Allen & Unwin/ASAA.

Jones, G. W. (1976), 'Religion and Education in Indonesia', *Indonesia*, 22: 36–56.

—— (1984), 'Links between Urbanization and Sectoral Shifts in Employment in Java', *Bulletin of Indonesian Economic Studies*, 20(3): 120–57.

—— (1986), 'Differentials in Female Labour Force Participation Rates in Indonesia: Reflection of Economic Needs and Opportunities, Culture or Bad Data?', *Majalah Demografi Indonesia*, 26: 1–28.

—— (1987), *The 1985 Intercensal Survey of Indonesia: The Labour Force*, Department of Demography, Australian National University, Research Note No. 78, Canberra.

—— (1988), *Economic Growth, Changing Employment Structure and Implications for Educational Planning in ASEAN Countries*, NUPRI Research Paper Series, No. 47, Tokyo: Population Research Institute, Nihon University.

—— (1992), 'Dilemmas in Expanding Education for Faster Economic Growth: Indonesia, Malaysia, and Thailand', in N. Ogawa, G. W. Jones, and

J. Williamson (eds.), *Human Resources and Development along the Asia–Pacific Rim*, Singapore: Oxford University Press.

Kabul Santoso Mangku Adimuljo, R. (1977), 'The Income Distribution and Employment in Desa Sumberejo, Kecamatan Pandaan, Kabupaten Pasuruan', Postgraduate thesis, Institut Pertanian Bogor.

Krijnen, J. F. (1982), 'Presentation of Data: Dairy Cattle Survey in the Pujon Area', Konto River Project, Internal report, Malang.

Kristianto, B. (1985), 'East Java Labour Force Participation: Dimensions and Changing Employment Patterns, 1971–1980 and Labour Force Projection to 2000', MA thesis, Australian National University.

KRP (Konto River Project) (1982), 'The Kali Konto Upper Watershed Area in East Java; The State of the Forest Land and Its Meaning for the Rural Population under the Prevailing Socio-economic Conditions', Konto River Project, ATA 206, Internal report, Malang.

____ (1985), *Final Report, Second Phase*, 4 vols., Konto River Project, ATA 206, Malang.

KSJT (Kantor Statistik Jawa Timur) (annual), *Jawa Timur dalam Angka* [East Java in Figures], Surabaya.

____ (1970), *Survei Perusahaan Industri Tahun 1970: Daftar Nama dan Alamat Perusahaan Industri Besar dan Sedang* [Survey of Industrial Firms, 1970: Register of Names, and Addresses of Large- and Medium-scale Firms], Surabaya.

____ (1983), *Penduduk Propinsi Jawa Timur Menurut Kecamatan: Hasil Pencacahan Lengkap Sensus Penduduk, 1980* [Population of East Java Province by Subdistrict: Results of the Complete Enumeration of the 1980 Population Census], Surabaya.

KSM (Kantor Statistik Malang) (annual), *Kabupaten Malang dalam Angka* [Malang District in Figures], Malang.

____ (1982), 'Penggunaan, Luas Tanah, dan Angkatan Kerja Kabupaten Daerah Tingkat II Malang, 1980–81' [Use, Land Area, and Labour Force in Malang District, 1980–81], Mimeo, Malang.

____ (1983), *Kabupaten Pati II Malang: Fakta dan Penjelasan* [Malang District: Facts and Explanations], Malang.

____ (1985), *Sensus Pertanian, 1983: Data Hasil, Pendaftaran Rumahtangga di Kabupaten Malang* [Agricultural Census, 1983: Results of the Household Survey in Malang District], Malang.

KSP (Kantor Statistik Pasuruan) (annual), *Kabupaten Pasuruan dalam Angka* [Pasuruan District in Figures], Pasuruan.

____ (1986), *Sensus Ekonomi, 1986* [Economic Census, 1986], Pasuruan.

Landbouwatlas (1926), *Landbouwatlas van Djawa en Madoera, Mededeelingen* van het Centraal Kantor voor de Statistiek No. 33, Batavia.

Lewis, W. A. (1954), 'Growth with Unlimited Supplies of Labour', *Manchester School of Social and Economic Studies*, 1(2): 131–91.

Lindblad, T. (1989), 'The Petroleum Industry in Indonesia before the Second World War', *Bulletin of Indonesian Economic Studies*, 25(2): 53–77.

Lipton, M. (1977), *Why Poor People Stay Poor: A Study of Urban Bias in World Development*, London: Temple Smith.

LMOD (Landbouw Maatschappij Oud Djember) (1909), *Gedenkboek* [Commemoration Volume], Amsterdam.

MacAndrews, C.; Sibero, A.; and Fisher, H. B. (1982), 'Regional Development

Planning and Implementation in Indonesia: The Evolution of a National Policy', in R. P. Misra (ed.), *Regional Development: Essays in Honour of Masahiko Honjo*, Tokyo: Maruzen Asia.

McCawley, P. (1971), 'The Indonesian Electrical Supply Industry', Ph.D. thesis, Australian National University.

McCutcheon, L. (1977), 'Migrant Adjustment in Surabaya, Indonesia', Ph.D. thesis, Brown University.

McDonald, P. F. and Sontosudarmo, A. (1976), *Response to Population Pressure: The Case of the Special Region of Yogykarta*, Yogyakarta: Gadjah Mada University Press.

McDonald, P. F.; Mohammad Yasin; and Jones, G. W. (1976), *Levels and Trends in Fertility and Childhood Mortality in Indonesia: Indonesian Fertility–Mortality Survey, 1973*, Jakarta: Department of Demography, University of Indonesia.

McFalls, J. A. and McFalls, M. H. (1984), *Disease and Fertility*, New York: Academic Press.

McGee, T. G. (1969), *The Southeast Asian City*, London: Bell.

Mackie, J. A. C. (1961–2), 'Indonesia's Government Estates and Their Masters', *Pacific Affairs*, 34(4): 337–60.

____ (1980), 'The Concept of Dualism and Its Application to Indonesian Agriculture', in J. J. Fox, R. G. Garnaut, P. T. McCawley, and J. A. C. Mackie (eds.), *Indonesia: Australian Perspectives*, Canberra: Australian National University, Research School of Pacific Studies, pp. 295–306.

____ (1985), 'The Changing Political Economy of an Export Crop: The Case of Jember's Tobacco Industry', *Bulletin of Indonesian Economic Studies*, 21(1): 113–39.

Mackie, J. A. C. and Djumilah Zain (1989), 'East Java: Balanced Growth and Diversification', in Hal Hill (ed.), *Unity and Diversity: Regional Economic Development in Indonesia since 1970*, Singapore: Oxford University Press.

Mackie, J. A. C. and O'Malley, W. J. (1988), 'Productivity Decline in the Java Sugar Industry from an Olsonian Perspective', *Comparative Studies in Society and History*, 30(4): 725–49.

McStocker, R. (1987), 'The Indonesian Coffee Industry', *Bulletin of Indonesian Economic Studies*, 23(1): 40–69.

Mamas, S. G. M. (1983), 'Tren dan Variasi Angka Kelahiran Indonesia Menurut Propinsi' [Trends and Variations of Indonesian Fertility Rates by Province], Paper presented at the Indonesian Fertility Seminar, Central Bureau of Statistics and National Family Planning Co-ordinating Board, Jakarta.

Manning, C. (1987), 'Public Policy, Rice Production and Income Distribution: A Review of Indonesia's Rice Self-sufficiency Programme', *Journal of Southeast Asian Social Science*, 15(1): 66–82.

____ (1988), 'Rural Employment Creation in Java: Lessons from the Green Revolution and Oil Boom', *Population and Development Review*, 14(1): 47–80.

Mantra, I. B. (1986–7), *Migrasi Penduduk di Indonesia Berdasarkan Hasil Supas, 1985* [Migration in Indonesia Based on the Results of the 1985 Supas], Jakarta: Biro Pusat Statistik.

MARIF (Malang Agriculture Research Institute for Food Crops) (1986), *Palawija: Food Crops Other than Rice in East Java Agriculture: An Overview with Special Reference to Research Strategies*, Malang.

Mather, Celia E. (1983), 'Industrialization in Tanggerang Regency of West

Java: Women Workers and the Islamic Patriarchy', *Bulletin of Concerned Asian Scholars*, 15(2): 2–17.

Mears, L. A. (1961), *Rice Marketing in the Republic of Indonesia*, Jakarta: P. T. Pembangunan.

Meijer, A. M. E. (1915), 'De Aardappelcultuur door de Inlandsche Bevolking in de Residentie Pasoeroean, met Naschrift der Redactie' [Potato Cultivation by the Native Population in Pasuruan Residency, with a Postscript by the Editor], *Pemimpin Pengoesaha Tanah*, 1(7): 24; 1(8): 3.

Moeljarto Tjokrowinoto and Dwi Retnandari (1990), *Kopi* [Coffee], Yogyakarta: Universitas Gadjah Mada, Village and Regional Research Centre.

Montgomery, R. D. (1975), 'Migration, Employment and Underemployment in Java: Changes from 1961 to 1971 with Particular Reference to the Green Revolution', *Asian Survey*, 15(3): 222–34.

Mubyarto (1977), 'The Sugar Industry: From Estate to Smallholder Cane Production', *Bulletin of Indonesian Economic Studies*, 8(2): 29–44.

Munneke, H. H. and Vorsterman van Oyen, E. (1987), *Socio-economic Conditions in the Hamlet Cukal: A Study on the Impact of the Bendosari Agroforestry Schemes*, Konto River Project, ATA 206, Phase III, Working Paper No. 11, Malang.

Nagib, L. and Jones, G. W. (1987), *The 1985 Intercensal Survey of Indonesia: Employment by Industry and Occupation*, International Population Dynamics Program, Department of Demography, Australian National University, Research Note No. 83, Canberra.

Netherlands Mission (1982), 'Feasibility Study, Dairy Development, East Java', Unpublished report.

Nibbering, J. W. (1986), 'Socio-economic Conditions and Developments, Kali Konto Upper Watershed, East Java', Konto River Project, ATA 206, Internal report, Malang.

____ (1988), 'Forest Degradation and Reforestation in a Highland Area in Java', in J. Dargavel, K. Dixon, and N. Semple (eds.), *Changing Tropical Forests: Historical Perspectives on Today's Challenges in Asia, Australasia and Oceania, Workshop Meeting, Canberra, 16–18 May 1988*, Canberra: Centre for Resource and Environmental Studies, Australian National University.

Nibbering, J. W. and Schrevel, A. (1982), *The Role of Additional Activities in Rural Java: A Case Study of Two Villages in the Malang Regency*, Discussion Papers of the Department of Social Geography of Developing Countries, No. 17, Utrecht: Geographical Institute, State University of Utrecht.

NUDS (National Urban Development Strategy) (1985), *NUDS Final Report* , Jakarta: Directorate of City and Regional Planning.

Oetomo, D. (1987), *The Chinese of Pasuruan: Their Language and Identity*, Pacific Linguistics Series, Canberra: Research School of Pacific Studies, Australian National University.

O'Malley, W. J. (1990), 'Plantations', in Anne Booth, W. J. O'Malley, and A. Wiedemann (eds.), *Indonesian Economic History of the Dutch Colonial Era*, Yale Southeast Asian Studies Monograph Series, No. 35, New Haven.

Oshima, H. (1983), 'The Industrial and Demographic Transitions in East Asia', *Population and Development Review*, 9(4): 583–607.

Palte, J. G. L. (1984), *The Development of Java's Rural Uplands in Response to Population Growth: An Introductory Essay in Historical Perspective*, Yogyakarta: Faculty of Geography, Gadjah Mada University.

____ (ed.) (1981), *Socio-economic Structures and Developments in the Rural*

Uplands Surrounding the Upper Serayu River, Yogyakarta: Faculty of Geography, Gadjah Mada University.

Pelzer, K. J. (1957), 'The Agrarian Conflict in North Sumatra', *Pacific Affairs*, 30(2): 151–9.

Perhepi (1984), *Perkebunan Indonesia di Masa Depan* [Indonesian Plantations in the Future], Jakarta: Yayasan Agro Ekonomika.

PLN (Perusahaan Listrik Negara) (1986), *Commercial Information, 1984–85*, Jakarta.

Rafferty, E. (1982), *Discourse Structures of the Chinese Indonesians of Malang*, Monograph Series No. 12, Jakarta: Nusa.

Raharjo, Y. and Hull, V. J. (1984), 'Employment Patterns of Educated Women in Indonesian Cities', in G. W. Jones (ed.), *Women in the Urban and Industrial Workforce: Southeast Asia and East Asia*, National Centre for Development Studies, Australian National University, Monograph No. 33, Canberra.

Remenyi, J. V. (1986), 'Issues in Smallholder Tropical Dairying', *Bulletin of Indonesian Economic Studies*, 22(1): 57–87.

Rietveld, P. (1986), 'Non-agricultural Activities and Income Distribution in Rural Java', *Bulletin of Indonesian Economic Studies*, 22(3): 106–17.

____ (1988), 'Urban Development Patterns in Indonesia', *Bulletin of Indonesian Economic Studies*, 24(1): 73–96.

RIN (Research Institute for Nature Management) (1984), *Evaluation of Forest Land: Kali Konto Upper Watershed, East Java*, Vol. 3, *Natural Forest*, Leersum, Netherlands.

Sajogyo (1977), 'Golongan Miskin dan Partisipasi dalam Pembangunan Desa' [The Poor and Their Participation in Rural Development], *Prisma*, 6(3): 10–17.

Santoso, A. (1986), 'Public Policy Implementation: Rice Policy at the Regional Level in Indonesia, 1970–84', Ph.D. thesis, Australian National University.

Santoso Djoko (n.d.), 'Profil Kelistrikan Desa di Djawa Timur' [Profile of Electrification in Villages in East Java]', Unpublished paper.

Schmit, L. (1981), 'Desa Pagersari: Een Onderzoek naar Werkgelegenheidspatronen binnen de Sociaal-culturele Context van een Hooglanddorp te DAS Kali Konto in Oost-Java' [Pagersari Village: A Study on Employment Patterns within the Socio-cultural Context of a Highland Village in the Konto River Watershed Area in East Java], M.A. thesis, University of Leiden.

Schuitemaker, B. (1949), 'Maatregelen tot het Behoud van de Bodem in het Inheemse Landbouwbedrijf op Java' [Soil Conservation Measures in Indigenous Farming on Java], *Landbouw*, 21(4/5): 153–76.

Segers, W. A. I. M. (1988), *Manufacturing Industry, 1870–1942, Changing Economy in Indonesia*, Vol. 8, Amsterdam: Royal Tropical Institute.

Shand, R. T. (ed.) (1986), *Off-farm Employment in the Development of Rural Asia*, 2 vols., Canberra: National Centre for Development Studies, Australian National University.

Simandjantuk, E. S. and Widiyanto (1983), 'The Rise of the *Kretek* Giants', *Prisma*, 27: 63–81.

Sinaga, R. S. (1978), 'Implications of Agricultural Mechanization for Employment and Income Distribution', *Bulletin of Indonesian Economic Studies*, 14(2): 102–11.

Singarimbun, M. and Penny, D. H. (1976), *Penduduk dan Kemiskinan: Kasus Sriharjo di Pedesaan Jawa* [Population and Poverty: The Case of Sriharjo in Rural Java], Jakarta: Bhratara Aksara.

Slamet, E. J. (1985), 'Population Trends in East Java', MA thesis, Australian National University.

Soegiyanto Padmo and Edhie Djatmiko (1990), *Tembakau* [Tobacco], Yogyakarta: Research Centre for Rural and Regional Development, Universitas Gadjah Mada.

Soelistyo (1975), 'Creating Employment Opportunities in the Rural Areas of East Java', Ph.D. thesis, University of Colorado.

Soemitro, R. (1986), *Pajak Bumi dan Bangunan* [The Land and Buildings Tax], Bandung: P. T. Eresco.

Soewito, T. and Harahap, Z. (1984), 'Cisadane: Varietas Padi Tahan Wereng Coklat dengan Rasa Nasi Enak' [Cisadane: Brown Planthopper Resistant Rice Variety with Good Taste Qualities], *Pemberitaan Penelitian Puslitbangtan*, 6: 29–38.

Steele, R. M. (1980), 'Origins and Occupational Mobility of Lifetime Migrants to Surabaya, East Java', Ph.D. thesis, Australian National University.

Sullivan, J. M. and Wilson, S. E. (1982), *The Second Round (1981) of the East Java Population Survey: A Final Report*, Technical Report No. 3, Jakarta: Central Bureau of Statistics.

Supriyatna, B.; Lande, M.; Sama, S.; and Hasanuddin, A. (1983), 'Sadang dan PB 56: Dua Varietas Baru Padi Sawah' [Sadang and PB 56: Two New Sawah Rice Varieties], *Pemberitaan Penelitian Puslitbangtan*, 1: 7–11.

Sutherland, H. (1979), *The Making of a Bureaucratic Élite*, Singapore: Heinemann.

Tempo (1985), '*Yang Besar Yang Banyak Tidur: Dapatkah G.G. Bertahan*', 29 June: 52–8.

Tennekes, J. (1963), 'De Bevolkingsverspreiding der Residentie Besoeki in 1930: Drie Geografische Studien over Java' [Population Distribution in Besoeki Residency in 1930: Three Geographical Studies of Java], *Tijdschrift van het Nederlands Geografische Genootschap*, 80.

Timmer, C. Peter (ed.) (1987), *The Corn Economy of Indonesia*, Ithaca: Cornell University Press.

Tirtosudarmo, R. (1985), *Migration Decision Making: The Case of East Java*, Jakarta: Indonesian Institute of Science, National Institute of Economic and Social Research.

Titus, M. J.; de Jong, W. M.; and van Steenbergen, F. (1986), 'Explorations into the Economic Structure and Role of Small Urban Centres in the Serayu Valley Region, Central Java', in P. J. M. Nas (ed.), *The Indonesian City: Studies in Urban Planning and Development*, Dordrecht, Netherlands: Foris Publications.

Todaro, M. P. (1976), *Internal Migration in Developing Countries*, Geneva: International Labour Office.

Tukiran (1986), 'Population Mobility and Migrant-village Ties: A Case Study of Two Villages in East Java', MA thesis, Australian National University.

Unibraw (Universitas Brawijaya) (1984), *Soil and Soil Conditions, Kali Konto Upper Watershed, East Java*, Malang.

United Nations (1980), *Patterns of Rural and Urban Population Growth*, Population Studies No. 68, New York.

____ (1989), *Demographic Yearbook, 1988*, New York.

Universitas Gadjah Mada and BPS (1980), *Sensus Penduduk, 1961: Penduduk Desa Jawa, Buku III: Propinsi Jawa Timur* [Population Census 1961: The Rural Population of Java, Volume III: East Java], Yogyakarta: Pusat Penelitian dan Studi Kependudukan.

van der Broek, P. J. (1946), 'Bevolkingstabak' [Smallholder Tobacco], in C. C. J. Hall and C. van der Koppel (eds.), *De Landbouw in den Indischen Archipel*, Vol. II B, The Hague: van Hoeve.

van der Kolff, G. H. (1953), 'An Economic Case Study: Sugar and Welfare in Java', in P. Ruopp (ed.), *Approaches to Community Development*, The Hague and Bandung: van Hoeve, 188–296.

van Setten van der Meer, N. C. (1979), *Sawah Cultivation in Ancient Java*, Canberra: Australian National University Press.

Vatikiotis, M. (1989), 'Eastern Promise', *Far Eastern Economic Review*, 29 June: 57.

VD Research Institute of Indonesia (1953), *The First Two Years: Development of the Venereal Disease Research Institute of Indonesia—Sourabaya*, Surabaya.

Veth, P. J. (1903), *Java: Geographisch, Ethnologisch, Historisch* [Java: Geography, Ethnology, History], 2nd edn., Part 3, Haarlem: Bohn.

Vivekananthan, M. N. (1987), 'Rehabilitation of Irrigation Systems in East Java, Indonesia', *International Congress on Irrigation and Drainage, Thirteenth Congress*, Q.40–R.9: 147–73.

Ward, K. (1974), *The 1971 Election in Indonesia: An East Java Case Study*, Monash Papers in Southeast Asia No. 2, Clayton: Centre of Southeast Asian Studies, Monash University.

Wasono, H. S. and Partosudjono, S. (1986), 'Mobilitas Sirkuler Penduduk ke Surabaya' [Circular Mobility in Surabaya], in I. B. Mantra (ed.), *Studi Mobilitas Sirkuler Penduduk ke Enam Kota Besar di Indonesia* [Study of Circular Mobility in Six Main Cities of Indonesia], Yogyakarta: Universitas Gadjah Mada, Pusat Penelitian Kependudukan.

White, B. N. (1976), 'Population, Involution and Employment in Rural Java', *Development and Change*, 7(3): 267–90.

____ (1979), 'Political Aspects of Poverty, Income Distribution and Their Measurements: Some Examples from Rural Java', *Development and Change*, 10(1): 91–114.

Wibowo, H. (1983), 'Migration and Squatter Settlements in Indonesia: A Chi-square Approach to Systemic Social Problems as a Basis for Policy Formulation', Ph.D. thesis, University of Texas.

Wilson, S. et al. (1985), 'East Java Population Survey: Third Round Report', Unpublished paper.

Wolf, Diana (1984), 'Making the Bread and Bringing It Home: Female Factory Workers in Family Economies of Rural Java', in Gavin W. Jones (ed.), *Women in the Urban and Industrial Workforce: Southeast and East Asia*, Canberra: National Centre for Development Studies, Australian National University.

World Bank (1988), *World Development Report, 1988*, Washington.

____ (1990), *World Development Report, 1990*, Oxford: Oxford University Press.

Yerita (1985), 'Pengaruh Kemiskinan Keluarga Terhadap Permilihan Pekerjaan Wanita di Daerah Pedesaan: Suatu Studi Terhadap Pergeseran Tenaga Kerja Wanita Pedesaan ke Sektor Industri', Honours thesis, FISIP, Universitas Airlangga, Surabaya.

Yusuf Saefuddin and Yuni Marisa (1984), *Perubahan Pendapatan dan Kesempatan Kerja*, Bogor: Studi Dinamika Pedesaan, Yayasan Penelitian Survey Agro Ekonomi.

Zelinsky, W. (1971), 'The Hypothesis of the Mobility Transition', *Geographical Review*, 61(2): 219–49.

Zonneveld, J. M. (1988), *Soil and Water Conservation Engineering: Experiences in the Konto River Project*, Konto River Project, ATA 206, Phase III, Working Paper No. 19, Malang.

Author Index

Subject Index